A Guide To CHICAGO'S HISTORIC SUBURBS
On Wheels & On Foot

*Lake, McHenry,
Kane, DuPage,
Will, and Cook
Counties*

by IRA J. BACH
**Assisted by
Susan Wolfson**
With Photographs by
Harold A. Nelson

A Guide To
CHICAGO'S
HISTORIC
SUBURBS
On Wheels
& On Foot

SWALLOW PRESS
OHIO UNIVERSITY PRESS
Chicago   Athens, Ohio   London

Library of Congress Cataloging in Publication Data

Bach, Ira J.
    A guide to Chicago's historic suburbs on wheels and on foot.

    Includes index.
    1. Architecture—Illinois—Chicago metropolitan area—
Guide-books. 2. Historic buildings—Illinois—Chicago
metropolitan area—Guide-books. I. Wolfson, Susan. II. Title.
NA735.C4B33   917.73'110443   81-9516
ISBN 0-8040-0374-2   AACR2
ISBN 0-8040-0384-X (pbk.)

*This book is dedicated to
those individuals and historic
societies fighting so courageously
to preserve our heritage in landmarks.*

CONTENTS

FOREWORD   xiii
INTRODUCTION: The Region's Communities and
Buildings
C. W. Westfall   1

LAKE COUNTY   62
    Barrington   65
    Long Grove   81
    Mundelein   85
    Libertyville   89
    Gurnee   93
    Waukegan   97
    Lake Bluff   113
    Lake Forest   123
    Fort Sheridan   141
    Highland Park   147
MCHENRY COUNTY   160
    Union   163
    Marengo   169
    Woodstock   183
    Richmond   199
    Crystal Lake   203

KANE County   218
    Carpentersville   221
    East Dundee   229
    West Dundee   235
    Elgin   247
    Wayne   265
    St. Charles   269
    Geneva   283
    Batavia   303
    Aurora   321
DuPAGE COUNTY   340
    Elmhurst   343
    Lombard   353
    Glen Ellyn   361
    Wheaton   365
    Wayne   377
    Winfield   387
    Warrenville   391
    Naperville   395
    Lisle   413
    Oakbrook   417
WILL COUNTY   422
    Plainfield   425
    Lockport   435
    Joliet   453
    Frankfort   469
    Peotone   481
COOK COUNTY 1   494
    Evanston   497
    Wilmette   533
    Kenilworth   549
    Winnetka   565
    Glencoe   575
    Northbrook   587
    Glenview   591
    Des Plaines   595
COOK COUNTY 2   602
    River Forest   605

Oak Park   623
Lyons   659
Riverside   663
Brookfield   681
Western Springs   685
Forest View   697
Palos Hills   701

APPENDIX OF HISTORICAL SOCIETIES AND MUSEUMS   707
APPENDIX OF NATIONAL HISTORIC LANDMARKS AND
      NATIONAL REGISTER OF HISTORIC PLACES   709
INDEX   711
GLOSSARY   717

A REMINDER

**MOST OF THE STRUCTURES
INCLUDED IN THIS BOOK
ARE PRIVATE RESIDENCES.**

**MOST MAY BE SEEN
FROM PUBLIC WAYS.**

**PLEASE RESPECT THE RIGHTS
OF THEIR OCCUPANTS
AND DO NOT TRESPASS.**

FOREWORD

BECAUSE CHICAGO'S suburbs were not touched by the Great Fire of 1871, it is there we turn for a fascinating history of structures built before that time.

Architecturally, some of these dwellings are of interest because of their extreme simplicity, or as examples of styles infrequently used today. There are houses in the Greek Revival style, fashionable during the ante-bellum days; some are noteworthy for their Victorian ramifications; there are also many sophisticated Prairie School houses of such prestigious architects as Frank Lloyd Wright and George Washington Maher.

Historically, many are valued as homes of early settlers. Some were the birthplace or one-time abode of famous people. Many sites are National Historic Landmarks or are listed on the National Register of Historic Places.

For many years these houses were allowed to deteriorate or be destroyed, but many survived and the 1970s brought a new interest in preserving the past. Perhaps new buildings were becoming too costly; perhaps there was a pure concern for roots. For whatever reason, the historical societies of town after town, staffed by volunteers with an enormous enthusiasm for preserving their heritage, grew and actively protected their landmarks. Upon seeing the results of their efforts, we quickly shared their enthusiasm.

Many of the older houses were designed and built by carpenters and masons who, anxious to please their clients, often included in one structure forms from many styles. We have included a glossary to assist the architectural buff who might otherwise become confused by the multi-style features of many of the homes.

The book is structured in seven chapters, each an automobile or bus route. The five outlying counties (Lake, McHenry, Kane, DuPage, and Will) have one route each, and Cook County has two. Most stops within each town are at locally designated historic buildings, where the thirty-five Walking Tours begin and end.

Although the Chicago area is internationally known for its important contributions in the field of architecture, the suburban area has been largely neglected. I am grateful to Lewis W. Hill, Chairman of the Regional Transportation Authority, for recognizing this. He had previously invited me to make recommendations for a series of Suburban Culture Bus Tours, which initiated my interest in the area.

The work of identifying some 800 buildings by address along with descriptions of style and design, while fitting each into a walk that in turn fits into a network of automobile or bus tours, was indeed a colossal task. To accomplish this, a field task force was organized. We prepared an inventory of buildings located in various towns. Next, we drafted the initial routes and walks. Many field trips were made to prepare accurate descriptions of each building, photograph them, and prepare the maps for the rides and walks.

The staff consisted of seven persons. Although these individuals worked together for the first time as a team, their efforts were cooperative and cohesive, making them a first-rate task force.

Our architectural historian, Carroll William Westfall, performed the most demanding task of identifying the various styles, many of which were a mixture of designs. In many cases he uncovered additions that, to the inexperienced eye, might pass as part of the original structure. Dr. Westfall is Associate Professor of History of Architecture and Art at the University of Illinois, Chicago Circle. In addition to his invaluable guidance in the field, he has prepared an essay which follows this introduction, describing the variety of architectural styles indigenous to the Midwest. He also prepared the glossary.

Harold A. Nelson, being an architect as well as a photographer, brings photographs to this book with a special sensitivity. Lawrence Young, who prepared the maps that illustrate routes for driving and walking, acceded to the tedious task of demanding accuracy. Julie Siegel, Ellen Kaufman, and Pamela Marsden deserve thanks for their special efforts.

It was the monumental task of my assistant, Susan Wolfson, to coordinate the work of all these people as well as to prepare certain drafts. Her passion for accuracy and perfection has proved to be an invaluable asset.

I would be remiss if I did not mention the legal technical assistance of my good friend Marshall M. Holleb and the patience of my dear wife Muriel who aided in reviewing innumerable drafts.

Included among the many persons who assisted us in the field are:

Verna Beaver
Larry Bidderman
Marvin Block
John Bourg
   Mayor, City of Joliet
Marcella Brownson
Ellen Bryant
Gussie Conrad
Addie Cook
Myra Cosgrove
James A. Cowan
   Mayor, City of Marengo
Mrs. Richard K. Dompke
Edward Emmerling
Teresa Fraser
Sandi Friedman
Mr. and Mrs. Robert Gobin
Lucille Gustafson
Mark Haggitt
Jim Hansen
Will Hasbrouck
Richard Haussman
Virginia M. Hayter
   President, Village of
   Hoffman Estates
Tom Heinz
Winkle Hirschfield
Sue Hornat
Chief Fred Huscher
Don S. Johnson
Sidney Kaplan
Vivian Kaplan
Shuji Kimura

Bob Kincaid
Bill Klingenberg
Ruth Kretschmer
Vivian Kreuger
A. B. Krisciunas
Mary Alice Lambert
Richard Lambert
Bud Lidicker
Jeanine McLaughlin
Chris Meier
Ruth Mogg
Jim Morgan
Bill Morris
   Mayor, City of Waukegan
Patricia Morris
Gilbert Morrison
Michael R. Morrison
Mrs. John Nordsell
Steven Olderr
Florence Parkhurst
William E. Peterson
   Vernon Township Supervisor
Ray Piepenbrink
Charlotte L. Pierce
Eileen S. Ramm
Dora Rasmussen
Esther Rasmussen
Gillian Roberts
Bob Robinson
Pamela Rogosh
Ellyn Ross
Frances Ryan

Chester J. Rybicki
   Mayor, City of Naperville
Donna Schmidt
Keith Sculle
Mary Ann Serenda
Sandra Sheibley
Barb Smith
Marge Smith
Louise Spanke
Robert Topel
Dorothy Unger
and Debbi Reed

Fred Valentine
Ruby Van Camp
Mr. and Mrs. Arthur Veysey
Isabel R. Wasson
Gene F. Westergren
   Police Chief,
   City of Marengo
William Wood
   Mayor, City of Glencoe
Gladys Yirsa
Mary Zinke

IRA J. BACH
Chicago, November 1980

INTRODUCTION: THE REGION'S COMMUNITIES AND BUILDINGS

Carroll William Westfall

Y OU MUST picture in your mind a time very different from our own to see all there is to see in the six-county area of the nineteenth century.

Most people in the country were farmers, and the towns outside the major cities served the needs of the land. Each town was a tight little community. Its citizens were concerned more with the town's affairs than with those of a large city or a world beyond the horizon.

Chicago contrasted sharply with the towns in the surrounding region. It received the cheese, butter, milk, eggs, fruits, berries, and vegetables sent from the towns. It took in the grain and livestock to be shipped to markets in the east. Its banks supplied the farmers with credit, and its huge stores stocked goods never seen for sale in the towns. Its congestion, diversity, and quick tempo of daily affairs made it unlike anything found beyond it.

Whether in the countryside, towns, or metropolitan center, a man in that time sought stability and security. He believed he had to work for a while to raise the money required to marry. When he moved into the house which was to serve as his family's home—outside the city he might help build it himself—he looked forward to a large family but expected to lose every third or fourth child to death before the age of five. The city offered risk and fortune, but the towns offered a different reward. In return for hard work it promised a modest security for a man and his family and the enjoyment of life in a community of neighbors.

The first settlements in the six-county area grew slowly and steadily, adding a house now and again to the few unpaved streets scattered around a

1

central cluster of stores. Then, after less than a generation, the rural tranquility of the area's first towns was disrupted by the railroad.

The railroad was the most important agent of growth and change in the towns, cities, and suburbs of the six-county area. The first one, the Galena and Chicago Union (now the Chicago and Northwestern Railroad) connected the Des Plaines River to the Chicago River in 1848, and reached Elgin in 1850. The Illinois Central, the largest railroad in the world when finished in 1856, began its 703-mile system in 1851. In 1852 others were begun. Soon a web of rail lines tied the area's towns to Chicago—St. Charles in 1849, Aurora and Batavia in 1850, Joliet in 1852 and by another route in 1858, and Waukegan and Woodstock in 1855.

The railroads were built to haul the rich prairie harvests to the port at the Chicago River mouth. Soon they were also hauling commuters to and from the city. By the time of the Fire of 1871, much of today's radial network was the system familiar to the commuters of that day. Suburbs were laid out only to be absorbed by the expanding city—for example, Hyde Park, Austin, Irving Park, and Rogers Park. As the city grew, older commuter lines were pushed out to new suburbs farther out, new lines were added in between, and new suburbs were planted in the spaces left by the original leapfroging expansion of the metropolitan region along the rail lines.

Barely a generation after the plow had first broken the virgin prairie, the rail lines had penetrated every corner of the region. In another generation, the region's towns could be divided into three broad categories. In the far distance were farming communities. They used the railroad to move crops to market and carry goods back to the local stores. Along the rail lines in the middle distance were small industrial centers, especially along the Fox River where water power was abundant, and beside the Illinois and Michigan Canal, opened in 1848 to connect the Great Lakes and the Mississippi River by way of the Chicago River and the Illinois River. Here people sought a balance between the bucolic charms that drew them there and the factories and railroad that brought them prosperity. Finally, along the lake and in the nearer distance were commuter suburbs. Totally dependent upon Chicago for their livelihood, many were sponsored by speculators, but others began as farming communities only to be absorbed within the city's explosive expansion.

As the century progressed the suburban belt pushed outward at an ever increasing rate, but the suburbs and towns along the rail lines remained like knots in a rope. Surrounded on every side by farmland, their built up area stood in sharp contrast to the open spaces around them. Their size remained limited to the distance a man would willingly walk to the commuter station.

After the First World War the automobile brought increased mobility and independence from both the commuter lines and the walk to the suburban station. Gradually the distinction between rural towns and suburbs became blurred, and the land between the area's settled towns began to be filled in with houses. After the Second World War came a new and larger burst of building activity aided by a federal highway program and a federal mortgage guarantee policy that encouraged suburban growth at the expense of the central city.

Now the open land around the older towns has nearly disappeared, and with it the distinct identity they had. Even distant towns have expanded across the land and lost their distinction from the land. Left in the original core are old houses, commercial structures, public buildings, and churches, some languishing in neglect, others already reduced to mere memories held by older residents.

During the last decade a new attitude about these older cores has begun to change their character. The "find it, fix it, use it" spirit has taken hold, and many of the nearer suburbs of Chicago have begun to recover their identity. People are restoring the older buildings—public, private, commercial, and residential—and protecting whole streets and districts. In more distant parts of the region many communities have so far escaped the worst ravages of mindless expansion. They have begun to protect and preserve their heritage. And in between, some stretches of open land which still reveal the agricultural riches that attracted early settlers while providing a buffer between their towns are finding friends.

When the first railroad left Chicago for the Des Plaines River, a mere ten miles away, it left the city behind at Halsted Street. Even a decade later a popular winter sport was to ice skate on the open, frozen marsh stretching from Ashland Avenue out to where the Des Plaines River widened into a broad plain around today's Riverside and Brookfield. As growth constantly ate into the open land, the city attempted to set aside some open space for its crowded citizens. First, in 1869, it developed a ring of parks and boulevards (Lincoln, Humboldt, Garfield, Douglas, Washington, and Jackson parks), but the city soon reached beyond them. Next, the Cook County Forest Preserve began buying up an open band between the city and the towns in the middle distance. Now even the most distant open spaces in the six-county area are threatened with suburban growth, both tawdry and ritzy, but suburban growth nonetheless, and various ways are being found to preserve and maintain an open barrier against the ceaseless dullness of metropolitan expansion—here a patch of prairie, there a farmstead with a house and out-buildings of early settlers, and elsewhere a county forest preserve with a grove or a stream and protected open space.

What remains today in the near-in older towns and suburbs, in the remaining open land, and in distant parts of the six-county area is a living record of the lives of early settlers, of what they found when they arrived, of the changes they made willingly and had inflicted upon them, of their adaptation to those changes, and of the rapid rise in population and the steady rise in prosperity during the two thirds of the nineteenth century when westward expansion transformed the region.

THE BUILDINGS of the six-county area reveal the far-reaching changes in technology introduced during the nineteenth century.

The earliest settlers turned to local groves which contained a wide range of good woods for building. These they hacked and sawed with hand tools they had carried to the frontier to make oak and walnut timbers and pegs for the structural frame, cedar or butternut shingles for the roof, walnut and oak clapboards for the siding, and oak and pine boards for the floors of their houses. With smaller hand saws they fashioned oak and walnut boards for trimming openings and with hand planes and other tools they produced the doors, windows, and whatever mouldings and cabinets they might be willing to sacrifice the time to furnish. They or a blacksmith made nails. For hinges, door latches, and other hardware, and for the glass, putty, and paint, they turned to dealers selling items made on the east coast or in St. Louis, Louisville, or Cincinnati. The most common luxury was a beautifully finished walnut newel post and bannister occupying pride of place in the central stairhall immediately inside the front door.

In 1833, the year Chicago's few hundred residents decided to make the settlement into a town (it would be incorporated as a city four years later), Augustine Taylor, a carpenter and parishoner, (another story includes George Snow on the job) built for Chicago's colony of about 125 catholics, mostly of French extraction, their first church. Dedicated to St. Mary, it was a rather rude building costing all of $400. Taylor used dimension-cut lumber brought by scow from St. Joseph, Michigan, which he trimmed with a saw and pinned together with nails. In this job Taylor had invented and introduced a revolutionary, new building technique.

The new technique allowed a semi-skilled carpenter and a small boy to build in a few days what would take several experienced carpenters using the centuries-old framing technique much longer to produce. The old technique used a structural frame with custom-cut timbers and braces that were notched, slotted, and pegged together. When finished, the frame was enclosed with roofing and siding to keep out the weather. The new technique used thin struts of dimension-cut lumber nailed together and kept in place by siding and roofing nailed to the struts to form a continuous structure.

Buildings using the new technique suddenly appeared everywhere, seemingly popping up along Chicago's streets and out across the opening frontier wherever lumber, nails, a saw, and a hammer could be brought together. The buildings were strong and would not blow down, but because they weighed little they could blow away unless firmly anchored to the ground. Thin-walled, appearing suddenly, and light enough to blow away— any one of these factors may have been the one that gave the name "balloon frame construction" to the new building technique. People could now quickly build themselves a shelter and settle down to develop the land. Chicago's invention helped make the rapid development of the west possible.

Even before the railroads appeared to haul its products to the countryside, Chicago was supplying tools, nails, hardware, lumber, finished doors, windows, cabinets, and furniture. Building supplies were among Chicago's earliest industrial products, and the six-county area provided a ready market.

In addition to wood, the area possessed good resources for masonry construction. Clay pits furnished material for bricks, and along some stretches of the Fox River the soil had been worn away to provide easy access to a soft rock suitable for walls. While digging the Illinois and Michigan Canal in the mid 1840s a better building stone was unearthed, and soon quarries in the Joliet-Lemont region were supplying the yellow and grey-yellow stone used for foundations, sills, lintels, and other large structural pieces incorporated into brick construction and the stone for whole buildings. Quarried stone was expensive. It was often used over brick as a veneer of thin slabs popularly called "Athenian marble." It was neither from Athens (although Lemont's earlier name was Athens) nor a marble, but merely a humble local limestone.

The expanding railroad network soon made stone from distant places available, but at a price. The hard, grey, almost light blue Indiana limestone gained popularity after the Civil War, especially for lintels, sills, string courses, arches, columns, and veneers. The Romanesque Style made the dark red and brown granites of New England popular, while the classical styles sometimes used east coast marbles. Because polished granites and marbles were expensive they were often used only where they could produce the greatest effect, for example in the porch and entrance area in structures built of less expensive stones.

The railroads also brought iron and plate glass, the first new building materials since antiquity. They found little use in residences, but they made possible a new type of commercial building which quickly became standard. The age-old desire of the merchant has been to display his wares attractively and provide light to show them off to prospective purchasers. Wood, brick, and stone buildings allow large openings in a wall only with great expense, but with cheap and strong pieces of cast and wrought iron to span long openings and with large sheets of plate glass to put in them, the merchant could have a nearly transparent shop front for lighting his store's interior and displaying his goods to the outside world.

At first cast iron and plate glass were used only on the ground floor. The story or two above were usually of brick or stone which offered greater protection from fire than did wood. A sheet metal industry soon developed in Chicago to provide these upper floors with projecting bays, elaborate cornices, and even whole sheet metal facades, though these facades are rare in northern Illinois.

The style of these commercial structures in the six-county area changed little from their first appearance at mid-century until they were displaced by a new type of shopfront in this century. The main streets of towns throughout the region were once lined with these buildings, and many survive today.

Not only new materials but also new technologies gradually changed the appearance of the region's towns. By the time of the Civil War it was possible to discern the difference between towns linked to the larger world and the others still attached to the farming regions they served, a difference that became accentuated as the century progressed. Gas lines were laid in larger, outlying towns, and by the turn of the century electricity was installed, but in many communities people were still using kerosene for light. After 1870 plumbers could connect houses to a town's water supply and sewage system, and install running water and toilets, and steamfitters could hook up radiators to coal-fired boilers, but in the smaller, more distant towns people still pumped water by hand, hurried outside to toilets, and carried in wood to feed fireplaces, Franklin stoves, and kitchen ranges. Only well after the turn of the century did most of the conveniences we take for granted find their way into the houses, both old and new, in many parts of the six-county area.

These new conveniences were paid for with the increased prosperity of workers in towns and cities, and they usually remained beyond the reach of those depending on agriculture for a living. Farm prices remained depressed during the last third of the nineteenth century while the real income of those engaged in commerce, trade, industry, and the professions rose steadily throughout the country. In Chicago they increased even faster.

The result was that the houses of those in the farming regions remained closer to the relative simplicity of the earlier settlers, while the residences of those tied to the city by the rail lines changed. Some of the new conveniences required more complex designs—for example, bathrooms and larger kitchens had to be worked into the plan. Other new devices necessitated greater size—for example, gas lighting required a higher ceiling to provide sufficient distance between the burning gas and the ceiling to prevent scorching and still allow the chandelier to clear the heads of those in the room. The increased prosperity also called forth new suburbs with larger lots. Those building on them now wanted something grander, and with the grandeur they wanted something more stylish. The larger buildings from the last third of the century rapidly developed a more distinctive image that set them off from those typical of the earlier generation.

BEYOND SATISFYING utilitarian needs a building provides an appearance, an image, that is thought to be the right one for the circumstances.

Today, we generally believe that the architect provides this image and that what he suggests must be acceptable to the client. We might also believe that much of what is built today—suburban tract houses, shopping centers, franchise food outlets, and industrial buildings—do not really belong to the realm of the architect and are new, twentieth century building types.

Some of these are new types, but suburban tract houses and industrial buildings are almost as old as the oldest towns in the six-county area, and architects were involved in their design, at least indirectly, by providing the basic styles they display, even if they display them in quite diluted form.

We often tend to think that a style is a well-worked, highly polished design, but this is to confuse the word's adjectival form with the noun form. A style is a particular, characteristic image or appearance shared by a group of buildings. Suburban tract houses and industrial buildings, whether old or new, have a style, but in these building types it is not developed as richly and as carefully as the same style would be when used for a monument meant to proclaim the grandeur of a community or for a residence built by a wealthy man willing to display his wealth and his highly cultivated taste.

Today, we generally accept the notion that architects provide the styles for buildings and that we are left to figure out what those styles are, and why they are used. The styles descend from them to us, even if we happen to be a client. Few clients will quibble with an architect about what a proposed building will look like after the architect has proven that his design will satisfy utilitarian requirements and the budget. If it functions well, the architect may give it whatever appearance he wishes.

The architect began to assume this god-like position during the later part of the nineteenth century. In the gradual change from having him adapt an accepted style for a particular application to having him provide an original and unique design, one that displayed his architectural abilities and revealed the individuality of his client, the decade of the 1880s is an important watershed although the full effect of the change was not felt until the twentieth century.

Architects have always sought original designs, but in the earlier period they were more willing to acknowledge that there actually is no such thing as an original design, that there is instead a modification of previous designs. They worked within an established style that stressed similarities. These similarities allowed buildings to present a clear stylistic image which buildings shared because that image conveyed important meanings. The similarities also allowed the differences among buildings to reveal their relative importance instantly and without ambiguity. Increasingly, however, after the Civil War the architect sought to display his originality and the client to portray his individuality, and this could only be done at the expense of a style's role in conveying a meaning and revealing relative importance.

The newer styles, like the buildings, were more complex, and this made the stylistic unity displayed by the buildings less clear. It also made the role of the architect more important and produced a sharper distinction between the buildings designed by architects and those that were not. In the earlier styles architects knew better than others how to handle the design of buildings, but others could still do a quite credible job simply by working within the fairly simple framework of the styles they learned by looking at other buildings or at pattern books and other builders' manuals.

The newer styles required a more sophisticated understanding of design and of the various options available within each style. The newer styles became less a model for the architect to follow and more a catalogue of visual effects to draw upon. To use them a person had to know more, and for those working in the six-county area, this required familiarity with east coast and European trends because that is where the styles originated. The well-traveled, well-informed architect gained a tremendous advantage over the local builder, and this remained the case until nearly the end of the century when, for the first time, a small group of architects working in Chicago began to develop a new style. Perfected as the style of the Prairie School, this was the first residential style whose major examples could be studied locally and be judged according to locally-developed standards.

The major imported styles were not left unaltered when they arrived in the six-county area. They were often extensively modified to satisfy local materials, needs, and tastes. This sometimes leads people to consider local buildings to be inferior, especially when compared to the "prime monuments" and "high examples" of the various styles appearing in the histories, guide books, and glossaries that have made a sometimes arcane procedure of stylistic analysis available to anyone interested in looking at buildings. They may be poor examples of one thing but quite good examples of something else, something that is ignored and left unenjoyed.

The fault is not in the buildings but in the procedure. The styles were not so tightly segmented and compartmentalized as historians sometimes make them seem. Historians, after all, seek to present their stories in neat, clear-cut, easily graspable form, and they usually write for a wide, generalized audience, which inhibits the presentation of regional variations. All the styles prevalent during the nineteenth century possess a greater regional and personal diversity than historians have so far admitted.

In addition to allowing buildings to be categorized according to style, stylistic analysis also allows for a judgment about the quality of a design. This presents a ready trap for the unwary. A person often assumes that the building's designer knew the same things about the style and believed the same things about it as he does. If he finds the building to be a "poor example" of a style, he may be presuming that the designer failed to achieve the stylistic purity or the full embodiment of the style, and this leads him to censure the architect and dismiss the building.

We hardly ought to presume that we know more than the designer did or that the style is more important than the building. A building is less enjoyable as an example of current notions about what a building ought to have looked like and more enjoyable as an example of certain stylistic characteristics that the designer used in a certain way to achieve the effect, to produce the appearance, to make the image he, and we might assume his client, wanted in the building.

A better procedure than one of stylistic censoriousness is to look at a building with a knowledge of what sorts of images the designer might have drawn on, to discover how he used them, and to judge the effect or the image he produced in using them. In doing so the building will begin to tell tales about the time and the place in which it was built and tales about the designer and the client, tales that are revealing, rewarding, and enjoyable.

IF WE see during the sixty year period from 1840 to 1900 a bewildering complexity of imagery and diversity of styles in the buildings of the six-county area, and if we think of that period as having a stable cultural and social order, then we have got things exactly backwards.

That period was almost unimaginably different from our own. During the most recent similar span of sixty years, since about 1920, we have produced around Chicago one of the most visually cacophonous suburban and regional scenes ever made by man. In comparison, the nineteenth century suburbs are harmoniously monotonous. Meanwhile, we have promised to institute a progressive cultural and social order and have hailed even the smallest adjustment in traditional customs as evidence of dramatic progress toward that goal. The contrast to the nineteenth century is acute. That was a period of thoroughgoing change in every aspect of culture and society, but those who endured that change believed the old values were prevailing.

Is it any wonder that the nineteenth century is difficult for us to understand? Unlike us, its people valued and preserved old images and distrusted new ones. When a new architectural style was introduced, it was accepted only if it provided a new and clearer way of conveying old values. Our century is the one in which architects began to declare (and people have believed them!) that the old is meaningless, false, and without value, that only the new is progressive and good. During the relentless and tumultuous cultural and social change of the nineteenth century, people believed that America offered stability and security for oneself and one's family in return for hard work and respect for old values.

Even as the six-county area was receiving its first settlers to plant its towns and fields, society was changing. The social structure was becoming more complex, people were becoming more prosperous, and buildings were being constructed to serve a wider range of quite specific and specialized needs. A deepening gulf developed between the farmer and laborer on the one hand, and the banker, industrialist, capitalist, and merchant prince on the other. The settlers arrived with an idealism akin to Thomas Jefferson's belief that the basis of the American republic was the farmer tilling the land. But growing around them was the other model of society, Alexander Hamilton's society of merchants and manufacturers in contact with the international world of commerce. The farmers ignored it, remaining rooted in the soil and venturing into the nearby market towns only to trade, while the merchants and manufacturers traveled to the east and to Europe, establishing a large network of contacts and returned with knowledge of the latest that the world had to offer.

The two societies lived in relative harmony. The less fortunate, whether rural farmer or urban mechanic, often hoped they might join the more privileged, but in the meantime they willingly contributed to a stable society by occupying the niche that destiny had prepared for them. During the labor troubles of the 1870s, 1880s, and 1890s, the mechanics and their fellow wage-earners assailed not the privileges enjoyed by the salaried and the wealthy but the injustices inflicted on them because they were workers. During the Granger and Populist movements of the period, the farmers were less distressed by the wealth accumulating in the pockets of the few in the cities than by the low prices paid for what they brought forth from the land.

Social distinctions were accepted as part of the necessary order of things. That they paralleled distinctions based on wealth and ascended from the many out on the land and in the city's factories up to the few in the urban offices and mansions only provided evidence that the promise of America could become reality. This was not a hierarchy of peasants and feudal barons but an orderly society of free men engaged in farming, manufacturing, and trade, all with the opportunity to rise, all enjoying the promise of security. Jefferson's and Hamilton's societies had merged to produce a peaceful, prosperous, growing, and expanding America.

This was possible because the extremes were buffered by a new class, the middle class, which hardly existed when the republic was founded. Its members did not live off the land they tilled or the wages of their labor. But neither did they enjoy the return from capital they had inherited or the vast, sudden wealth they had garnered through persistence, pluck, or luck. They were, instead, salaried clerks, middlemen, and manufacturers' agents, dealers in wholesale and retail goods and in real estate, small manufacturers and aspiring professionals, and they formed a new class.

After the middle of the century, while the number of farmers in the six-county area increased slowly and the laboring population increased rapidly in Chicago but slowly elsewhere, the number of people forming the middle class increased very rapidly. These people headed for the towns and suburbs accessible from Chicago, as a commentator on Chicago and its suburbs observed as early as 1874. In discussing them Everett Chamberlin said, "The fact is thoroughly established that ninety-nine Chicago families in every hundred will go an hour's ride into the country, or toward the country, rather than live under or over another family, as the average New Yorker or Parisian does." As New York and Paris were being built up with tall, blocky apartment buildings, Chicago's suburbs were expanding outward with single family houses.

Each of these three classes—the working class, the middle class, and the wealthy—assumed responsibilities for maintaining an ordered society. As circumstances changed around them—as differentials in wealth widened, as the numbers of the various classes increased unequally, as the towns grew into cities, as Chicago coaxed suburbs from farmland and commandeered market towns for suburban use, as towns and cities installed conveniences and stocked goods unavailable in rural areas, as railroads facilitated travel and broadened horizons—as all this happened in a brief span of years, people sought stability in a changing world by embracing images that conveyed enduring values. Their buildings were meant to reassure them that the American ideals were secure and the social order sound.

It is difficult for us to see buildings in this way because we seldom use buildings for these purposes and we too often falter when we try. Public bodies have too often shown pride in a town hall, library, or school that is distinguishable from an insurance office or appliance store by little more than the sign it displays. It has become unfashionable to build mansions that display private wealth. Instead, the monuments are built by corporations and these display neither civic values nor private wealth but only the values of corporate efficiency and impersonal, corporate wealth.

People during the nineteenth century did things differently. Those entrusted with public affairs and those who were wealthy believed they were to provide a model of public behaviour and of taste which would percolate through the community and reinforce the accepted cultural and social order. The town hall, public library, and school were monuments to the community's aspirations and achievements. All contributed to their grandeur—the wealthy often made special contributions to the library—and all took pride in their presence in the community. The mansion of a wealthy man was an emblem of his success and a promise of similar success for others. The still unsuccessful might envy the mansion, but they did not despise it. They pointed to it with pride, and they emulated it in diluted form when they built their own houses.

The result is that a community's older buildings display easily discernable differences between those built by the few of class and the many of the mass, as the nineteenth century so euphoniously put it. They reveal the increasing distinctions between class and mass that accompanied the century's increasingly unequal distribution of an increasing prosperity. These distinctions are evident not only in the comparative size and obvious cost of buildings but in the quality of their design and the currency of their styles as well.

To complicate visual matters, two styles were often fashionable concurrently.

Although perhaps of different styles, the older buildings in the earliest towns of the six-county area differ little from one another in either size or quality of design, but gradually the distinctions became sharper. As the century progressed new styles were introduced, and these offered a greater potential for elaboration and for distinctive, unique development. Those who built the more pretentious buildings seized upon this potential and produced an ever sharper contrast between their buildings and the more humble structures. In communities tied to Chicago by the commuter railroads, the contrast was even more heightened.

Aiding in accentuating these distinctions was an increasing number of well-trained, professional architects to design buildings, and of highly organized, competent contractors to construct them. In 1850 the area had few professionally trained architects. At the time of the Fire in 1871 the Chicago business directories listed ninety-three, but the only residences designed by the best of them were mansions for the wealthy. During the next two decades the profession expanded tremendously, and there were many more good designers in it. Now good architects began to design modest houses for the middle class and to supply builders with typical plans that were reproduced again and again. Builders also used standard plans obtained from pattern books and magazines, but they were not brought in to design buildings of much pretense. The wealthier members of the community, therefore, built not only the bigger houses but the ones that were more up to date and better designed as well.

During the earlier period building practices within the region were often quite diverse. Using materials and techniques readily at hand, a man could build his own house as he tilled the land, and a mason or carpenter could build one from time to time for a client or even on his own account to sell to a future resident. These local materials and practices produced a distinct regionalism. The cobblestone houses of Crystal Lake, the riverstone houses of the Fox River towns from Dundee to Aurora, and the limestone buildings in Lockport and Joliet are examples.

Even longer lasting in some towns was the continued dependence on strong local traditions or on an able, local carpenter with his own bag of tricks and decorative motifs which he worked into buildings as he adapted his designs to new stylistic models. The heavy, grooved, channeled, and bossed wooden ornamental pieces abounding on houses in Richmond or the abundance of sunburst motifs in Naperville's houses are examples.

Gradually, as houses became more complex, these regional practices gave way to the economies made possible by catalogue supply houses richly stocked with prefabricated pieces, and to changing tastes. Increasingly, middle class buyers wanted something resembling the houses that appeared in pattern books and magazines or approaching the works of professional architects and contractors. Builders responded by erecting whole streets of buildings for the choosey Chicago commuters, often by producing diluted versions or small-scale examples of the stylish mansions of the wealthy.

Meanwhile, the humblest buildings continued to be built in styles and forms of decoration that had long before fallen out of fashion in more pretentious buildings. Some seem to have an almost timeless quality—they were never important examples of the latest styles, but they have never been out of date.

The result of more than three generations of building activity during a period of drastic change accompanied by a longing for stability is a regional architecture, rich and diverse, more or less based on eastern styles, often revealing the traditional building methods and stylistic traits of diverse localities, a unique collection of buildings belonging to the communities which built them.

THE REGION'S STYLES

Terms referring to styles can heighten one's enjoyment of the rich diversity and general homogeneity of design found in the region's nineteenth century buildings. When properly used they focus one's vision on the formal qualities of buildings. They also make accessible the meanings the buildings' images conveyed to the people who built, used, and encountered them.[1]

During the last twenty or so years several terms for styles of nineteenth-century buildings have come into common use. Some of them derive from nineteenth-century sources, others from modern interpretations. They were not developed from an analysis of the buildings in the six-county area, and, therefore, their unstudied use could lead to misjudgments about these buildings. Needed is an understanding of how well they apply to the region's buildings. The stylistic sketches that follow attempt to provide an introduction to this understanding.

These sketches were developed after examining every structure presented in this guide book and many more as well, but not every nineteenth-century structure in the region, and so the sketches lack the balance needed for a comprehensive guide.

In addition, this guide is limited to the region around Chicago but excludes the city itself. One result of that exclusion is silence about one of the region's major contributions to international architecture, the invention of an architectural form appropriate to the tall, skeletal-framed commercial building. Another result is the lack of attention paid to another important building type, the multifamily residence, whether walk-up flat or elevator apartment building.

Each sketch includes five topics: the source of the style, the meanings it was thought to convey, its adaptation to local conditions, its penetration across the spectrum of the region's building activity, and its major visual characteristics.

Finally, notes accompanying each sketch refer to discussions of the style in four other publications. The first one, Marcus Whiffen, *American Architecture since 1780: A Guide to the Styles* (Cambridge, Mass., and London: MIT Press, 1969) was selected because it was the earliest and most comprehensive of this genre of literature. The debts to it of later authors are often quite conspicuous even if not always acknowledged. The second was included because it is easily available to people interested in old buildings: John Poppeliers, S. Allen Chambers, and Nancy B. Schwartz, *What Style is It*, originally a series of four articles in the quarterly of the National Trust for Historic Preservation, *Historic Preservation*, spanning from the April-June, 1976, through the January-March, 1977, issues, and published as a book in 1977. The third was selected only because it includes terms defined with reference to photographs of buildings rather than with words: John J.-G. Blumenson, *Identifying American Architecture: A Pictorial Guide to Styles and Terms, 1600–1945* (Nashville, Tennessee: American Association for State and Local History, 1977). The final one presents in an easy format a guide to the styles of a neighboring state: R. P. Meyer, D. J. Stith, and J. M. Dean, *Styles and Designs in Wisconsin Housing: A Guide to Styles* (Madison, Wisconsin: Cooperative Extension Programs, University of Wisconsin, October, 1974).[2]

THE FEDERAL STYLE (1785–1850)[3]

The Federal Style was the first variant within the classical styles produced in America. Classical architecture had been current for more than three hundred years when the new republic was formed. The Renaissance architects of Florence first began supplanting Gothic designs with classical ones in about 1420. The new classicism had swept all of Italy by 1460, penetrated into France before 1500, and by the time of the English colonization of America it was the reigning style in England.

Classical architecture is more a vocabulary than a statement, more a language to be manipulated to convey specific meanings than a fixed, inflexible, unsupple image. Since 1420 it had conveyed a number of different meanings with a wide variety of very different visual images. The revolutionary colonialists had grown up with an architecture that today we would call Georgian. It was based on the style developed by English architects around 1700 working from sixteenth-century Italian and seventeenth-century French and Dutch sources. Its American versions constitute the Georgian Colonial Style.

The Georgian Colonial Style was considered unsuitable for the buildings of the new republic. When building activity picked up after the capitulation of the British a new style, broadly called the Federal Style, took its place.[4] It was as varied as the former colonies and regions included within the new republic, and it could be as different in the effect it produced as the needs the new buildings were meant to satisfy.

The Federal Style was the product of several different architects, among them Thomas Jefferson. While minister to France during the Revolutionary War he had visited ancient Roman buildings in the south of France, and in Paris in 1785 he designed the new Capitol for Virginia in Richmond. It was to be a Roman temple with a full columnar portico supporting the pediment across its front. In 1817, after retiring from the presidency, he began the campus of the University of Virginia at Charlottesville. Facing one another across a central green were two rows of free-standing, temple-fronted residential structures for the professors linked by a colonnade tying them together into an ensemble. The green was headed by the library with a design based on that of the noblest building of ancient Rome, the Pantheon.

These buildings show Jefferson's belief that whole Roman building types could serve the institutional needs of the republic. He modified them as little as possible, and he showed a penetrating knowledge of the Roman orders in their design. He, and many of his countrymen, believed that the institutions of the new republic should not be housed in the building types of the royalist and aristocratic regimes of the old world. Instead, just as the virtue of the ancient Romans had inspired the early patriots, so, too, would their buildings provide model accommodations for the civil activities of the new republicans.

Jefferson had built his own house at Monticello before the Revolution, but he rebuilt it later to the form it has on the nickle coin. Its final design was based less directly on Roman models than on his study of the learned, rational, Roman-based theories and buildings of Andrea Palladio. Palladio, a late sixteenth-century architect active around Venice, produced books and buildings that were more important than those of any other single foreign architect in shaping America's buildings. Jefferson, following a long classical tradition, made a distinction in his works between the more monumental and proper public buildings and the residential structures which required a different scale and conveyed a different meaning.

Jefferson's legacy is primarily in larger, public buildings and in villa-like plantations. Other architects produced Federal Style designs for a wide range of building types—cathedrals, state houses, mansions, townhouses, waterworks, etc.—which showed how to draw on Rome, use severe massing similar to Jefferson's, and include precisely worked classical elements.

They drew on a different source from the ones Jefferson did, preferring the works of the brothers Adam to those of Palladio and the Italians. John, James, and especially Robert Adam were the most popular architects among the English aristocrats and nobility who fought and lost the war that made America independent. In American usage, however, the Adams' forms were straitened by a Palladian chastisement, and they were used sparingly. They appeared primarily in interior decoration and at the opening containing the front entrance where well-detailed pilasters, half-columns, or columns flanked sidelights below a fanlight, although they also occasionally found their way into window surrounds and appeared as a balustrade across the top silhouette.

Federal Style buildings, unless they are rare and important institutional buildings, have a composition and massing that remains independent of ancient buildings and so they do not resemble ancient buildings as much as they resemble one another. They have a simple massing that is worked into a tougher, tighter design than the Georgian Colonial Style had allowed. The refined, aristocratic elegance of the colonial period had given way to buildings which, whether Jeffersonian or Adamesque, suggested a disciplined mentality. Federal Style buildings, with their tauter surfaces and sharper edges, with fewer suggestions of shadow and less variation in outline and silhouette, and with a greater emphasis on proportion and the proper and studied use of a few, well-chosen decorative elements, seem to be worked out in the mind rather than spring forth from the senses. Whether in august public buildings or simple, refined private dwellings, these designs correspond to the rational basis of the United States Constitution, one of the great documents of the Enlightenment, the Age of Reason.

The six-county area was an unsettled wilderness beyond the frontier when the Federal Style began to give way to its successor, the Greek Revival Style. Only a few houses have designs based on it, and fewer yet show Jefferson's plantation Palladianism. Many more houses have prominent traces of the Federal Style in their lighter, more delicate classical elements, a legacy, perhaps, of the New England or middle Atlantic training of the builder during a period when the Federal Style was dominant or an indication that the owner wanted something familiar to him from his earlier residency in those areas.

THE GREEK REVIVAL (1820–1880)

The Greek Revival style eased the Federal Style from domination rather quickly after its introduction. The new style extended the trend toward severity, displacing Roman and Renaissance Palladian sources with those of ancient Greece.

The popularity of the style revealed a new assessment of the roles of Rome and Greece in early civilization. Greece was still part of the Islamic Ottoman Empire and largely unvisited during Jefferson's younger years.

Ancient Greeks were considered crude when Roman civilization was accepted as the highest attainment of the ancient world. As Enlightenment sentiment penetrated farther into first principles, however, Greece became an ever more enticing goal of travelers and its accomplishments began to replace Rome's in the popular estimation of greatness. Greek democracy now became the ideal against which the republic's citizens measured their own achievements.

Government buildings therefore began to appear in Greek-derived designs. In 1818 William Strickland's scheme for the Second Bank of the United States in Philadelphia used archaeologically precise elements in a pattern that came close to reproducing a whole ancient Greek temple. Its austere Doric order properly lacked a base and used fluted column shafts to support an entablature complete with triglyphs and metopes and supported a full and correct pediment.

Its interior was spanned with a barrel vault, a Roman rather than a Greek element, but he buried it within a roof pitch to make it invisible from the outside. Unlike Federal Style architects, the Greek Revival designers were willing to distort interior spatial configurations to satisfy the blocky requirements of exterior design, but one Roman element common in Federal Style buildings remained unpurged. That was the axial approach.

An ancient Greek temple stood free and had a colonnade and steps running around all four sides. The Romans designed temples as elements integrated into large, open spaces. They placed free-standing columns only along the front; those along the sides and back were flattened onto the wall as pilasters, and the steps were limited to the front and were framed by podia. This produced an emphatically axial design with a single, central and frontal viewing point, and it invited a person to approach and enter the building rather than simply walk admiringly around it.

The Greek Revival retained the frontal emphasis but combined it with plain walls, simple cubic massing derived from the form of the Greek temple, and elements such as columns, pilasters, window and door frames, and entablatures or cornices with a Greek simplicity and, at times, an archaeological correctness.

America's first professional architect, that is, the first person who depended upon his architectural practice for his livelihood, was Strickland's teacher, Benjamin Henry Latrobe, and Strickland was one of several in his generation. They had available an increased number of publications illustrating ancient Greek buildings and their details, and increasing numbers of builders' guides provided patterns for designing the new style's elements. Examples of the new style also became available to the general public in the early magazines of the period. The new style quickly spread into all corners of the new republic and out to the advancing frontier.

The Greek Revival Style became the dominant style of the public buildings, banks, mansions, and town houses in the growing towns and cities of the east which the first settlers bound for northern Illinois were leaving. It was also the style they saw on the trip west and in Illinois. The 1836 Bank of Illinois in Shawneetown, the main entry point from the Ohio River country, is an excellent example of the style. Built with an inspiring augustness and correctness, it has an odd rather than the canonic even number of Doric columns supporting its pediment. Even the one-story courthouse in Chicago that served Cook County between 1835 and 1856 was a Greek Revival Doric temple.

The style's simple massing and austere decorative elements made it ideal for use on the new frontier. It was easily built in traditional brick, stone, or braced frame construction, and in the new balloon frame method. The first building using that construction technique was Greek Revival.

The earliest industrial buildings in the six-county area were also based on the same style. America's industrial revolution began along the New England and the middle Atlantic water courses a bare generation before it found a foothold in northern Illinois. Surviving buildings along the Illinois and Michigan Canal and the Fox River reveal a close and satisfying match between the prevalent building technology, the materials available for its use, and the Greek Revival traits of the builders of these unpretentious structures. This match probably accounts for the longevity of the style among this humbler class of building. Throughout the six-county area many simple masonry mills, warehouses, and factories, and many small wooden houses as well, differ little in appearance whether built as early as 1830 or even after 1880.

More important buildings, those meant to have important imagery and with greater pretense and conscientiousness in their design, date from a more limited period. They span the years between about 1835, the earliest that people in the area had sufficient time and money to produce more than the routine, to about 1860, when the Greek Revival was replaced by a different version of classical architecture.[5]

Lurking within every Greek Revival design, whether a completely finished residence with columns and pediment or a mere industrial building with rough-faced ashlar walls and regularly disposed linteled windows, is the formal pattern of a Greek temple with a Roman axiality. A few churches provide the most vivid interpretations of the form. The temple prototype is clearest in a pedimented stone church with pilasters on all four walls and placed on a high basement which contains the entrance. It is still present, however, in a pedimented clapboard-clad frame structure with an entrance placed within a porch framed by columns, an element that survives from the Federal Style, and marked with a steeple which comes from the Colonial Georgian Style.

Only a few of the area's residences use the style's full temple form with a row of columns supporting a pediment. The entablature returns down the sides and across the back to provide a crown for the walls. In the most common type the entrance is placed at one end of the gable elevation which faces the street. A variant has the entrance on the long side. Here the columns support an entablature which supports the roof pitch, and the porch is carved out of the block of the building. A rare type has a square plan with a hipped roof and a colonnade on three sides but no pediment.

The area's residences use Doric columns but they are not always the stout, baseless Greek Doric. They will often be fluted, but smooth shafts are also common. These and other liberties found in the proportions and details were taken either from a sense of license or out of ignorance of what is "correct," but they do not necessarily detract from the quality of the design. Indeed, the handling of proportions, the placement of openings, and the treatment of details reveal how skillful the designer was, or wasn't.

Greek Revival houses are typically one, one-and-a-half, or two stories high. Those lower than two stories almost never light the upper story with roof dormers (when they exist they are almost certainly later additions). Instead, windows are placed in the gable (if there is no pediment) with a lintel set above the crown of the long walls. If a pediment precludes these windows, small ones may be set into the entablature or cornice of the long wall and sometimes across the front as well.

Wings could be added to increase the interior volume. Most commonly in this area only one was used, producing an "L" plan; a "T" plan is extremely rare. The wing is lower than the main block—for example, a one-and-a-half story wing might be added to a two story structure. The wing was placed well back from the front in order not to detract from the force of the gable-front design. The wing would often have a porch along its entire length and a secondary entrance, and it might have wall dormers to increase the space available for use and provide light in the attic.

Ancient Greek temples were built of white marble or the best quality stone available, but wood is the most common material used for Greek Revival structures in America and in the six-county area. Brick and stone examples also abound with cornices and door frames in wood. The wood was meant to suggest but not imitate the stone originals, and so the clapboard-clad frame buildings were painted white. The clapboards are now often hidden under the asbestos, metal, and vinyl siding disfiguring many fine examples of the style. In brick buildings the lintels are usually stone, although some of the earliest examples use flat brick arches. Because the round arch was never used by the Greeks in important works, it does not appear in Greek Revival buildings. Roofs were shingle, although most now have modern roofing materials.

The prototypical design, the one that most resembles a Greek temple, was usually diluted. Buildings lacking the frontispiece of columns suggest it by reducing the columns to pilasters, often placing them only at the corners and even reducing these to simple corner boards. The cornice crowning the long wall and following the pitch up across the gable may be anything from a wide entablature to a thin board; to suggest the pediment it may be extended horizontally across the gable or, more commonly, be stopped after a few inches to form a cornice return that makes a clipped pediment.

Gable-front houses lacking the full frontispiece often had porches, although most of them have been removed or replaced, even during the nineteenth century, to "modernize" the house. Typically, an original porch was only in front of the entrance with columns, or perhaps piers or even simple posts, supporting an entablature or cornice like the one crowning the wall.

If the builder of a pitch-front building was not willing to sacrifice the interior space required for a porch, he would add one with columns, or piers, or even simple posts, along the long side. The porch's slope was the same as the one used for the main roof, but it began a bit below the upper roof's cornice.

Even a humble house with simple corner boards and a clipped pediment could be given great dignity by lavishing attention on its openings, allowing them to differ little from the treatment given more pretentious buildings. This tends to occur earlier rather than later in the style's currency. The typical entrance is a single door with a rectangular transom light and sometimes with side lights framed with columns, half-columns, pilasters, or, most commonly, piers. A version of the framing elements used for the door was repeated for the windows. These were rectangular and approximated the proportions of a double square with each sash of the double-hung window approximately square. The windows were sometimes extended down to the floor level. In wood construction the lintel, sometimes crowned by a thin cornice moulding, might project slightly beyond the vertical members of the frame. In wood or stone, the lintel's upper edge might have a slight upward pitch.

The design of these elements may be severe, plain, and archaeologically correct, and even include acanthus leaves or other decorative forms, but they will never be elaborate. Richness was characteristic of the earlier styles which the severity of the Greek Revival was meant to purge, but it soon returned after people grew weary of Grecian restraint.

THE GOTHIC REVIVAL STYLE (1840–1885)

If the Greek Revival was the last clear emblem of the Enlightenment mentality, the Gothic Revival was the first product of Romantic sentimentality to penetrate American architecture.

Architects and builders working from Colonial and Federal traditions had developed the Greek Revival Style. A few clients, architects, and skillful publicists challenged its hegemony with the Gothic Revival. Its earlier history had been passed in England, where, since early in the eighteenth century, gothic designs had been used for occasional follies and other light-hearted structures decorating aristocratic country estates. By the end of the century it was used for entire country houses, and people had begun "restoring" churches to a supposed gothic splendor. Still, the gothic was more a fancy than a style and did not yet merit an initial capital letter.

When the Houses of Parliament had to be rebuilt following a destructive fire in 1834, the English had decided that the Gothic was their own early invention and believed it carried true English values just as surely as the classical styles revealed those of the Mediterranean world. Their history was wrong—the Gothic was French, not English, in origin—but the new Houses of Parliament were still rebuilt in a style that looked Gothic.

In the United States, the Gothic Revival did not so easily dislodge the classical styles from public buildings and other urban building types. Instead, it took root as the proper setting for the family living in domestic suburban isolation and for suburban churches and schools.

The classical styles produce formal buildings in an urban setting and were best seen from a single viewpoint. A Gothic Revival building is informal. It is meant to sit in a landscape and be seen from a number of different view points. It is the material from which one might make a picture, or it is a picture made concrete on the land, and hence the term picturesque refers to the style's aesthetic category. Its broken, asymmetrical massing, silhouette, and detail should delight the eye from various vantage points and from near and far. The design should not present one clear and memorable image as a Greek Revival building does. Greek Revival designs are orderly and are meant to move the mind to think noble thoughts about civic life and virtue. The appeal of the Gothic Revival is romantic; it is meant to enchant and to stimulate the sentiments to reveries on the virtues of domestic life.

The Gothic Revival never did displace the Greek Revival but settled in beside it. On the basis of taste, or of conviction, or of cost, or on some other grounds, an individual chose one over the other much as he selected one candidate for office over another. Free American voters, after all, determine their own destinies and representatives in government. The people accept a position if it stands on its own merit, not because it is advanced by a person in a position of authority or is sanctified by historical traditions. In England, the style's promoters appealed to authority and history, and some of its supporters in America tried the same tactic, but ultimately individuals, whether choosing between political candidates or styles for houses, decided for themselves on whatever basis they wished. The result was an American tradition rich in diversity and with a necessary complement, a tolerance for conflicting beliefs, the combination required for the American tradition called pluralism.

The easy cohabitation along American streets of the Greek and Gothic Revivals is an architectural manifestation of the pluralist tradition. The earliest settlers may have known some of the earliest Gothic Revival country estates along the Hudson River and in the middle Atlantic suburbs, and builders with experience in the style were doubtless among later settlers, but the main avenue bringing the style to the frontier was a spate of books that began appearing in the 1840s. Intended for the householder rather than the professional house builder, they differed from the builders' guides that had assisted in disseminating the Greek Revival Style. These had supplied patterns for individual elements to be assembled into the finished building, as did the new books, but the new ones added whole house patterns with plans, views of the exterior and of interior rooms, designs for furniture, and even discussions of plumbing, heating, ventilating, and tasteful decorating. They were written to be read and enjoyed by those who would live in the new houses as well as to inform the carpenters who would build them. One of the most popular was *The Architecture of Country Houses* by Andrew Jackson Downing first published in 1850 with nine printings producing more than 16,000 copies by the end of the Civil War.

These books showed plans based on interior use rather than exterior appearance. Unlike Greek Revival plans with their formal arrangement of rectangular rooms, these allowed a variety of room configurations, each suitable for a particular domestic purpose, all assembled into easily habitable combinations. This could produce an asymmetrical and irregular exterior massing quite appropriate for the picturesque aesthetic, anathema to that of the Greek Revival, and easily constructed in balloon framing.

The books favored stone construction but recognized that wood was the more common building material. Most of the decorative elements—the door and window mouldings in particular—, while drawn from the practice of medieval masons, could easily be rendered in wood, while other parts—particularly bargeboards, porch posts, and lintels—had no precedent in stone. These pieces were exactly suited to the new technology of woodworking based on powerful saws and other instruments for shaping wood, especially the jigsaw or scroll saw which cut curvilinear shapes. The Greek Revival Style had no place to put the fanciful pieces made possible by the new tools, but the styles presented in the new house pattern books reveled in them and used them to picturesque advantage.

The new books illustrated a number of different picturesque styles. The first to catch the popular imagination in the six-county area was the Gothic Revival Style.[6] A few churches illustrate it as it had been developed in the east by 1840, although the region's examples are later. Among the houses are some high-style examples derived from the pattern books or based on eastern practice with local modification.

The plans of these buildings are based on the shape of an "L" or, more commonly in the earliest examples, of a "T." The disposition to symmetry remained so strong that although there was much talk of irregular massing, the "T" plan usually had a porch on both sides of the stem which projected toward the street. Typically, Gothic Revival houses have porches large enough to be called verandas and were used for enjoying the out-of-doors, an activity that began with the Romantic period.

The wings forming the building's mass are generally rather narrow, a proportion that is emphasized by their steeply pitched roofs. Their eaves generally begin below the lintel of the gable windows, and they extend into broad overhangs both along the sides and over the gables. Both roof and wall dormers are common features; the angle of their pitched roofs follows that of the main roofs. Windows are generally tall and narrow, and may be of various sizes in different parts of the same building. Although the east's stone buildings' pointed arches are common and are also found in wooden ones, in the six-county area there are no stone examples, and the brick and wood buildings only very rarely have pointed arches over their openings. When they do, they are usually nailed on the wall over flat-headed windows. The massing is often broken by protruding bay windows and sometimes by balconies.

Whether built of brick or wood, the building often receives the products of woodworkers using power-driven tools to produce what is often called the "Carpenter Gothic" style. They are used as frames for the openings, sometimes to suggest a pointed arch but more commonly making a hood moulding. They provide a rich variety of turned and curved wooden forms for porches. And they furnish the finials and pendants at gable tops, the punctured fillets in gable peaks, and the punctured and moulded barge-boards on the gables and dormers.

The siding is generally clapboard, although a few examples of the board and batten commonly used since the style's introduction survive in the region. While Greek Revival houses were almost invariably white, Gothic Revival houses were often painted in muted shades based on greens and browns. Grey, varying from off-white to a middle shade, or lighter tints of yellow, from near white to a middle tone, were often used for the trim, mouldings, and frames around the openings.

The six-county area has as few prime examples of high style Gothic Revival houses as it does Greek Revival ones of similar finish and pretense. It also has relatively few pure dilutions of the high style, although there are examples with the typical massing but lacking the rich woodwork and many that appear to have been diluted Gothic Revival houses before they were altered. Much more common—indeed, almost as common as diluted Greek Revival houses—are buildings that fuse the general configuration of the Greek Revival with some of the most common characteristics of the Gothic Revival. The result is not so much an impure example of one or the other as it is a Greek-Gothic hybrid. This was obviously an acceptable house type to buyers and a common product of carpenter-builders.

The plan of this house type is generally like that of a Greek Revival structure but it seems taller and is topped by a steeply pitched roof with broad overhangs. The frames for the openings may be Greek or Gothic, and the ornamental elements used for the porch in the same structure may be the opposite. The building may be symmetrical except for a bay window or a porch in the reentrant angle of an "L" shaped plan which breaks up that massing with a suggestion of the picturesque aesthetic.

The Greek-Gothic hybrid appeared as soon as the Gothic Revival did, and it persisted long after the waning of the style in its more self-conscious form, just as the diluted versions of the Greek Revival did.

One of the hybrid's main attributes, which it shared with the diluted Greek Revival, was its relatively small size. Both of the six-county area's first styles were used for smaller houses than the styles that followed them, and they remained the typical design for small houses until a different pattern for smaller houses displaced them, a time which may have coincided with the time the carpenter-builders who produced them began to retire and be superseded by others trained in the later styles.

The Gothic Revival was gradually nudged from prominence among high style buildings by the Italianate, but after the Civil War it reëmerged as a richer, more complex style. It retained many of the same picturesque qualities, now emphasized by combining brick and stone in the walls, using slate of various colors on the roof, and placing rich cast iron cresting along the silhouette. Often called the High Victorian Gothic or, more broadly, the Victorian, it had been brought to America from England where it had become the vogue in the 1850s. It enjoyed a little over a decade of popularity before being swamped by the Queen Anne, leaving behind a few enjoyable examples of large houses and some churches in the six-county area, but it did not percolate into the more humble levels or spread broadly across the area's building activity.

THE ITALIANATE STYLE (1845–1900)

The house pattern books that broadcast the Gothic Revival included other styles but only one of these, the Italianate, captured the popular imagination in the six-county area.

Like the Gothic Revival, the Italianate reached into the past for a style adaptable to the needs of Americans. It was not promoted with any moral fervor about its being a true and proper style, nor as the only appropriate one for some high and noble purpose. It became popular because it satisfied the increasing appetite for picturesque designs and imposing buildings.

The English and American architects and authors popularizing the style cited the villas of Tuscany as their source, but their designs were very free interpretations of these often quite somber buildings. They, and their Italianate adaptations, were very different from the ones used by Colonial Georgian and Federal architects. Indeed, one characteristic of the new style is that the designer shows imagination rather than reverence in interpreting and adopting his sources. The result was an independence that made the term Italianate rather than Italian or Renaissance the name of the new style, although the others were used at times.

The Italianate reigned as a high style through two generations, the second distinctly different from the first. The first generation extended from the style's introduction in the 1840s to the Civil War, the second from the late 1860s to the end of the century, although the style quickly lost out to others in important buildings during the 1880s.

Both generations found it a style of pride. The second generation built on the first generation's experience using a greater profusion of elements and complexity of details to achieve a grander effect. By enhancing its massing with large-scale decorative elements, designers could produce the highly valued memorable and forceful image and overbearing presence which people of the period called "character."

Its "character" made it popular for the new public buildings and institutional structures—courthouses, schools, colleges, insane asylums, etc.— required as the frontier matured. Railroads used it for commuter stations, although they turned to an even more impressive style for the main terminal. And it was favored by those who wished to display their new wealth, especially during its second generation. This led later critics to stigmatize it as the style of vulgar, parvenu display, a style, they said, that revealed a lack of cultivated taste and ability by the designer matched only by the owner's luxurious love of the display of wealth.

Quite early on, the style had become associated with commerce. Its early popularity coincided with the introduction of cast iron, sheet metal, and plate glass and of the commercial building types those materials made possible. The Italianate became the dominant style for the imposing two- and three-story business and commercial structures lining the downtown streets of the towns in the six-county area. As the century wore on its forms became heavier and more ponderous, but the style remained current in new commercial construction around Chicago until after the turn of the century.

The style used the picturesque aesthetic but it also drew heavily on the clean-cut massing of the classical styles, and it used two different major compositional patterns, one asymmetrical, the other symmetrical.

One of the asymmetrical patterns is sometimes set aside as a separate style called the Italian Villa Style.[7] It has an L-shaped plan with each wing rising two stories and with each wing topped by pitched roofs. Rising in the reentrant angle is a three-story tower with the entrance which is fronted by a porch. Other configurations are also common for bringing together the two or more blocks and the taller, hip-roofed tower.

The symmetrical version of the Italianate came in two basic patterns. The early and rarer form is a cube topped by a gently sloped hipped roof truncated to produce a flat top. The central section of the cube's front is stepped forward slightly and extended upward into a three-story tower with its own hipped roof. The other pattern, by far the more common, is a similar cube but now with a two-story veranda crossing the entire front and projecting forward in the center marking the entrance and substituting for the tower. A cupola atop the hipped roof reinforces the central axis of the two-story mass. A lower service wing often added at or towards the back adds interior space without disturbing the basic symmetry.

Whether asymmetrical or symmetrical, the clear-cut massing is sharpened with quoins when possible. The building is set high off the ground requiring imposing steps to reach the first floor. The ceilings are also higher than those in earlier styles. When augmented by a tower or cupola the result could be quite impressive.

Various elements were added to the mass to produce "character." During the earlier generation carpenters displayed the products of their power tools; during the later period architects and designers showed off their inventiveness.

The most common element was the bracket. Indeed, brackets are so much a required element in the Italianate that the style is sometimes called the "Bracketed Style." Its most common form was that of a double curve. Pendants or knobs were often added at the bottom, and the surfaces of the brackets were often incised, punctured, and grooved. They were often used in pairs, although sometimes only at the corners and in reinforcing the lines of the edges of the porch projecting beyond the veranda. They were obligatory under the eaves and appeared elsewhere, for example in supporting lintels at the window heads, along the porch lintels, and atop the posts holding the porch lintel.

Bay windows, either flat-fronted or polygonal, were another favorite element. Along with verandas, they could break up the blockiness of the masses to produce a picturesque appearance and add "character" to the design. The veranda across the front often returned down one side to terminate at a projecting wing toward the rear. A projecting central porch marking the entrance might be enriched with a pediment. Like the bays, the veranda and porch were usually in wood with robust square posts, octagonal posts, or stout Tuscan columns supporting solid lintels. During the earlier generation lintels and cornices often had scroll cut tracery of quite liberal dimensions draped underneath or attached to the face along with spindels, knobs, and other forms. This produced the "Steamboat Gothic," the Italianate's analogue to the "Carpenter Gothic."

The large bracketed cornices often had panels and sometimes small windows, like those in the entablatures of Greek Revival buildings, to light attic rooms.

Openings were large. The typical entrance had double doors and a transom light, but side lights were rare. Windows often extended to the floor. The wooden construction that dominated the earlier generation's Italiante houses prevented using the fully rounded window arches with prominent keystones found in the east, but the institutional buildings of the period were in stone and they have them.

The second generation of the Italianate relished heavy ornament, particularly around openings, along the cornice line, and in the porch. The forms are sometimes drawn from the "U.S. Grant" or the Eastlake decorative styles, which are discussed later, but high style examples commonly use Roman, Renaissance, and Baroque forms that are enlarged, enriched, and abstracted.

Particularly favored was the Renaissance tabernacle window, a full frame fitted around an opening. Its mouldings were made large and heavy, the lower and upper sections of the jambs (or side members) were extended out to form feet and shoulders, and the lintel and pediment were forced together to form a single element. This enlarged lintel was sometimes supported by brackets, consoles, or other shoulder devices extending from the jambs or even from the wall beyond them.

Such a window was expensive, so for slightly humbler buildings the favored opening was a segmental shouldered (or stilted) arch with a prominent keystone. In brick buildings this was often built in stone or in a color of brick differing from that of the walls. Even though this was a masonry form it was commonly used in wooden buildings.

Below the high style the Italianate left two important legacies, both prominent in the area's building practice up to the end of the century.

One was a repertoire of forms used for decorating a basic, gable-front clapboard Greek Revival house. Instead of Greek Revival forms, the standard wood frame structure was given brackets, oversized Italianate window surrounds, and a full-length porch with square posts and bracketed lintel, while a bay window might protrude from one or both sides to provide a picturesque touch.

The other descended from more substantial aspects of the style. This was the standard, older "grandmother's house" type. It is the basic cube in clapboard-clad balloon frame or in brick and topped with a hipped roof and with bracketed eaves, a full or partial porch, Italianate window and door surrounds, and bay windows. To enlarge it the cube could be extended at one corner with a wing, perhaps ending in a polygonal bay. This house type lasted as long as the diluted Greek Revival and the Greek-Gothic hybrid types did, providing slightly more space for a slightly higher cost.

THE SECOND EMPIRE STYLE (1855–1900)

Largely concurrent with the Italianate was a style providing an extra quotient of grandeur, the Second Empire Style.[8]

The style achieved instant popularity in the mid-1850s following its introduction in major government buildings in London and, slightly earlier, in Paris which the new Emperor, Napoleon III, set about rebuilding after he assumed imperial authority in 1852. The new style was based on earlier French styles but so loosely that it amounted to a new one. Its introduction served notice that a new civil order was being instituted, a civil order promising a progressive future firmly founded on past grandeur but independent of former errors. Like the new continental governments of the period, it was both a revival and an invention.

Paris was just then becoming the mecca of newly-rich Americans. Architects began going there to study architecture, and merchants began installing buyers there. The Parisian Second Empire style was used for Marshall Field's new store on State Street which was stocked with the latest Parisian fashions when it burned in the Fire of 1871, and it was the style of Potter Palmer's new hotel built at the same time and rebuilt even more grandly after the Fire to provide an even higher level of Parisian service.

In its fully-developed form the style had four major characteristics. One was in the composition of the massing. The design was divided into five blocks (in longer structures, the pattern could be extended, but always with an odd number of units). The central one was the highest, the ones on each end were like it but slightly smaller, and each of the three projected forward. Connecting these sections, which are called pavilions, were lower, recessed wings. This compositional pattern was often the only one finding its way into a building, especially an institutional one, that was otherwise Italianate.

The second characteristic was an abundance of columns (often paired, limited to one story in height, and repeated on each story), entablatures or string courses, pediments, tabernacle windows, quoins, dormers, chimneys, and balustrades. These were masonry forms rendered in stone and taken from the seventeenth-century Baroque rather than from the comparatively austere Renaissance which had preceded it. Because the historical Baroque's forms were inadequate for producing the "character" the designers and builders sought, they were enlarged and exaggerated, and used in greater abundance.

The third characteristic was in the vertical division of the facade. The ground floor was generally treated as a high basement with large, rusticated blocks, sometimes opened with arches, providing a firm base for the two or three "character"-filled stories that followed. The top floor was then given a special roof that could properly terminate the vertical subdivisions and emphasize the processions and recessions of the five-part division of the horizontal composition.

The fourth characteristic was the Mansart roof. Named for the great seventeenth-century French architect François Mansart who used it well but did not invent it, a Mansart rises from a cornice with a very steep pitch and then flattens out to a top hidden from view below. The result is an additional story which is lit by dormers usually aligned with the windows below. Roof intersections and the top of the lower slope generally have large, highly conspicuous mouldings. The upper one, called a curb, is usually ornamented with cresting of some sort to enrich the silhouette. The lower slope may be a straight plane, or it may have a convex outward bulge or be concave, running down to a flare near the base. This last form was the most popular in the six-county area. The roof is usually slate, often in a variety of colors and patterns.

The style added pomposity to pride. It was more common in large urban structures than in the types found beyond the urban centers. In the six-county area it was usually limited to the Mansart roof placed atop an otherwise orthodox Italianate structure. Found as early as the late 1850s, these roofs continue in vogue nearly until the end of the century. Sometimes one wing of a house will have a Mansart while another will have the mid-slope pitched roof of the Italianate. The Italianate Style did not use dormers; when they appear on an Italiante hipped roof, the designer was probably thinking the roof was a Mansart even if the curb is lacking and brackets rather than a Baroque cornice terminate its base.

After the turn of the century the Mansart again became popular, but it was now sleeker and used as the termination for a more learned Neo-Classical design rather than above the exaggerated and abstracted classicism of the early period.

THREE DECORATIVE STYLES: THE STICK, THE "U.S. GRANT," AND THE EASTLAKE

Architectural and decorative styles were often mixed in a seemingly helter-skelter manner during the second half of the nineteenth century. We often condemn this procedure because the architectural practice of the last fifty years has not distinguished between architectural and decorative styles. Building construction and architectural design have become intimately interdependent. The applied decoration used to enhance openings, porches, cornices, and other parts of nineteenth-century buildings has been banned for several generations as an article of faith about architectural styles. The result is that we hardly comprehend a nineteenth-century description that might praise a building because its "design is Italianate and its style is Norman." For us, design and style are the same; if the design is Italianate, then so too is the style, and vice versa.

The major architectural styles of the period were used principally as guides for establishing the larger, broader aspects of design, for example, the relationship between plan and massing, the character of the massing's composition, and the size, proportion, and placement of openings. In their earlier years, and for their more high-style applications, the major styles came equipped with a number of elements for use in the places requiring decoration. But architects, designers, builders, and clients were not bound by rules of stylistic consistency, especially as a style aged and as it was used for more humble building types within the rather rigid hierarchy of decorum that gave stability and order to architecture and society during the period. The public expectation was that among the higher level of buildings, just as in the upper levels of society, more proper codes of conduct were to be used. It was, after all, a period when people "called" on others by leaving a calling card, when a person might or might not be "at home" even if she was in her home, when people dressed for dinner, when gentlemen deferred to ladies and when ladies expected to be deferred to. It has been said of the period that the masses slept uncomfortably in nightgowns on hot nights because they believed those of class wore nightgowns.

Many of the most interesting buildings in the six-county area are humbler structures built by and for middle class and working class residents which show a greater independence in combining design and style than do high-style examples. This may be because their builders knew no better, or because the builders' clients or the builders' guesses about their market were ignorant of what was proper, or because there was a willing indulgence in whimsy at the expense of strict obedience to a decorum they did know. Whatever the case, it is important to recognize that in these buildings the styles of the design and decoration may be different.

During the generation or more of building activity after mid-century three major decorative styles were applied to the major architectural styles. These decorative styles did not develop into an architectural style in the six-county area although elsewhere in the country one of them did. That one was the Stick Style, the earliest of the three.[9] It was among the styles in the house pattern books that carried the Gothic Revival and the Italianate to the Midwest, and it appeared most often in designs based on those two styles. It is the first decorative (or architectural) style developed in this country that did not use wood to imitate or emulate decorative forms originally used in stone buildings.

In this region it provided the design for sheathing, especially in gables and bay windows, of frame houses by using flat boards to form panels and often to crisscross them with diagonals often over a background of clapboard or shingles. It also furnished verandas and porches with flat boards, squarish timbers, and small pieces of lumber, sometimes with rounded or moulded edges, that built up a rich decorative pattern. Wooden bosses, roundels, diamonds, and other plaque-like shapes were often included in these elements and in cornices, along porch lintels, and on gable rafters.

The second decorative style, the "U.S. Grant" Style, was introduced after the Civil War.[10] The name reveals the early popular esteem in which the General and President was held, particularly in Illinois. The house given him in Galena, which he left to move into the White House in 1869, was an Italianate villa with proper if spare Italianate ornament, and the decorative style was most often used within that architectural style and in those of the Second Empire and the later Gothic Revival.

It drew its decorative forms from Greek ornament, particularly from anthemia, palmettes, meanders, and other patterns, and it included the stout obelisks sitting atop the ends of sheet metal cornices on commercial structures. The original, delicate Greek forms were abstracted into robust, heavy, and sometimes quite coarse forms, and they were often enriched with spherical knobs, globular patera, and other pieces produced on a lathe. The material of the originals was marble, but those in the "U.S. Grant" style were often wood, sheet metal, and terra cotta. Eventually the cycle turned back on itself and these forms were rendered in stone.

The Eastlake was the third decorative style.[11] It was named for an English furniture designer who in 1868 published a book in England on design that was reprinted in Boston in 1872 to a very popular reception. It became the successor to the earlier generation's "Steamboat Gothic."

The Eastlake Style made two important contributions to the six-county area. One is an incised decorative pattern that quickly spread across lintels and on their flat stone and wooden surfaces.[12] Produced with a simple V-shaped or U-shaped gouge that left a tight line of unaltered width, its forms are quite distinctive. Favorites were a thistle, palm, lily, or other floral form rendered with a wiry abstraction. The other was a love for turned and chiseled wooden elements—spindels, knobs, struts, brackets, posts, balusters, etc.—used to construct elaborate porches and other elements protruding from the mass of the building.

The Eastlake Style was usually used to make a simple design, generally a Gothic Revival or Italianate one, more elaborate. The juxtaposition of richly complex Eastlake porches with spare, clapboard houses is sometimes quite enchanting. The style was so extensively used farther west, both among buildings of all kinds and on each individual building, that it assumed a dominant role in design and therefore nearly produced an architectural style. The result was generally called Eastlake construction; it had an appearance that left the English furniture designer aghast when he learned of it. He had intended, he claimed, to refine the taste for furniture and not to spawn a vulgar and decorative architecture.

THE QUEEN ANNE STYLE (1880–1905)

The Queen Anne style represents a triumph—of the middle class as patrons of architecture, of the architect as skillful designer, and of transportation and industry as supplier of building materials.[13]

The Queen Anne style is the first architectural style used in America to spread upward from the bottom—that is, it was first used for residences and only later for public and institutional buildings. The residences were not the urban mansions that in earlier styles provided diluted designs to serve lower uses and suburban needs but the seaside villas and country houses of the wealthy that offered a relaxed and open charm lacking in their formal and stoney mansions. The new residential style was quickly appropriated by the middle class and spread across their rapidly expanding suburbs. Only then was it adapted for other suburban uses, particularly for churches.

The style appeared as an increasingly populous and affluent middle class began to need architects. To handle the flood of new commissions, architects now began to appear from schools and, more usually, from the offices of older practitioners. Architects now began to receive professional periodicals with handsome renderings and, shortly after, with reproductions of photographs which quickly spread the latest fashions across the country and throughout the profession. Young men eager to make their mark in the profession often made the renderings—Frank Lloyd Wright produced them for Joseph Lyman Silsbee, his first employer, in 1887. Popular illustrated magazines and newspapers consumed by middle class subscribers also carried them. The extreme picturesque qualities of the Queen Anne Style are partly the result of designing buildings that would look good in published renderings.

By now the building industry could supply all kinds of materials in all kinds of shapes from all kinds of places at a reasonable price. Architects took pride in using a wide variety of materials and in manipulating the balloon framing technique in ever more flexible patterns. A Queen Anne house often seems to be the result of forcing into one picturesque design all the skills of the designer and all the riches of the builders' yards.

Because the style had begun with domestic architecture, domestic needs dictated its development. The style extended the Gothic Revival principle of subordinating the exterior to interior requirements, but now the buildings were much larger and catered to a wider range of requirements. To enter required at least a porte-cochere, veranda, interior vestibule, and reception room. The public rooms included a parlor, library, dining room, conservatory, and breakfast or morning room. The service area had to have a butler's pantry, storage pantries, kitchen, laundry, and maids' rooms. The private area contained bedrooms, some with recesses, alcoves, or balconies, and closets and bathrooms.

In the Queen Anne Style, for the first time, it was possible to design each of these to its own best advantage. For example, the morning room could be oriented to the east and the library to the west, the dining room could enjoy a prospect of the garden, the parlor could be separated from the library, the conservatory could protrude to catch more light, and so on. The design could be precisely adapted to the site as well. For example, houses on corner lots could differ from those on interior lots. No previous style had offered so much, or, to put it the other way around, no earlier combination of clientele, design profession, and building industry had called forth a style to satisfy such a complex set of requirements since the boom period of seaside villa construction in early Imperial Roman times.

The Queen Anne Style, like all major styles, conveyed a meaning, even if it was a spurious one for its form. The style had been introduced to great numbers of people by a small group of English-designed buildings housing the British commissioners at the American Centennial Exposition in Philadelphia in 1876. Their form was based on recent trends in residential design in England and America. The popular and professional press in this country associated the style with the pre-Georgian colonial period of the last Stuart queen (reigned 1702–14) even while properly recognizing that it was closer to Elizabethan styles (Queen Elizabeth, reigned 1558–1603) which were closer in date to the establishment of the first New England colonies. Pedantry has never checked popular acceptance, however; people could see that these buildings were different from those in the aristocratic Georgian Colonial Style, and they accepted the Queen Anne as the indigenous style used by the early New Englanders to satisfy their own special domestic needs with the available building materials while using local craft habits. Thus, the Queen Anne was taken as the first authentic American style, one that had been grown at home and not imported from England, France, or Italy. But pedantry can revile error, and a generation later when a revival based on the Georgian Colonial Style became the rage, the Queen Anne was condemned as a bastard offspring of error and license.

It was also excoriated as a style of "shingled castles." In a sense it was the Chateauesque style of the middle class, with corner turrets of wooden construction, but it was much more than that. It represented a half-century's experience with wood used for domestic architecture, and it was preëminently a style for wooden buildings. But soon brick construction, which had always been considered a poor substitute for stone, began to emulate the rich textures, patterns, colors, and variations in scale found in the wooden structures. The barb was a veiled complaint that the style was working upward from the bottom through the hierarchy of construction materials just as it was through the similar one of building types.

The High Victorian Gothic Style popular in England and on the east coast had made little headway in the six-county area, but it had called forth from brick yards a variety of machine-moulded brick forms and various brick colors beyond the ones the raw clays themselves yielded. These provided the variety required in Queen Anne designs. Similarly, the terra cotta industry, which flourished in the Chicago area as it did nowhere else, developed rapidly during the 1880s to supply an increased quantity of textured, sculpted, and patterned pieces for Queen Anne structures. But brick construction was always more expensive than wood, so it was used only where required by fire laws or to the extent that a client's sense of importance was accompanied by a generous building budget. This excluded it from most suburban residences and limited it to a few suburban commercial and public buildings.

The appearance of the style is more easily described with design principles than with actual visual elements. The point of using the style was to produce something different, and in that, the designers were very successful, time and again, even in relatively small structures. The major principles and their implementation seem to have been the following:

Each floor level will have a different texture:

Generally having two stories and a full attic, the building is usually set on a high basement of rough-faced yellow limestone. This masonry base often rises to the level of the ground floor window sills and, in places, through the whole ground floor and sometimes into a conspicuous exterior chimney. The first floor is sometimes brick but clapboard, often of very thick dimensions, is more usual. The second floor is often shingled as is the roof which it sometimes slides into through an indistinct cornice, although a clear and distinct cornice is common. The wall shingles usually have a variety of patterns, especially in the gables, which may have pent roofs.

The massing will be broken up:

Interior spaces often push outward into wings and exterior bulges or recede with indentations. The upper floor may project in places beyond the first floor or be recessed to form a balcony. Similarly, gable ends often extend beyond the walls below, or the wall may have splayed corners beneath a projecting gable.

Every window will be different, or at least the windows for each room will be different:

Bay and bow windows abound, not as elements attached to the wall but as protuberances pushing out the exterior sheathing. Window lintels and sills often extend across the wall as string courses. Upper story windows are generally smaller than ground floor windows. Multilight sashes may be mixed with single pane ones, casement or double-hung windows may be arranged in continuous strips, and windows may be bent or curved around corners. Two window types are particular favorites. One is a tall, thin oval window set in the gable or elsewhere with a keystone-like wedge set between each quadrant. The other is the Palladian window with its distinctive combination of square-headed windows, usually double-hung, flanking an arched window with the arch springing from the lintel of the flanking windows.

The roof will change pitch often and produce a varied silhouette:

Hipped roofs occur, but pitched roofs are more common, as are various forms of dormers. Chimneys are also worked into the composition. The result is a plethora of shapes breaking up the form and adding picturesque interest.

Whenever possible, use an oriel or a corner bay window, and extend one corner oriel as a tower above the roof's eaves to terminate in a roof shaped like a bell, cone, spire, or pyramid.

There will be a large and inviting veranda:

The veranda may be carved out of the interior space or placed against the exterior wall. Either way, it covers more than one face, often sweeping around a corner with a great curve. The entrance is often marked by some special feature, and the entire veranda is enriched with a variety of turned elements often based on the classical orders but with an unclassical thinness. Especially popular were clusters of porch posts separated by spindles so tightly packed they produce a balustrade with a visual texture rather than a pattern. The Eastlake experience made possible this proficiency in woodworking, but the general delicacy and refinement of the turned pieces and their disciplined arrangement separate the Queen Anne spindle work from Eastlake examples.

Finally, whether in wood or brick, a variety of colors will be used:

The colors generally provide a distinctive contrast between the clapboard and shingle fields and the borders, frames, string courses, and cornices crossing and defining them. Buildings in the six-county area were apparently never gaudily painted with various pieces of a single post, spindle, or window frame receiving different, bright colors. Instead, the preference was for broad contrasts within a range of sympathetic rather than complementary colors—for example, yellow for trim, green for shingles (except those on the roof—they remained untreated), and buff for clapboards. The paints used were often oil paints which produced a smoother texture and a stronger color rather than stains with their more muted colors and protection of the original wood textures.

Only a relatively few houses were large enough to include all that. The Queen Anne Style was the dominant residential style in the six-county area during the very busy building period spanning from the recovery of building activity around 1880 through and even after the slump that followed the depression of 1893. Many modest houses incorporated many of its elements. Even the most humble ones could have a varied surface pattern, broken silhouette, and spindly porch, even if the underlying structure was a Greek Revival L-shaped structure or a Greek-Gothic hybrid. Only the blocky, stolid Italianate remained inhospitable to the style.

The Queen Anne was so pervasive it swallowed up the incipient Stick Style before it could develop broadly as an architectural style in the six-county area. Its ubiquity also excluded the Shingle Style which developed on the east coast, particularly in New England, alongside the Queen Anne.[14]

It may be that the area's designers resisted the discipline required by the Shingle Style which was a style of limitation—the masses were simple and clear-cut, the surfaces were wrapped in shingles stained to preserve the color and texture of the wood, the veranda supports were understated and often clad in shingles as if the veranda were cut out of the wall, and the windows were repetitive in shape, carefully placed within a coherent composition, and set into the shingle wall as if the taut surface had been cut into to make the opening. A few excellent Shingle Style architects were active in Chicago and its suburbs, for example J. L. Silsbee and W. C. Zimmerman, and examples of their work survive, but the principal role of the style was to serve as a predecessor to the Prairie Style which benefited from its disciplined handling of masses, volumes, surfaces, and patterns.

The Shingle Style came closest to being used with stylistic consistency in churches. A church was hardly a proper place for the exuberant vigor of the Queen Anne. In taming it by smoothing out the wall planes, simplifying the roofs, using shingles extensively for the surface, and breaking into the surface with simple, large windows, the area's ecclesiastical Queen Anne came close to becoming the Shingle Style.

RICHARDSONIAN ROMANESQUE (1880–1905)

While the domestic and light-mannered Queen Anne enjoyed popularity, the monumental, heavy-handed Richardsonian Romanesque provided an alternative style for those who wished vigorous masonry construction.[15]

The style had been used for rugged stone structures featuring large arches and rough-surfaced walls in medieval Spain and southern France. But its use now was based on the very personal interpretation of those buildings in the works of Henry Hobson Richardson, the second American to be trained in architecture at the Ecole des Beaux Arts in Paris—so personal, indeed, that his name is appropriately included in the name of the new style.

In the 1870s, a few years before he designed some of this country's first Queen Anne and Shingle Style residences, Richardson invented the new architectural style. It quickly became the standard one used throughout the country for the important buildings that formerly had achieved a monumental presence by using the later Italianate or the Second Empire Style. The new style apparently had no special meaning beyond that provided by the indubitable presence that a massive, controlled pile of masonry always possesses.

Richardson's office was in Boston, but he enjoyed a very wide practice and produced three buildings in his mature style in Chicago shortly before his death at age 47 in 1886. Only one of them, the fortress-like Glessner House at 1800 South Prairie Avenue, remains standing. The style was more popular in urban centers than in suburban fringes and distant towns and cities. In the six-county area outside Chicago, examples of the style are less domineering than is usual elsewhere. Not only are these buildings smaller, but they are often rendered in the lighter limestones available locally rather than in the dark red and brown stones that Richardson used even when he had to import them to Chicago from Massachusetts.

Buildings in the style use large blocks of stone, maintain a simple silhouette, and have large round arches over their ample openings. The main entrance is usually through a massive arch springing from near the bottom of the opening and protecting a deep porch. Walls, which are often battered, often carry massive, swelling bows and oriels. Oriel roofs are conical and usually kept below the silhouette of the main roof which is usually hipped and covered with slate forming a single color and pattern. Dormers are common, and they, too, are usually hip-roofed.

Within this general compositional framework, the style allowed a great deal of variety, including linteled windows. A common form is a tall, thin slit covered with a massive lintel; such a window forms a distinct contrast to the typical broad-arched opening. Contrasts also appear from setting smooth-faced blocks against rough-faced ones or from using contrasting colors of stone for different purposes—for example, light colored ones for walls and dark ones for string courses or around openings, or vice versa. Columns and piers are stout and massive; also common are tall, thin colonnettes gathered into bunches. Capitals are typically crudely carved foliate designs.

Whole buildings in the style are found, but so too are the lower sections of Queen Anne houses. Richardson himself had used the combination of massive stone basements and chimneys and smooth, taut shingle walls in some of his Shingle Style houses. In this area the contrast is usually between the somber heaviness of masonry and lighter Queen Anne forms. Such a base seldom rises high enough to furnish a ground floor entrance through a typical Romanesque arch, but it might rise in chimneys.

As important to six-county area architects as the massive, arched, stone buildings were Richardson's brick ones. These assisted architects who were translating the Queen Anne Style from wood into masonry in finding models for using brick, terra cotta, and stone. Some of their masonry Queen Anne buildings became more vigorous, disciplined, and coherent than their equivalents in wood might have been, while others stopped short of spilling over into the full-blown robustness of the Richardsonian Romanesque. For these buildings, which are somber in ways Queen Anne designs never are but less massive than Richardsonian Romanesque ones become, the term Romanesque is often useful.[16]

Such buildings are large and substantial, and are usually devoted to some public purpose. Their lighter colors and smoother surfaces and the smaller pieces used for their construction make these buildings appear less grave, somber, massive, and forbidding than the more orthodox Richardsonian Romanesque buildings. They have smooth brick walls made distinctly planer by using pressed brick (it has a denser, smoother, almost shiny surface) laid with very thin joints of red mortar rendering the joints almost invisible. The wall is enlivened with moulded and patterned terra cotta panels and with large pieces of stone, usually the same color as the brick and with a smooth face, used for structural elements such as lintels, sills, string courses, voussoirs, spring blocks, and so on.

Among large masonry mansions a third style, supplementing the Queen Anne and the Romanesque, was available, but there are so few remaining examples in the six-county area—there never were very many—that it need not be discussed in a separate section. That was the Chateauesque.[17] It was a style for the wealthy, and it borrowed its forms from the period of the French king who patronized the arts and lived royally, Francis I (reigned 1515–47).

In the Chateauesque, the walls are built of smooth ashlar or smooth brick. A basic cubic shape is extended with regularly placed bows and bays, and with oriels or tourelles terminated by conical roofs. The main roof is hipped and covered with slate, carries dormers, and is edged by chimneys often with elaborate tops. Windows are linteled and framed with medievalizing Renaissance forms which, like the design as a whole, could be learned through study in France, or on Fifth Avenue in New York which during the later part of the century was faced with these chateaux to an extent that the midwest could never rival.

THE LEARNED REVIVALS: CLASSICAL, TUDOR, AND OTHERS (1892–1930)

A sustained slump in building activity often spells the end of a style's popularity and prepares the ground for new fashions in architecture. The deep depression of 1893 produced just such a slump in the six-county area. When activity picked up again toward the end of the century, times had changed and so had the architecture.

Architects had assumed an increasingly important role. They were more professional, and they were generally better educated and better informed about larger trends in design. Their clients were also more cosmopolitan, and they were anxious to use buildings to represent the stable and decorous social order they had built. As a result the exuberant individualism of the Queen Anne and the solid originality of the Romanesque styles gave way to designs based on historical examples. Architects reached back into the past as they displayed their learning and their abilities in producing images of conservative respectability for their clients.

Conservative society now embarked upon a long generation of unexcelled tranquility and prosperity. World War I was more a distraction than a disruption. The sustained boom was considered normal while the occasional busts were taken as mere economic adjustments that accompanied the perpetual prosperity promised by the future. For this class, the period from the

Spanish-American War of 1898 to the Depression of the 1930s had a single identity.

The buildings of these privileged optimists hardly hint at the period's far-reaching innovations—the automobile came into general use; movies and mass-distribution photo magazines spread images at an accelerated pace; advertising introduced a new, snappy language and imagery; and radio made distant events instantly accessible. While other architectural currents during the period acknowledged these changes, the architecture of conservative society continued to clothe itself in a time-tested architecture.

This architecture may be divided into two broad categories. For public buildings and for others meant to suggest stability in society, the classical styles dominated. For residences and other structures associated with domesticity, the Gothic, generally in the form of the Tudor, was used.[18] Architects were expected to be adept in either style, and clients might commission one or the other depending on which image he thought best for the building. He might leave his Tudor home in the suburbs to work in a classical office building, have dinner in a Gothic club, visit his widowed mother in a classical apartment building, meet his commuter train at a classical railroad station, and pick up a newspaper at a Gothic drugstore on his way home. Each was as much a part of the decorum of his society as was a formal dinner in which a fish plate was followed by a meat plate, and not the other way around, and neither one without the other.

Compared with the revival styles of earlier periods, these were more learned and correct, but they had no less potential for producing a design of high quality. Originality and quality now resided more in sophistication and less in exuberance, more in the manipulation of an historical formal language than in the invention of something new.

The propensity to use historical examples appeared first in east coast residences and summer homes produced by Queen Anne and Shingle Style architects who, in some designs in the later 1870s and 1880s, drew on the general configuration, symmetrical massing, and classical elements of the Georgian Colonial Style. During the same years they produced some libraries and museums, that is, public buildings devoted to cultural activities, and some mansions in a studied neo-classical style. The Colonial Revival Style and the Neo-Classical Style that resulted from these early examples were not necessarily related in their meaning. The one referred to the colonial roots of Americans, the other to the belief that America's growing wealth should usher in an age of artistic achievement rivaling the brilliance of the Italian

Renaissance. This belief in America's great destiny was served up in a rich, impressive, and learned architectural display based on the grandest examples of the Rome of the ancient emperors and High Renaissance popes and princes, a display which established Neo-Classical architecture as the official architecture of all things progressive and cultural in America.

That display was at the World's Columbian Exposition in Chicago's Jackson Park in 1893, which an estimated quarter of the people living in America visited. At the Fair they were bathed in an image of sublime order, a dream, a White City of classical purity and order, and they hastened home inspired to make over their cities, towns, and houses in that image.

The Fair was Chicago's coming-out party in America. Hosting it brought a change of mind to Chicagoans. Before preparations for the Fair began to preoccupy them, Chicagoans had stood proudly aloof from the east. They flouted their western independence and unashamedly devoted themselves to the pursuit of gain. With the Fair came a desire to justify their gain by demonstrating that it enabled them to be the equals of easterners in manners and culture. Raw frontier attitudes were melted down and recast in the image of the American Renaissance of which the Fair proudly built by Chicagoans was the most prized emblem.

Because the first wave of post-Fair Neo-Classicism followed the design tenets taught at the Ecole des Beaux Arts, it is often called the Beaux Arts Style or Beaux Arts Classicism. The Ecole, which by now a number of Americans had attended, promulgated a method of design rather than a style, however. Those with talent could learn how to design competently and in a number of different styles. As that method spread, competent designs in many styles flourished, sustaining a period of learned revivals lasting up to the Depression of the 1930s.

Buildings formerly designed in a rough-hewn Romanesque style now appeared in smooth-surfaced ashlar classical designs. Asymmetrical bulk gave way to symmetrical massing, and fenestration became a regular disposition of solids and voids. Some designs were adaptations of historical prototypes—for example, for the combined Cook County Building and Chicago City Hall of 1907–1911, the Chicago firm of Holabird and Roche drew on J.-A. Gabriel's design for the Ministry of Marine erected for Louis XVI in Paris' Place de la Concorde. To work from models in this way is no different in kind from the interpretation each architect makes of his own previous designs or of the designs of others in a current style. The willingness to reach back to specific buildings rather than to general stylistic characteristics of an earlier period, as Queen Anne architects did, or to general building types, as Jefferson and Greek Revival architects did, is what makes the difference between this revival style and the others that preceded it.

Major buildings (or parts of major buildings) in major cities by major architects built for important patrons were often selected as models for major American Neo-Classical buildings. For residences and churches the favored source was the Georgian period in England and the Georgian Colonial Style in America. The new examples differ little from their predecessors except they are larger, more refined in their composition and in the use of the classical elements, more formal in their siting, and more often brick than wood—and found in the midwest, which had hardly been explored much less settled at the time of the style's first currency.

The third favorite source of models, especially for residences, country clubs, and other domestic, suburban buildings, was the England of Henry VIII and of Elizabeth I, the last of the Tudor monarchs. Individual motifs were appropriated more often than whole designs. At first they were applied to an armature provided by the Queen Anne Style which, in a way, was another version of what is broadly called the Tudor. The Tudor Revival differs, however, in having much less variety in the massing and silhouette and using a more limited range of surface treatments. Half-timbering on the second story and in the gables and extensive brick work (sometimes ashlar limestone) become standard. Window types are reduced to only a few with strips of casement windows with diamond pane leaded glass a special favorite. Verandas are now supported by Tudor timber work rather than the spindles and other lathe-turned elements favored by the Queen Anne.

To produce a Tudor Revival rather than a Queen Anne design required only a little disciplining of the massing and taming of the elements. But before the Colonial Revival could appear in full-fledged form, the Queen Anne required a more thorough transformation. In the process, which began in about 1895, some of the six-county area's most interesting houses were built. In this phase the Queen Anne was straitened by imposing clear-cut massing and using large, classical elements. From a distance the result might seem to be a Queen Anne, but when one moves closer he sees a subdued asymmetry with a veranda extending beyond one face and a porte-cochere from the other, with classical columns supporting both extensions. A pair of dormers appears in the hipped roof atop the clapboard-sheathed mass, perhaps with a pair of projections near the back, each different, but together balanced in their composition.

Gradually the proper Colonial Revival structure will appear from further manipulation of the design, but in the meantime a simplified version of the transitional type became established as a standard building type among modest houses in brick or frame with clapboard cladding. The columnar porch is limited to the front and does not project beyond the sides, and the projections toward the back may be little larger than bay windows or be lacking altogether. It may be that this house type is the Colonial Revival version of the Italianate "grandmother's house."

Finally, in the six-county area the same design could be reduced a bit more to produce a bungalow.[19] In the simplest bungalow the second story is replaced by a relatively low pitched roof with the gable to the street. Variations were made by drawing on plans from the Greek-Gothic hybrid. Instead of porch columns based on the classical elements, square posts that are often tapered become common. This motif seems to have been suggested by the Tudor. The bungalow began to appear around the turn of the century and is not really a nineteenth-century building type although it is extremely common in the six-county area.

Another twentieth-century building type ought to be mentioned because it is so common in the commercial areas and shares its style with suburban schools. That is the Gothic commercial building, the replacement for the Italianate which had reigned since the middle of the nineteenth century. Wood construction was inappropriate or illegal for these buildings, but they were expected to conform to the prevailing Tudor tendencies in the suburbs, and the Tudor required wood. A solution was found by using terra cotta to build designs based on the English ecclesiastical architecture of the Perpendicular period. The original style had featured large windows with tracery of straight verticals and horizontals; in its commercial application, the shop windows are left bare and the tracery is moved to the side and up into the parapet where it may erupt into a number of cusps to provide a delightful cornice.

THE PRAIRIE STYLE (1890–1925)

Chicago area architects made a significant contribution to international architecture while the learned revivals were the prevailing styles. That contribution was the Prairie Style.[20] It has, ever since, brought fame and visitors to the region.

The Prairie Style flourished as an alternative to the revival styles. Its promoters claimed that, except for one thing, it was everything the learned revivals were not. Each side claimed that its buildings were suitable for their uses—all architects always make that claim. But the Prairie Style architects claimed that theirs was not a foreign architecture but an American one. It required not a studied replication of an imported style but the free play of the architect's imagination. And its discipline came not from the studied application of a design methodology to produce a preconceived visual result no matter the site, the materials, or the use. Instead, it arose from the conditions of the site, the nature of the building materials, and the requirements of the Americans who were to use the building.

These claims were exaggerated as occurs in all lively polemics, but two conclusions are not overstated: This was a new style; and, it was the first fully developed new style to grow out of initial successes in domestic design.

This second point reveals the style's origins. It appeared after the freedom and originality first explored in the Queen Anne Style and later in the Shingle Style had been exploited by a genius who wrestled from the tradition of architecture a new synthesis of meaning and form. The genius was Frank Lloyd Wright. The new meaning was that of an American architecture. And the form was a disciplined conjunction of space, geometry, and materials to produce a richly articulated integration of interior and exterior and of solids and voids with a dominant horizontality.

Wright was largely self-taught. Born in Wisconsin, he worked briefly for J.L. Silsbee, Chicago's leading Queen Anne and Shingle Style architect, and his first designs, from around 1890, reveal a rare talent for using the Queen Anne in its local Shingle Style and Colonial Revival forms. He then worked for Louis Sullivan as his own independent genius slowly unfolded.

For Wright, Sullivan remained the "lieber meister" or beloved master teacher. Sullivan taught that every problem, properly stated, contains its own solution, that structure is the basis of architectural design, and that the role of ornament is to decorate structure by calling attention to its character and enriching its architectonic form. He believed fervently that American democracy was a bulwark against the feudalism of the old world and of its new world counterpart, the baronial business practices of American moguls. He taught that a building has to contain a big idea, an idea as big as that of American democracy and of any one man's genius.

Wright spurned an offer to develop his talent through study at the Ecole des Beaux Arts. Instead, he established his own practice and developed what he had learned from Sullivan. As is usual with young architects, his first commissions were for houses. In their design he sought a domestic architecture suitable for uniquely American conditions. By the turn of the century he had brought a new house type to full maturity. At the center of the house is a hearth with a fireplace and a great chimney unifying the members of the family and the spaces of the house. Spreading out from it are the rooms where the family lives. Their spaces sweep into one another, each one giving into another with ease, allowing the family to live as a unit and use it as a family's home. In contrast, a revivalist's house seemed to be used by a number of individuals who were forced into separation and confinement within a series of boxes labeled "reception room," "parlor," "dining room," "bedroom," and so on.

Wright's ideas about the new house were accompanied by a new architectural form. It was founded on the rigors of geometric organization which disciplined the design by arranging the home's several spaces along two axes meeting at right angles at the hearth. Conversely, the spaces extended horizontally across porte-cocheres, porches, and verandas and beyond the long, low roofs defining and enclosing them. The design was then farther extended beyond the bounds of the building through podia and planters in the landscape, unifying the house and the flat site which was inevitable in the Chicago area.

Already in the 1890s Wright had attracted a group of young architects who began working in loose coordination with one another. Some produced richly articulated Shingle Style designs, others preferred simplified Tudor designs, but after the turn of the century they all used the broad horizontals extending across the flat landscape that made the term Prairie School appropriate for them. By 1905 they had worked out their own personal idioms for the new plan types and visual forms that Wright had first explored and that unmistakably identify the Prairie style: low hipped roofs with broad eaves and deep overhangs, strips of casement windows with intricate, geometric leaded glass, sparse ornament derived from the way brick is laid, the way boards and stucco are used together or the way boards are used alone, and the extension of the design across the landscape.

During the next decade Prairie School architects produced a broad range of designs but the bulk of their work was houses, and houses for the middle class at that. It never became fashionable among the wealthy, it failed to dislodge the Beaux Arts style from eastern architecture or its methodology from the curriculum in the schools of architecture, and it failed to produce "any transcendently beautiful or very important piece of work"; therefore, the Prairie Style never achieved dominance in American architecture, as was observed already in 1927 by Thomas Tallmadge, one of its practitioners and an historian of Chicago and of American architecture

After Wright left in 1909 for Europe to prepare several of his projects for a Berlin publication, never again to live in Illinois, his circle broke up. Those who remained in the Chicago area drew on the new outlook the new style had brought to architecture, but increasingly they did so within designs that were more clearly revival styles, usually Tudor, than Prairie School designs. Meanwhile, European architects studied the Prairie School designs, and they incorporated aspects of it into their own new architecture which they brought back to this country as the unsettled conditions of the 1930s and 1940s made Europe uninhabitable for modern architects.[21]

Despite its gradual and premature demise, the Prairie Style changed the form of the six-county area's buildings. By the second decade of the new century some of the style's most conspicuous visual characteristics had been absorbed into the design of houses produced by contractors. This "Contractor's Prairie" with its broad horizontals, low hipped roofs, strips of casement windows, stucco and board walls, and careful brickwork lacking in historical reference and calling attention to the structural character of the wall and the spatial disposition of the interior proliferated in building types ranging from low apartment buildings and commercial shop fronts to tract houses, new garages behind old houses, and the basic, cubic "grandmother's house" type of the earlier generation. Local architects also learned from the Prairie style. Although he might continue to use the classical styles, an architect often, especially when the style was at its height, used his interpretations of the classical elements, perhaps in response to the Prairie School's success in remaining altogether independent of historical precedents. The same reason may have prompted other architects who would otherwise have been more historically correct in using the Tudor to produce designs with an abstraction approaching the simplicity of the Prairie Style.

"Contractor's Prairie" and variants on the learned revivals are very numerous in the six-county area. They reveal the deep and extensive penetration of the style into the building practices and architectural styles of the region, and they are perhaps the strongest testimony to the power of the new imagery developed by the Prairie School architects. That power, along with the independent frame of mind of the architects working before the World's Columbian Exposition of 1893, make the appearance of the cities, towns, and suburbs of the six-county area of high quality and unique in America.

NOTES

1.

The term style is used here as discussed above, that is, as "a particular, characteristic image or appearance shared by a group of buildings." (p. 7, supra) This means that the concept of style is *only* part of a system of categorization useful for analytical purposes when reviewing the works of builders and architects and that, from the point of view of the nineteenth-century architects discussed here, a style provided "a model for the architect to follow" and "a catalogue of visual effects to draw upon." (p. 9, supra) The term is also used here to refer to an image common to a group of buildings with the assumption that during the period under review here that image "conveyed important meanings. . . and allowed the differences among buildings to reveal their relative importance instantly and without ambiguity . . ." while allowing the architect "to display his originality and the client to portray his individuality." (p. 8, supra) Finally, the term is used here to refer to a conceptual ordering within an analytical procedure that "allows for a judgment about the quality of a design." (p. 9, supra)

There is no suggestion here that it is possible "to avoid vagueness in stylistic categories." Such vagueness is inherent in the approach and is no reason to eschew it, as one critic, Christian Otto, has suggested. (Christian Otto, letter to *Historic Preservation*, vol. 28, no. 4, October-December, 1976, p. 47). Nor is there an attempt to work with "our historic laundry list [which] was rinsed in stylistic analysis by the German art historian [Heinrich] Wölfflin," although it is hoped that the "suspect methodology, the notion of 'development' in the Darwinian sense," another of Otto's points, has been avoided and that "concerns [sic.] such as patronage, purpose, personality and meaning" which Otto believes are proper questions for engaging "the richness and complexity of [the art historians'] discipline" have been worked into the discussion of the region's buildings.

Two final technical observations: Nowhere in this essay does the word "influence" appear. The locution "This design was influenced by the Italianate Style," or "This design shows Italianate influences" hurls the speaker into the murky abyss of turn-of-the-century historiography that is as ambiguous and treacherous as the Darwinian overlay Otto objects to in his letter. To use the word "influence" in this manner is to suggest that styles, not people, design buildings. It seems better to turn that around and suggest that people design buildings which, at least during the nineteenth century, they themselves and, today, critics may subject to analysis based on the concept of style as discussed in the first paragraph of this note.

Finally: Notice that the term vernacular is not used, although most of the buildings in this guide belong to various vernaculars. The term is often used to refer to the products of craftsmen and builders rather than of architects, and to humbler buildings not needing (or not receiving) pretentious designs. It has also wittingly, but not accurately, been used to refer to buildings whose designers remain unknown from lack of research—inaccurately, because often, nothing of value would be learned through having names of craftsmen-builders, although more about them and precise dates for buildings would be useful fruits of research. The term has too often been substituted for a more precise characterization of a design and of its sources. After those have been defined for a region or a locale, the term may become a useful generalizing term, but not enough is now known about the buildings in the six-county area to allow broad application of that meaning of the term.

2.

The emphasis throughout this book is on the general exterior appearance of buildings. For the investigation of particular characteristics of individual structures, a useful guide appropriate for Illinois is James R. Allen, "Investigating the Fabric of a Building," in *Preservation Illinois: A Guide to State and Local Resources*, edited by Ruth Eckdish Knack (Springfield, Illinois: Illinois Department of Conservation, Division of Historic Sites, December, 1977), pp. 197–207, with drawings by Carl Fischer and Charles William Brubaker. The entire publication is quite useful.

3.

Except for the first two styles, the Federal and the Greek Revival, the dates in parentheses refer to the earliest and latest use of the style in the six-county area. More buildings are produced in a style in its earlier years than in its later ones; some indication of the period of greatest popularity will be given in the discussion. The dates given for the first two styles refer to their introduction at their source and the latest currency they enjoyed in the six-county area.

4.

Whiffen divides the Federal Style into two separate styles, the Adam Style, primarily a domestic style, and Jeffersonian Classicism, used primarily for public and monumental buildings. The National Trust guide also divides the style into two. Whiffen's Adam Style becomes the "Federal or Adamesque," and his Jeffersonian Classicism becomes "Jeffersonian or Roman Revival." Blumenson makes Whiffen's Adam Style the Federal Style, and Whiffen's Jeffersonian Classicism he calls Roman Classicism. The Wisconsin guide only mentions the Federal Style.

5.

Whiffen, the National Trust guide, Blumenson, and the Wisconsin guide discuss the Greek Revival Style.

6.

Whiffen calls it the Early Gothic Revival, and stresses churches as the major building type that used it. This was less the case in the six-county area than it was in the east. Whiffen had used the adjective "early" to set this phase off from his High Victorian Gothic which followed (see below). The National Trust guide does not distinguish between the two phases; it puts them together and calls them the Gothic Revival. Blumenson follows Whiffen, calling the two periods the Gothic Revival and the Victorian Gothic. The Wisconsin guide presents the Gothic Revival as the first of the Early Picturesque Styles and includes in the Gothic Revival the later phase that the others separate as the High Victorian Gothic or Victorian Gothic.

7.

Whiffen, having to deal with the entire United States and working with many more examples that display a greater variety of regional variations within the formal and stylistic patterns of an increasingly complex taste in architecture, breaks the general Italianate Style discussed here into the following: The Italian Villa Style; The Renaissance Revival—The North Italian Mode; The Octagon Mode; and The High Victorian Italianate. Most of these, as well as the Italian Villa Style, were too little used in the six-county area to warrant separate discussion here. They are differentiated from one another primarily by the historical source suggested by their decorative elements, although they also differ by favoring either asymmetrical or symmetrical massing.

The National Trust guide collects Whiffen's many styles and modes into two, the Italianate and the Exotic Revivals. Again, there are too few exotic revivals in the six-county area during the period of the Italianate's dominance to call for separate discussion. Blumenson returns to Whiffen's basic scheme and names as separate styles the Italian Villa, The Italianate, The Renaissance Revival, The Romanesque Revival (here, as in Whiffen, this is not to be confused with the Richardsonian Romanesque), the Victorian Romanesque (again, not Richardsonian), and the Octagon which he presents as a "concept" which he says was "accepted across the country and adapted to various styles;" compare Whiffen who calls it a "mode" as did its originator, Orson Squire Fowler. The Wisconsin guide includes the "Italianate or Bracketed" style as the second of its three "Early Picturesque Styles."

8.

Whiffen designates it the Second Empire Style. He notes that because its heyday was during the expansionist period following the Civil War and its most conspicuous uses were for government buildings, it is also called the "General Grant Style." For another use of this term, see the discussion above of the Italianate Style and in the next section for the "U.S. Grant" style. The National Trust guide follows Whiffen, as does Blumenson. The Wisconsin guide includes this as the third of the three "Early Picturesque Styles" and calls it the Mansard (an alternative spelling for Mansart) or French Second Empire. It notes that the Mansart roof was often added to older buildings to make them stylish, and it also indicates that the term "French Provincial" is often wrongly used for this style. Another name for the style is Second Empire Baroque, a term introduced because of the strong dependence of the style on French Baroque models.

9.

Whiffen includes it as an architectural style. The National Trust guide includes a section on it with the statement that it is one of the "major forces that shaped American architectural design after the Civil War" occurring with others in the free mixture of elements from several styles. Blumenson names an Eastern Stick Style (Whiffen's Stick Style) and a Western Stick Style, a style found on the west coast during a later period. The Wisconsin guide names the Stick Style as the first of three "Late Picturesque Styles."

10.

Whiffen, as we have seen, mentioned the term "General Grant" as a term of limited utility for referring to the Second Empire Style. This acknowledges its use within an Italianate context and as a decorative style, and Whiffen quite usefully states that the term "fails to acknowledge the international background of this style." The National Trust guide follows Whiffen without repeating the useful comment about its limitation as a term. Blumenson and the Wisconsin guide do not mention it.

11.

Whiffen used the term for a style but states that "Most Eastlake buildings would be classifiable as Stick Style or Queen Anne if they were not transmogrified by a distinctive type of ornament." (p. 123) The National Trust guide does not refer to the style. Blumenson illustrates it as "a popular decorative style of ornamentation found on houses of various other styles, e.g., Victorian Gothic, Stick Style, and Queen Anne. The Wisconsin guide does not mention the style.

12.

This is sometimes called Neo-Grec ornament; it can predate the Eastlake and is French in origin.

13.

Whiffen, the National Trust guide, and Blumenson include it as a style, as does the Wisconsin guide which calls it the Queen Anne Revival and makes it the second of the three "Late Picturesque Styles."

14.

Whiffen, the National Trust guide, and Blumenson discuss it as a separate style; the Wisconsin guide includes it as the third of the "Late Picturesque Styles" but notes that it "is rare in Wisconsin."

15.

Whiffen, the National Trust guide, Blumenson, and the Wisconsin guide include this style.

16.

None of the style guides makes a place for this variant by setting it off as a separate style. Buildings such as Burnham and Root's Rookery in Chicago from 1885 (which Whiffen illustrates as an example of the Richardsonian Romanesque) and the courthouses in DuPage and Kane counties lack many of the Richardsonian Romanesque elements and also stand apart from the Queen Anne; hence the suggestion here that Romanesque without Richardson is an appropriate term for them.

17.

Whiffen and Blumenson include it as a style; the National Trust guide and the Wisconsin guide do not.

18.

Other authors have used various smaller subdivisions for this period, but they seem inappropriate for the building activity in the six-county area, especially for a study that only touches on the twentieth century. Whiffen includes among the classical styles the following: Beaux-Arts Classicism, The Second Renaissance Revival, The Georgian Revival, and The Neo-Classical Revival; among the Gothic he includes these: The Late Gothic Revival and the Jacobethan Revival (a compound adjective made from Jacobean and Elizabethan, now generally called the Tudor). The National Trust guide uses the following: The Beaux-Arts, the Classic Revival of the 20th Century, and The Period House (Georgian house, Spanish hacienda, English cottage, New England farmhouse, etc.). Blumenson includes these: Mission Style, Pueblo Style, Spanish Colonial Revival, Colonial Revival, Egyptian Revival, The Second Renaissance Revival, Beaux Arts Classicism, and Neo-Classicism. The Wisconsin guide includes among the "Battle of the Styles at the Turn of the Century" the following: Eclectic Resurgence, with English Tudor, Georgian, and the Mediterranean.

19.

The bungalow is more a building type than a style, but the extreme reduction of the high styles when worked into the bungalow design so obscures their origins, and the type is so prevalent and soon begins to be so modified with disregard for high style designs, that it may be treated as a style rather than as a building type. See Whiffen, the "Bungaloid." The National Trust guide does not mention the bungalow, Blumenson includes the Bungalow Style, and the Wisconsin guide includes the Bungalow Style in its section on "A Battle of the Styles at the Turn of the Century."

20.

This is the final nineteenth-century style encountered in the six-county area outside Chicago. It is generally considered a twentieth-century style, but see the discussion below. Architects are not always punctual in ending and beginning architectural styles at the turns of centuries.

Concurrent with it another revolutionary, new, indigenous style with equally broad importance in international architecture was being developed in Chicago, primarily after the example of Louis Sullivan. Called the style of the Chicago School and also the Commercial Style, it was related to the Prairie School's principles but was used for a very different building type, the tall commercial building with skeletal construction. This building type was largely limited to the dense commercial centers of major cities, and is therefore only rarely encountered in the six-county area outside Chicago. For some important rarities, see the buildings in Aurora by George Grant Elmslie.

For these styles see Whiffen (The Commercial Style, Sullivanesque, and The Prairie Style). The National Trust guide lists the Chicago School and the Prairie Style. Blumenson has the Sullivanesque and the Prairie Style. The Wisconsin guide includes the Prairie School with The Battle of the Styles at the Turn of the Century; because that guide is devoted exclusively to residential architecture, it does not discuss the commercial buildings of the Chicago School.

21.

One of the finest testimonies to the interpenetration of Prairie School forms and the ideas of early modern European architects is perhaps the Farnsworth House near Plano, Illinois, in Kendall County. Designed by the German émigré Ludwig Mies van der Rohe in 1946 and built in 1950, this small

Farnsworth House

structure is one of the prime monuments in modern architecture in America. In 1981 the American Institute of Architects acknowledged the building's role of serving a generation of architects as an inspirational icon by conferring on it their prestigious 25-Year Award.

Built as a retreat residence for a Chicagoan forty-five miles west of the metropolis, the building at first glance appears to be a mere steel and glass box belonging to an entirely different realm of architecture from the one that includes the Prairie School.

No matter how simple it may appear, it is richly complex. Only a terrace stands between the ground and its floor level. Eight steel I beam columns support the floor beams five and a half feet above the ground and extend unbroken to carry similar beams holding the roof. Both horizontal slabs extend slightly beyond the easternmost and westernmost supports, as do the similar ends of the terrace. The floor and roof are formed from precast concrete panels; the terrace and house floor are paved with rectangles of travertine. Nothing is seen projecting above the roof, and only a single inconspicuous tube may be found running between the floor and the ground.

Inside, a free-standing core containing a fireplace and the heating and plumbing equipment divides the interior into living, dining, sleeping, and kitchen spaces. This core is placed slightly northeast of the main enclosure's center, a position that balances the terrace's placement on the south side of the structure and extending beyond its west face. That face is left open to serve as a veranda that begins a little to the west of the first support east of the west end.

The structure is meticulously detailed and has recently been carefully restored to its original condition. The points where the steel horizontals and verticals intersect are welded, and the steel surfaces are ground smooth and painted white. Sheets of glass stretch unbroken from floor to ceiling to provide nearly invisible diaphragms between interior and exterior. The travertine decks are unencumbered by porch or step rails.

The building has no applied decoration or ornament, and the architectural quality of the design arises from the scrupulous care in handling the materials, two traits shared by the early modern European and Prairie School architects. The construction in steel and glass came from European beliefs about the potential for a new architecture of new materials provided by modern technology, but the spatial design, which here is every bit as brilliant as the careful detailing and as essential for understanding the achievement this building represents, came from Chicago's Prairie School, not from Europe.

The building may be seen as Mies' interpretation of the fully developed Prairie Style house. Like one of them, it was designed as if it were a mere minor adjustment to its setting. For example, Chicago's Robie House by Frank Lloyd Wright from 1908–09 at 5757 S. Woodlawn Avenue is on a deep, narrow corner lot in a residential area (now with intrusions from the expansion of the University of Chicago). On the south side, the site of which the house forms a part begins with the flat sweep of 58th Street and continues through the street's curb, the planting strip with a row of trees, and the sidewalk. The architect's tinkering with the site begins at the low wall along the sidewalk, extends into the play court, and then moves along the building's parapets, walls, fenestration, eave fascia, and hipped roof planes. Along the west end is Woodlawn Avenue where a curb, sidewalk, and grassed yard are followed by the pointed prow of the elevated porch with its brick parapet and then by the narrow end of the long hipped roof and the next roof and chimney penetrating up through the house. These forms are balanced and adjusted to acknowledge the site's character which is a flat, urban corner lot with the entrance deep along the house on the side opposite the street and with the porch and family spaces running into one another on the west end and the closed, service spaces and garages tucked back out of the way in the rear of the house at the east end.

The country retreat is a thorough transformation of the type of design represented by the Robie House, a transformation of the same principles that took a different form in Wright's design. Now the Fox River provides the flat sweep of a horizontal channel fronting on the site. Along the river is a growth of deciduous trees providing a veil between the river and the house. Similar trees, more densely clustered and separating the site from the outside world, surround a nine-and-one-half-acre meadow. Only a few trees, most of them small, disturb the meadow's nearly flat grassland. The house stands on the edge of the site near the river. Between the house and the river is a very large, gnarled oak tree toward the eastern end of the house and balanced at the western end by the terrace.

The meadow lacks the rigidity of an urban building site, but its enclosure and its careful tending make it different from a totally rural or natural setting.

Similarly, the building lacks the complexity required for an urban, family residence, but it contains the geometric discipline, balance of spaces, and character of design in its interior and exterior configuration of a fully developed Prairie Style house. And, like the best Prairie Style houses, it is a thoroughly rational or mentally contrived extension of the uses it was built to satisfy.

Questions such as where is the lawnmower kept, where is the car parked, and where are the garbage cans, while important in the complexities of urban life, become pointless here where the architect can ignore them. Like the best Prairie School designs, which in renderings were shown set within trees and shrubs and trailing vines and flowers from their podia urns and parapet planter boxes, this design clearly extends from a belief that nature provides a setting for man's art and asks that his art be an equal partner with nature's paradoxical clear simplicity and subtle complexity.

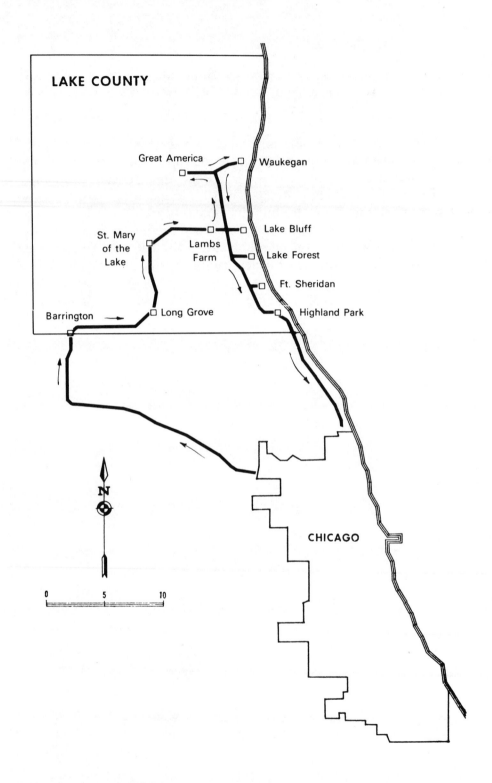

LAKE COUNTY

Great America   Waukegan

St. Mary
of the
Lake

Lambs
Farm

Lake Bluff

Lake Forest

Ft. Sheridan

Barrington   Long Grove   Highland Park

N

CHICAGO

0   5   10

Lake
County

BARRINGTON

BARRINGTON

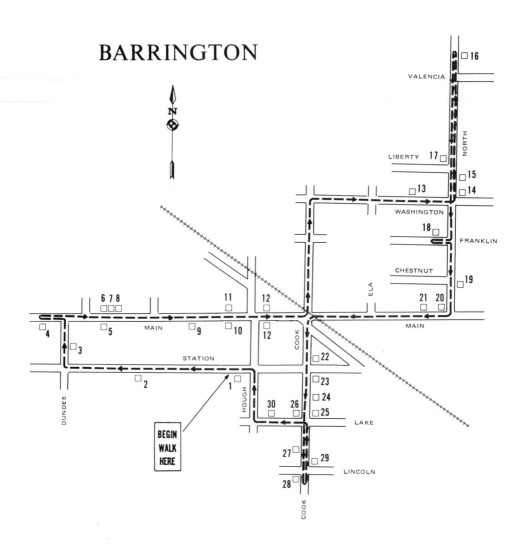

From downtown Chicago, take the Kennedy Expressway to the Northwest Tollway. Exit Barrington Road North. Drive north 6.1 miles. Barrington Road becomes Hough Street as you get into town. Turn left (west) on Station Street and stop.

BARRINGTON WALKING TOUR

1. Barrington Historical Museum
111 W. Station Street—1929

This building from 1929 was built as a blacksmith's shop. On display are many artifacts reminiscent of the farming origins of the town, household items from the nineteenth century, and books on the history of Barrington. The Historical Society regularly schedules two-hour bus tours of the surrounding countryside.

Leaving the historical society, walk left (west) on the south side of the street, past the fire station. The fifth house on your left is

2. 201 W. Station Street—pre-1853

This house, built prior to 1853, was first moved in 1859, then again in 1917. Its most prominent features are the bay window and the siding. The bay window was probably added in 1917 (possibly in the 1940s when the siding was added). Only the general form of the house represents 1859.

Continue west to Dundee Avenue. Turn right (north). The third house on your right is

3. 109 Dundee Avenue—1880s

This is a straightforward, frame, clapboard-covered house from the 1880s that has an Italianate double-arched window on the ground floor, a very pretentious feature relative to the mass and configuration of the house itself. The house is a relatively humble type, like the one to the south of it, but those windows give it an added importance. The porch is a later addition.

Continue north on Dundee Avenue to Main Street. Turn left (west). The second house on your left is

4. 323 W. MAIN STREET—1873

This building, built in 1873, was originally at 401 E. Main Street. It was originally used by the St. Paul United Church of Christ for the teaching of religious classes in the German language, then in the 1880s for the overflow of pupils from the public school on Hough Street. In the early 1900s it was used to teach confirmation classes, then moved to its present site in the 1920s. The only aspect that represents the building's original appearance is the general outline, especially of the roof. The surfaces and the front porch and the protection over the front door are all twentieth century, as are the foundation, windows, and wrought iron porch posts.

Backtrack east on Main Street past Dundee Avenue. The third house on your right (south side) is

5. 223 W. MAIN STREET
The Octagon House—c.1860

This house was built by a Mr. Brown soon after he arrived from New England, in 1860. It was probably there that he became acquainted with a book by Orson Squire Fowler called *A Home for All, or The Octagon Way of Building*. It shows that with an equal perimeter, eight walls enclosed more space than four. Fowler was also among the first to integrate central heating, gas lighting, and plumbing into a house's design. Because builders had problems with the left-over wedge-shaped pieces, the house style proved impractical and died out before 1900. This house is a very fine example and displays excellent integrity. All of the pieces are present showing both the octagon and the style of the early 1860s. It has scroll-cut brackets in the cornice, a fancier version of scroll-cut brackets with incised and scalloped details in the porch capital, cut-out porch posts, and, at the base and under the porch, scroll-cut patterns abstracted from the Greek anthemion shapes. The clapboards terminate on corner boards which have little capitals on them on the upper floor. The window surrounds have nice entablatures, all of which show a high level of carpentry skill and a great delight in using the mechanized building industry, namely power driven saws, lathes, and planers. The building is on the National Register of Historic Places.

This block is significant because there are three buildings, two of which are in excellent condition and one of which has nice features, that are next to the Octagon House. It would be fair to characterize this street as representing the appearance of a downtown residential area at the turn of the century.

5. Octagon House
223 W. Main Street

Pay particular attention to these buildings: 204–206 W. Main Street (Barrington #8), and 218 W. Main Street (Barrington #6), which preserve almost all of their features in pristine condition; and 212–214 W. Main Street (Barrington #7), which has some extremely interesting features. The highlight of the block is the extremely important Octagon House (Barrington #5) which gave the neighborhood special distinction and is in itself an exceptionally rare and fine building.

Directly across from the Octagon House is

6.   218 W. MAIN STREET—c.1890

This standard L-shaped cottage with Queen Anne detail from the late 1880s or early 1890s stands on a limestone foundation with a porch tucked into the reentrant angle. The porch has a great deal of spindle work, large turned posts, and a Mansard roof. On the face of the front projecting wing is a slightly projecting bay window with the roof treatment repeated. The window has a leaded cut-glass transom and two side bars, and there are double windows above. The gable, both there and on the wing facing to the east, has scalloped shingles, and everything else is clapboard. A newer wing projects in the back.

   This house is an excellent example of a typical house type which is often ruined by changing the porch, putting on false vinyl or metal siding, changing the bay window, etc. This one is in excellent condition.

Continue east. The next house on your left is

7.   212-214 W. MAIN STREET—1880s

This is a very different kind of house (from Barrington #6). Probably dating from the 1880s, its style derives from the broad Italianate manner. It has windows on the second floor set far apart and an attic window in the top with a fancy pediment. The windows on the second floor have fancy entablatures which match the windows on the ground floor, something which is made even grander for the entrance. The porch still has most of its original turned posts with scroll-cut corbels acting as a kind of capital. Unfortunately, the rest of the building is covered with asbestos siding.

Continue east. The second house on your left is

8.   204-206 W. MAIN STREET—late 1880s

This is an example of a rather large house from the late 1880s with Queen Anne features dominant. It is a double house which is appropriate because it's near the downtown where they would build a big house for two families. It has two separate entrances and two separate porches, each leading to a residential unit.

The Queen Anne style is prominent in the variety of projections, the variety of textures, and the use of the Palladian windows in the gable, which is a much liked feature in that style. Note how the clapboard contrasts with the two different types of shingle textures, one between the first and second floors and the other in the gable. Also worthy of note is that the gable is treated sculpturally. The peak of the gable is projected outward in a curved shape and held up by a little bit of a bracket, and the bottom of the gable flares out to join at the extreme corners with the bargeboards of the gable itself. Also note the porches, apparently both original, complete with spindles.

Had it been a single-family house instead of a double house, a little bit more money would have been spent on it, for example, in having twice as many ballisters holding the porch rail. The ballisters are standard items bought in a lumberyard, but they did cost a certain amount. The porch on the second floor at 204 Main Street (on the east side of the building) is worth noting, as is the shingle field between the first and second floor, flared like the gable above, adding a sculptural richness to the form that corresponds with the way, on the ground floor in the front, both the corners that project are splayed at an angle but the area above is not, so there is a little cove above the corner window.

Cross to the south side of the street and continue east. The third building on your right is

9.   145 W. MAIN STREET—c.1900

This frame building dates from around the turn of the century and shows a blending of the variety of the Queen Anne motifs with the strict Classicism popularized by the Chicago World's Fair of 1893. The Queen Anne elements are the bulging bay window on the east side underneath the porch, the polygonal window on the west side of the porch, the rather elaborate dormer in the hipped roof, the flared bottoms of the hipped roofs, and the use of the

8. 204–206 W. Main Street

Palladian motif (rather freely, both in the dormer in the roof and in the second floor window on the east side).

The classical elements include the columns that hold up the porch, clustered in threes in the corners and also concentrated at the entrance because the porch projects at the entrance. Also classical is the use of the wreath motif above the flat-headed windows in the Palladian window and the swags used in the upper level of the Palladian window on the second floor. Also classical is the general symmetry of the building with large dormers projecting on both the east and the west, and the asymmetry introduced by having the central entrance offset to the west balanced with a large porch toward the back of the building on the ground floor, and projecting to the east.

Continue east. The third building on your right is

10. 117 W. Main Street—c. 1862

Built about 1862 by an early pioneer, this Greek Revival, L-shaped house has details added that show the impact of the new technology with power-driven wood-working tools. The general configuration and proportions of the building, the windows, front door, and corner pilasters represent the broadness of the Greek Revival. But the paired brackets in the gable are closer to the Italianate, a style that depended very much on making pieces with power-driven tools. The front porch is spurious and detracts from the character of the original design. Also an addition is the double door in the porch itself, but the configuration of the front door is original.

Across the street, on the north side, is

11. Catlow Theater—1927

Built in 1927 by the Chicago architectural firm of Betts and Holcomb, this small vaudeville and movie theater with shops on the ground floor and apartments on the second is done in the English half-timbered medieval style popular at that time in residential architecture and in suburban downtowns that wanted to maintain a residential character. Praised as a proper English theater, it has the mixture of materials and variety of forms characteristic of the style.

Inside is a surprise. The decoration was done in a fetching mixture of medieval, Prairie, and Art Deco styles under the personal direction of Alphonso Iannelli, who executed the nude in white art stone in the lobby.

Iannelli was an important collaborator of many famous architects including Frank Lloyd Wright. His designs allow the fantasy, so important in early movie theater designs, to turn to Arthurian England, one of the rarer themes in theaters of the period. The exterior and interior have been altered somewhat, but the general character survives.

Continue east past Hough Street. The second building on your right is

12.   119 E. MAIN STREET (and across the street)
124-126 E. MAIN STREET—1880s

Both of these buildings have altered ground floors, making them look like Williamsburg, Virginia. The brick fabric above, however, is the kind found on a typical midwestern "Main Street" building in the 1880s. Both buildings are very interesting because each has its original sheet-metal cornice. 124–126 E. Main Street includes the heavy "U.S. Grant" detail (the little stubby obelisk and the great big acanthus leaf) on either end, and 119 E. Main Street uses a delicate, classically derived motif. These standard sheet-metal cornice details could be ordered from a catalogue to dress up the top of a brick building.

Continue east on Main Street to the railroad tracks. Turn left (north) onto Cook Street. Walk 3 very short blocks to Washington Street. Turn right (east) 1 block. Pass Ela Street, then, the fourth house on your left (north side) is

13.   320 WASHINGTON STREET—1866

Built in 1866, this was once a secondary school (although not an accredited high school) taking pupils who had finished elementary school. In its nineteen years of use, thirteen different teachers taught here. This building has much greater historical significance than architectural, because the surface is new, but the general configuration of the building and the simplicity of the openings indicate a relatively humble building from the 1860s.

Continue east. On the NE corner of Washington Street and North Avenue is

14.   404 WASHINGTON STREET—c.1880

This frame double house on a limestone foundation has all the characteristics of a clapboard Italianate structure. It is symmetrical with a hipped roof

14. 404 Washington Street

and double scroll-cut brackets along the cornice and front and along the side. It has a porch with turned posts and scroll-cut brackets. It still has something rarely retained, the cast iron crestings along the top of the porch. In the front, windows are almost symmetrically arranged except their placement does not correspond with the regularly spaced brackets above.

Walk north on North Avenue. The second house on your right is

15.   311 NORTH AVENUE—c.1870
This house, built about 1870, was once on Main Street, where until 1894 it served as the parsonage of St. Paul Church. It now has a completely twentieth century facade covering the original building.

Continue north on North Avenue 2 blocks. The fourth house on your right past Valencia Avenue is

16.   511 NORTH AVENUE—1864
This charming two-story frame house was built in Cuba Township in 1864 and later moved to this location. The porch represents the type being built at the time the house was moved rather than in 1864.

Backtrack south on North Avenue. On the NW corner of North Avenue and Liberty Street is

17.   334 E. LIBERTY STREET—1867
This is a standard L-shaped house built in 1867. It has a marvelous porch, added in the corner, which has very nicely done mill work, turned spindles, and porch posts (except that the bottom level, the ballisters, and porch railings are spurious). Especially noteworthy: around the windows is a different style, commonly known as "U.S. Grant," which is more often found in furniture than on buildings.

Continue south on North Avenue. Walk 2 blocks to Franklin Street. Turn right (west) and the second house on your right is

18.   328 FRANKLIN STREET—c.1855
This is said to be the first milled lumber house built in Barrington. It was built about 1855 by Ed Lamey. The family held Catholic masses here until the local church was built. The one-story entrance on the east side is not

original. Otherwise, the building represents the standard design from the 1850s: a relatively simple clapboard structure, corner posts vaguely derived from the Greek Revival, but with some of the tall, thin proportions from the Gothic Revival.

Turn back east on Franklin Street to North Avenue. Turn right (south). On your left, just past Chestnut Street, is

19.   117 NORTH AVENUE
The Greenery Restaurant—1883

This 1883 building was once part of the Hough Street School. When the new school was built in 1905, the four wings of the old structure were sold and moved to new locations. This is one of the wings. In its present configuration it has been altered along the ground floor.

Continue south. On the NW corner of North Avenue and Main Street is

20.   334 E. MAIN STREET—c.1862

Built about 1862, this is a standard L-shaped cottage. It is noteworthy that this house has porch posts which are a carpenter's version of the more elaborate posts found on the Octagon House (Barrington #5), which were probably added later.

Walk west on Main Street. The fourth building on your right (north) is

21.   312 E. MAIN STREET—c.1862

This house was also built about 1862. Unfortunately, most of the building has been covered with asbestos brick, but the building does show the Queen Anne style addition put onto the front of the older building. This addition, which constitutes the front of the house, is probably from the 1890s. It has large turned posts, and a two-story projecting bay in the front that rises into bracketed and latticed corners supporting the large roof, which sweeps out over the front of the house. What is now visible is the addition of a new style onto a building which probably originally looked much like 334 E. Main Street (Barrington #20).

Continue west on Main Street to the railroad tracks (Cook Street). Turn left and walk 1 block on the left (east) side of the street. On the NE corner of Cook and Station streets is

22. 119 S. Cook Street
Town Shop—c. 1860

This is the oldest store building in Barrington. Built about 1860, the downstairs was a general store, the upstairs a hall, and the back a jewelers. In 1916 the building was moved and turned around to its present location. As is common with commercial buildings, the front has been completely altered. Only a few traces and the general configuration remain to indicate the original building. Its significance is historical rather than architectural.

On the SE corner of Cook and Station streets is

23. 201 S. Cook Street
The Village Green—c. 1873

This building, built about 1873, once boasted one of the four dug wells with a hand pump in Barrington; it was used for watering horses. As is typical with commercial buildings, this has been so altered that very little of the original facade or configuration remains.

Continue south. The next building on your left is

24. 207 S. Cook Street—c. 1862

This house, built about 1862, was enlarged in the early 1870s. It started as a standard L-shaped cottage, but its present surfaces all date from the 1870s, with clapboard and scalloped shingles. The placement of the porch is from the 1870s, as are the turned posts, but the filagree work at the top of the porch is a very recent addition, probably taken from the interior of a house and added here. The porch railing is spurious. This shows that houses are constantly rebuilt and altered to meet the changing needs of their occupants, and then when they get adapted to commercial use they tend to be changed again.

Continue south. The second house on your left, on the NE corner of Cook and Lake streets, is

25. 219 S. Cook Street—pre-1862

Built before 1862, this building was originally Boyse Tavern. It was enlarged in 1862 to be used as a residence. Millius B. McIntosh, the first occupant, was also the first resident of Barrington to have a kerosene lamp in his home.

Nothing now visible represents the nineteenth century, and even the original configuration is masked by the projecting porch.

On the NW corner of Lake and Cook streets is

26. 218 S. COOK STREET—c.1862
This house, except for the front porch, dates to about 1862.

Continue south. The third building on your right is

27. 312 S. COOK STREET
Masonic Temple Association—1872
This building was originally built for the Methodist Church congregation in 1872. The nicest feature that shows the original building is the entrance, which has excellent Gothic Revival carpentry work.

Continue south. On the SW corner of Cook and Lincoln streets is

28. 400 S. COOK STREET—c.1862
This house was built about 1862. Numerous additions, such as the shutters, porch railings, screen door, and the wings show that buildings change and grow over the years.

On the NE corner of Cook and Lincoln streets is

29. 319 S. COOK STREET—1870s
This is a standard L-shaped building from the 1870s with a porch added sometime in the early twentieth century. Especially noteworthy are the windows. On the ground floor, facing Cook Street, is a large flat-fronted projecting window and on the south side is a bay window which has scroll-cut and incised corbels. The rest of the windows have a device which is not often seen: a hood molding derived from the Gothic Revival.

Backtrack north 1 block on Cook Street to Lake Street. Turn left (west) and cross to the north side of Lake Street. The third building on your right is

30. 110 E. LAKE STREET
The Raleigh House—c.1862
This house, built about 1862, was moved from its original location to make

room for a gas station. It is in adaptive reuse as a tearoom and gift shop, which accounts for the addition on the front. The shutters are not original.

Continue west on Lake Street to the corner. Turn right (north) on Hough Street, 1 block, to Station Street. Turn left, returning to the Barrington Historical Society on your left.

This concludes the Barrington Walking Tour.

Drive west on Station Street 1 block to Dundee. Turn right (north) 1 block. Turn right (east) on Main Street which becomes Lake-Cook Road. Continue until it ends at Route 12.

LONG GROVE

LONG GROVE

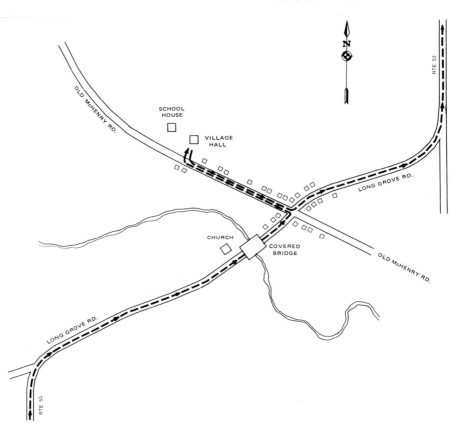

Turn right on Route 12, ½ mile to the first light (Route 53) then turn left onto Route 53 North. Continue 2.7 miles to Long Grove Road, which angles to the left. Turn left onto Long Grove Road and continue about ¼ mile. Stop at the Long Grove Church on your left.

THE LONG GROVE CHURCH—1846

Originally built in 1846 as a simple Classical Revival structure clad in clapboards with a stout tower, it has subsequently received additional elements. The chancel was extended, the windows heightened, and the steeple added in 1874. The tracker organ, originally hand pumped, dates from 1902. The pedimented front porch and an addition to the rear date from 1947; later additions are from 1952 and 1967. The cemetery has been in use since the 1840s and has a surviving gravestone dating from 1849.

Continue to the crossroads and turn left on Old McHenry Road about ¼ mile to the Village Hall (just past the new school). Turn right into the drive and stop in front of the Village Hall.

Parts of the Long Grove Village Hall were once a tavern. Across the creek is Archer School, an 1840's one-room schoolhouse, now stocked with period antiques. It was moved to this site in order to preserve it. Also note the wild flowers that grow around the area.

Walk down the drive and turn left 1 block to the crossroads of Old McHenry Road and Long Grove Road.

Long Grove has been an attractive community ever since German farmers settled here in the 1840s. Drawn by the grove of hardwood trees, a large section of which survive north of the town, and by the convenient location on major country roads an easy day's drive from Chicago, the town became a milk supplier to Chicago.

The town grew slowly after mid-century, and many of its early buildings, utilitarian, wooden structures typical of early mid-western settlements, survived in their original condition up to World War II. During the first post-war decade, Long Grove's residents recognized that the authentic country charm of their rural community was threatened by the expansion of Chicago's suburbs, stimulated in part by road improvements proposed for the vicinity. In response, they instituted one of the earliest local preservation ordinances in the state. It specified that all future construction had to correspond to the general character of the original "Long Grove style," as they called it.

The result of subsequent growth is the pleasant collection of shops and other buildings, some old, some new, spread along the original crossroads. Behind them are parking lots discreetly tucked from view. Recently, the steel truss road bridge, typical of those built on country roads around the turn of the century, was given a wooden superstructure to produce the effect of an old-fashioned covered bridge, now the emblem of the town.

Leave Long Grove on Long Grove Road East, about ½ mile until it ends at Route 83. Turn left (north).

MUNDELEIN

ST. MARY of the Lake

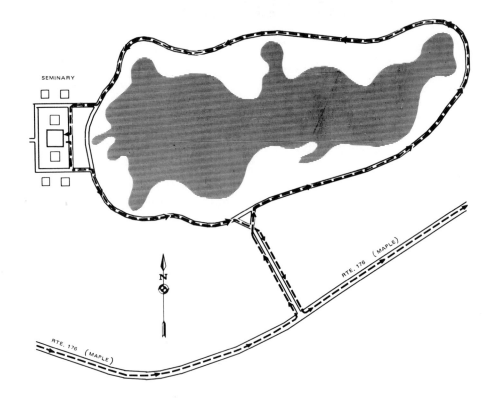

SEMINARY

RTE. 176 (MAPLE)

RTE. 176 (MAPLE)

N

Drive north on Route 83, 4 miles, continuing north on Route 45. Continue 3 miles. Turn right (east) on Route 176 about 1 mile. On your left is

SAINT MARY OF THE LAKE SEMINARY—Circle around the lake, noting the beautiful surroundings and the matched bridges. *Stop* in the circular drive near the church.

The principal work of the seminary is the training of young men for the Catholic priesthood. This unique institution was founded in 1920 by the late George Cardinal Mundelein. The town now bears his name. The seminary master plan called for clustering nearly all the buildings, designed by Joe W. McCarthy, near the main entrance and facing the lake. There, neo-classic, Georgian, red brick buildings include classrooms, residence halls, offices, chapel, gymnasium, and other athletic facilities on about 900 acres of land, including the 100-acre lake.

It is an enchanting rustic setting with the lake, magnificent trees, bushes, and grassy meadows. Except for the buildings clustered at the main entrance, the grounds are free of structures.

The extensive landscaping is in keeping with eighteenth century gardening that fits with the neo-classic design of the buildings. The full cluster of buildings which overlook the lake is reminiscent of Sir Christopher Wren's design for the Royal Naval Hospital at Greenwich, near London. The hospital, of course, faces the Thames River.

Turn left out of the driveway onto Route 176 (east).

LIBERTYVILLE

LAMBS FARM

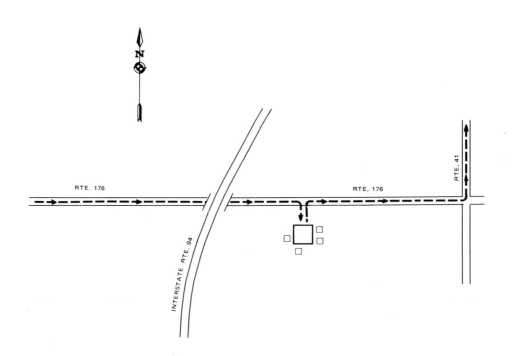

Drive east 4.3 miles on Route 176. Just past the tollway, on your right is

LAMBS FARM—This not-for-profit complex provides training and jobs for the mentally retarded. It is a good place to bring the children, with animals to touch, a pet shop, and hay rides. There are several shops. One specializing in silkscreened works allows you to watch the whole process before you buy. At the bakery, you can watch people working behind a glassed area. There is also a restaurant.

Leaving Lambs Farm, turn right (east) on Route 176, 2 miles to Route 41 North. Turn left (north), curve to the left, then turn right (north) onto Route 41. Continue north 5 miles to exit Route 120 West. Drive west 1.3 miles.

GURNEE

GREAT AMERICA

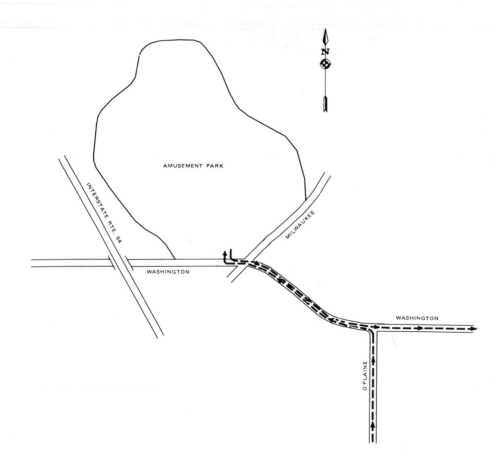

Turn right (north) on O'Plaine Road .8 miles to Washington Street. Turn left (west) on Washington Street 1 mile. On your right is

MARIOTT'S GREAT AMERICA—This theme park offers rides and attractions for the whole family. Various shows and big-name entertainers are scheduled throughout the season. (Seasonal.)

Leaving Great America, turn left (east) on Washington Street 5½ miles.

WAUKEGAN

WAUKEGAN

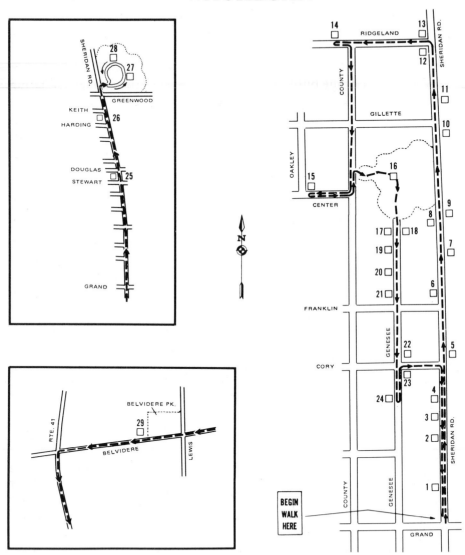

Turn left (north) on Sheridan Road 3 blocks. Stop.

WAUKEGAN WALKING TOUR

Walk north on Sheridan Road. The first house on your left is

1. 320 N. SHERIDAN ROAD—1852

The second brick home built in Lake County, and the oldest still standing, this 1852 Greek Revival house is of special interest because its foundation is of boulders encased in cement. In the original part of the house, the foundation is waist high and three feet wide. It survives in excellent condition, except the porch has been altered and the building repainted.

Continue north. The second building on your left is

2. 408 N. SHERIDAN ROAD—1875

This 1875 home is an example of an exuberant use of the Italianate style. The tall, thin, first floor windows, pronounced moldings with scroll-cut and incised and cut-out brackets, and the heavy window surrounds with keystones have become extremely decorative. In the center on the second floor, the heavy shoulders for the window surrounds and, in the gable of the third floor, the punched out bargeboard indicate a great deal of fun was had with the Italinate style. The only visible alteration is the two-story porch on the south side which was sympathetically added sometime shortly after the turn of the century. The building is in adaptive reuse as a funeral home.

Continue north. The next house on your left is

3. 414 N. SHERIDAN ROAD—1847

Built in 1847, this frame house is one of the finest examples of the strictly formal Greek Revival style house in the state of Illinois. It was built by John H. Swartout. The architectural purity is concentrated at the portico, where fluted Doric columns support a stark entablature and an almost canonic pediment. Inside the portico are three openings, each the same, except the windows have shouldered moldings acting as frames which the door lacks, but it has a transom. At each end of the front wall, reflecting the columns in front, is a pilaster. The restrained details and excellent proportions give the

3. 414 N. Sheridan Road

building a distinctively fine character. A large rear porch was added in 1858 and a north bay window in 1877. The south porch was enclosed in 1933.

Continue north. The fourth house on your left is

4. 438 N. SHERIDAN ROAD—1840s

The Italian Villa style home you see was built around a small 1840s house that was in the Greek Revival style. Added to make it an Italian Villa was a tall central tower, a porch with the customary columns and shouldered lintel, the double brackets under the eaves, and the pediments above the windows which include the windows on the original Greek Revival section. Especially noteworthy here are the double windows in the second floor of the tower and the rope moldings above the double doors. The rope moldings are also used as spiral columns for the double arched window and on the third floor. The same window is used on the east and west faces of the third story of the tower and on the east face of the second story of the tower. The Italian Villa style here is characteristic of the mid-1850s. Inside are a walnut staircase, six fireplaces, and a dumbwaiter. The house has double brick walls with an air space between, and glass windows imported from Europe. It is now owned by Shimer College.

Cross to the east side of the street and continue north. The first house past Cory Avenue, on your right, is

5. 505 N. SHERIDAN ROAD—1850s

Probably built in the 1850s, this house shows its early date by having a central tower with a steeply pitched roof (indicating a Gothic Revival style) set in the middle of a block with two windows on either side, which have slightly flared segmental arches. More proper to the Gothic Revival style is the double window in the central tower, with its peaked, arched pediment. The doorway, with its heavy robust forms, more closely matches the breadth of the tall windows on either side of the ground floor.

Cross to the west side of the street and continue north. The fourth house on your left is

6. 526 N. SHERIDAN ROAD—late 1840s

This late 1840s house reflects the Ohio influence of Greek Revival style. The

4. 438 N. Sheridan Road

front windows (under the pediments between the pilasters of the front section along the north) have very simple surrounds. The corner pilasters rise to a Greek Revival gable that has slight returns. Later additions, probably between the late 1850s and the mid 1870s, include: the present porch, with its octagonal columns; the front doorway, with its heavily bracketed canopy; and the polygonal bay window projecting to the south at the end of the one-story wing. This one-and-one-half-story frame structure is characteristic, and an excellent example, of its type. It forces the upper story windows into the gable area of the structure, reducing the headroom on the sides, but making a smaller building to construct.

Cross back to the east side of Sheridan Road and continue north. The sixth house on your right is

7.   619 N. Sheridan Road—1840s

Many Victorian houses were built around earlier structures, since it was considered unlucky to take down an earlier structure. This house was built around an 1840s house. The small, symmetrical, formal structure embodies all the best of the Victorian Gothic style. The steep gables for the wall dormers in the front, the central towers, and the dormer on the wing on the north are striking. The unornamented double doors and window trim give a functional simplicity.

Cross to the west side of Sheridan Road. Continue north. The fifth house on your left is

8.   710 N. Sheridan Road—1872

Restored to its 1872 Victorian elegance, this Second Empire and Italianate frame house features tall, arched, double entrance doors with glass panels, a veranda-like columnar porch, Mansard roof, elaborate window surrounds, and a rich double-bracketed cornice.

Cross to the east side and continue north. The fourth house on your right is

9.   721 N. Sheridan Road—1926

Leonard J. Latz, Sr. designed this brick house in 1926, employing the rectilinear lines of the Prairie School of architecture. He extended the eaves of the hipped roof well beyond the walls, creating a horizontal and low-to-the-ground quality. The horizontal emphasis is reinforced by the stone belt line between the first and second stories. The arched central doorway, and the three arches in the center of the second story, show an historical revival style occurring at the time this building was built; but the overall character of the house, augmented as it is by the care in which the brick is used to produce a pattern, makes it a strong example of the Prairie School.

Continue north. The third house on your right is

10.   837 N. SHERIDAN ROAD—1858

This 1858 brick house is in the Italianate style. Carefully added to it, probably around 1910, was a front porch and a polygonal bay with clear representation of the Prairie School style. The addition works very well with the original structure.

Continue north. The second house on your right is

11.   907 N. SHERIDAN ROAD—Early 1930s

Built during the depression, this Lannon stone, English Tudor house has a slate roof with only the slightest projections. A tall, wide chimney, flanked by casement windows in its wall dormers, dominates the facade. The ivy-covered entrance has a medieval-derived, pointed arch. The garage on the north is nicely worked into the composition.

Cross to the west side of the street and continue north. On the SW corner of Sheridan Road and Ridgeland Avenue is

12.   946 N. SHERIDAN ROAD—1876

This Italian Villa frame house from 1876 is notable primarily for the openings in the tower. On the ground floor is a doorway, above that is a pair of windows under a circular pediment, and above that, a triplet of windows under a triangular pediment.

On the NW corner of Sheridan Road and Ridgeland Avenue is

13.   1004 N. SHERIDAN ROAD—late 1890s

This large, frame structure, rising a full two stories to a full attic, probably dates from just before the turn of the century. On the east facade, in the gable, is a Palladian window. A porch wraps around the ground floor to the south side of the building where it intersects a one-story polygonal bay, projecting from a gambrel-roofed projection. In the gambrel roof's gable is another Palladian window. The porch is sustained by Tuscan columns set between tightly spaced ballisters.

Walk west on Ridgeland Avenue past County Street. On your right (north side of the street) is

14. 310 RIDGELAND AVENUE—1894

This 1894 house is an example of the Eastern Stick style as it was interpreted by midwestern carpenter contractors. The main roof is steeply pitched and repeated lower down on the front. A large front porch is stopped at the east by a diagonally placed bay. Vertical, horizontal, and diagonal lines form a highly decorative pattern. Porch posts and railings in a patterned design complete the picture of "stick-work."

Backtrack east on Ridgeland to County Street. Turn right (south) 2 blocks. Turn right (west) on Center Street. On the NE corner of Center Street and Oakley Avenue is

15. 324 CENTER STREET—1896

Unique in Waukegan, according to experts, this 1896 house was built as a double house. It is in the Queen Anne style and shows characteristic liberties taken with the classical elements, especially evident in the pillared porch. The roof curves gently to a peak above the arch over the third-floor roof windows.

Backtrack east on Center Street to County Street. Turn left (north). Just past 809 County Street is a path leading into a park. Turn right onto the path (walking east). In the park is

16. 732 N. GENESEE STREET—1853

This 1853 house is a large, brick, Gothic cottage or villa. It has steeply pitched roofs, a heavy columnar porch, wall dormers, hooded window moldings, and one window with a pointed arch. In the section added on the west timbered bargeboards with knob pendants along the eaves contribute to its exemplary representation of the Gothic Revival style.

15.   324 Center Street

Standing with your back to the front of 732 N. Genesee Street, walk straight ahead and you will be walking south on Genesee Street. The third house on your right, on the west side of the street, is

17.   710 N. GENESEE—c.1850

This Greek Revival house was built about 1850. Wings were added to the house in the 1860s or early 1870s with tall windows and a porch made up of stout posts holding a bracketed entablature, under which is an incised hipped molding. The entrance with its outsized, incised corbel also dates from the later period.

Directly across the street is

18. 709 N. GENESEE STREET—1924

This house, designed by Leonard J. Latz, Sr., was built in 1924. It is very much like the later structure designed by Latz at 721 N. Sheridan (Waukegan #9). It, too, has a broad hipped roof with ample eaves and very careful brick work. Here, however, set within the arched opening of the doorway, is a small columnar porch. The arch of the doorway is matched by similar three-part arches on either side which contain the windows. This is a highly stylized version of the Palladian motif that had been popular since the sixteenth century and revived in the Queen Anne style of the 1880s. The roof tiles have been removed.

Cross back to the west side of the street and continue south. The first house on your right is

19. 638 N. GENESEE STREET—pre-1886

The pre-1886, frame, one-and-one-half-story house has a Greek Revival body and an Italianate extension with a porch and bay. It is said to have been a model house which appeared in Godey's Lady's Book.

Continue south. The next house on your right is

20. 628 N. GENESEE STREET—c.1867

One of Waukegan's wealthiest citizens in the 1860s, brick magnate John B. Legnard, built his home of wood. The delightful frame house has a wraparound circular porch with very recent and unsuitable supports, but the hooded arched windows, tall and thin in the Italianate manner, and attic windows in the cornice, survive.

Continue south. The third house on your right is

21. 614 N. GENESEE STREET—1872

This 1872 Italianate house features a frame structure with hooded and arched, needle-thin windows on the tower, and incised scrollwork design in the bracketed cornice and flanking the door.

Cross to the east side of the street and continue south past Franklin. The fifth house on your left is

22. 509 N. GENESEE STREET—1872

Although the basic style of this frame, 1872 house was originally Greek Revival, with the many additions it can easily be called Italianate. Note: the tower with the Mansard roof has small pediments inserted on each face; the south corner has an octagonal turret between the arched window; the cornice has incised moldings; the steeply pitched roofs; the arched, hooded windows; and the decorative bargeboard, on the small pediment above the window, between the tower and the corner turret. The floor-to-ceiling windows, which betray the early date of the building, make the rooms light and airy.

Walk south to the corner. On the SE corner of Cory Avenue and Genesee Street is

23. 445 N. GENESEE STREET—1917

Designed by well-known architects Thomas Tallmadge and Vernon Watson, this 1917 Prairie School house has the materials often found in such structures: brick along the basement, and stucco walls trimmed with boards used as window frames, timbers, and gable rafters. Characteristic of Tallmadge and Watson are the pier-like projections on the wings, the arched window on the second floor of the west facade, and the leaded glass in the casement windows. Leaded glass is also found inside, where it is used extensively in room dividers and bookcases.

Cross to the west side of the street and continue south on Genesee Street. The third house on your right is

24. 438 N. GENESEE STREET—late 1880s

This small Queen Anne style house is probably from the late 1880s because it is still very simple in its detailing which produced the style by adding carpentry work to the walls. Note, for example, the boards: used under the windows on the ground floor, used around the window on the second floor, and used instead of turned spindles for much of the intricate detailing on the porch.

Backtrack north to Cory Avenue. Turn right (east) 1 block to Sheridan Road. Turn right (south) 1 long block to Grand Avenue.

This concludes the Waukegan Walking Tour.

Drive north on Sheridan Road. The third house on your left past Stewart Avenue is

25. 114 N. SHERIDAN ROAD—1913

This outstanding example of the Prairie School of architecture embodies the distinctive blocky shapes, horizontal styling, combination of stucco and flat boards, and carefully detailed casement windows indicative of the style. Designed by Purcell and Elmslie (protegees of Frank Lloyd Wright) the 1913 house is similar in design to Wright's 1906 "Fireproof House for $5,000." The wrought iron fence in front is not in the Prairie style.

Continue north on Sheridan Road 3 blocks. On the NW corner of Sheridan Road and Harding is

26. 1524 N. SHERIDAN ROAD—1928

A fine example of the Mission style of architecture, this 1928 house features the characteristic tile, hipped roof, and arched windows. It was designed by Leonard J. Latz, Sr. Notice the rough and smooth materials and varied colored bricks which give interest to the basically rectangular silhouette.

Continue north 2½ blocks to Bowen Park on your right (east).

JOSEPH T. BOWEN COUNTRY CLUB,
now Bowen Park

This rolling, ravine-cut site was originally laid out in 1843. It occupies slightly more than sixty acres and contains large areas that have remained unaltered. These give an idea of the original topography and forested character of the Lake Michigan shoreland. The park is most important as a gift in 1911 to Hull House by Mrs. Louise DeKoven Bowen, Chicago social figure and philanthropist, given in memory of her husband who was important in the development of the Chicago and Northwestern Railroad. Mrs. Bowen bought it so that it could serve as a country club for the slum children cared for by her friend Jane Addams (Mrs. Bowen was President of the Hull House Woman's Club whose membership was otherwise exclusively from the Hull House slum neighborhood. She cared for Miss Addams in her final hours at the Bowen Astor Street mansion). Many of the structures in the park were built for the use of the Hull House children. Since 1963, the park has been part of the Waukegan Park District. It is listed on the National Register of Historic Places.

The building on the east side of the circular driveway is

27. THE JACK BENNY CENTER
1917 N. Sheridan Road

This cultural arts center is housed in what was a nineteenth-century summer estate building, now much altered. It now provides arts classes in music, dance, drama, art, and needlework for Waukegan's young people.

The building on the north end of the circular driveway is

28. WAUKEGAN HISTORICAL SOCIETY
Haines House Museum
1917 N. Sheridan Road—1843

The structure housing the Waukegan Historical Society was the residence of the earliest owner of the site. It is named after its 1857 purchaser, John Charles Haines, an early Mayor of Chicago who used it as a summer home. The building's oldest section dates from 1843, but most of what is visible are additions from about 1873–76.

The Waukegan Historical Society has gathered hundreds of antiques to display the house as it might have been in the last century. The Victorian parlor is set up as a music room; the library contains antique books, as well as a collection by Waukegan authors; the schoolroom is furnished as a typical turn-of-the-century school; there is a wonderful communications display; one room boasts a bed (rather short) in which Abraham Lincoln is said to have slept; a farm kitchen is stocked with utensils as well as packaged foodstuffs of a bygone era. There are extensive photographs of Waukegan's landmark buildings along the walls. The museum is staffed by friendly, well-informed volunteers.

Leaving Bowen Park turn left (south) on Sheridan Road 2.2 miles to Belvidere Street. Turn right (west) 1.8 miles. On your right is

29. TUBERCULOSIS SANATORIUM
2400 Belvidere Street—1940

William A. Ganster and William L. Pereira designed this 1940 building in the International Style popularized in America by Mies Van der Rohe and Lazlo Moholy-Nagy. Ganster received the Philadelphia Art Alliance medal in 1948. It is aesthetically pleasing with its juxtaposition of glass walls and abstract planes. The walls are planes, as are the windows, arranged in long strips that open up almost all of the wall. Contrasting with these planes are those of the roof and of the balconies, both treated as thin slabs. The balconies are lined with carefully detailed pipe railings.

Continue west on Belvidere Street 1½ miles to Route 41 South (towards Chicago). Continue south 5 miles on Route 41.

LAKE BLUFF

LAKE BLUFF

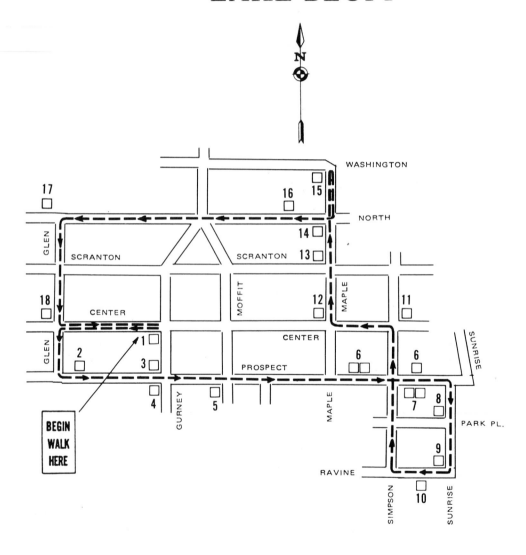

Exit Route 176 right, then turn a sharp left (U-turn) at Shagbark Road onto eastbound Route 176, continuing east onto Center Avenue (a total of 1.8 miles) to the SW corner of Center and Gurney avenues. Stop.

LAKE BLUFF WALKING TOUR

On the SW corner of Center and Gurney avenues is

1. 345 CENTER AVENUE—c.1877

This home, built about 1877, is a lovely rebuilt example of the Camp Meeting Cottage. Visible here is very interesting work from an early period (for example, the struts under the gable, the notched eaves, and the brackets holding the outer gable rafters). The parapet across the roof of the porch is also an example of early carpentry work, related in its period of construction to the Gothic arched openings in this frame structure.

Walk west on Center Avenue 1 block to Glen Avenue. Turn left (south) 1 block. Turn left (east) on Prospect Avenue. The third house on your left is

2. 314 E. PROSPECT AVENUE—c.1880

Built about 1880 or earlier, beyond the recently rebuilt porch is an excellent example of a rare type of construction called "board and batten." The massing is that of the Gothic Revival Cottage style, although the roofs here have a lower pitch than is usual, as are the proportions of the thin, very tall windows, the same size used for the opening for the door. The board and batten walls stressed the verticality characteristic of the Gothic style then being revived, but it also proved to be a very efficient way of sheathing early frame structures.

Continue east to the corner. On the NW corner of Prospect and Gurney avenues is

3. 346 E. PROSPECT AVENUE—c.1887

This house was built about 1887 by Solomon Thatcher, Jr., who helped organize the Lake Bluff Camp Meeting Association and became its first president. Note the similarities in its shape and details to 345 Center Avenue (Lake Bluff #1).

On the SW corner of Prospect and Gurney avenues is

4.   345 E. PROSPECT AVENUE—c.1912

This house was built about 1912. The Prairie influence can be seen in the strips of casement windows set into areas on the stucco walls defined by boards, although the general massing of the house is tall and blocky, whereas the Prairie style is usually thought of as long and low.

Continue east 1 block. The last house on your right is

5.   419 E. PROSPECT AVENUE—c.1883

This house, built about 1883, was constructed from brick made in the local Ben Cloes brickyard. It was later stuccoed, leaving exposed the stone arches over the windows, producing an anomaly, because stone arches belong on brick buildings and stucco is usually placed over frame construction.

Continue east past Maple Avenue. The third, fourth, and sixth houses on your left are

6.   618 E. PROSPECT AVENUE,
    624 E. PROSPECT AVENUE, and
    710 E. PROSPECT AVENUE—early 1910s

These three houses, variations on a similar design, are examples of what might be called "contractor's-Prairie." Each has a ground floor distinctly set apart from the upper floor. The ground floor is given a strong horizontal emphasis, with porches with broad eaves, and windows grouped together in bunches. The ground floor carries through to the sills of the second floor windows, where a different treatment begins. It might be stucco and wood as with 618 E. Prospect, or a revival of board and batten construction as at 624 E. Prospect, or smooth boards as at 710 E. Prospect which also has very finely done Prairie leaded glass. The design is then topped with a simple pitched roof. All three structures date from between 1910 and 1915.

Across the street, on the SE corner of Prospect and Simpson avenues, are

7.   701 PROSPECT AVENUE (and to the east)
    707 PROSPECT AVENUE—c.1885

This delightful pair of houses stands where the Chicago meat packer Gustovus Swift built two buildings about 1885, the one on the corner for the use of

6. 624 Prospect Avenue

8. 456 Sunrise Avenue

his son. These buildings are fine examples of the suburban resort houses from the period just before World War I. Both have indications of the historical style of the period and of the Prairie School. Notice the use, on the corner building, of bunched windows and on 707 Prospect Avenue, of a simple board acting as a stringcourse in broad stucco surfaces.

Continue east to Sunrise Avenue. Turn right (south). On the NW corner of Sunrise Avenue and Park Place is

8.   456 SUNRISE AVENUE—c.1889

Originally a duplex cottage facing north, this house, built about 1889, was later turned to face the lake and enlarged to its present size. It has a marvelous exuberance of architectural expression with two tiers of porches and towers on either side. It just misses being symmetrical, a characteristic which lends it a great deal of interest.

Continue south to Ravine Avenue. On the NW corner of Sunrise and Ravine avenues is

9.   404 SUNRISE AVENUE—c.1890

This house, built about 1890, has solid concrete construction, imitating masonry, holding up a great gambrel roof with three dormers.

Turn right (west) on Ravine Avenue. The first house on your left is

10.   727 RAVINE AVENUE—c.1935

This is a two-story, frame structure covered in stucco with casement windows grouped together and a flat parapet marking the top of the building. On the east side is a foresquare entrance block. These are characteristics of the late 1920s and 1930s architectural style known as Moderne. It is an interesting precursor of the later modern styles used for residential architecture.

Walk west on Ravine Avenue to Simpson. Turn right (north) 3 short blocks. On the NE corner of Simpson and Center avenues is

11.   700 CENTER AVENUE—c.1899

The house, built about 1899 by Horace R. Cook, was later enlarged by his daughter Marion Claire Cook Weber, a noted opera singer of that day. It shows traces of the earlier, blockier composition of the 1890s with its variety of roofs and its corner tower; but the surfaces, covered as they are with stucco and boards, and its simple casement windows with transoms indicate the stylization of that design characteristic of the post World War I period. Especially interesting is the metal casement window above the front door, a building component derived from industrial construction. Extensive garden wells extend the design across the ample grounds.

Walk west on Center Avenue. On the NW corner of Center and Maple avenues is

12.   550 CENTER AVENUE—c.1900

This house was built about 1900. Recently covered by metal siding, probably obscuring more extensive textured surfaces like the fragment seen on the gable facing south, the massing survives to show the variety of forms characteristic of this period. Especially interesting is the porch facing east on the third floor, from which one probably had a marvelous view of the lake.

Walk north on Maple Avenue 1 block. On the NW corner of Scranton and Maple avenues is

13.   548 SCRANTON AVENUE—1880s

This tiny, one-and-one-half-story frame house is a good example of early Cottage style architecture. It is possibly from the 1880s.

Continue north on Maple Avenue. The next house on your left, on the SW corner of Maple and North avenues, is

14.   618 MAPLE AVENUE—c.1910

Designed by Webster Tomlinson (a protege of Louis Sullivan), this brick, stucco, and board house, built about 1910, is a good example of Prairie School architecture. Especially notable is the care with which it has been designed for its corner site, with the porch projecting from the brick ground floor at the reentrant angle. Also notice the thinness of the roof as it projects beyond the stucco walls, and how on the second story, windows projecting at an angle echo the angle of the roof pitch.

Continue north on Maple Avenue. On the SW corner of Maple and Washington avenues is

15. 666 MAPLE AVENUE—c.1886

This house, with vague Italianate massing, was built about 1886 by Ben Cloes, using brick from his brickyard across the street.

Backtrack south on Maple Avenue to North Avenue. Turn right (west). The ninth house on your right is

16. 500 NORTH AVENUE—c.1875

Built about 1875, the Lake Bluff Camp Meeting Association office moved here from Prospect Avenue. The building has been remodeled by adding the stucco surface and inserting a new porch on the east side and one similar to it on the west. The elaborate window frames, with fine incised detailing and elaborate cut-out forms, and the roof shapes and roof carpentry work with nice brackets in the gable including a date plate, remain intact and give an indication of the original character of the structure.

Continue west. On the NW corner of Glen and North avenues is

17. 244 NORTH AVENUE—c.1910

Built about 1910, this structure, once used as a tearoom, is unusual because above its ground floor rises a three-story roof. The top story forms a small attic. It shows the board and stucco surfaces derived from the English Tudor but with a simplicity characteristic of the Prairie style. The roof treatment and general massing represent an approach of notable Prairie School architects Tallmadge and Watson and of a similar proficient practitioner, Dwight Perkins.

Walk south on Glen Avenue 2 short blocks. On the NW corner of Center and Glen avenues is

18. GRACE UNITED METHODIST CHURCH—1903

The church was built in 1903 and sympathetically enlarged in 1948.

Walk east on Center 1 block to the corner of Gurney Avenue.

This concludes the Lake Bluff Walking Tour.

Drive west on Center Avenue 3 blocks, jogging left before the underpass. Turn left (south) on Sheridan Road, continuing south on McKinley Road a total of 2 miles to Deerpath Road.

LAKE FOREST

LAKE FOREST

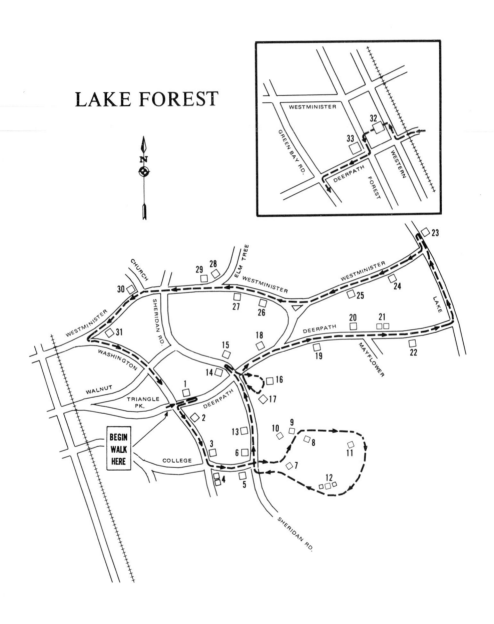

Lake Forest was founded soon after the first railroad was pushed from Chicago to Waukegan in 1855. In 1857 Jed Hotchkiss, a St. Louis landscape architect, laid out the town. His design is based on picturesque principles developed in eighteenth-century England and used in America first for cemeteries. It takes full advantage of the rolling, ravine-ridden topography, a landscape unusual in the Chicago region. The site's natural beauty and easy access by rail from Chicago, as well as its foundation on strict moral principles (its original, 1861 city charter forbade the manufacture and sale of liquor), established it even before the Chicago Fire of 1871 as an exclusive (if distant) suburb for important Chicagoans. Much of Lake Forest including its downtown is a district listed on the National Register of Historic Places.

Drive east on Deerpath Road, across the railroad tracks to Triangle Park. Start from the NE corner of Deerpath Road and Washington.

LAKE FOREST WALKING TOUR

Walk east on Deerpath Road. On your left is

1. 550 E. DEERPATH ROAD—1859
Part of this building was originally the house of Sylvester Lind (an important person in the founding of Lake Forest, active in Chicago lumber, real estate, and insurance who arrived in Chicago in 1837 as a carpenter). It was built in 1859, but what is now visible is a formal design from the 1920s.

Backtrack west on Deerpath Road to Washington. Turn left (south). The second house on your left is

2. 595 WASHINGTON—20th century
This two-story, pitched roof house is a twentieth-century building but is based upon a common nineteenth-century type, showing how nicely old styles can be used as a basis for newer buildings.

Continue south on Washington. At the end of the block on your left is

3. 561 WASHINGTON—1860
Buried within the present building, which is a post World War II structure, is

an 1860 house which was originally an auxillary building of "The Homestead" at 570 Sheridan Road (Lake Forest #6).

Turn left (east) on College Road. The first house on your right is

4. 605 E. COLLEGE ROAD (and behind it)
449 WASHINGTON—1903

"Linden Lodge" was built in 1903. The architects were Frost and Granger. These were originally the house and coachhouse of Henry Calvin Durand, wholesale grocer and important benefactor of Lake Forest University. The house is a highly formalized version of an English country house. Note, for example, the carefully done Doric columns which derive ultimately from the Parthenon in ancient Athens.

The coachhouse is a small and less formal building. Notice the columns, on the back facing over the gardens, are like the ones on the main house but done in stucco with little capitals, a dilution of the correctness found in the main house that is appropriate for this service building.

Continue east on College Road. The next house on your right is

5. 621 E. COLLEGE ROAD—1902

This Frost and Granger house was built in 1902. The general mass is similar to 605 E. College (Lake Forest #4), but is covered in shingles instead of stucco and, instead of a columnar porch, it has a simple, broken, swan's-neck pediment framing the doorway.

Continue east. On your left, on the NW corner of Sheridan and College roads, is

6. 570 N. SHERIDAN ROAD—1860

"The Homestead" is an 1860 house (see Lake Forest #3), home of D.R. Holt, Chicago lumber dealer and one of Lake Forest's original land owners. This is an excellent example of a formal, clapboard covered, frame, Italianate structure. On the east end is a porch, on the west a polygonal bay projecting on the lower story only. Across the front is a porch with square piers and open arches. On the first and second floors are very generously proportioned windows with segmental arches, above is a cornice with paired brackets, between are small windows lining the attic. The hipped roof above rises to a widow's walk, complete with its ballisters, something that is often blown off in the Midwest in tornadoes, but here, survives.

Continue east on College Road, entering

THE LAKE FOREST COLLEGE CAMPUS
Lake Forest grew from the establishment of Lake Forest Academy, a private Presbyterian "Seminary for Young Ladies" opened in 1859. Its founding in 1856 gave the original impetus for establishing the town. Its building burnt in December, 1877, and the oldest of the present structures date to its resurgence.

As you enter Lake Forest College from Sheridan Road, on your right is

7.   THE REID MEMORIAL LIBRARY and
THE REID HOLD MEMORIAL CHAPEL—1899
These buildings were designed as a complex by Frost and Granger in 1899, based upon the model English abbeys. The tower marks the chapel, but the entrance facing the road indicates the library complex. The slate roofs cover a building with smooth limestone walls, opened and broken up by forms very similar to the late Norman, early Gothic forms in England. The combination of openings, projections, and massing is a very pleasant one and an excellent design for this type of historical revival style.

Continue into the campus. To the north and east of the library you can see three of the original structures. To the right is

8.   COLLEGE HALL—1878
This is an 1878 building rising above a basement through three tall stories to a great Mansard roof. Each end is given a special treatment, by coming forward from the wall, with a peaked roof and a tower in the center. The entire mass marks the building as a major dominant building of the original college design. Unfortunately, the porches on the front have been lost.

The building to the left (in the center) is

9.   NORTH HALL—1880
This 1880 building retains its porch, rises slightly lower, and has a similar

composition except that the ends have been moved in a bit and it lacks a central tower.

The building on the left is

10.   PATTERSON LODGE—1879

Built in 1879, it has a central tower but no pavilions on the ends, marking it as the residential structure in the complex. It too has a Mansard roof, but it rises only three stories.

Follow the road around to the right. On your right is

11.   THE GYMNASIUM—1890

The gymnasium was built in 1890, designed by Henry Ives Cobb. It shows the importance that the Romanesque style assumed in significant structures such as college buildings, on the basis of the designs by Henry Hobson Richardson for academic buildings at Harvard. This building is a great massive redstone building with battered bases on the corner towers and a great hipped, ridged roof that crowns the heavy walls. The entrance is through a steeply gabled porch holding an arch with very large voussoirs under which is a massive lintel.

Continue around to your right. On your right is

12.   BLACKSTONE HALL, HARLAN HALL, and
CALVAN DURAND COMMONS—1906

The 1906 complex of Blackstone Hall and Harlan Hall designed by Frost and Granger, and the Calvan Durand Commons forms a pleasant complex of brick with stone trim, a few towers, and broad roofs and windows which convey a character that combines English country houses with the Gothic image of English colleges.

Continue on the pathway returning to Sheridan Road. Turn right (north) on Sheridan Road. Past College Road, the second house on your left is

13.   660 N. SHERIDAN ROAD—1860

This 1860 house originally belonged to Harvey Thompson, the first mayor of Lake Forest and owner of an important early Chicago hotel, the Brevoort

13. 660 Sheridan Road

House. An excellent example of the Italianate used in an informal composition, this two-story building has a large projection on the left which rises to the roof. In that projection is an arched window under its own roof. On the other face of the building is a three-story octagonal tower that rises above the roof to a spindle with a pointed spire on top. The window frames and the attic windows are similar to other Italianate structures in the grand scale of the elements, as is the porch with its large square piers supporting the roof. On the octagonal tower, in order to maintain the symmetry of the design, some of the windows were never opened, known as "blind windows."

Continue north. Just beyond the corner on your left is

14.   700 N. SHERIDAN ROAD
Presbyterian Church—1887

This 1887 church, designed by Charles Frost, is an excellent example of the Shingle style used in East Coast resort towns such as Tuxedo, New York and Newport, Rhode Island. Only myth has it that its stones came from the Second Presbyterian Church in Chicago destroyed by the Fire of 1871.

It has a strong stone basement. Above it rise shingle walls and roofs laid on as thin planes. A delicately modeled Palladian window is set into the broad end wall formed by the slope of the roof. In the tower notice that the octagon of the roof is given added interest by having small roofs tucked in at each corner; below that, the shingle walls swell out to form a balcony under the broad arch that opens under the top of the tower. The entrance, added recently, is done sympathetically with the rest of the building.

Almost due north across Sheridan Road is

15.   725 N. SHERIDAN ROAD—c. 1890

This house was built during the 1890s. It shows a restrained version of the Queen Anne style in that the usually quite exuberant forms are here tucked under the roof planes, but at least the roofs are broken into the variety of shapes characteristic of that style. The massing is also considerably tamed by having a porch stretch across the entire front and project (toward the right) to form a porte-cochere and (toward the left) to wrap around the corner of the building. The entrance is indicated by a decorated pediment in the porch, beyond which is a bulge to hold the broad front door. The entrance is framed by very restrained carpentry work. Above that, tucked into the gable, is a repetition of the decorated porch pediment.

14. Presbyterian Church
700 Sheridan Road

Cross to the other side of Deerpath Road. Reenter Lake Forest College Campus at the SE corner of Sheridan and Deerpath roads. On your left is

16.   DURAND ART INSTITUTE—1891

This 1891 structure was designed by Henry Ives Cobb and built in redstone. Another version of Henry Hobson Richardson's model of the Richardsonian Romanesque developed in New England in the 1880s, it features a large, arched entrance above which are five arched windows, with a steep pediment above and knobs at the base and the top. At the base of the gable are two owls. Between five windows and the entrance arch is a frieze with foliate ornament including pine cones (like the knobs in the gables) and letters spelling out "Henry C. Durand Art Institute" on the top. Notice also, in the entrance arch, the inner arches are richly decorated. The entrance area is set to one side, to lend a sense of informality, and the entire structure is covered with a red slate roof, to continue the character of stoniness conveyed by the entire building.

Continue on the path. On your right is

17.   LOIS DURAND HALL—1897

This 1897 building was designed by Frost and Granger. It is a long structure with broken roof forms and a lantern in the center. It is modeled on the English Tudor country lodges and is an early example of that style's use on the north shore, indicating the civility of English country life appropriate for a college.

Backtrack to Deerpath Road. Turn right (east). The third house on your left is

18.   644 E. DEERPATH ROAD—1860

This 1860 house was called "Forest Lawn." Built for real estate man David Lake, one of the founders of Lake Forest, it originally had the same informality observed at 660 N. Sheridan Road (Lake Forest #13). After the turn of the century, however, the building was modernized by giving it a coating of stucco, changing the projection toward the front, putting on new surrounds, and adding a small porch on the left side next to the polygonal two-story projection. It remains a handsome structure.

Walk east on Deerpath about 1 block. The second building past the campus on your right is

19. 747 E. DEERPATH ROAD—1916

This delightful 1916 brick house was designed by Frederick Perkins. It was built for the prominent Chicago grain dealer Finley Barrel on the site of an 1875 house which burned. Trees from the original landscaping still remain. It has a number of elements based on very sophisticated models and assembled in a quite picturesque manner. A highly stylized columnar loggia frames the left side of the ground floor, and a metal and glass porch fronts the entrance. The building is topped by a balustraded parapet and by a high, hipped, ridged roof on the left side. The assemblage has the style considered very chic immediately before World War I.

Continue east on Deerpath Road about ½ block. On your left (north) is

20. 808 E. DEERPATH ROAD—1910

This 1910 house was designed by Shepley, Rutan, and Coolidge, who produced a number of these excellently designed, finely detailed, formal, Georgian houses. This one is especially delightful because of its excellent proportions and details most notable in the columnar, circular porch, topped by an opening with a six-over-six window and sidelights, all set below an arch.

Continue east. Just past Mayflower Road, on your left, are

21. 888 E. DEERPATH ROAD and
920 E. DEERPATH ROAD—1869

This house (and carriage house), built in 1869 by J.V. Farwell, a prominent Chicago dry goods dealer and one-time partner of Marshall Field, was the first concrete house in America. The cement and the contractor who knew how to use it were imported from England. The building is a very interesting combination of styles and obviously experimental, both from the point of view of style and from that of construction. The design shows clear indications of the English Victorian Gothic style, but the overall massing follows the American Italianate style. The pattern cast in the cement walls resembles stone ashlar construction. In the middle, on the ground floor, is a simple ogive arch. In the slate Mansard roof (the roof being associated with the Italinate style) are the steeply pointed dormers (characteristic of the Gothic style), including pointed arches in the windows. The carriage house, to the east, at 920 E. Deerpath Avenue has been extensively remodeled since World War II.

Continue east, about ½ block. Cross to the south side of the street. On your right is

22.   965 E. DEERPATH ROAD—1893

This house was built in 1893 by Robert A. McCann, a leading Chicago industrialist. At the end of the drive can be seen the formal entrance to a neatly detailed Georgian Revival building. Its front porch has a swan's-neck pediment with a finial centerpiece.

Continue east to Lake Road. Turn left (north). Just past Westminster, on your right (east side of the street) is

23.   955 LAKE ROAD—1917

This 1917 house in pale, mortar-washed brick was designed by David Adler, Howard Van Doren Shaw's successor as the prominent society architect in Chicago, on the basis of notions of how ancient Roman villas looked. Two wings reach out to the street, one with the entrance. These lead to a two-story block with a tile covered, hipped roof. Inside, between the wings, is an open atrium with busts looking down into it. Extending along the road from either side of the house are walls that enclose the ample grounds.

Backtrack south to Westminster. Turn right (west). On your left (south side of the street) is

24.   941 E. WESTMINSTER—c. 1900

Built about 1900, this building shows two main sources in styles current at the time. The boards against the stucco show the Tudor style. The spread out extent of the design, with the entrances tucked under a projecting central portion, shows knowledge of designs being done at the turn of the century in the Lake District of England.

Continue west. The fourth house on your left is

25.   855 E. WESTMINSTER—c. 1920

Built about 1920, this English Tudor design is built up and out to a point that makes it baronial in character. Notice the variety of roof shapes and wall surfaces, some stucco, some half-timber, some brick, and the clustering of chimneys into vents. Notice also the careful attention given to the front

25. 855 E. Westminster

entrance where a number of brick patterns are used and the wood elements are carved, bent, and molded to provide an inviting and rich entrance to the house.

Continue west on Westminster, taking the right fork in the road. The first house on your left is

26. 735 E. WESTMINSTER
Hawthorne House—c.1917

Built during the decade that included World War I, the formality of the house as seen from the roadway changes to informality on the south side where the forms are broken up as they look over the wide secluded lawn. From the street, one is presented with a formal turn-around beyond two gateways which have whimsically designed tops with acanthus leaves in the corners and cannonballs over the sills that hold squat urns. The house front has a broad slate roof with a formal entrance in the center and gabled ends on the projecting wings, one with a chimney, the other with a finial.

Continue on Westminster. The second house on your left is

27. 645 E. WESTMINSTER—1917

Built in 1917, this is an excellent example of a brick English country house very characteristic of the style favored in large suburban estates around the time of the First World War.

Across the street, on the NW corner of Westminster and Elm Tree Road, is

28. 880 ELM TREE ROAD
"Eastover"—1897

Architect Charles Frost designed the 1897 home as his own residence. His basic model was the formal one of the Georgian Revival, but he broke it up with various forms characteristic of the waning Queen Anne style. Notice that the polygonal bay on the left side projects from the second floor, that next to it is the steeply pitched roof of the entrance porch with a scallop in the pediment, and that on the right a broad flank of wall must be traversed before a polygonal bay matching the one on the left is finally encountered. This bay, however, is different from its left mate because it rises through two stories rather than one. The asymmetry produced by this contrast is balanced by having a porch project from the wall at the opposite end. This was a sleeping porch, very popular at the turn of the century because it was thought to be healthy to sleep out of doors in the winter cold.

Continue on Westminster. The next house on your right is

29.   600 E. WESTMINSTER—1897

This 1897 house was designed by Charles Frost for his next door neighbor. It shows the same Georgian armature (as Lake Forest #28) but a much subdued use of asymmetry. The simple entrance is slightly to the left of center, and slightly to the right is a Palladian dormer window, set into a gambrel roof.

Continue on Westminster 1½ blocks. On the NW corner of Westminster and Church Road is

30.   400 E. WESTMINSTER
               Church of the Holy Spirit Episcopal Church—1902

This 1902 church was designed by Alfred Granger and has several additions, each sympathetically matching the English country Gothic style of the original building.

Continue to the corner and cross the street. On the SE corner of Westminster and Washington is

31.   777 E. WASHINGTON—1873

This 1873 house was originally a dairy barn on the Ezra Warner, Sr. property called "Oakhurst." When the structure was converted to a residence sometime after 1910, it received its present appearance. Especially notable is something rarely encountered: the juxtaposition of the textured, shingled walls with wooden features on the central projecting element that reproduce masonry features, namely, quoins and fragments of the entablature.

Walk south on Washington past Walnut Road. On your right is Triangle Park.

This concludes the Lake Forest Walking Tour.

Drive west on Deerpath Road across the railroad tracks. Turn right (north) on Western Avenue. On your left, across from the railroad station is

32. MARKET SQUARE
700 N. Western Avenue—1916

This shopping center designed in 1916 by Howard Van Doren Shaw, a prominent local resident and important Chicago architect, is meant to reproduce the character of a small English market center. It has half-timbering, broken roofs, brick and stucco, and distinctive entrances to the various shops. The forecourt of the precinct is effectively terminated at the west by a great columnar market hall originally built as a bank but now occupied by Marshall Field and Company. The complex is known as the first shopping center designed in America and constitutes the downtown of Lake Forest. Its English Tudor style is similar to that used for many of the mansions in Lake Forest to allow villages to emulate English country life. Note that the homogeneity of the shopping center complex is accomplished by making certain that the storefronts contribute to the overall character of the place rather than being designed as individual and aggressive prominent pieces.

Leave Market Square from the west and turn left (south) on Forest Avenue. On the NW corner of Forest Avenue and Deerpath Road is

33. CITY HALL
200 E. Deerpath Road—1898

This English Tudor building, designed by Frost and Granger in 1898, shows a very interesting design because the architects (very prominent citizens of Lake Forest and important in architecture in Chicago) had to combine into one design the character of a public building and that of a domestic building. They did so by regulating the scale and the materials to make it look somewhat domestic but enlarging the elements slightly and adding a tower to one side. They also used a very simple block-like mass rather than the broken shapes that we associate with domestic architecture.

Drive west on Deerpath Road to Greenbay Road. Turn left (south) until it ends at Old Elm Road.

32. Market Square
700 N. Western Avenue

FORT SHERIDAN

FORT SHERIDAN

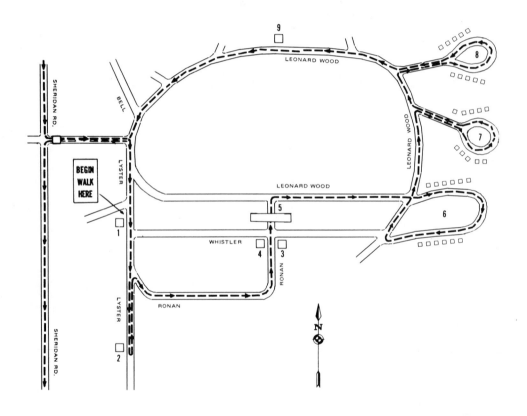

Turn left (east) on Old Elm Road until it ends at Sheridan Road. Turn right (south) 1 block to Fort Sheridan, on your left.

Fort Sheridan is listed as a district on the National Register of Historic Places.

Pass the main gate, then turn right on Lyster Road. 1 block south, just past Westover Road, on your right is

1. THE MUSEUM/DETENTION FACILITY—1890

Originally constructed as a stockade in 1890, this steamheated structure is made of brick and stone, producing an appearance of strength.

Walk south on Lyster Road.

Stretched along Lyster Road is a handsome row of buildings differing slightly but all dating from the same period, 1890 to 1893, and having the same general character. They have light brick walls with arched openings; some have stone corbels holding the roof projections and hipped roof dormers. The homogeneity of materials used for the walls, the similar roof lines, and the similar setback makes the ensemble quite handsome. It should be pointed out that these are utilitarian and service buildings.

2 blocks south, on your right is

2. POST OFFICE—1890

Originally constructed as a veterinary hospital in 1890, this brick, stone, and cement structure was converted to a full-service post office after World War II.

Backtrack north on Lyster Road to Ronan Road. Turn right (east) 3 blocks. Turn left (north) continuing on Ronan Road 1 block. On the SE corner of Ronan and Whistler roads is

3. FIRE STATION—1893

This 1893 building is one of the few still serving its original function.

On the SW corner of Ronan and Whistler roads is

4. THE GYMNASIUM—1893
This 1893 building was originally an infantry drill hall.

Across Whistler Road to the north is

5. COMMAND HEADQUARTERS, BARRACKS, AND THE TOWER—1891

This is a very impressive ensemble of buildings, barracks at either end and the command headquarters dominating the long central section. Built in 1891, projecting in the center of the command headquarters is a great fortress-like tower with large bulbous corners rising to knobs at the top within which is an octagonal structure with three arches on the four major faces. The tower is brick and rises from a strong stone base with an arch on each side leading to a vaulted chamber under the tower. Note that the arch in the chamber has ribs with rich carvings on their surfaces. The segmental arched windows on the ground floor of the command headquarters give a sense of stability to the ground floor, while the round arches on the second story open that story up. Each building is topped by a hipped roof. The ends of each building come forward to form pavilions again producing a sense of strength, solidity, and seriousness for the center of the fort. Bronze cannons appear at intervals adding a sense of ornamentation. The barracks structures at either end have a central projection with a two-story porch and a gable above, featuring a simple, straightforward, no-nonsense, Palladian window characteristic of the period. The structure is listed on the National Register of Historic Places.

Be certain to walk through the tower and view the exquisite arch above you. When you emerge on the north side of the tower turn right (east) on Leonard Wood Avenue to Logan Loop. Continue east into Logan Loop.

6. LOGAN LOOP
The far east end of the drill field is lined with large free-standing houses, appropriate for higher officers in the Army. On each side of Logan Loop are four identical houses with the single one (on either end and nearest the lake) the more elaborate. Notice the fine wrought iron porch rails and stair rails on the identical structures. The four on the north are mirror images of those on the south. The most elaborate houses (nearest the lake) each have octagonal pavilion corners, a projecting porch, simple, heavy carving in the gable, and a fine strap iron brace for the chimney.

5. The Tower

Coming out of Logan Loop, turn right (north) on Leonard Wood Avenue (east of the drill field). Continue north to Scott Loop on your right.

7. SCOTT LOOP

This is an officers compound with more houses than those found in Logan Loop. However, they are built to the same design.

Emerging from Scott Loop, turn right and continue to MacArthur Loop on your right.

8. MACARTHUR LOOP

This features the same structures as those on Scott Loop.

Along the north side of the drill field are found houses similar to those in the two loops and the double houses at the east end of the drill field.

Leaving MacArthur Loop, continue west on Leonard Wood Avenue, on your right is

9. THE BACHELOR OFFICERS QUARTERS

The original structure has a row of piers rising to paired Romanesque columns and, in the roof, three large dormers that retain their original pointed, cut shingles. An addition has been placed on the west end more recently.

Continue west to George Bell Road. Turn left (south) then immediately right (west) back to Sheridan Road. Turn left (south) on Sheridan Road, following it as it turns into St. Johns Avenue.

HIGHLAND PARK

HIGHLAND PARK

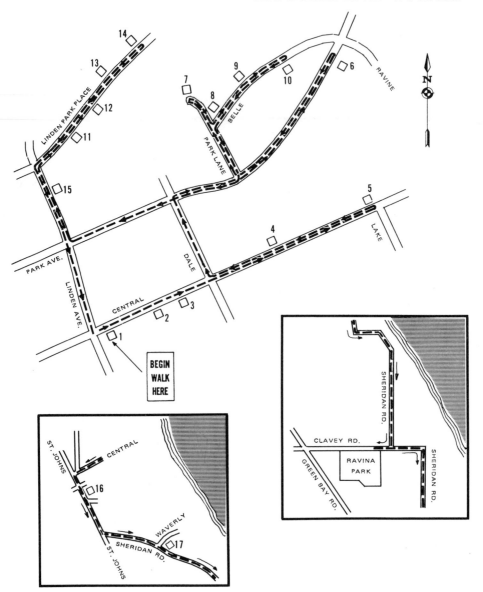

Continue south on St. Johns Avenue (a total of 2.6 miles) to Central Avenue. Turn left (east) on Central Avenue to Linden Avenue. Stop.

HIGHLAND PARK
WALKING TOUR

On the SE corner of Central and Linden Avenue is

1. HIGHLAND PARK HISTORICAL SOCIETY MUSEUM
326 Central Avenue—1871

Built in 1871, the Mrs. Jean Butz James museum is in a brick building in the Italianate style. The porch and the projection on the east are very nicely restored. Of special interest is the way the bricks on the second floor are handled to produce the effect of a hipped, stone, segmental arch. The museum features several permanent and one rotating exhibit. The permanent features include a parlor furnished with Victorian period pieces, the Ravinia Room (highlighting Ravinia's history), a marvelous toy collection, and an authentic doll-house that belonged to Elizabeth Orton Jones, notable children's author. There is a friendly, well-informed staff. The museum is open 1:00 p.m.-5:00 p.m. Tuesday–Saturday, and Sunday from 2:00 p.m.-4:00 p.m.

Walk east on Central Avenue. The third house on your right is

2. 288 CENTRAL STREET—1870s

This structure is a symmetrical version of a brick Italianate structure probably from the mid-1870s, although the porch on the east side is a later addition. The wooden cornice on top has paired brackets and immediately below are several courses of brick which define the lower level of the cornice. The segmental windows and door are framed by brick panels and the first and second floors are separated by a brick belt course running out to the panels on either end, which suggest the enframing pilasters. The original porch has been replaced by a later one.

Continue east. The next house on your right is

3. 274 CENTRAL STREET—1870s

Although somewhat altered by the addition of a porch on the west side and the loss of the original entrance porch, this structure presents a fine example of a brick Italianate building from the 1870s. It rises through two stories to a hipped roof below which paired brackets define the wooden cornice.

The corners of the building on each side of the front facade are treated differently. On the west corner is a pilaster running the entire distance; on the east side is a small window next to the entrance door, which cuts into the pilaster necessitating the apparent doubling of it. This throws the three windows slightly off center relative to the peak of the roof. The brick on the front wall is handled to suggest window frames for the typically tall, segmentally arched window.

Cross to the north side of the street and continue east. The fifth house on your left is

4.   175 CENTRAL STREET—1890s
This tall frame structure topped by a truncated hipped roof conveys the Colonial Revival style of the late 1890s. The middle one of the three dormers (on the front facade) is larger, indicating the central axis of the design, which is marked on the ground floor by the entrance porch with its clusters of Tuscan columns supporting its simple linteled roof. A bay window on the east side suggests the extension of the open columnar porch. Beyond it swells a bay window through both stories. On the opposite side is a small polygonal porch. The corners are crisply edged by edge boards that rise to a full, but simply detailed, cornice.

Continue east. The next house on your left is

5.   147 CENTRAL STREET—c.1875
This structure presents a curious juxtaposition of two separate styles, both said to date from about 1875. On the eastern section is a straightforward, but slightly broad, Gothic cottage with a pitched roof running parallel to the street, intersected by a pitched gable to provide space in the second story which faces south across the ample grounds. Abutting it on the west is a structure of approximately the same size with the second story contained within a Mansard roof. In place of a gable there is a large Palladian window with very ample cornices, including a large keystone atop the fully rounded central arch. Below it, on the ground floor, is a square-fronted bay with two segmental windows in its front face separated by pilasters.

5. 147 Central Street

The entrance is below a broad segmental arch opening in the pitched roof section immediately next to the Mansard section. The porch begins where the two sections join, spreads across the rest of the south front, then returns across the entire east side, providing a very broad veranda. Its lintel is shouldered with brackets and sustained on square chamfered posts with single bottle ballisters forming the balustrade. At the northern end is a modern addition. Extending in the opposite direction (toward the west) is a one-story porte-cochere, probably a later addition, topped with a balustraded parapet. On the ground floor of the pitched roof section are very broad (but very high) segmental arched, double-hung windows.

The entire structure is board and batten and is an excellent example of this construction technique, topped under the bracketed cornice in the Mansard section by fine carpentry detail work. Note also the two strips of saw-tooth shingles in the Mansard roof and the fine rope moldings around many of the openings.

Backtrack west on Central Avenue to Dale Avenue. Turn right (north) 1 block. Turn right (east) on Park Avenue past Park Lane. The last house on your right (at the ravine) is

6.   160 PARK AVENUE—c.1890
This structure from about 1890 is an excellent representative of the Shingle style. It began as a coachhouse and has been adapted to serve as a residence. The gambrel roof extends the entire length of the building and is intersected on the street or north side by a gambrel gable with a large Palladian window flanked on each side by an oval window. The intersection of the gable with the gambrel roof is marked by a louvered cupola, a usual device to ventilate the hayloft. The ground floor is clad in clapboard and the original stable entrance is at the east end. This was the coachhouse for 147 Central (Highland Park #5).

Backtrack west to Park Lane. Turn right (north). The house in front of you, where Park Lane dead-ends, is

7.   2122 PARK LANE—1882
This Stick style house, built in 1882, forms a fine contrast to the brick building of the same date just south of it, 175 Belle Avenue (Highland Park #8). The ground floor has panels of clapboards, framed by boards as the sheath-

ing, separated from the second story by diagonally cut shingles. Parts of the second story begin with vertical siding, the rest is completed by shingles.

The south facade breaks forward in the center to place a gable above the base of the front pitch of the hipped roof. It contains a vertical siding upper section with a round-headed window set between the quadrants of the half-circular window to produce a variation on the Palladian motif. The entrance, set in the reentrant angle in the west side, has lost its original porch but contains the rich variety of motifs that would eventually be exploited to produce the Queen Anne style from the Stick style represented here.

Backtrack south on Park Lane. On the NE corner of Park Lane and Belle Avenue is

8. 175 BELLE AVENUE—1882

This 1882 building shows the use of Queen Anne massing to present a picturesque face to the corner site but it contains the conservatism of the Italianate seen elsewhere on this block. The cubic shape of the building has a two-story projection on the west with a gable extending back to the hipped roof. On the south facade a polygonal bay begins, only to extend toward the southeast with a square bay set at a 45° angle to the south facade. The angle connecting the bay with the front door is topped by a pediment with radial carpentry work; the bricks, above the segmental arch on the second story immediately below the cornice, are set at an angle to introduce additional interests at that important point in the design.

Unfortunately the original porch has been removed. It would doubtless have been an eye-catching device composed of extensive spindle work. Some small indication of that richness is provided by the small, thin, scroll-cut brackets in the cornice and in the west pediment, which is shingled and contains a bull's-eye window.

Walk east on Belle Avenue. The first house on your left is

9. 151 BELLE AVENUE—1875

The original core of the house is brick and portrays very well the formal Italianate style of 1875, the year of its construction. The hipped roof is supported by a dignified cornice with paired brackets and ample dentils. There were originally five openings facing the street to the south, the central one on the second story broader than the others, all with keystones in their segmental, brick, shouldered arches. The original entrance must have been in the center.

Sometime soon after the turn of the century, the building received its present outriggers, involving a new entrance porch on the west and a two-story sunporch on the east, erupting into a broad two-story bay facing the east. That sunporch was connected to the original structure by incorporating the outer windows, and at the opposite end a new entrance was broken through on the west facade. The east and west porches were connected by a trellis supported by a pair of the same substantial Tuscan columns used on the ground floor of the structure.

Cross to the south side of the street and continue east. The second house on your right is

10.   120 BELLE AVENUE—1875

This two-story frame structure has a low hipped roof which rises directly from the very broad eaves, supported by paired brackets, which give the impression of a Mansard roof. The cubic shape of the block is extended (toward the south side of the west front) by a full projection with its corners framed (as is the case with the north face) by pilasters rising the full two stories and containing a diamond at the midpoint. The windows throughout the section have scroll-cut boards attached to the inner and outer edges to produce impressive frames that only vaguely recall their Italianate origins. The horizontal wood siding is treated in a manner rarely encountered, with horizontal and vertical flat bottomed grooves to give the impression that the structure is built of broadly drafted, regular stone ashlar.

Toward the south side of the east facade is a hipped roof projection and a service wing extending to the southeast. It has shingled sides on the upper stories but the same fictive ashlar on the ground floor. The shingles, however, betray its origins from at least a decade after the original building. The screen porch in the reentrant angle probably dates from this period also. The combination is quite handsome and the structure a fine example of the masonry Italianate rendered in wood.

Backtrack west on Belle Avenue to Park Lane. Turn left (south) 1 block. Turn right (west) on Park Avenue to Linden Avenue. Turn right (north) 1 block. Turn right onto Linden Park Place. The second house on your right is

11. 296 LINDEN PARK PLACE—1870s

The original section of this house dates from the 1870s. It is a T-shaped brick structure with steeply pitched roofs and the leg of the "T" set slightly to the west of the center, to contain a one-story section on the east side which holds the entrance. The cast iron cresting along the ridge of the roof conveys a sense of the original richness of the design as do the scroll-cut bargeboards that survive on the gable rafters. The windows are topped by brick segmental arches and on the ground floor (of the west top of the "T") is a polygonal bay window from the original period of construction.

The building probably originally would have been crossed on all three sides of the front wing by an elaborate porch. Sometime shortly before the turn of the century that porch was removed and the present entrance porch constructed as was the second story of the bay on the east side of the top of the "T" with its shingle walls splaying out over the brick of the polygonal bay of the original construction. Despite the alterations and the loss of the original porch the building conveys the original character of a popular Gothic Revival cottage of the period.

Continue on Linden Park Place. The second house on your right is

12. 274 LINDEN PARK PLACE—c.1870

This L-shaped Italianate building from about 1870 has two porches (in the reentrant angle and a front entrance porch) from after the turn of the century, but the original building is an excellent example of the Italianate style. It has thin corner boards along its clapboard covered walls and a firm cornice with generously scaled paired brackets. The low hipped roof meets the walls rather than the outer edge of the cornice, a suggestion of the concurrent Mansard roof style of the Second Empire. The windows are crowned by generous segmental cornices.

Cross to the other side of the street and continue on Linden Park Place. The second house on your left is

13. 243 LINDEN PARK PLACE—1869

Beyond the open columnar veranda that crosses two sides of the building and extends to the east for an enclosed porch rises an excellent example of the Italianate style, built in 1869. The relatively thin, very tall windows on the ground floor are like their mates above, topped by segmental arches. The cornice has paired brackets with panels between and attic windows to light the space in the hipped roof. On the west side (toward the back) is a flat-fronted projection through the full two stories and, beyond that, a full height polygonal projection. A smaller flatfronted projection appears on the east side. These projections are characteristic of the style and provide greater interest for the spaces of the cubic rooms of the interior.

Continue on Linden Park Place. The second house on your left is

14.   211 LINDEN PARK PLACE—1870s

The original L-shaped structure from the 1870s represents a transition between the Gothic Revival and the Italianate styles. The configuration, especially prominent in the steeply pitched roofs, is that of the Gothic Revival, but the flattened brackets, extending more as modillions than as brackets under the eaves, are characteristic of the Italianate as are the details in the original carpentry work (in the cornice of the polygonal bay projecting in the front). The windows above that bay, the present entrance, and the wrought iron work are all more recent modifications.

Backtrack on Linden Park Place to the corner. Turn left (south) on Linden Avenue. The second house on your left is

15.   2023 LINDEN AVENUE—1910s

This simple structure from the years just before World War I is a characteristic example of the designs of Tallmadge and Watson, important Prairie School architects. A frame structure covered in stucco, it used boards to define the lower and upper levels, to separate the floor levels from one another, and to line the windows which are placed in strips. The plan is simple and straightforward with a hipped roof projection extending toward the street and an entrance in the wing toward the north. Opposite it, and closer to the front, is a two-story porch (originally open). The enclosure of the eave soffits with stucco helps to reinforce the effect produced by the boards of a neat, square-cut mass whose design is based upon simple geometric principles, rather than upon the allusion to historical styles.

Continue south on Linden Avenue to Central Avenue.

This concludes the Highland Park Walking Tour.

Drive west on Central Avenue to St. Johns Road. Turn left (south) 1½ blocks. In the park on your left is

16. STUPEY CABIN—1847

This authentic one-room, pioneer cabin, built in 1847, is a delight to explore. It features all the typical furnishings a pioneer family might have had in the 1850s. It was moved to this site to preserve it. From May to November, it's open from 2:00 p.m.-4:00 p.m. Otherwise, you may inquire about access at the Historical Society.

Continue south on St. Johns Road to Sheridan Road. Turn left and continue on Sheridan Road to Waverly Road. The first house past Waverly Road, on your left, is

17. 1445 N. SHERIDAN ROAD
Ward W. Willits House—1902

This extremely significant Frank Lloyd Wright house built in 1902, a standard illustration in history books devoted to world architecture, represents the fully developed Prairie School house in its classic form. The plain stuccoed surfaces are spread across the ample grounds along a cross-shaped plan and are anchored to the earth by a brick chimney at the center. Broad lower wings extend to the north and south, one serving as a porte-cochere and entrance, the other as an open porch.

The building rises to a second story in the center with the open, two-story living room in the front indicated by the strips of casement windows while the open stairhall leading to the second story bedrooms in the back is revealed by the strips of casement windows next to the porte-cochere. The wings are covered by low hipped roofs with broad overhangs that seem to extend across the landscape, an effect reinforced by the broad, low base with its prominent mudsill and coping, and the wooden belt course at the sill level of the second story windows. Prairie School urns and high quality leaded glass complete this seminal design. The house is listed on the National Register of Historic Places.

Continue south on Sheridan Road 1.8 miles to Ravinia Park on your right.

RAVINIA PARK

Operating only in the summer, Ravinia has an indoor theatre, as well as the outdoor, covered pavilion. Dance, drama, and music are offered. One can picnic on the lovely grounds while listening to the music from the pavilion. Food service is available.

Leaving Ravinia, exit south (right) onto Sheridan Road and follow it into Chicago.

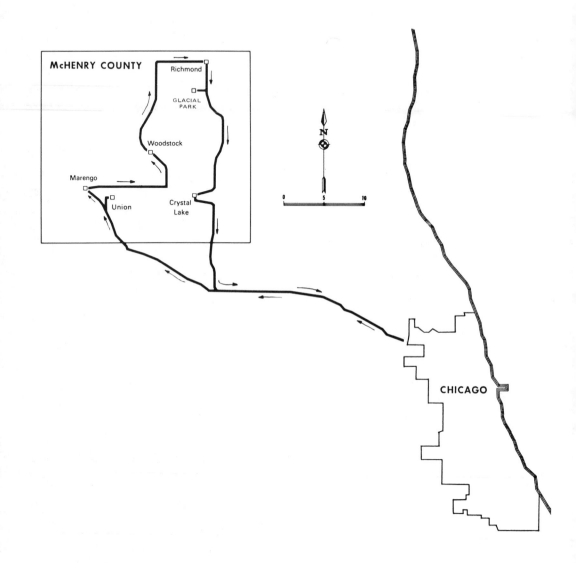

McHENRY COUNTY

Richmond

GLACIAL
PARK

Woodstock

Marengo

Union

Crystal
Lake

N

0   5   10

CHICAGO

McHenry County

UNION

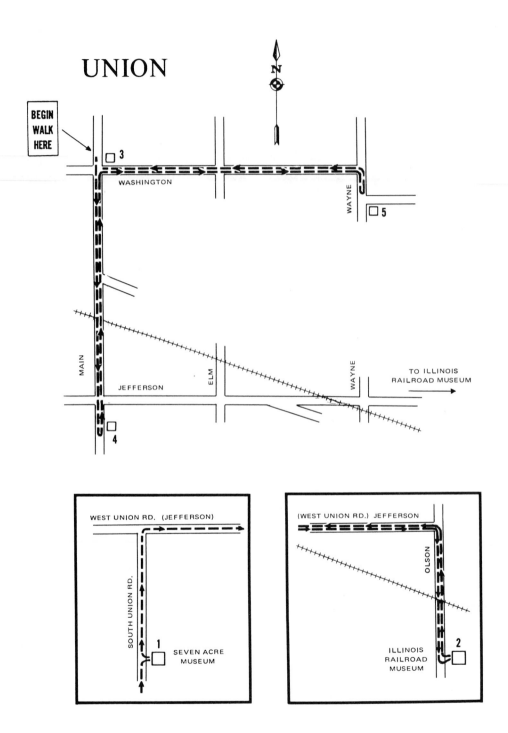

Leaving Chicago, take the Kennedy Expressway north to the Northwest Tollway. Follow the Northwest Tollway north to the intersection of Route 20. Exit Route 20 North 4.6 miles to South Union Road. Turn right (north). On your right is

1. SEVEN ACRES ANTIQUE VILLAGE & MUSEUM

This delightful museum is full of fascinating items, ranging from the largest collection of antique phonographs in the Midwest to an extensive military collection that includes a 1932 Nimbus motorcycle. Seven Acres has an antique village, completely reconstructed from a western-style town of the early 1900s, and a museum divided into three sections: antique phonograph collection (including a model of the rare Edison tinfoil phonograph from 1877), World War I military collection, and a reconstruction of an 1890s street complete with regularly shown Laurel & Hardy movies. Daily: April-October; Weekends: November-March. Closed January.

Leaving Seven Acres, turn right (north) on South Union Road and continue until it ends. Turn right (east) on West Union Road, which becomes Jefferson Street east of Main Street, and continue 1 mile until it ends at Olson Road. Turn right (south) past the railroad tracks. Stop. *On your left (east side of road) is*

2. ILLINOIS RAILROAD MUSEUM

The museum's historic collection of railroad equipment is comprised of over 140 cars and locomotives. Much of the equipment has been completely or partially restored and is operated over the museum's one-and-one-half-mile-long demonstration railroad. Sundays only: March 1-October 31; Saturdays and Sundays: May 1-September 30; Daily: Memorial Day-Labor Day.

Leaving the Railroad Museum, turn right (north) on Olson Road, across the railroad tracks, to the first road on your left (Jefferson Street). Turn left (west) to Main Street. Turn right (north) 2 blocks to the NE corner of Washington and Main streets. Stop.

UNION WALKING TOUR

On the NE corner of Washington and Main streets is

3. MCHENRY COUNTY HISTORICAL SOCIETY—c.1870

The main section of the building, which was built about 1870, is a two-story schoolhouse structure built in carefully cut limestone ashlar with the conservative lines of the Greek Revival, but with a cornice with paired brackets, derived from the Italianate. The pitched roof is topped by an octagonal cupola with brackets and a small octagonal dome. Later additions to the structure include a school auditorium.

The museum is filled with artifacts from all over the county. There is a music room displaying instruments and furniture from the turn of the century. A much larger room, once a school auditorium, has many exhibits, ranging from doll collections to ancient pharmaceutical gadgetry to a Civil War flag.

A small log cabin has been recently moved to the site from a farm about five miles away. Cabins of this sort were used to shelter the early settlers of the region in the 1840s.

Walk south on Main Street.

As you walk along Main Street, notice the many old buildings and storefronts. Most of the buildings are difficult to date specifically. However, as with the majority of the buildings in town, Main Street probably sprang up around the 1860s or 1870s, at the time the first railroads came through the town.

On the east side of Main Street, just south of Jefferson Street, is

4. THE FIREHOUSE—1860s

This large structure, which has been altered by the additions of new windows and a new door, is still of interest. Notice that the limestone blocks are not nearly as carefully finished as those at the schoolhouse. The window lintels are treated differently: behind the cast iron plates, which give the building a bit of sophistication, are wooden lintels; they, together with the stone blocks, indicate an earlier date than the 1870 date of the schoolhouse.

Backtrack north on Main Street to Washington Street. Turn right (east) 2 blocks. On the SE corner of Washington and Wayne streets is

5. HARLEY WAYNE HOUSE—1857

Built in 1857, this red brick, Italianate house is easily the nicest building in town. Notice that the limestone blocks of the foundations on the side of the

5. Harley Wayne House

house are cut more neatly than those under the porch, which were not meant to be seen. The porch, which extends across the entire front, has the heavy mid-century forms that were associated with the Italianate. Especially nice are the fat, single-bottle balusters and the substantial posts with chamfered corners. The windows, opening onto the porch on either side of the entrance, reach to the floor. The entrance has sidelights and a transom. The six openings on the front all have neatly dressed, limestone lintels, as do the rest of the windows. The cornice is an especially fine example of mid-century carpentry work in the Italianate style, with finely turned pendants suspended from the paired carved brackets. Between the brackets are large dentils. The hipped roof has an unusually low pitch, and the cupola has been lost.

Especially nice is the strict symmetry of the front where the broad flank of the projecting central section greets the visitor who enters through the broad segmental arches of the porch. Extending from the back of the house is a lower one-and-one-half-story service wing, also in brick, with wooden cornice detailing in a simplified version of the more elaborate carpentry used on the main block of the house.

Traces of the original landscape are visible with indications of where the sunken garden, surrounded by the circular drive, was placed. Inside are surviving interior features in excellent condition, including the heavy door and ceiling moldings. The marble and cast iron coal fireplaces are intact. Harley Wayne, who built the house, was an early supporter of the Union cause in Illinois and perished in the Civil War.

Backtrack east on Washington Street 2 blocks to Main Street.

This concludes the Union Walking Tour.

Drive south on Main Street 2 blocks to Jefferson Street. Turn right (west) on Jefferson, which becomes West Union Road, 1.6 miles until it ends at Route 20.

MARENGO

MARENGO

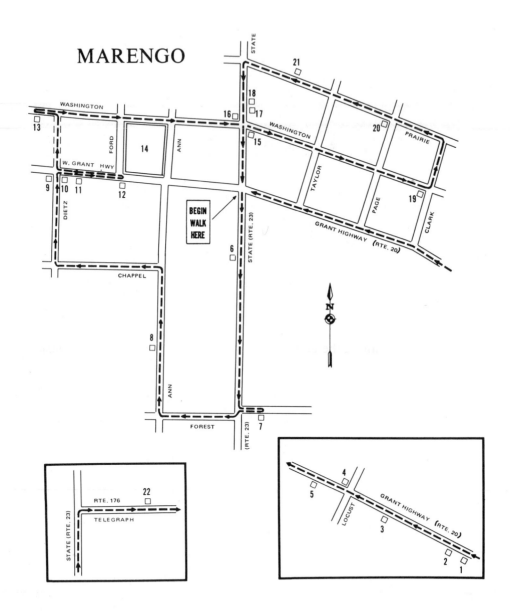

Turn right (west) on Route 20, .3 miles. On the left (south side) is

1. 19621 E. GRANT HIGHWAY
Anson Rogers House—1846

These two nearly identical houses, the other is 19809 E. Grant Highway (Marengo #2) farther along the road, were built by two brothers, born in Vermont, who arrived with their father as early settlers in the county. The one by Anson Rogers was built in 1846. Anson was an innovative farmer. He used the first cotton gin in McHenry County in the 1840s and was the purchaser of one of the earliest McCormick reapers. His brother, Orson, built his house at the same time or slightly later. Orson was active in banking and business in Marengo, although he too had a farm. It supplied butter and cheese for Chicago hotels including the Palmer House. See Marengo #2, below.

Continue west. The next house on your left is

2. 19809 E. GRANT HIGHWAY
Orson Rogers House—c.1847

Both houses, this one and Marengo #1, are representative of a type of Greek Revival architecture found in New England. They have a porch carved out from the overhang along the side. The pitched roof is supported by six Doric columns with the center ones set farther apart to reveal the location of the entrance. The entrance has a refined doorway without transoms but with sidelights and is framed by piers. The Orson Rogers house has columns framing the door within the recess. It is probable that, originally, neither house had a balustrade across the eaves. The polygonal bays projecting from the end of each house are probably also later additions. The extensions projecting to the south beyond the original one-and-one-half-story structures are certainly later additions to the original, small but elegant, buildings. The Orson Rogers House is listed on the National Register of Historic Places.

Continue west on Route 20 (E. Grant Highway). Continue .7 miles. On your left (south) is

3. 927 E. GRANT HIGHWAY—1870

This clapboard house from 1870 is an excellent example of the surviving Greek Revival style used in a frame structure. Especially nice are the dentils

2. 19809 E. Grant Highway

along the frieze and the pediment, and also on the top of the one-story addition on the east. Also nice are the thin pilasters on the corners which are repeated in smaller size for the recess forming the front entrance. The porch, with its four Ionic columns, was added later but lends a dignity to the original structure. Notice to the east of the building a two-story carriage house with a pitched roof clad in board and battens. The one-story clapboard addition to the carriage house is later.

Continue west on Grant Highway 2 blocks. On your right, on the NW corner of Locust Street and E. Grant Highway, is

4.   658 E. GRANT HIGHWAY—1890s

This tall, two-story, frame, clapboard structure with a full attic is made elaborate and rich by extensive use of spindle-work and texture in the gable facing east. The spindle-work is concentrated in the two gables and the porch. The porch has half fan wheels, beads, porch spindles, and turned posts producing an elaborate polyphony of carpentry. In the gable are scalloped and diamond-shaped shingles spread between yoke-patterned boards. The structure sits on a heavy rubblestone foundation. It may date from as late as the 1890s, but is characteristic of the 1880s.

Continue west on Grant Highway. The tenth building on your left (south side of the road) is

5.   553 E. GRANT HIGHWAY
Tauck House—1850

This frame structure was built in 1850 and is an excellent example of the Carpenter's Gothic but displays the symmetry of the Greek Revival with a porch on each side of the projecting center which rises into the characteristically high pitched roof of the Gothic Revival. The porch on the right (to the west) retains a feature unfortunately lost on the other side: a small rib tucked under the broad shouldered arch of the front porch. Otherwise, the building retains all of its original features in excellent condition. On the second story are windows with pointed window heads. The ground floor has tall thin windows, a proportion exaggerated by having double panes of glass in each sash. The gable bargeboards are made from wood and have a series of loops, each with an acorn pendant, rising to a large pendant at the peak of the gable, atop which is a knobbed finial. The same large elements are used even

(detail)   **5.**   553 E. Grant Highway

for the small gables at the reentrant angles. The porches have shouldered arches sustained by cut-out posts. At the front of the building on the ground floor is a broad, arched window with three arched lights; below is an open balcony; above, projecting on wavy corbels ending in acorn pendants, is another balcony with a railing made of fat spindles or thin balusters (a curious transition element between the spidery Gothic and the more bulbous Italianate). At the top of the gable in the front is a quatrefoil window characteristic of the Gothic Revival.

Continue west 5 blocks to the NE corner of E. Grant Highway (Route 20) and State Street (Route 23). Stop.

MARENGO WALKING TOUR

Walk south on State Street. The third house on your right is

6. 320 STATE STREET—c.1868

This two-story frame structure, built about 1868, is a very simple version of the Italianate. It has simple paired brackets for the eaves and on the ground floor, a projecting polygonal bay on the north side, and in the center a slightly larger polygonal porch (again with paired brackets), and hexagonal posts with chamfered corners, topped by a balustrade.

Continue south on State Street 1 long block. Turn left (east) on Forest Street. The second house on your right is

7. 209 E. FOREST STREET—1852

This 1852 yellow Georgian house was saved from demolition by being relocated here. Modifications made in 1887 and 1933, and more recently, have produced the present, pleasant residence.

Backtrack west on Forest Street, past State Street, 1 block to Ann Street. Turn right (north) on Ann Street. Between the sixth and seventh houses on your left (west side of street), set back, is

8. 436 S. ANN STREET—1855

This one-story 1855 brick cabin is said to have served originally as slave quarters.

Continue north to the corner. Turn left (west) on Chappel 1 block to Dietz Street. Turn right (north) on Dietz 1 short block. On the SW corner of Dietz Street and Grant Highway is

9. 413 W. GRANT HIGHWAY
Cupola House
Charles H. Hibbard House—1846

This Italianate house from 1846 is believed to have served as a depot on the Underground Railroad. The octagonal cupola served as a look-out tower while, at one time, a sandstone tunnel leading to a secret room under the front lawn provided a hide-away. Architecturally notable here are the characteristically heavy Italianate forms, with pendant scroll-cut brackets at the corners and porch posts. Also notable is the porch, which on the ground floor spreads across the entire front and in the center projects forward to carry a second story. Also extremely interesting are the cut-out traces of arches between the posts, a rhythmic motif repeated as broad cut-out shapes on the cornice of the second floor. The house is listed on the National Register of Historic Places.

On the SE corner of Dietz Street and W. Grant Highway is

10. 329 W. GRANT HIGHWAY—c.1840
This very simple and early structure, possibly from as early as 1840, began as a Greek Revival building but sometime after the middle of the century simple Italianate brackets were added in the pediment and along the front which contains the entrance, to bring it to the then-modern style. Subsequently it has undergone several interior structural changes, but it preserves the essentials of its original appearance. The two houses after this one (Marengo #11 and Marengo #12) show a similarity of construction and a different kind of elaboration based upon other prototypes.

Walk east on Grant Highway. The next house on your right is

11. 309 W. GRANT HIGHWAY—1850s
This structure is a simplified version of one seen earlier at 553 E. Grant Highway, the Tauck house (Marengo #5). It also probably dates from soon after 1850 and shows the diffusion of similar prototypes throughout the community. It was originally constructed elsewhere and moved to this site in

9. 413 W. Grant Highway
Cupola House

the 1870s. It shows a simple frame structure with Italianate brackets under the eaves, but the Gothic detailing of the porch remains conspicuous.

Continue east. The next house on your right, across from Ford Street, is

12.   301 W. Grant Highway—1850s
This is an even simpler version of the house next door (Marengo #11). Notice that the corner brackets are thick but the other paired brackets are thin as are the boards at the corners rising up to curves to join the cornice.

Backtrack west on Grant Highway. Across from Dietz Street is what appears to be an alley between 328 and 402 Grant Highway. Turn right (north) and walk 1 block. When the alley ends at Washington Street, turn left (west). The fifth house on your left (south side of the street) is

13.   429 W. Washington Street—1870s
This foursquare brick Italianate structure probably dates from the 1870s. It rises two stories to a hipped roof. The cornice has pairs of brackets set into a tier of bricks acting in substitution for the usual wood of a cornice. All of the windows have brick laid to reproduce lintels and sills, usually done in stone on brick Italianate structures. The square porch also has simplified versions of the usual Italianate elements. Projecting to the east is a lower, and still simpler, service wing. The entire building serves as an example of the more economical manner of constructing an impressive Italianate house.

Backtrack east on Washington Street. Just past Ford Street, on your right, is

14.   Louis Sullivan School—1870s and 1897
This limestone and brick building is actually two different structures designed by the same architect. The windows have recently been considerably altered by enlarging them and inserting glass block. On the west end of the older structure an even newer extension has been added. The original building, fronting Grant Highway, is of limestone and was built in the 1870s. Notable on its east and west ends are slight projections topped by sheet metal terminations, probably indicative of the treatment once found along the roofline but subsequently removed. The addition, built in 1897, is seen from Washington Street and is of brick of similar color to the limestone.

Especially impressive here is the battered limestone foundation of the projecting central section with its broad semi-circular arch and the words "high school" set within a foliate background and the date "1897" similarly placed above. Walk around this impressive structure to view it from all sides.

When back to the starting point, continue east on Washington Street to the intersection with State Street, the downtown of the original settlement. Pause at the intersection and notice four conspicuous structures which convey the early character of this prosperous town in an early farming area.

On the SE corner of Washington and State streets is

15. 205-209 S. STATE—1875

This is a two-story structure from 1875 with Italianate brackets, quite elaborate arches made from three pieces of stone (the middle one a keystone), and with heavy quoins on the splayed corner set into the brick walls. The ground floor shops have been modernized as is characteristic of commercial structures. The corner shop contains traces from the modernization of about 1900.

Kitty corner, on the NW corner of Washington and State streets, is

16. 100 W. WASHINGTON STREET—1882

This tall brick structure dates from 1882. It has a seemingly small Mansard roof above a thin, double-corbeled cornice. On the front facade is a series of stone arches over windows which unfortunately have been radically altered.

Across the street and slightly to the north, on the east side of State Street, is

17. 119–121 S. STATE STREET
Bank Block—1883

This 1883 building still retains its sheet metal cornice complete with an anthemion atop a pediment. Notice here how the bricks have been arranged under the cornice to produce a feature that resembles the corbels of the cornice just above. Also nice here is the slightly projecting bay window in the center.

The building immediately north is

18.   113 S. State Street—c.1887

This building has three bay windows and some nice brick work. It dates from only a few years later than Marengo #17.

Walk east 3 blocks on Washington Street. On the SW corner of Clark and Washington streets is

19.   321 E. Washington Street—1881

Under the unfortunate addition of asphalt shingle siding may be clapboard and shingle fields matching the richness of the rest of this 1881 structure. Projecting at an angle is a flat-fronted, three-story tower rising to a steeply pitched roof well above the gables facing the two streets, each handled differently. The gable facing north has a small porch, rich with carpentry work; the one facing east, with equally rich carpentry work, is much larger. Above it is a polygonal projection rising to a gable with broad turned posts and scallop-cut rafters. On the northeast side of the building is a one-story oriel with colored glass in the transom, held up by a quarter round support and covered with a conical roof.

Walk left (north) 1 block on Clark to Prairie Street. Turn left (west) 1 block. On the SW corner of Page and Prairie streets is

20.   225 E. Prairie Street—1855

The original design of this 1855 white clapboard structure is marred only by the replacement of the ground floor window with a modern one. The blocky forms, the very broad projecting bay on the east, the Mansard roof rising to a flat top above, and a very conspicuous top curb indicate the Second Empire style. Italianate influences are seen in the brackets, both of the porches and of the cornice, but they are handled differently at this early period. Notice the brackets are paired in the center and thickened at the corners. Notice also, on the porches, the pendants are square rather than round as is usual.

Continue west on Prairie 1½ blocks. Past the police and fire departments, on your right, is

21.   132 E. Prairie Street
Old City Hall—c.1905

This masonry building was built just after the turn of the century. It has been much modified but retains traces of the rich carving that originally made it an important civic building.

Continue west to State Street. Turn left (south) on State 2 blocks to Grant Highway (intersection of Route 20 & 23).

This concludes the Marengo Walking Tour.

Drive north on State Street ½ mile to Telegraph Street (Route 176). Turn right (east) .4 miles. Behind the white wall on your left is

22.   640 E. TELEGRAPH STREET
Clemens House—1850

This Italianate house was built in 1850, an early date betrayed by the large forms used for the brackets and the relatively tall proportions on the brick block. The paired brackets at the corners project below the cornice line and contain knobs on the upper curve. The windows here are topped by segmental stone arches, and the double door entry is framed by a finely done rope molding.

Continue east on Telegraph Street (Route 176) 8.8 miles until it ends at Route 47. Turn left (north) on Route 47, 3.4 miles to Lake Avenue.

WOODSTOCK

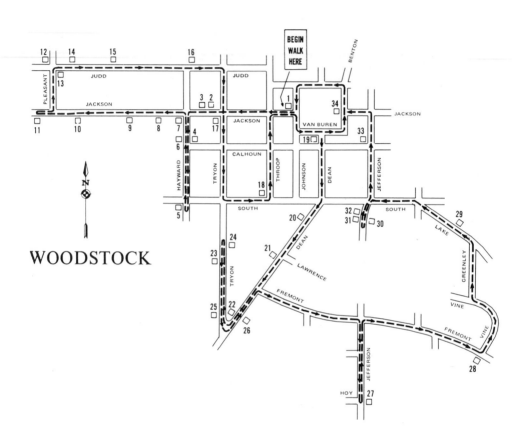

WOODSTOCK

Turn left (west) onto Lake Avenue, which angles into South Street at the stop sign and continue on South Street 3 blocks. Turn right (north) on Throop Street 2 blocks to Jackson Street. Turn right to the Woodstock Square. Stop.

WOODSTOCK WALKING TOUR

On the NW corner of Jackson Street and Johnson is

1. 101 N. JOHNSON
Old McHenry County Courthouse —1857
and Jail—1887

The imposing, brick and stone, Italian Renaissance Revival Courthouse, built in 1857 and designed by the prominent Chicago architect John Mills Van Osdel, dominates one side of the square. The dome is visible from some distance. (The building resembles Van Osdel's Cook County Courthouse and City Hall which were destroyed by the Chicago Fire of 1871.) The adjoining sheriff's residence with its jail was built in 1887; its most famous prisoner was Eugene Debs, jailed for his role in the Pullman strike.

The two-story courthouse, with a hipped roof and projecting center section containing the entrance, is an excellent version of the Italianate style. The cornice with paired brackets is constructed of sheet metal. Until 1972 the buildings served as McHenry County's official headquarters. At that time, the structures were saved from demolition and restored. They are now in adaptive reuse with boutiques and restaurants which are reached by the imposing staircase within. Notice on the outside of the courthouse the iron fence which surrounds the small lawn, setting off the structure as a major public building. Both structures are on the National Register of Historic Places.

Walk west on Jackson 2 blocks. Then the second house on your right is

2. 310 W. JACKSON STREET—1895
This 1895 house is in the Queen Anne style. The corner projects into an additional floor and is topped by a pointed roof, next to which is a gable with curved brackets holding the gable rafters. Sweeping around two sides of the house is a porch supported by thin Ionic columns. Between the columns are turned balusters, providing a tight rhythm behind the landscaping.

1. Old McHenry County Courthouse and Jail
101 N. Johnson

Continue west. The next house on your right is

3.   326 W. JACKSON STREET—1875

This frame Italianate house was built in 1875. Especially nice are the paired brackets in the cornice, and the porch across the front with full-length, thin Tuscan columns. Still remaining on the building is the widow's walk, at the top of the hipped roof, complete with its thin-spindled balustrade.

Continue west to the corner. Turn left (south) on Hayward Street. On the NE corner of Calhoun and Hayward streets is

4.   123 S. HAYWARD STREET—1852

This minuscule one-and-one-half-story brick house, built in 1852, is patterned after the much grander Greek Revival houses of the period. It imitates with a brick pattern, here brought out by the change in paint color, the details of the classical prototypes. Unlike the usual Greek Revival houses, however, it has its entrance on the long side and has a porch across the entire front, sustained by posts. The posts that sustain it in place of the expected columns are in keeping with the small size of the house. The frame structures in the back of the house are later, but quite early, additions.

Continue south on Hayward Street 1 block. On the SW corner of South and Hayward streets is

5.   403 W. SOUTH STREET—1883

This white clapboard frame house was built in 1883.

Backtrack north on Hayward Street. The fourth house on your left is

6.   128 S. HAYWARD STREET—1906

This 1906 frame structure, clad in thin clapboards, shows the influence of the Classical Revival brought about by the World's Columbian Exposition of 1893. It is formal and blocky with a great many classical elements worked into it. The hipped roof has a pair of dormers. Below them, on the second story, is a slightly projecting section flanked by pilasters which carry through the entire two floors. These pilasters are repeated, wrapped around the corners. Across the front is a porch, extending to the south to form a porte-cochere. The porch is sustained by Tuscan columns set on pedestals.

4. 123 S. Hayward Street

Continue north. The next house on your left, on the SW corner of Hayward and Jackson streets, is

7. 401 W. JACKSON STREET—c.1870

This house was built about 1870 and subsequently has been altered by the addition of the stucco and the portico facing east. Surviving from the original structure are the impressive bracketed cupola on top of the hipped roof and the bracketed entrance porch facing toward Jackson Street.

Walk west on Jackson Street. The first house on your left is

8. 421 W. JACKSON STREET—1894

This frame structure from 1894 shows the characteristics of the Queen Anne style with remnants still surviving from the earlier Stick style. Notice the great variety of turned ornaments: for example, in the gable and at the porch end is mill-produced work in the polygonal bay projecting through three stories on the northeast corner. Atop the bay is a marvelous cast iron finial, a rare survivor of something often destroyed. The house was a gift by George Bunker to his daughter Florence on her wedding day on May 17, 1894. It cost them $5,000 but Bunker could easily afford it since he owned half of Woodstock. He was mayor twice and of the same family that gave its name to Bunker Hill, Massachusetts.

Continue west. The second house on your left is

9. 457 W. JACKSON STREET—c.1890

This frame structure from the 1890s is notable for a different variety and use of turned spindles, used to dress up its otherwise rather simple massing.

Continue west. The sixth house on your left is

10. 481 W. JACKSON STREET—1889

This house, built in 1889, is a frame structure with a simple hipped roof and stuccoed walls. Its symmetry is broken by placing the entrance on the west side in the front and marking it with a pediment containing a tooth-cut shingle pattern. The metal siding detracts from the original quality.

Continue west. The fourth building on your left is

11. 535 W. JACKSON STREET—1858

The initial construction of this simple, Greek Revival, clapboard-covered, frame house was in 1858. Either at that time or soon after, at the back of the structure, a two-story wing was added. Another addition was made to form a termination to that wing, finally producing the gable front. The result is a building that rambles more than would be expected of a city house, but this was most likely originally a farm house located outside Woodstock, which grew to it and subsequently beyond it.

Backtrack to Pleasant Street. Turn left (north) 1 block. On the NW corner of Pleasant and Judd streets is

12. 502 W. JUDD STREET—1900

This clapboard Greek Revival house was built in 1900, the late date apparently accounting for the use of pilasters on the front face under the gable.

Kitty-corner, on the SE corner of Pleasant and Judd streets, is

13. 491 W. JUDD STREET—late 1890s

This blocky, shingle-covered house dates from just before the turn of the century. It has a porch across the front that extends outward in the center with a dramatic pediment, above which is half of an octagonal porch covered by a conical roof with a flared base.

Cross to the north side of Judd Street and walk east. The second house east of Pleasant Street, on your left, is

14. 488 W. JUDD STREET—1905

Built in 1905, this two-story frame house with a full attic is shingle-clad. It has a small balcony on the second floor and a broad, full porch shielding a large window with an art glass transom and an entrance with art glass sidelights.

Walk east on Judd Street. The fourth house on your left is

15. 452 W. JUDD STREET—1907

This clapboard house, built as late as 1907, is a resumé of earlier styles. It has a shingle pattern in the gable and porch pediment, set off against tight clapboards, and bulging porch balusters. The porch swings around the corner and has cut-out shapes forming the enclosure underneath.

Continue east on Judd Street. On your left (north side of Judd Street) at Hayward Street, is

16.   330 W. JUDD STREET—1890s

This imposing two-story structure with a full attic has a dramatic gable with a rich shingle texture and a projecting upper section above the pair of double windows. Under the projecting gable are two floors of clapboards, the ground floor broken open under a decorative foliated pediment, supported by coupled columns to form the entrance porch. The columns, like the ones on the west side of the house, are supported by a large stone foundation built of rubblestone. The design dates from the late 1890s.

Continue east on Judd Street 1 block to Tryon Street. Turn right (south) 1 block. On the SW corner of Tryon and Jackson streets is

17.   301 W. JACKSON STREET—1862

This frame Italianate structure was built in 1862 although the addition on the east is later. Note the oversized elements, often used for smallish houses of this sort. The window frames, the cornice with its brackets, and the elements in the porch are especially generous in size and lend the structure a sense of grandeur.

Continue south on Tryon Street 2 blocks. Turn left (east) on South Street, 1 block. On the NW corner of South and Throop streets is

18.   202 W. SOUTH STREET—c.1900

This turn-of-the-century, eclectic, clapboard house has a turret facing the corner which, with its multi-sided porch, acts as a dramatic entrance. Also interesting is the variety of textures achieved by using shingles and clapboards.

Walk north on Throop Street 2 blocks to Jackson Street. Turn right (east). Follow the square around to your right to

19. Woodstock Opera House
121 Van Buren—1889

Built in 1889, the Opera House originally contained the city hall, the public library, the fire department, and a second floor auditorium. The Opera House became McHenry County's center for entertainment with touring vaudeville, minstrel shows, and dramatic companies using the stage. The building was designed by Smith Hoag and since reopening in 1977, after two years of restoration, has been on the National Register of Historic Places. There are exhibits on the first floor.

In comparison with the courthouse (Woodstock #1), this building shows the dramatic change in style that had occurred in the thirty interim years. This is a Romanesque structure, characterized by using large pieces of stone to form broad arches and strong stringcourses supported by bulging foliated capitals. Also characteristic of this period is the richness of the terracotta seen here in modeled panels under the windows, under the stringcourses, on top of the gable, and in the panels near the top of the tower. Giving an indication of the rich colors and fine decoration to be found inside, in the auditorium proper, are stained glass lunettes visible from the exterior as well as the two colors of stone used for the structure.

Walk around the square and enjoy the renovated old stores that surround the lovely park in the middle. If you wish to end the walk at this point, spend more time exploring the square.

If you wish to continue the Walking Tour, walk south on Dean Street. The second house on your right, past South Street, is

20. 324 Dean Street—1901

This Queen Anne frame house clad in clapboards and shingles was built in 1901 and features a polygonal corner turret and a Palladian window in the small gable on the south side.

Continue on Dean Street. The first house on your right, past Lawrence Avenue, is

21. 410 Dean Street—1892

This 1892, mid-Victorian, frame house features a rich textured shingle pattern and, on the ground floor, a flat-fronted projecting window with art

19. Woodstock Opera House
121 Van Buren

glass in the transom and curved sides from its slightly projecting front window. The small Mansard roof shielding the window echoes the one on the porch.

Continue on Dean Street. On the NE corner of Tryon and Dean streets is

22.   522 DEAN STREET—1855

The major portion of the 1855, brick, Greek Revival, one-and-one-half-story structure presents a pediment to the street. Its date from Woodstock's earliest period is betrayed by the smallness and simplicity of the door which is slightly off center from the window above and has a segmental arch rather than a stone lintel like those above the windows. Pride and pretense are present, however, in the careful brickwork which describes a rich cornice. Along the tops of the side walls and returning at the front to form a split cornice, the brickwork suggests the full entablature of the Doric order. The wing projecting to the left is a later addition.

Turn right (north) on Tryon Street. Halfway down the block, on your left, with a fire hydrant in front, is

23.   336 TRYON STREET—1905

This 1905 frame structure shows the way in which the classical style began to tame Queen Anne's exuberance. A square-fronted projection rises above the entrance; it has a simplified Palladian window on its second floor; but tying all of the forms together is a broad porch, projecting beyond the porch to the south as a porte-cochere, sustained by a series of thin Tuscan columns.

Cross to the other side of the street and continue north. The second house on your right is

24.   329 TRYON STREET—c.1895

Although the replacement of the original clapboards by metal siding has disrupted this building, it is a fine example of the 1890s Queen Anne style used to make a small building look larger. This is especially noticeable at the corner where a two-story porch is topped by a polygonal, pyramidal roof and sustained by thin turned posts.

Backtrack on Tryon Street. The last house on your right, before the school, is

25. 382 and 384 S. Tryon Street—1884

This white clapboard, Italianate house was built in 1884. The late date accounts for the thinness of the brackets as well as the elaborateness of the porch which stretches across the front and returns down the south side of the house. The porch is decorated with a spindled lintel and hipped, cut-out, post corbels.

Turn left on Dean Street. The red brick house on your right is

26. 517 Dean Street—1855

This Colonial style brick house, built in 1855, is a variation of the one across the street at 522 Dean Street (Woodstock #22). It has a hipped roof instead of a pitched one, but still uses an elaborate brick pattern to define a top cornice. Projecting to the north is a one-story wing which contains a porch (not original) and another hipped roof ending in a gable. One of the original entrances has been bricked up.

Continue on Dean Street, then turn right (east) on Fremont Street 2 blocks to Jefferson Street. Turn right (south) on Jefferson to Hoy Avenue. On your left is

27. 631 S. Jefferson Street—1898

This clapboard house was built in 1898 and features a second-story balcony with a gable roof projecting out from the main face. Next to it is a larger gable for the front wing of the house. Each has a different texture treatment in the gable, one a board pattern, the other a shingle pattern.

Backtrack north on Jefferson 2 blocks. Turn right (east) on Fremont Street. On your right, on the south side of Fremont Street at Vine Street, is

28. 450 Fremont Street—1896

This white clapboard house was built in 1896 and features a radial shingle pattern in the gable. The brick porch in front is a later alteration.

*Walk north on Vine Street, following it around to the left. Turn right (north)
on Greenley 1 block. Turn left on Lake Avenue. The third building on your
right is*

29.   329 LAKE AVENUE
McHenry County Housing Authority—1840

This 1840 brick house is unusual because it has brick flat arches for the
windows and for the front door in place of the usual stone. Projecting to the
left is a one-story extension with a porch whose roof is supported by a single,
fluted, Doric column emphasizing the Greek Revival heritage of this early
structure. Two possible explanations for the substitution of the flat brick
arches for the usual stone: it was built before a quarry had been opened in
the area to supply stones that large; it was built at a time of the year or a
period of the settlement when the roads would not allow hauling a piece of
heavy stone so far from a quarry.

*Continue on Lake Avenue, turning left on South Street and left again on
Jefferson Street. The fourth house on your left is*

29.   329 Lake Avenue

30.   327 S. JEFFERSON STREET—1901

This Victorian house was built in 1901. Notable here are two features not often found: the basket weave motif in the porch pediment, and the keyhole in the attic gable.

Directly across the street is

31.   328 S. JEFFERSON STREET—c.1900

This turn-of-the-century frame structure has an unusual roof configuration: a swooped, hipped roof with two dormers with polygonal, hipped roofs topping them.

Backtrack on Jefferson Street to South Street. On the SW corner of Jefferson and South streets is

32.   126 E. SOUTH STREET—1894

This clapboard house, built in 1894, is a large frame structure which occupies the corner site very effectively. It has a large gabled roof facing each street, one with a hooded Palladian window, the other with a pair of heavy hooded windows. The gables project beyond the second floor. A broad porch supported by clapboard-encased piers project from the first floor.

Continue north on Jefferson Street to Calhoun Street. On the NW corner of Jefferson and Calhoun streets is

33.   EVANGELICAL LUTHERAN CHURCH—1898

This handsome, 1898, Gothic Revival, brick structure corresponds to a type of design used throughout the nineteenth century. It features a fine tower with pier buttresses projecting from each corner. The tower rises into small corner spires above which rises the tall spire. Presently unused, it survives in relatively sound condition.

Continue north on Jefferson Street, 1 block to Jackson Street. Turn left (west), returning to the square. Directly in front of you, in the square, is

34.   THE SPRING HOUSE—1873

Although much restored, the 1873 gazebo still conveys the original festive character of this ornament in the town square, originally constructed over a mineral spring.

This concludes the Woodstock Walking Tour.

Exit the square on northbound Benton Street to the stop sign. Turn right (east) on Church Street 1 block to Madison Street. Turn left (north) 2 blocks to McHenry Avenue. Turn right 1 block to Route 47 (Seminary Avenue). Turn left and drive 11 miles on Route 47 to Route 173 (Maple Avenue in Hebron).

RICHMOND

RICHMOND

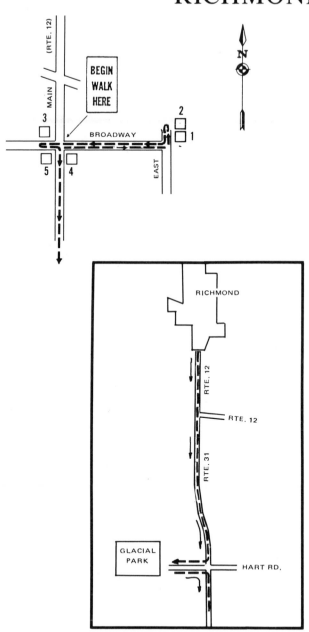

Turn right (east) on Route 173, 6.7 miles to Route 12. Turn right (south) on Route 12 (Main Street) to the intersection of Main Street and Broadway. Stop.

Richmond is a charming town. There are about a dozen antique stores, several restaurants, and many interesting shops.

RICHMOND WALKING TOUR

Walk east on Broadway 1 block. On the east side of East Street at Broadway is

1. 10314 EAST STREET—1880s
This frame Italianate structure from the 1880s, covered in clapboards, has a marvelously heavy porch with broad brackets and incised boards under the lintels with pendant keystones between. The brackets are repeated in the gable. Notice the heavy shouldered moldings around the windows and the door.

Walk north on East Street. The first house on your right is

2. 10316 EAST STREET—1880s
This is a slightly smaller version in the same style, also from the 1880s. It has scroll-cut details in the gable top and scroll-cut boards nailed onto the upper part of the double window on the second floor. The porch has a heaviness like its neighbor to the south, but is composed of very different elements.

Backtrack west on Broadway to Main Street.

The turn-of-the-century intersection of Main Street and Broadway still shows the original crossroads forming the town, formerly typical of many places but now mostly mutilated.

On the NW corner of Main Street and Broadway is

3. 5506 BROADWAY—1880s (and two buildings north)
10321 MAIN STREET—1882
These buildings show two variations on cast iron storefronts with brick

structures above. The cast iron columns on 5506 Broadway have a spiral pattern, while the ones on 10321 Main Street are closer to classical elements. The brick walls above portray the Italianate forms with 10321 Main Street having a complete sheet metal cornice.

On the SE corner of Main Street and Broadway is

4.   10310 MAIN STREET—1905

This building shows a later, slightly more elaborate version of the same type of construction seen on the two previous buildings.

On the SW corner of Main Street and Broadway is

5.   10313 MAIN STREET and
5601–5609 BROADWAY—c.1910

This building has a sheet metal bay window on the second floor, midway along the Broadway facade.

An enjoyable side trip is to walk west on Broadway where there are a number of houses, predating the turn of the century, exhibiting a variety of carpentry forms in the Italianate and Victorian styles.

This concludes the Richmond Walking Tour.

Drive south on Main Street (Route 12).

Continue south on Route 31, .4 miles to Hart Road. Turn right (west) to

GLACIAL PARK—This is the District Headquarters for all the Conservation Districts in McHenry County. On the grounds are a marsh, a bog, and a prairie to demonstrate wildlife in its natural habitat. Guided tours are available.

Backtrack east on Hart Road to Route 31. Turn right (south).

CRYSTAL LAKE

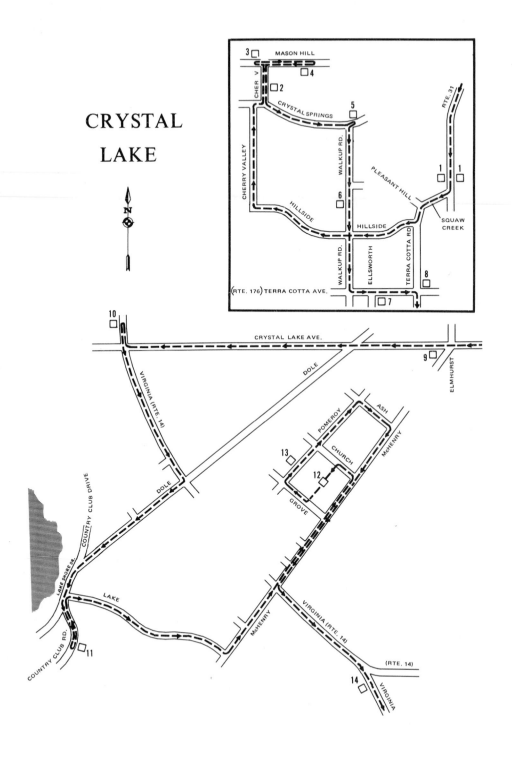

CRYSTAL
LAKE

CRYSTAL LAKE DRIVING TOUR

Drive 11½ miles on Route 31. Stop. On your left (east), across from the factory building, is a small building.

1. TERRA COTTA INDUSTRIES—c.1850

This pre-Civil War structure is an excellent example of an early stage coach stop in the Greek Revival style, flawed only by the addition of a small enclosed entrance replacing the original porch and front door. Especially noteworthy is the cobblestone foundation, under the porch to the right, and two features that are very rare in this type of construction: the use of long pieces of stone to form the porch posts, and the wall dormer inserted in the roof on the wing.

Notice the very large terra-cotta urn in front. It was produced across the street in the factory that produced much of the terra-cotta used in the building industry in Chicago in the last years of the nineteenth and early years of the twentieth centuries.

THE FACTORY AT TERRA COTTA—1881

The factory here started out in 1881 and grew into one of the three major terra-cotta factories in the midwest. William Day Gates's American Terra Cotta and Ceramic Company first produced tiles for draining the local farm land, but it quickly expanded to become a major supplier of the fireproofing materials used to protect the steel construction of Chicago's new, early skyscrapers first built in the 1880s. The artisans of the factory also produced ornamental terra-cotta for facades and artistic vases and other small pieces as a part of one of Chicago's major activities in the arts. The company's competitors were in Chicago, but here Gates was near good clays, a source of straw for packing his easily breakable products, and a line of the Chicago and Northwestern Railroad for shipping his products. In 1892 Gates moved into a terra-cotta house designed for him in Hinsdale by the important architectural firm of Jenney and Mundie. Gates remained a loyal friend of Chicago's most famous architect and designer of terra-cotta, Louis Sullivan, and supplied the materials for many of that master's last designs. Like the other terra-cotta companies, this one was greatly harmed by the collapse of building activity during the Great Depression and by the introduction of new materials when building revived after World War II, but lasted longer than its competitors, manufacturing terra-cotta up to 1966.

Continue south on Route 31, 1 block. Turn right (west) on Squaw Creek Road ½ mile to Pleasant Hill Road. Turn left (south) ½ mile to Hillside Road. Turn right (west) on Hillside Road and follow it west past Walkup Road 2.2 miles until it appears to end at Oak Street. Turn right and continue on Hillside Road 1.2 miles to Cherry Valley Road. Turn right (north) on Cherry Valley Road until it ends at Crystal Springs Road. Turn right 1/3 mile. Turn left (north) on Cherry Valley Road. Drive 1/3 mile. On your right is

2.   1904 CHERRY VALLEY ROAD
Stickney House—1849–56

This unusual, if not unique, structure is a two-story brick residence with tall, thin pilasters, segmental arched windows, brick corbels in the cornice, and other elements typical of the Italianate style, but these are handled in a highly unusual way. The building was begun in 1849 and completed in 1856 by George Stickney, the first farmer in the region, who arrived in 1835 from New England. Stickney was a member of the Spiritualist sect and used the house for séances, fortune telling, and other activities connected with spirits and the dead. The rounded corners, a feature made visually conspicuous by setting the pilasters well in from them, reveal the layout of the interior rooms. In the front on the first floor are large parlors and across the second floor a ballroom. These have rounded corners so that there are no square corners where evil spirits may lurk. Long abandoned, the building is again occupied and is being restored. It is listed on the National Register of Historic Places.

Continue on Cherry Valley Road to Mason Hill Road. Ahead of you on the north side of Mason Hill Road is

3. 7920 MASON HILL ROAD
Terwilliger House—c.1845

Built in 1849 by Samuel Terwilliger, the third settler in the region who arrived from New York State in 1836, this Greek Revival structure is more representative of the established East Coast than of the recently opened western frontier. Its prominence reveals the early prosperity made possible by hard work on the rich northern Illinois farmland. The square, two-story brick structure originally had a ballroom on the second floor stretching across the front. The well-proportioned brick core is surrounded on three sides by a wooden peristyle porch with seventeen fluted Doric columns. The formal entrance faces east while lesser entrances appear on the north and

2. Stickney House
1904 Cherry Valley Road

3. Terwilliger House
   7920 Mason Hill Road

south sides. Atop the low hipped roof is a large cupola with generous windows, an unusual feature for the classical pedigree of the design but soon to become common with the Italianate. The building is listed on the National Register of Historic Places.

Drive east on Mason Hill Road 1.0 miles. Behind a clump of pine trees on your right is

4. 6907 Mason Hill Road
Salisbury House—pre-1862

This white clapboard, Georgian house was built in stages, the two-story section on the right and the mid-section with the porch dating from before 1862. The slightly lower two-story addition on the left is later, but it does not disturb the overall character of the structure. The house is frame, covered in clapboards, with fine chamfered posts for the porch and very restrained Greek frames around the windows of the original section. Note the small windows lighting the second story in the central section above the porch. This structure, like the Stickney and Terwilligar houses (Crystal Lake #3 and #4), stands on the highest spot of the landscape, indicating the early settlement of these houses as the area was developed for farmland. The fully matured trees around the house also date from a very early period of planting.

Backtrack west 1.0 miles on Mason Hill Road to Cherry Valley Road. Turn left (south) to Crystal Springs Road. Turn left (east) on Crystal Springs 1.8 miles to Holcombville Corners. On your left is

5. 6310 CRYSTAL SPRINGS ROAD
Holcombville School—1858

This red brick, one-room schoolhouse was built in 1858. Its pattern follows the Federal style but is rendered in extremely simplified means by manipulating the brick in the pediment and entablature levels to suggest the full classical forms. The brickwork throughout has been very carefully done. Especially notable are the molded bricks near the bottom of the wall where the wall thickens slightly to cast the rainwater away from the foundation. The foundations are of riverstone.

Turn right (south) on Walkup Road 2.7 miles. One block past the electrical tower, on your left are tennis courts, on your right is

5. Holcombville School
6310 Crystal Springs Road

6.   5215 N. WALKUP AVENUE
Walkup House—1856

Built in 1856, the two-story pitched roof structure has the general configuration of the Greek Revival, complete with large windows. The walls are built of finely scaled cobblestones with large stones for the basement and foundations and graduated, smaller stones up the walls. Strength is added to this rare form of construction by adding large, carefully dressed stones above and below the windows, in the front on the level of the first floor, and at the corners where they are called quoins. Additional ornament is added by placing large cobblestones, surrounded by rings of small ones, between the first and second floor windows. Projecting to the left is a one-and-one-half-story wing which is part of the original construction although the porch is new as is the cornice of the taller structure. This form of construction was imported to northern Illinois from upstate New York.

COBBLESTONE HOUSES

The cobblestone houses in Crystal Lake are examples of a rare building type. The first to use stones worn into smooth shapes by glaciers were Irish laborers digging the Erie Canal in the 1820s. At first, the construction technique was limited to the Lake Ontario region of New York State.

These Illinois houses are similar to the "middle cobblestone period" New York houses built between 1835 and 1845 and must have been built by settlers from that region. The stones might have been collected by small boys or by neighbors in a great social "gathering bee." After being graded by size, with the best looking and most homogeneous ones destined for the front facade, two masons who knew the secret mixes of mortar required for their construction could build as much as sixteen vertical inches of wall in a day. The walls are usually as much as a foot and a half thick with a layer of insulating air between the inner and outer layers of stone.

It was possible to produce a sound, snug, and attractive house quite quickly and cheaply but only in areas with the proper glacial deposits. Rockford, Illinois and Beloit, Wisconsin have such houses, and the Gifford House, 363–365 Prairie Street (Elgin #16) from 1849–50 is another example. Only a limited number could be built, however, because the land surface yielded only a limited quantity of useable stones. The houses in Crystal Lake (Crystal Lake #6 and Crystal Lake #10) were built by some of the area's earliest residents.

(detail)

6. Walkup House
5215 N. Walkup Avenue

Continue south on Walkup Road to the stop sign at Route 176 (Terra Cotta Avenue). Turn left (east) ½ mile to the SE corner of Ellsworth Street and Terra Cotta Avenue.

7. 155 E. TERRA COTTA AVENUE
Ellsworth House—pre-1860

The distant relative of this impressive brick building from the late 1850s is found in sixteenth-century Italian villas as translated to Virginia by President Thomas Jefferson. It has the formality associated with the Federal style. The central section is two stories with a pedimented roof facing the front, flanked on each side by a lower wing each with a porch. The classical detailing is rendered by intricate brickwork like that observed at the Holcombville School (Crystal Lake #5) and characteristic of this settlement.

Continue east on Route 176 to the intersection of Terra Cotta Road. Turn left. On the NE corner of Terra Cotta Road and Terra Cotta Avenue is

8. THE COLONEL PALMER HOUSE—1840s

This red brick house, in the Federal style, probably dates from just before 1850. It is owned by the town of Crystal Lake and is being restored to its original condition. The carefully detailed wooden cornice is the type rendered in brick at the Ellsworth House (Crystal Lake #7) and at the Holcombville School (Crystal Lake #5).

Drive south on Terra Cotta Road to Crystal Lake Avenue. Turn right (west) on Crystal Lake Avenue 1½ miles. On the SW corner of Elmhurst and Crystal Lake avenues is

9. 100 W. CRYSTAL LAKE AVENUE—c.1900

This impressive turn-of-the-century structure has reddish rubblestone used on the bottom story and is constructed to produce robust arches over the openings. Above it is a two-story area, covered by two great intersecting gambrel roofs. Across the front of each street face is a broad porch sustained by solid-looking columns. The roofs originally had wood shingles like the ones that appear on the gabled ends.

Continue west on Crystal Lake Avenue .9 miles to Route 14 (Virginia Street). Turn right. The second building on your left is

10. 36 N. Virginia Street
Wallace House—c.1850

This Greek Revival house is said to be the oldest house in Crystal Lake and dates from about 1850. Built of cobblestone, it is a more pretentious representation of the style than is usual. The windows in the two-story, gable-topped section have stone lintels, but they are covered with wooden panels to reproduce the character of a more archaeologically pure Greek Revival. The porch has thin, canonic, Doric columns, with the lack of bases again indicating a selfconscious archaeological exactness.

Backtrack south on Virginia Street. Turn right on Dole Avenue until it runs into Lake Shore Drive. Turn left on Lake Shore Drive 1 block. Veer left onto Country Club Road 1 block. Then turn left into the second driveway.

11. 401 Country Club Road
Dole Mansion—Lakeside Center—1864

This expensive mansion took three years to build. It was begun in 1864 by C. S. Dole, partner in the important Chicago grain company of Armour and Dole. Dole moved here after its completion and laid out a half-mile race course (since destroyed) and extensive landscaping which survives in the many large trees. Here he hosted large, social gatherings that were unrivaled in the area. After 1901 the house was used by the superintendent of the Knickerbocker Ice Company which supplied Chicago with ice from the pond. Four years after it became a country club in 1922, the wing was added stretching south from the original mansion. The country club failed, and the building later served as a Catholic seminary for boys. In 1977 it was bought by its present owner, the First Congregational Church of Crystal Lake, which is restoring the interior.

The north end of the house is the original structure; the south end is an addition. The original, elaborate, Italianate building has very fancy double brackets and similarly elaborate woodwork used for the projecting bay windows on the first and second floors and for the sunporch on the left front corner, which has been enclosed. Both towers have been altered. The original interiors survive in excellent condition and are quite opulent.

Backtrack on Country Club Road to Lake Avenue. Turn right to McHenry Avenue. Turn left (north) on McHenry to Church Street. Turn left (west) onto Church, then left again into the parking lot. On your left is

12. 210 S. Michigan
Parish Offices—c.1855

This brick, mid-nineteenth-century house is in the Federal style. It is a T-shaped structure although, on the front facing the street, there has been an addition. The front section rises a full two stories, but the leg in the back has a one-and-one-half-story area indicated by the small windows tucked into the cornice. Notable also are the large grounds with a very early iron fence running next to the sidewalk.

Drive out the far end of the parking lot and turn right on Grove Street 1 block to Pomeroy Avenue. Turn right. The second house on your left is

13. 160 Pomeroy Avenue—1850s

This frame, clapboard-covered structure, surrounded by ample grounds, is an excellent example of the configuration given to Gothic Revival cottages probably dating to the middle of the nineteenth century. It has a steeply pitched roof intersected in the front by a gable of equal pitch and size, decorated with bargeboards which are in pristine condition and show the early use of scroll saws to produce elaborate patterns. The bargeboards terminate at the bottom with long loops and at the top are nosed into a turned pendant. Rising into a gable is a narrow pointed window. Across the front is a porch which could be original. On each end of the front section of the house, the same pattern found in the front gable is repeated. Gothic Revival cottages of this sort were popularized by the publication of an extremely influential book that appeared in 1850 by Andrew Jackson Downing, called *The Architecture of Country Houses*. The book sold more than 16,000 copies by the end of the Civil War.

Continue on Pomeroy Street to Ash Street. Turn right 2 blocks to McHenry Avenue. Turn right (south) on McHenry Avenue to Route 14 (Virginia Street). Turn left on Route 14, jogging right at the "Y" intersection. The first house on your right is

14. 7101 Virginia Street—pre-1872

The eastern section of this Italianate complex pre-dates 1872, and the structure extending to the west contains additional later pieces, although much of

13. 160 Pomeroy Street

what is seen now is the result of its adaptive re-use as Fuhler Real Estate. Especially notable on the oldest section and on the section to the right is the delicate carpentry work in the gable.

Continue east on Virginia Street 3¼ miles until it ends at Route 31. Turn right (south) on Route 31, 9.6 miles to Route 90 East, toward Chicago.

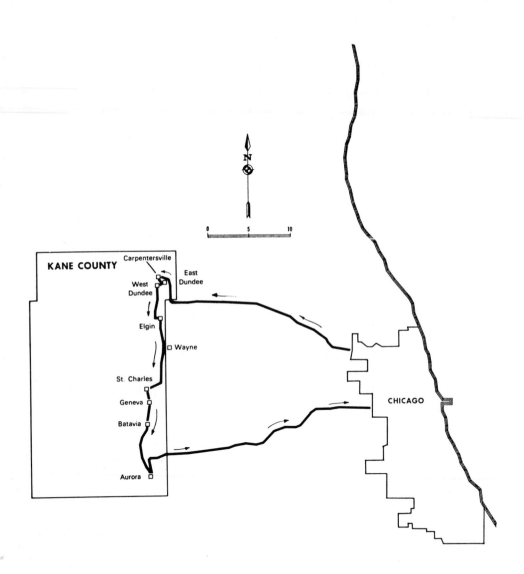

KANE COUNTY

Carpentersville

East
Dundee

West
Dundee

Elgin

Wayne

St. Charles

Geneva

Batavia

Aurora

CHICAGO

N

0   5   10

Kane
County

CARPENTERSVILLE

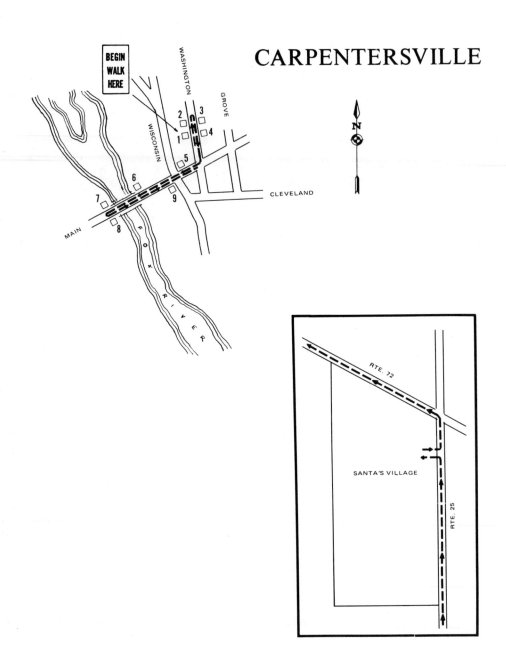

CARPENTERSVILLE

BEGIN
WALK
HERE

WASHINGTON

GROVE

WISCONSIN

1 2 3 4

5

6

9

7

8

MAIN

CLEVELAND

N

FOX RIVER

RTE. 72

SANTA'S VILLAGE

RTE. 25

Leaving Chicago, take the Kennedy Expressway to the Northwest Tollway. Continue on the Northwest Tollway and exit at Route 25 North. Drive north 1.8 miles. On your left, on the west side of the road, is

SANTA'S VILLAGE—Three Worlds of Fun
This theme park for children is open only in the warmer months.

Leaving Santa's Village, turn left (north) on Route 25, 1 block to the first stop light. Turn left (west) on Route 72. Drive 1 mile to Water Street. Turn right (north) on Water Street, 1.1 miles (Water Street becomes Washington Street). Just past Main Street, in the middle of the block, stop.

CARPENTERSVILLE WALKING TOUR

On your left (west side of the street) is

1. 21 N. WASHINGTON STREET
Old Library Building—Library Hall—1885
This 1885 building once served as the Carpentersville library, then as the headquarters of the Dundee Township Historical Society, and is now owned by the Dundee Township Park District. It is on the National Register of Historic Places.

The basic configuration of the building is based on the Romanesque style, with a broad, hipped roof topping a brick structure with large pieces of stone used to dress the opening and quarry-faced stone used as a basement. The central projection contains a broad arch which rises from spring blocks. The gable, above, ends in similarly rich carving. On either side are pilasters with rich foliate capitals; there are incised flowers in the lintels they support. The interior survives virtually untouched. Especially notable are the great quantity of beveled art-glass from the period and the woodwork, including a wooden wainscoat.

Walk north on Washington Street. The first house on your left is

2. 29 WASHINGTON STREET—1850
This small, brick, Greek Revival, one-and-one-half-story house has flat

brick arches. Especially interesting here are the metal stars anchoring rods that run through the building to hold the walls together. These were manufactured at the Illinois Iron and Bolt Factory (Carpentersville #8) in 1850. The wooden addition to the south and the additions in the rear are later.

Directly across the street (on the east side) is

3.   32 WASHINGTON STREET
Congregational Church—1884

Built in 1884, the original section of this building is a fine example of the Romanesque style rendered in brick.

Walk south on Washington Street. The first house on your left is

4.   26 WASHINGTON STREET
Congregational Parsonage—1884

This 1884 Queen Anne residence, with its clapboard siding, enclosed front porch, and a variety of window treatments departs from the usual configuration of the Queen Anne by keeping most of its elements within the basic cubic mass of the tall roofed structure. Especially interesting on the front is the set of three windows rising one after another to indicate the location of the stairway within. Above is a balcony opening through rounded corners to the outside.

Walk south on Washington Street to Main Street. Turn right (west). Walk 1 short block. On your right, on the NE corner of Wisconsin and Main streets, is

5.   48 E. MAIN STREET
Carpenter Store—1846

This 1846 building has lost the bracketed cornices under its flat roof, but the brick pattern that formed part of the cornice survives. Notable also are the ornamental arches over the windows, although the windows have been partially filled in.

Continue west. On your right, at the river bank, is

6.   2 E. MAIN STREET
Star Manufacturing—1873

In operation since it was built in 1873, this company still makes farm implements and steel plow shares. The original structure is the two-story block on

3. Congregational Church
   32 Washington Street

6. Star Manufacturing
   2 E. Main Street

the corner, with a pitched roof adding a low attic. Notice how the brickwork is treated to produce the character of an Italianate cornice, but extremely simplified. On top of the building is a small penthouse, for the hoisting machinery found in the structure.

As the company prospered, additions were built, two in the direction of the river, the second with a sheet metal cornice that gives the name of the company. Other additions along the railroad tracks include a section two stories high and a second, a single story high. Beyond, is a manufacturing shop with a monitor roof characteristic of structures containing forges and other heat producing equipment. The monitor roof allowed for ventilation within the structure. This handsome complex is a fine example of nineteenth century industrial architecture. Additional expansion took place in two more phases along the river, visible from the bridge.

Cross the river. On your right, on the NW corner of Main Street and the river, is

7.   10 W. MAIN STREET—1870s

This three-story industrial structure has even more elaborate cornice brick-work. Notice, toward the west end of the building, the large arch, subsequently filled in, which originally would have served as a loading dock. Also notice, midway along the building and at the river corner, projecting bays which allowed for office workers and supervisors to survey the river and street outside. This structure also dates from the early 1870s.

Across the street, on the SW corner of Main Street and the river, is

8.   10* W. MAIN STREET
Illinois Iron and Bolt—1871

Much of the decorative iron work on old buildings in this area came from this company, whose present structure was built in 1871. Visible both on this structure, and on the Star Manufacturing Company (Carpentersville #6) original section across the river, are stars anchoring tie rods and floor beams within, which were manufactured in this building. The building is best viewed from the bridge on the east side of the river. At the west end is a two-story detached addition.

*This address, although unusual, *is* correct.

Backtrack east on Main Street. On your right, on the SW corner of Main and Wisconsin streets, is

9.   39 E. MAIN STREET
The Old Grist Mill—1864

Built in 1864, the brick veneer was applied in the late 1890s. The original use of the building is shown by the penthouses, from the roof, and by the variety of large loading doors on the east side of the building.

Continue east on Main Street to Washington Street. Turn left (north) to the Old Library Building on your left.

This concludes the Carpentersville Walking Tour.

Drive south on Washington Street .8 miles to Barrington Avenue (just past the foot bridge in East Dundee).

EAST DUNDEE

EAST DUNDEE

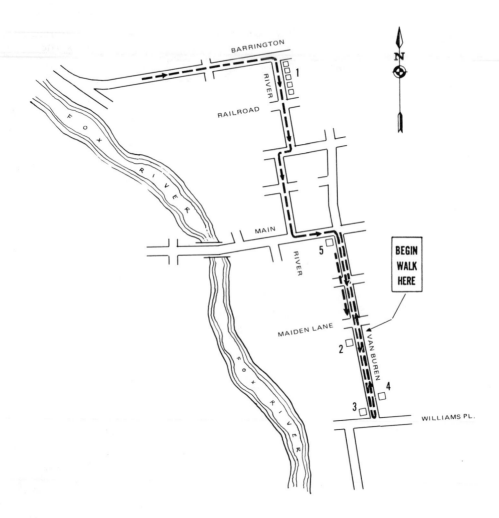

Turn left (east) on Barrington Avenue 4 blocks to River Street.

1. EDWARDS BLOCK
Eastside of River Street between Barrington
Avenue and Railroad Street—1855

Begun in 1855, and constantly expanded and altered, this complex originally had a general store, hotel, livery stable, and other buildings. The shops
on the west side of the tracks were built later. Above the ground floors, the
buildings are for the most part well preserved and now contain a variety of
charming shops.

*Drive south on River Street 4 blocks to Main Street. Turn left (east) 1 block
to Van Buren. Turn right (south) 5 blocks. Stop.*

EAST DUNDEE WALKING TOUR

On your right (west side of the street) is

2. HAEGER POTTERY
7 Maiden Lane

In 1897, David H. Haeger purchased a brick manufacturing plant. The
business began producing brick, but changed to art pottery and lamps, and
has expanded continuously ever since. There are free guided tours available.
Pottery and other items are for sale at discount prices.

*From Haeger Pottery, walk right (south) on Van Buren Street to the end of
the block. On the NW corner of Van Buren Street and Williams Place is*

3. 222 VAN BUREN STREET—c.1865
This small brick house from about 1865 rises one-and-one-half-stories to a
pitched roof under which the brick are laid to represent the pattern of the
Greek Revival. The frame extension on the north, although extensively rebuilt, represents something like the original configuration of this small
house.*

Backtrack north on Van Buren Street. The third house on your right is

*One will notice that many of the brick structures are built of a local brick
called "Dundee white brick."

(detail)

3. 222 Van Buren Street

4. 215 VAN BUREN STREET—c.1864

This L-shaped house from about 1864 shows the taller proportions and steeper roof of the Gothic Revival but here it is rendered in the same brick used for 222 Van Buren Street (East Dundee #3). Notice that the second story has a double arched top for its window opening and the bricks under the roof are laid in a simpler pattern, suggesting the corbels of the Greek Revival. The porch, stretching around the south wing, has turned posts and scroll-cut corner brackets.

Continue north 2½ blocks. On the SW corner of Main and Van Buren streets is

5. 407 JOHNSON STREET
Immanuel Lutheran Church—1886

This imposing, but quite simple, 1886, Gothic Revival church has a central tower rising to a double pitched, pointed, slate roof built in the same local brick. The stepbacks of the buttresses and other elements are stone and the pointed arches above the tall windows are of red brick. The tall pinnacles on each outer corner are done in sheet metal as is the cornice on the section between the pinnacles and the tower.

Backtrack south on Van Buren, 2 blocks, to Haeger Pottery.

This concludes the East Dundee Walking Tour.

Drive north on Van Buren Street 2 blocks to Main Street. Turn left (west) on Main Street.

WEST DUNDEE

WEST DUNDEE

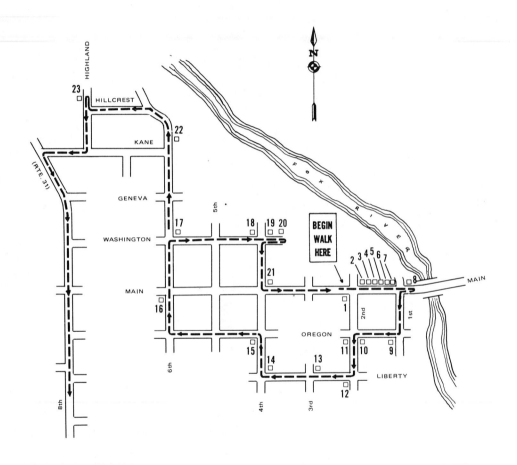

Drive west on Main Street, across the Fox River, to Second Street. Stop.

WEST DUNDEE WALKING TOUR

On the SW corner of Main and Second streets is

1. WEST DUNDEE VILLAGE HALL
102 S. Second Street—1909

This 1909 red brick building contains the massing characteristic of town halls of the nineteenth century, but the masonry details show the presence of the Prairie style. Especially notable is the care with which the windows are outlined by courses of brick raised slightly from the wall surfaces and, in the tower, the way in which the piers terminate in rows of brick that suggest classical capitals without actually being such. The entrance is sheltered by a hood molding supported by very simple geometrically stylized brackets.

The two blocks of Main Street stretching from Second Street to the river contain an excellent representation of a prosperous late nineteenth- and early twentieth-century downtown area.

On the NE corner of Second and Main streets is

2. 126-128 MAIN STREET—1887

This three-story building, named Hunt's Block, was called Hunt's Folly because it was so unusually tall for its time, 1887. Notice the paired Italianate brackets in the cornice and the ample arched windows.

Walk east on Main Street. The next building on your left is

3. 122–124 MAIN STREET—1880s

This structure is of more common height with the Gothic Revival detailing, characteristic of the 1880s.

Continue east. The second building on your left is

4. 118 MAIN STREET
First National Bank—1910s

This terra-cotta structure was built just before World War I.

Continue east. The next building on your left is

5.   116 MAIN STREET—1903

Built in 1903, the Dundee State Bank building shows a freer and more whimsical use of the same classical elements that gave identity to banks during the period when banks considered themselves trustees of a community's assets and therefore were public buildings.

Continue east. The fourth building on your left is

6.   106 MAIN STREET—c.1895

This is a double building with Italianate forms in its sheet metal cornice and broad arches in the windows on the second floor. The shopfronts here are characteristic of the period just before 1900, while the central entrance on the ground floor leads to apartments upstairs. Note on the western building, atop the small central pediment, the mortar and pestle to indicate the drugstore which apparently has always occupied the ground floor.

Continue east. On the NW corner of Main and First streets is

7.   102 MAIN STREET—1880s

This structure has a surviving sheet metal cornice and very elaborate arches on the upper story, framed by brickwork that represents the cornice and pilasters characteristic of the Italianate style. It probably dates from the 1880s.

Across the street, on the NE corner of First and Main streets, is

8.   98 W. MAIN STREET—c.1890

This three-story structure has Italianate forms and probably dates from the 1890s. The ground floor has thin cast iron columns opening up the shop fronts to the large expanse of plate glass. This is an excellent surviving example of an original shopfront.

Walk south on First Street 1 block. On the SW corner of First Street and Oregon Avenue is

9.   204 S. FIRST STREET
Whiting Hull House—c.1842

The central kernel of this tiny brick house was built about 1842. It is the one-and-one-half-story, brick, Greek Revival section. Later additions are to the

6. 106 Main Street

south and west. The old well in the garden once served the entire neighborhood.

Walk west on Oregon Avenue 1 block. On the SE corner of Oregon Avenue and Second Street is

10. 117 OREGON AVENUE—1870s

This tall, frame, Italianate structure dates from the 1870s. It has a paired-

7.   102 Main Street

bracket cornice. On the ground floor are floor-to-ceiling openings, the largest one serving as the entrance, the others as windows, all with elaborate
frames with feet and shoulders. Stretching across the north and west sides,
and accented by a pediment projecting diagonally at the corner, is a porch
sustained by Tuscan columns with a necking ring several inches below the
capital, characteristic of the liberties taken with the classical orders after the
rigidity of the Greek Revival style had wained. The house stretches south to
a lower wing which includes an elaborate polygonal projection on the west.

On the SW corner of Oregon Avenue and Second Street is

11.   203 OREGON AVENUE—1852

The large kitchen, called a "keeping room," was in the basement of this 1852
farmhouse, with an outside, ground level entrance. Characteristic of the
early date of this structure are the irregular lapped-board siding and the
windows which have eight panes in the lower section and twelve in the
upper. The thin window frames are also characteristic of the early date. The
moldings immediately around the front door are original, but the broken
pediment is not. A porch of some sort probably originally sheltered the
entrance.

*Walk south on Second Street 1 block to Liberty Street and notice the variety
of early twentieth century houses on either side. On the SW corner of Liberty and Second streets is*

12. 304 SECOND STREET—1879
This one-and-one-half-story Gothic cottage, built in 1879, displays the characteristic steeply pitched roofs from the Gothic Revival. It has a porch
across two sides with square posts holding scroll-cut knees. The porch ends
at the eastward projection of the structure. Projecting on the ground floor of
that east wing is a small polygonal bay with small scroll-cut brackets. Extending to the south is a slightly lower service wing which includes the back
porch.

*Cross to the north side of Liberty and walk west. The second house on your
right is*

13. 310 THIRD STREET—1916
This 1916 house has a tile roof and stucco exterior. The formality of the
composition derives from the Georgian Revival style but the free interpretation of the forms indicates the liberated attitudes characteristic of the Prairie
style. The porch on the east, which originally would have been a screen
porch, has been enclosed.

Continue west. On the NE corner of Liberty and Fourth streets is

14. 318 LIBERTY STREET—1894
Built in 1894, this beautiful house has black wood roof shingles on the
corner tower, carpenter lace with a pendant in the gables, and flat board
carpentry on the corner tower that contrasts handsomely with the clapboard
siding. Especially interesting here is the massing of the roofs, with pitched
gables intersecting a hipped roof, and a corner tower set into the same roof,
producing a great variety of roof planes.

*Turn right (north) on Fourth Street. Walk north 1 block. On the SW corner
of Oregon Avenue and Fourth Street is*

15. 403 OREGON AVENUE—1850 and 1873
Though the main portion of this brick house was built in 1873, the smaller
back portion is believed to be part of an 1850 school. The second story has a

(detail)   **14.** 318 Liberty Street

shingled Mansard roof with dormers lighting the interior rooms. Spread around the north and east faces is a porch sustained by porch posts and topped by cast iron crestings, which rarely survive. Projecting to the east from the "L" is a polygonal window which, like the other windows on the ground floor, has a segmental arched top. The windows under the porch are taller and narrower; their narrowness is accentuated by the vertical divisions of the glass.

Walk west on Oregon Avenue 2 blocks to Sixth Street. Turn right (north) 1 block. On the SW corner of Main and Sixth streets is

16. 601 MAIN STREET—1845
The brick structure nearest Main Street was built in 1845 as a hotel and stagecoach stop. It also served as a station on the Underground Railroad.

Continue north on Sixth Street. On the NE corner of Washington and Sixth streets is

17. 510 WASHINGTON STREET
St. James Episcopal Church—1904
Built in 1904, this copy, built in pale brick, of an English church features a Gothic doorway and landscaping by the Morton Arboretum.

Walk east on Washington Street 2 blocks. On the NW corner of Washington and Fourth streets is

18. 404 WASHINGTON STREET—c.1855
This two-story, frame, clapboard house was built about 1855. It shows the blocky massing of the Italianate but the pitched roof and central gable are characteristic of the Greek Revival. Spreading across the south and east fronts is a porch with Tuscan columns with necking rings below the capitals, characteristic of the Italianate. The overall restraint of the design indicates a very conservative, unpretentious, and serviceable approach to local construction.

On the NE corner of Washington and Fourth streets is

19. 318 WASHINGTON STREET—1847
The western section of this 1847 house is a Greek Revival structure with flat brick arches and star anchor ends between the first and second story. At a later date, before the turn of the century, a wing was added to the east to make a second unit, at which time the present porch, now carefully restored, was constructed.

Continue east. The next house on your left is

20. 310 WASHINGTON STREET—c.1864
This tiny, two-story, Greek Revival structure from about 1864 is barely large

enough to hold the openings or sustain the huge, cobblestone, fireplace chimney rising on the west. Although the ground floor, front window and the chimney are probably later alterations, the structure has a very appealing charm.

Backtrack west to Fourth Street. Turn left (south). On the NE corner of Fourth and Main streets is

21.   First United Methodist Church—1865

Originally, this 1865 building was the Old Baptist Church. The general composition of the structure, the careful rendering of corner pilasters and cornices, the double arched windows, and the arched doorway all indicate the New England source for this design, and perhaps for the carpenters who produced it. Note the pediments over the windows, the tight dentil molding in the cornice under the eaves, and the cobblestone foundation. The smaller upper elements in the tower are modern.

Walk east on Main Street 2 blocks to Second Street.

This concludes the West Dundee Walking Tour.

Drive west on Main Street 4 blocks. Turn right (north) 3 blocks to Sixth Street. On the east side of Sixth Street at Kane Street is

22.   405 Sixth Street—c.1870

Built about 1870, this tall, two-story, Italianate, school building stands above a high basement. The corners of the basement are defined by stone quoins. The rest of the structure is brick except for the richly worked, wooden bracketed cornice with eave returns at the four pedimented fronts of the south block. The corners are treated as pilasters and, by moving the brick out from the face of the wall, a similar treatment describes the segmental arches and the full semi-circular arches on the main story. The entrance to this structure was originally on the south face, indicated by the large central window. The building extends, with another block, to the north where the forms are slightly simpler and more subdued. The final section, at the far northern end, is a very carefully done addition, designed to correspond with the original sections. The structure sits on a high piece of ground overlooking the river and commanding the countryside around it, emphasizing its role as a major civic monument in the community.

Drive north on Sixth Street as it curves to the left (west) as Hill Crest Court, 1 block to Highland Avenue. On the west side of Highland Avenue is

23. DUNDEE TOWNSHIP HISTORICAL SOCIETY MUSEUM
426 Highland Avenue

The exhibits change, but usually feature turn-of-the-century displays, Indian artifacts from the area, and furniture or dress of a bygone era. Saturdays and Sundays: 2:00 p.m.-4:00 p.m.

Leaving the historical society turn right (south) on Highland Avenue 1 block. Turn right (west) on Kane Street 1 block. Turn left (south) on Eighth Street (Route 31).

ELGIN

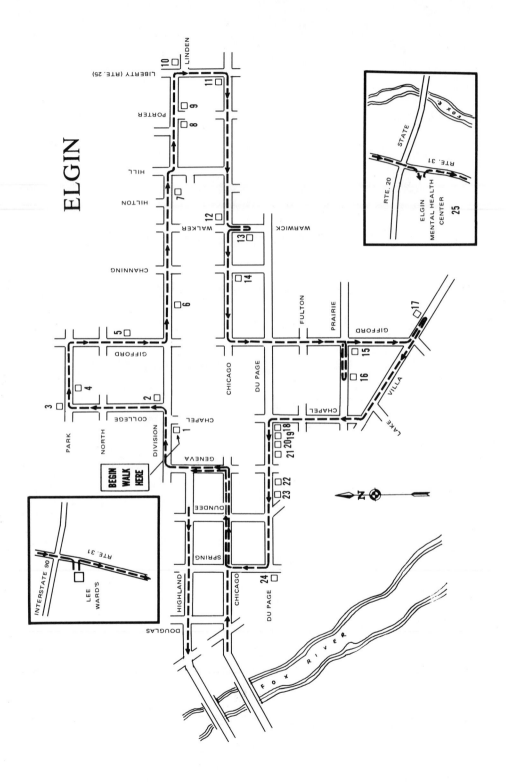

Drive south on Route 31, 3½ miles. On the right (west) side of the road is

LEE WARD'S CREATIVE CRAFT CENTER
Inside you will find the widest selection of handicraft items and supplies in the world.

Continue south on Route 31, 1.3 miles to Chicago Street (Route 20). Turn left (east) on Chicago Street 5 blocks. Turn left (north) on Geneva Street, 1 block to Division Street. Turn right (east) 1 block. Stop.

ELGIN WALKING TOUR

On the SW corner of Chapel and Division streets is

1. 321 DIVISION STREET
The Butterman's Restaurant—1889

Built in 1889, this three-story house is in the Queen Anne style. It has the mixture characteristic of the style: brick and carved stone, a high roof, a polygonal turret and a second one of sheet metal, prominent chimneys of modeled brick, a bell dome, a jerkin-head roof on the front dormer, and a full-scale spindled veranda with a pediment indicating the entrance. Restored to its original condition, it is in adaptive reuse as Butterman's Restaurant.

Almost kitty corner, on the NE corner of College and Division streets, is

2. 364 DIVISION STREET
O'Conner Funeral Home—1887

This 1887 Queen Anne mansion has a carefully preserved original interior. The exterior masonry forms have been painted white, but still visible is the variety of shapes, openings, and projections of bays and porches.

Walk north on College Street 2 blocks to Park Street. On the north side of Park Street at College Street is

3. 350 PARK STREET
Elgin Academy, Old Main—1848 and 1855

The bottom part of the structure was built in 1848, the top in 1855. It is a monumental but restrained classical building, conspicuously sited at the end of a street on the crown of a slope. Its long facade rises through three stories, a basement, main floor, and top floor, built of simply but well finished blocks of the local yellow stone. The center is marked by a temple front with its pediment providing an accent and held by two elegant columns set between piers at the ends of the balcony under the pediment. Below the columns is the entrance guarded by two very stout Doric columns, appropriate forms for the basement level. The building is listed on the National Register of Historic Places.

Cross to the south side of the street and walk east on Park Street. The third house on your right is

4.   373 PARK STREET—pre-1867

This pre-1867 cottage is one of the best examples in the Elgin area of the Gothic Revival style popular from 1830–1870. Tucked into the angle formed by the L-shaped plan is a tower rising to a slope-sided roof. In the front gable is a pair of pointed windows with heavy moldings and turned knobs. The square-headed windows below are shielded by small roof cornices supported by scroll-cut brackets. The bargeboards on the gables are punctured by quatrefoils. A projecting porch, supported by turned posts holding segmental arched traces, surrounds the corner. Above the front door and the windows in the tower are simple, square hood moldings. The vertical proportions and steep pitches of the roofs, characteristic of the Gothic Revival style, are emphasized by the board and batten siding. Also characteristic of the style, and now extremely rare: on the east side of the house is a wall dormer; beyond that, under the gable, is a one-story porch (now sagging a bit) with clusters of colonettes holding the roof of the porch, which is decorated with cut-out festoons. The hood moldings appear over the ground floor windows on this facade. A later variation of this design will be seen at 433 Division Street (Elgin #6).

Continue east to Gifford Street. Turn right (south) 1 block, then the fourth house on your left (east) is

5.   129 GIFFORD STREET—1860s

The central and southern sections of this house date from the 1860s and show the simple, blocky forms of the Greek Revival, but with simple

4. 373 Park Street

brackets on the cornice of the pediment on the one-story wing projecting to the south. Note the cobblestone foundation and the large, simple stones used for the window lintels.

Continue south to the corner. Turn left (east) on Division Street. The sixth house on your right is

6.   433 DIVISION STREET—c.1870

This structure from the decade after the Civil War is a variation on the configuration shown earlier at 373 Park Street (Elgin #4). The basic configuration is the same L-shape with a tower rising in the inner corner, but this building is covered in clapboards and the porch projects from the corner, bulging on the west side. The windows are square-cut and topped by delicately incised cornices. The two paired windows, on the top story of the tower, are topped by highly abstracted anthemion motifs. The tops of the gables contain scroll-cut filagree. On the ground floor, in the front, is a flat-fronted bay window with carved capitals on the pilasters at the corners. On the east side is another projection.

Continue east on Division Street. The second house on your left, past Hilton Place, is

7.   486-488 DIVISION STREET—c.1880

This structure, which dates from between 1875 and 1885, is a brick box with a pitched roof, a polygonal projecting bay on the ground floor, and a pair of windows above. The stepped-up brick pattern under the front gable recalls the Italianate, as does the front porch and the matching porch on the west side. The porches have square posts and scroll-cut, punched-out brackets. This is an interesting example of a relatively humble brick structure.

Continue east on Division Street to Porter Street. (There is a jag in Division Street.) On the SW corner of Division and Porter streets is

8.   34 N. PORTER STREET—1890s

This frame, clapboard structure is beautifully designed to satisfy the requirements of its corner site. The wrap-around porch, supported by stout Ionic columns, stands away from the main mass of the house which has pilasters at each corner. At the south end of the east face is a polygonal bay which balances the porch projection at the north. The symmetry is carefully reinforced by the careful placement of two nicely detailed dormers in the hipped roof. On the north face, a projecting wing terminates in a pediment carefully detailed to match the cornice below the roof. The structure is characteristic of the taming of the Queen Anne style by the neo-classicism of the 1890s, often termed a neo-Colonial style.

On the SE corner of Porter and Division streets is

9. 33 N. PORTER STREET—1890s

This large frame structure from the 1890s was originally covered in shingles. The roof shingles have been replaced by asphalt shingles, detracting only slightly from the strength of this design. The ground floor is overwhelmed by a two-story gambrel roof which extends beyond the ground floor wall on the north side, but in that area a bowed wall balloons into the covered space. There is a very flat, polygonal bay on the second story in the front facade; above it is a pedimented window, below a shed-roofed porch with a pediment containing a foliate design. The porch is sustained by clustered, tapered, square piers. To the south of the porch is a large, rounded, two-story bay rising to a conical roof. Additional elaboration in the design is provided by the diamond-shaped shingle patterns in the second floor and the saw-tooth motif crossing the tops of the windows.

Continue east on Division Street to Liberty Street. Cross to the east side of Liberty Street. On the NE corner of Linden Avenue and Liberty Street is

10. 55 N. LIBERTY STREET—1880s

Built in the early 1880s and remodeled in 1891, this Queen Anne home shows clear traces of both Shingle and Stick styles. The earlier period is visible in the general massing, which is blocky and clean-cut, with a three-story tower topped by a tall roof standing next to the one-and-one-half-story pitched roof structure. The later period is characterized by the variety of shingle patterns and clapboard base, the porch, and the variety of windows including the Palladian window in the tower. The wide transomed window on the ground floor, however, is characteristic of the earlier period. The inconspicuous two-story projection to the east is modern.

Walk south on Liberty Street, 1 block, to Chicago Street (Route 19). On the NW corner of Chicago and Liberty streets is

10.   55 N. Liberty Street

11. 600 E. CHICAGO STREET—1892

Built in 1892, this Queen Anne house was influenced by the Shingle style. The round tower and round arched side windows are common features of the former, while the latter features walls uniformly covered with shingles, which contrast with the sweeping, stone, veranda railing.

Walk west on Chicago Street (Route 19) 3 blocks. On the NE corner of Walker Place and Chicago Street is

12. 470 E. CHICAGO STREET—1887

This house, built in 1887, shows an exuberant diversion from the common L-shape plan. The L-shape is visible in the block topped by the steeply pitched roofs. Tucked into the corner is a stairwell, with the roof kept below the ridge of the pitched roof, entered by an octagonal porch topped by a parapet. The roof is carried on turned posts which appear here, as elsewhere, in elaborate carpentry work. The ends of the two wings are each treated differently: the one facing south is a polygonal bay complete with stained glass, and elaborated by extensive carpentry work; the other terminates as a bay, smaller on the second floor, topped by a balcony.

Cross to the south side of Chicago Street and walk south on Warwick Place. The third house on your right is

13. 18–20 WARWICK PLACE—1888

This 1888 house is eclectic in design. Wings and gables protrude in all directions; balconies, overhanging gables, and bay windows dot the facade; trim and ornament are elaborate. The San Francisco style paint-scheme emphasizes the decoration.

Backtrack north on Warwick Place to Chicago Street. Turn left (west) 1 block. On the SW corner of Channing and Chicago streets is

14. 443 E. CHICAGO STREET—1848

This 1848 Federal style brick residence, with a clipped pediment on the gable roof, has a handsome recessed entrance. The door, with a transom and sidelights, is framed by pilasters that support a frieze, decorated with abstracted anthemion ornaments. Note the fanlight in the pediment, a characteristic feature of the Federal style.

Continue west on Chicago Street 1 block to Gifford Street. Turn left (south) to Prairie Street. On the SW corner of Prairie and Gifford streets is

15. 150, 152, AND 154 S. GIFFORD STREET—1870s

These two-story, Italianate, brick townhouses are an unusual feature in a residential neighborhood. Built in the 1870s, they show a very simple, straightforward use of masonry to produce features associated with the more elaborate elements in stone, and an extremely restrained cornice, lacking brackets. The porches, with their small shed roofs above the entrances, are carried on the only extant elaborate detail: brackets incised with heavy, semi-circular tracery. Note that the building sits on very high bases producing front stairs (the present ones are later replacements), which were called stoops. (A great deal of courting took place on summer evenings when families sat on stoops and visited from house to house.)

Walk west on Prairie Street. The sixth house on your left is

16. 363–365 PRAIRIE STREET
Gifford House—1849–50 and 1871

This curious combination of two different architectural styles was begun in 1849 when James T. Gifford, who had come to the area from up-state New York, set the mason Edwin F. Reeves, who knew up-state New York cobblestone construction techniques, to work. The next year Gifford, who had founded Elgin in 1835, moved into the house, which long remained one of the town's showcases. Surrounded by a cast iron fence that kept a herd of deer within landscaped grounds that ran from Chapel to Gifford streets and from Villa to Prairie streets, "The Stone Cottage," as it was called, was the scene of many festive gatherings, but these were presided over by his eldest daughter and her husband, Orlando Davidson, because Gifford had died soon after moving into the house, in 1850.

In 1871 Davidson, by now proprietor of Elgin's Home Bank, rebuilt the house in the latest style. He added a wing and, more importantly, a Mansard roof with a balustrade above the cornice which was supported by evenly spaced modillions and with large, round-headed dormers and, finally, cast iron crestings along the top curb. The result was somewhat curious. Mansard roofs should go above a second story, and the two stories below should be massive enough to carry the visual load. Here, it sits atop the first story which is made of highly textured, multicolored, small-scaled cobblestones,

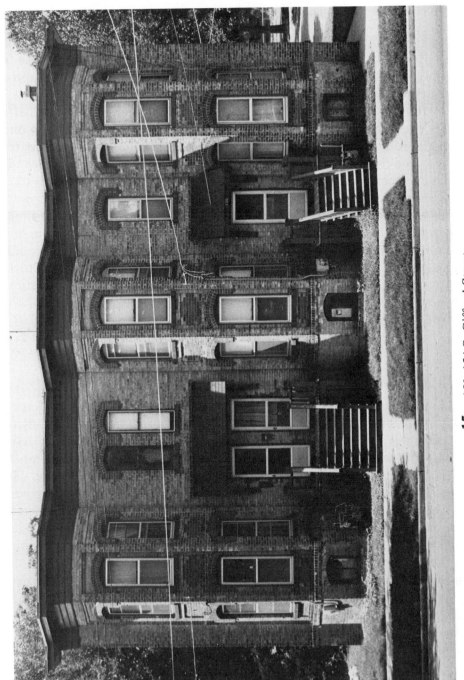

15. 150–154 S. Gifford Street

and it seems to press those walls into the ground. By 1871 there were not enough cobblestones available to extend the walls, or perhaps the founder's daughter had an attachment to the old house and this represents a compromise between her and her husband.

After Davidson died in 1899 the building was chopped up into apartments, the original front entrance (which faced west) replaced by a new one facing north, the outbuildings with their stables and servants' quarters removed, and the grounds subdivided into individual lots. What survives today is an excellent example of cobblestone construction with dressed stone for quoins and lintels, and with the columns Gifford wanted along the verandas because they reminded him of homes he had seen in South Carolina. Atop the "Stone Cottage" rests the stylish Mansard roof his son-in-law built, with its balustrade and cresting lost but with its pompous presence still quite evident. The building is listed on the National Register of Historic Places. (See Crystal Lake, p. 211, for additional information on cobblestone houses.)

Backtrack east to Gifford Street. Turn right (south) 1 block to Villa Street. Turn left (east). The second house on your left is

17.   259 VILLA STREET—1886

This structure, built in 1886, contains two features not often found together. One is a blocky, brick structure standing on a stone basement with dressed stone lintels and stringcourses. The windows on the second story have arches of brick and stone and, on one window, a separate terra-cotta molding. Terra-cotta also appears elsewhere as panels decorating the face. The masonry mass is topped by a sheet metal cornice, itself topped by a fragment of cast iron cresting which originally covered the entire cornice. Added to that is the other unusual feature, an elegant network of projecting wooden porches. One serves as an entrance and has a pediment set into a shed roof. On top of it is a semi-circular balcony. The other stands forth from the ground floor next to the porch. It projects farther and has elaborate carpentry work, with the stylistic character of the Stick style.

Backtrack west on Villa Street, past Gifford Street, to Chapel Street. Turn right (north) to DuPage Street.

The structures along the south side of DuPage Street from Chapel Street

(detail)   **17.** 259 Villa Street

two blocks to Phyllis Street portray an early form of house types which accommodated workers in the 1870s and 1880s. Other examples are found in other parts of Elgin. Here is a particularly fine stretch of them.

On the SW corner of Chapel and DuPage streets is

18.   327 DuPAGE STREET—1870s
This house is an excellent example of a more modest type of Victorian frame residence from the 1870s. It features a Mansard roof and dormer windows with segmental arches and, on the ground floor, polygonal bays flanking the entrance with its small roof supported by molded struts.

Walk west on DuPage Street. The first building on your left is

19.   321 AND 323 DuPAGE STREET—c.1885
This two-story Italianate structure has three entrances, two grouped under one wooden porch, the other set on the side with its own porch. The forms of the Italianate style are rendered, as is characteristic elsewhere in Elgin, in two different colors of brick. Dressing up the structure is a small panel of glazed tile under the most conspicuous front window.

Continue west. The second building on your left is

20.   315 AND 317 DuPAGE STREET—c.1870
This is an older four-flat from about 1870, done in brick with projecting bays across the front and a simple wooden cornice with bosses decorating it.

Continue west. The next structure on your left is

21.   307, 309, AND 311 DuPAGE STREET—1870s
This slightly later structure probably dates from the 1870s. It has flat bays instead of polygonal ones and a sheet metal cornice decorated with stamped metal ornament and brickwork of extreme simplicity. Notice that the transoms of the ground floor windows contain colored glass.

Continue west. On the SW corner of DuPage and Geneva streets is

22.   269, 271, 273, AND 275 DuPAGE STREET—1860s
This single building, probably from just before 1870, is the oldest of the

group. It contains twelve apartments, two entered from each entrance from the street level and the third entered from the areaway leading down to the basement apartments. (The original entry was probably on the lower level; the present ones probably date from the time the street grade was raised.) The building's extreme simplicity indicates the early date. The porches have been rebuilt; originally, there were probably Gothic Revival porches with extensive spindle work.

Continue west to Villa Street. On the SE corner of Villa and DuPage streets is

23. 55 VILLA STREET
First Universalist Church—1892

Built in 1892, this structure indicates the Romanesque Revival style as rendered in brick. A green-tinged stone was used as the foundation, terminated by a limestone sill. Limestone is used elsewhere in the building to demarcate stringcourses, act as lintels, and serve as copings for the gables of the two entrances, one on either side of the round tower set at the point of the triangular site. These entrances feed into a polygonal vessel containing the sanctuary. Beyond it is the lower structure of the ancillary areas within the church. The vigorous forms of the Romanesque Revival are conspicuous in the groups of windows in the round tower, the broad arches of the entrance, the slightly smaller arches of the sanctuary, and the broad arches on either side of the sanctuary. Note the extensive stained glass used throughout the design.

The design of the church was conceived and supervised by George Hunter, superintendent of the Elgin National Watch Company, to resemble the form of a hunting watch case. The body of the building is the case, the roof is the cover, the balcony with its choir loft is the hinge, and the tower becomes the snap of the case. The building is the largest physical reminder in Elgin that at that time the city had the largest watch factory in the world. Founded in 1866, at one time it produced 4,300 movements daily and employed 4,000 people. Indeed, the word pocketwatch and the Elgin brand name were synonymous. The church is listed on the National Register of Historic Places.

Continue west 1 block. On the SW corner of Spring and DuPage streets, at the beginning of the Elgin Mall, is

24. 167 DuPage Street

24. 167 DuPage Street
Ranstead Building—1892

This structure, built in 1892, is a fine surviving example of a relatively rare style: the Queen Anne rendered in masonry in a commercial application. Notice the variety of brick used with different colors and materials, and the characteristic mixture of materials, including modeled terra-cotta, limestone, quarry face stone used as lintels and stringcourses on the second floor, and as a lintel and as a flat arch on the ground floor. There is also sheet metal used for the polygonal bays on the second floor and for the cornice and the pediment containing the name of the building and the date of construction. Also noteworthy is the cast iron used for the shopfront facing DuPage Street, with a very thin, highly abstracted example of one of the classical orders used to support the wrought iron beam which holds the mass above. Immediately west of the shopfront is the entrance to the professional offices upstairs. This is a characteristic building of the period, although the finish and detailing of the design is extraordinarily fine.

Walk north on Spring Street to Chicago Street. Turn right (east) 2 blocks to Geneva Street. Turn left (north) 1 more block. Turn right (east) on Division Street 1 block.

This concludes the Elgin Walking Tour.

Drive west on Division Street, 1 block, to Geneva Street. Turn left (south) 1 block. Turn right (west) on Highland Avenue, 6 blocks. Turn left (south) on State Street (Route 31). Drive south 1.2 miles. On your right (west) is

25. Elgin Mental Health Center
750 S. State Street—1870s

The square mile of land for the State's grand, new asylum for the insane, as the people of the period called it, the third in the state, was acquired in the late 1860s and an architectural competition for the design of the buildings was won by S.V. Shipman of Madison, Wisconsin. Construction proceeded during the several years which were years of financial hardship for the State (it was assisting Chicago in recovering from the Fire of 1871 and then, in 1873, suffered with the rest of the country in a deep economic depression), but the monumentality believed appropriate for such an important institution appeared nonetheless.

The complex of buildings added over the next century of use is dominated by the oldest extant structure facing east across the lawns toward the highway. The composition is based on the balanced assemblage of structures tied together by long wings that is associated with Thomas Jefferson's Federal Style which provided the compositional form for some of the first major public buildings, for example the United States Capitol.

That conservative, institutional massing is also seen in the horizontal composition which is divided into nine sections, five of which project forward and rise higher, four of which serve as wings tying those major elements together. The low pitch of the roofs and the pedimental form of the gables also recall the Federal Style prototypes, as does the tri-partite vertical division of the elevations. It has a strong basement, here in stone across the entire distance, next a higher middle section, and finally a top section with the gables. In the three central pavilions with their additional story it includes the entire top story which is treated as an attic.

The design developed within that composition is not the refined, Federal Style, however, but Italianate, the reigning style of the period. It accounts for the tall, thin, round-headed or shouldered-arched windows, the simplified and oversized details in the pediments, the cupolas (both polygonal and square), and the verandas on the front of the central, dominant pavilion. The tier of verandas shows a particularly fine example of the adaptation of classical forms to the design demands of the Italianate style. The materials belong to both the Italianate style and to the regional building traits with various kinds of stone and brick used to reinforce the hierarchical arrangement of the forms in the overall composition.

This main structure originally housed all the activities of the asylum; note the grilled windows on the outer wings where the inmates resided. The numerous extensions on the west of the original building, and the other buildings farther to the west on the grounds, are later. They show the post World War I departure from the monumental design of the original structure to the later arrangement for such uses, the campus plan.

Drive south on Route 31, 2.1 miles to State Street.

WAYNE

WAYNE

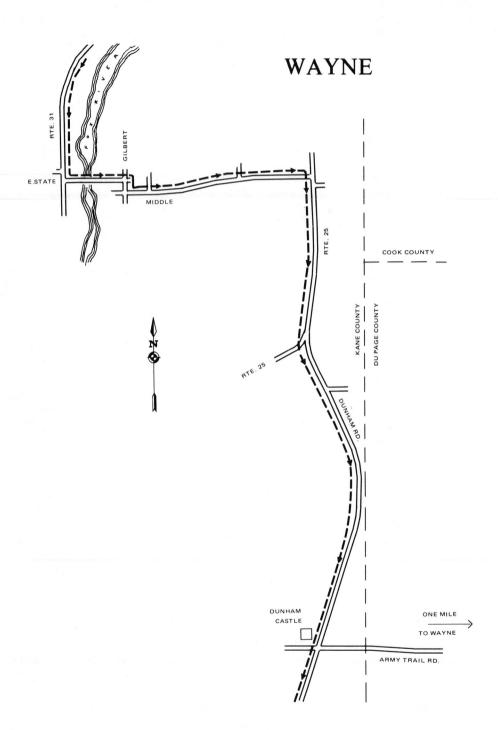

Turn left (east) 1/3 mile, across the river, to Gilbert Street. Turn right (south) 1 block. Turn left (east) on Middle Street 1.1 miles until it ends at Route 25. Turn right (south) on Route 25, 1 mile, then veer left onto Dunham Road. Drive 2.3 miles on Dunham Road. On the NW corner of Dunham and Army Trail roads is

DUNHAM CASTLE
Mark W. Dunham House, called Oaklawn—1880–83

This structure was built from 1880 to 1883 and designed by Mark W. Dunham with its construction supervised by Smith Hoag of Elgin. Commanding a prominent rise from the surrounding fields, the structure is surrounded by dense copse of woods and broad lawns setting off its august grandeur. The structure is sited so that a corner points down the hill at the access road and is prominently marked by a circular tower rising through the full two stories of the structure and well above the roofs to its own truncated, conical termination topped by an open lantern with a spire roof and a long rod reaching skyward. Facing to the east is the grand entrance porch with modeled columns supporting the porch roof. Projecting toward the south is a broad bow with a chimney rising through the roofs. The roof has several colors and textures and patterns of slate. The dormers, with their ogive arches and pointed windows, are topped by elaborate cast iron finials as is the tourelle on the southwest corner beginning above the windows of the second floor and extending above the roof. The window heads are incised with elaborate Eastlake patterning and assume a variety of shapes.

The only conspicuous disturbance to the character of the structure is the loss of the crowning element of the octagonal tower on the north side of the front facade, originally an element that would have competed successfully with the prominent circular one on the other side. The building is on the limestone base with cream colored bricks imported from Racine, Wisconsin to provide the coloristic character Mr. Dunham desired. The structure is listed on the National Register of Historic Places.

Mark Dunham was the proprietor of an extensive farm called the Oaklawn Farm at which place were raised percheron horses, the white draft horses that are seen in circuses but in earlier days were seen pulling heavy loads through the streets of Chicago. Many of the farm structures, including the barns and the operating headquarters, are maintained now as a part of the Wayne Dunham Woods Riding Club, which is diagonally across the street from the Dunham Castle. The fields on the other two corners of the intersection were originally used to raise the necessary grains fed to the horses and provided pasture land. The Oaklawn Farm (with the Dunham Castle) is listed on the National Register of Historic Places as an example of an early stock farm. The farm once embraced over 1,700 acres and now only a small section of it survives as open land. It remained in operation as late as 1929.

The farm was begun about 1835, but it was after 1865, when it became the property of Mark Wentworth Dunham, that it began to develop a significant place in history. Its original horses were imported from France (Perche district and hence the name) in 1868. Mark Dunham, enjoying the cooperation of about thirty area farmers, continued to perfect the breed and maintained close contact with officials in France. By 1883, he had imported over 1,300 mares and stallions. Dunham eventually issued a catalogue advertising the availability of his horses, one of which had illustrations by the famous artist Rosa Bonauer.*

Leaving Dunham Castle, drive south on Dunham Road 2.3 miles to Route 64.

* The town of Wayne, which is one mile east, is actually in DuPage County. If you want to go there now, drive east on Army Trail Road one mile. Cross the railroad tracks. *Stop*. (See pages 377-90 in DuPage County.)

ST. CHARLES

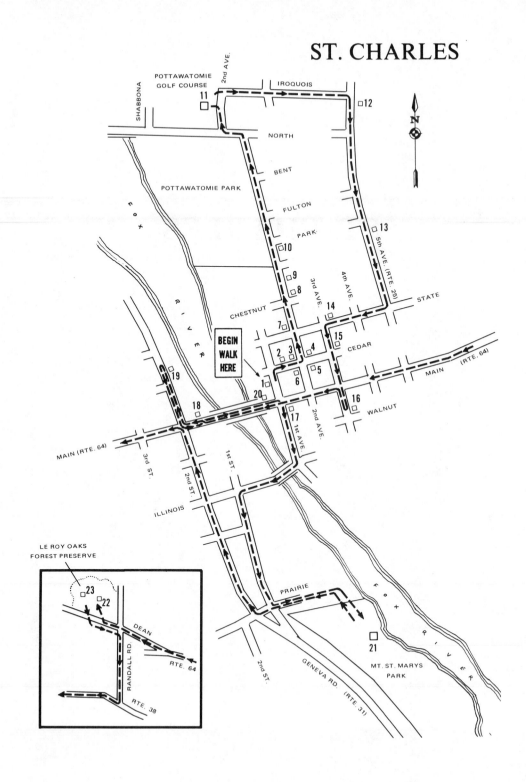

Turn right (west) on Route 64 (Main Street) 1½ miles to First Avenue. Turn right (north) and stop.

ST. CHARLES WALKING TOUR

Walk north on First Street. On your left, on the SW corner of First and Cedar avenues, is

1. 15 N. FIRST AVENUE
City Building—1892

This 1892 structure was built by F.W. Alexander to house the city offices and fire station. It presents the monumental forms characteristic of the Romanesque Revival, rendered in brick. Note the large opening on the south for the fire department and the same size arch, but smaller opening, for the entrance to the city building, as proudly labeled in the plaque. Above, in the central section, is a gable (with the date) which projects as a wall dormer from the hipped roof, which contains eyebrow dormers. Originally, the roof was slate.

Walk east on Cedar Avenue. The first house on your left is

2. 116 CEDAR AVENUE
Cedar House—1853

This 1853 building has the blocky configuration of the Greek Revival, but is topped by a paired bracketed, Italianate cornice. Similarly Italianate is the broad porch stretching across two sides of the building, ending at a one-story service wing projecting at the sides and back. The porch subsequently has been partially enclosed to adapt it to its present use as an art gallery.

Continue east. The next house on your left, on the NW corner of Cedar and Second avenues, is

3. 118 E. CEDAR AVENUE and
105 N. SECOND AVENUE
Wing Townhouse—1853

This structure, built in 1853, shows the survival of all the details and characteristics of the Federal style. Most notable is the segmental arched fanlight in the gable, complete with its small fan spokes. Also notable as belonging to

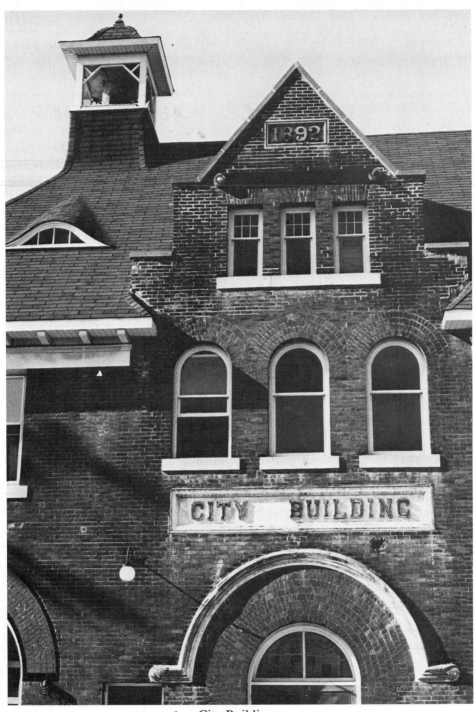

1. City Building
15 N. First Avenue

3. 118 E. Cedar Avenue and
   105 N. Second Avenue

that revival style is the more classically correct configuration of the porch piers and of the door frame. This structure also has had its broad, two-sided porch enclosed to adapt it to its present use as a book shop.

On the NE corner of Cedar and Second avenues is

4.   202 CEDAR AVENUE—1850

This 1850 structure is the oldest on this early intersection. Subsequent modifications have altered it substantially but the basic, simple, one-and-one-half-story structure with a low pitched roof is still visible.

On the SE corner of Cedar and Second avenues is

5.   201 CEDAR AVENUE—1853

This structure, also built in 1853, shows a very different way of achieving a pleasant sense of prominence (compared to St. Charles #2 and #3). Its basic massing is the same as the other two structures but its materials are very different. Here, riverstone, a very common material in this area, has been used. The building was then stuccoed, with small lines drafted into the wet stucco to make the wall look as if it were built of large blocks of ashlar. In this way the appearance is that of a very expensive form of construction, but it was achieved quite economically. The lintels over all of the openings and the sills of the windows are wood but those on the ground floor, except for the front entrance, have also been covered in stucco in order to obscure that humble origin. The riverstone is visible in the frame addition on the south of the structure, a one-story service wing built in the traditional clapboard materials of the period, but there is a classical column at the corner of the service porch, lending dignity even to that area. Except for the replacement of the original porch, minor alterations in the foundation, and the addition of a coat of paint, the structure survives in remarkable condition.

On the SW corner of Cedar and Second avenues is

6.   17 N. SECOND AVENUE—1870

This is a much more modest structure built in 1870. Frame and clapboard covered instead of brick with stone like the two houses across the street, it has higher proportions and cut-out porch brackets on the chamfered porch posts, which indicate a later date.

Walk north on Second Avenue 1 block. On the NW corner of Second and State avenues is

7.   116 STATE AVENUE—1840

This delightful structure was built in 1840 as a simple, steep, two-story, L-shaped, riverstone, Gothic Revival structure. Notice the scroll-cut barge-boards for the main gable, for the matching small gable under the front central ground floor window, and decorating the entrance to the porch on the west side of the south front. Notice also the summer kitchen, originally a free-standing board and batten structure with a pitched roof, on the west side of the building. Beyond it stands the original barn, also board and batten, probably from the same period.

Forty years later the dormers were added in the Queen Anne style. The largest one, nearest the corner, has the greatest variety of shingle patterns. The summer kitchen was subsequently connected to the main house by the brick service wing visible at the back.

Continue north 1 block. At the NE corner of Second and Chestnut avenues is

8.   304 SECOND AVENUE—c.1850

This structure, from the middle of the nineteenth century, is an excellent example of the Greek Revival rendered in a frame, clapboard-covered configuration. Especially notable are the generous proportions of the details. The cornice, both of the side walls and of the pediment, is quite broad and the front entrance has stout pilasters and a high entablature. The porch on the southwest corner has generous elements. Notice on the long sides of the building, small windows lighting the attic are cut into the cornice.

Continue north on Second Avenue. The next house on your right is

9.   312 N. SECOND AVENUE—1850

Compared to 304 Second Avenue (St. Charles #8), this 1850 brick structure has the same configuration, but less generous cornice elements. Its entranceway, however, is equally fine and grand. Notice the use of carefully cut riverstone to serve as sills and lintels of the windows, and that this structure lacks the small windows on the sides.

Continue north across the bridge. The first house on your right, on the SE corner of Second and Park avenues, is

10.   416 N. SECOND AVENUE—1875

The basic part of this structure dates from 1875 and was originally an Italianate design. Notice the projecting polygonal bays on either side, with paired brackets and oversized dentils, and the hooded segmental arches over the openings throughout the building. Notice that the foundations of the porch contain more precisely cut riverstone than is characteristic of nineteenth-century construction in this area. Added sometime in the present century, probably shortly before World War I, was the temple front with its extremely thin Tuscan columns and the false balustrade, simulating a second story porch, running across the wall.

Continue north on Second Avenue to North Avenue.

Notice the two-block stretch of fine houses overlooking the cemetery and park and enjoying the view of the river. These houses are representative of the various styles of the first thirty years of this century, ranging from late and rather formal Queen Anne, through Prairie, the Bungalow style, and the neo-Georgian style of the twenties.

As you enter Pottawatomie Park, on your left, is

11.   ABOUT 835 N. SECOND AVENUE—1936

The 1936 headquarters of the golf course is a long, spread-out structure, built in local riverstone, but suggests the expansive baronial structures of the Tudor style.

Leave Pottawatomie Park at the north end, walking east on Iroquois Avenue until it ends at Fifth Avenue. Turn right (south). The first house on your left (east side of the street) is

12.   820 N. FIFTH AVENUE—c.1905

Built on a stone foundation, this broad mansion on ample grounds is from the first decade of the twentieth century. It is a carefully done Dutch Colonial building with strict symmetry, broken only by the projecting porte-cochere on the north. It features an intersecting gambrel roof with a pent roof extending across the entire front. Tucked within the mass of the building (and seemingly protected by two thick, very stout, Doric columns) is the entrance, centered under the gable of the front gambrel. Interesting detail is provided by the fine glass work in the sidelights flanking the entrance. Also at the entrance are very broad, squat urns on the porch podia.

Continue south on Fifth Avenue. Just past Park Avenue, on your left, is

13. 404 N. FIFTH AVENUE—late 1880s

This farmhouse from the late 1880s has a very extensive series of projections from the basic, hipped roof, cubic block but has been marred by the recent siding.

Continue south 1 block to State Avenue. Turn right (west) 2 blocks. On the NE corner of Third and State avenues is

14. 304 STATE AVENUE—1853

This Federal style house was built in 1853. It has the lines of the Greek Revival and simple cornice brackets that later, in the Italianate, will be much more elaborate. Notice that the entrance to the house is set within a recess, protected by the high stone lintel, containing the usual transom and sidelights. Extending to the north is a service wing with a porch sustained by stout, square posts.

Walk south on Third Avenue 1 block. On the NE corner of Cedar and Third avenues is

15. 304 CEDAR AVENUE—1840

This 1840 brick building shows the fanlight, within the segmental arch in the pediment, characteristic of the Federal style. Peculiar, in this structure for this area, is the use of flat brick arches instead of riverstone lintels above the windows. Notice that the second floor windows are not arranged evenly; one is placed off-center. Also indicative of the early date and of the style is the division of the original windows into many small panes, here in a configuration of six over six. The rear porch projecting to the west is a slightly later addition. The second story of that porch and the front porch are much more recent additions.

Continue south 2 blocks on Third Avenue. On the NE corner of Third and Walnut avenues is

16.   18 S. THIRD AVENUE—1837

This frame, clapboard-covered, L-plan structure was built in 1837. The front porch was added later, but sympathetically. Notice how its heaviness and the polygonal bay disrupt the basic boxiness of the house. Indications of the very early date include: the somewhat crude construction of the foundation, a mixture of mortar and riverstone with a few bricks thrown in for good measure; and the lack of strict, linear, dimensional consistency in the clapboards; their waviness and slight irregularities indicate they were cut without benefit of powerful machine tools, either by hand or with water powered machinery.

Backtrack north on Third Avenue to Main Street. Turn left (west) 2 blocks. On the SE corner of First Avenue and Main Street is

17.   ARCADA THEATER
105 E. Main Street—1920s

This theater building, from the 1920s, is in the Moorish style similar to the facade of the Hotel Baker (St. Charles #18).

Continue west on Main Street, crossing the river. The first building on your right is

18.   HOTEL BAKER
100 W. Main Street—1927

Built in 1927, by the architectural firm of Wolf, Sexton, Harper and Trueax on the west bank of the Fox River, the Hotel Baker was meant to be a weekend and vacation resort center for the Chicago area, suitable for the new mobility that came with the automobile age. The depression frustrated the financial ambitions of its builder, Colonel Baker. The festive holiday-like character of the place is portrayed by the overt revivalism of the design, making it appear like Kubla Khan's pleasure dome, Xanadu, rendered in the Moorish style by extensive use of terra-cotta and an elaborate interior. Be sure to go inside. The sources can be detected in the ceiling beams, the stenciled wall patterns, and the Spanish balconies. The oval ballroom has a glass block floor with colored lights beneath, which were lit by drawing on the electricity originally generated by the building's own hydroelectric plant. The building is listed on the National Register of Historic Places.

Continue west to the corner. Turn right (north) on Second Street. Past the parking lot, on your right, is

19. 200 N. SECOND STREET
Hotel Baker Parking Garage—1929

Built as a garage for the hotel's guests (notice the ramp leading to the second story, projecting from the southeast corner), this elaborate brick and terra-cotta structure shows the glory of the automobile age. It was also designed by Wolf, Sexton, Harper, and Trueax.

Above the main doors, in the center of the building, are terra-cotta plaques depicting various means of locomotion including an Indian on a horse, a steam locomotive, an airplane, a covered wagon, and even a dinosaur; but above those is a great, 1920s, enclosed, touring car moving forward between crouched nymphs. This pattern is repeated in terra-cotta plaques above the four shop windows and the two entrances. The structural piers of the building are enclosed in terra-cotta and rise to basket-like finials, originally containing light bulbs which lit the way at night.

Backtrack south on Second Street to Main Street. Turn left (east) and cross the river. (Note the four cast metal foxes overlooking the Fox River.) On your left, on the NW corner of First Avenue and Main Street, is

20. ST. CHARLES HISTORICAL MUSEUM
St. Charles Municipal Center—1940–41

This stunning structure, built in 1940–41 and designed by R. Harold Zook, shows the use of the Art Moderne style for a civic structure. The basic configuration of a broad structure with a tower rising from it is honored here just as it was in the 1892 structure (St. Charles #1) northeast of it. The forms, however, are entirely modern, streamlined, and highly polished to represent machine-like finishes. Notice, inside the tower, the extensive terrazzo floors and the streamlined highly stylized stainless steel hardware and bannister rail rising through the circular staircase. Notice also the abstract Art Deco pattern in the colored glass in the tower, admitting light into the tower space to produce a dazzling brilliance. Monday-Friday: 1:00 p.m.-4:00 p.m.

This concludes the St. Charles Walking Tour.

Drive south on First Avenue 2 blocks to Illinois Avenue. Turn right (west) across the river. Turn left (south) on First Street 2 blocks to Prairie Street. Turn left (east), then right into Mount St. Mary Park.

21. WILLIAM BEITH HOUSE—1850

Built in 1850 by an early settler in St. Charles (who had learned stone masonry from his father in Scotland) this tiny, Greek Revival, two-story house with a single-story wing projecting to the right represents an early form of construction in the Fox River area. Its builder later became a prominent contractor in the region and constructed a number of important buildings. After he retired in 1865, he devoted himself to tiling fields to improve the agriculture of the region. At this writing, the house is to be moved to Mount St. Mary Park, to preserve it from demolition by the expansion of the industrial buildings that have grown up around its original site two blocks north. Here it will regain a semblance of the setting it originally had when it was one of the earliest structures surrounded by natural fields and looking out, untroubled, over the Fox River.

Leaving the park, drive west on Prairie Street to Second Street. Turn right (north) 4 blocks to Main Street (Route 64). Turn left (west) 6 blocks to Ninth Street. Turn right (north) 1 block on Ninth Street, which curves left (west) becoming Dean Street. Continue west 1.4 miles to the LeRoy Oaks Forest Preserve on your right. Turn right into the forest preserve to the first building on your right.

22. SHOLES SCHOOLHOUSE—c.1880-1890

This white, clapboard, one-room, late-nineteenth-century schoolhouse was moved to this location to preserve it. The cupola with the bell was added to this structure to convey an idea of an element commonly found on schoolhouses of this kind. It will be operated by Pioneer Sholes School Restoration Society with books, atlases, globes, and other objects commonly found in early schools to give today's pupils some understanding of the schoolroom of yesterday.

Continue north, curving to your left, then turn left. The building on your right is

23. DURANT HOUSE—1842

This simple, one-and-one-half-story, brick structure, built in 1842, shows the basic configuration of the Greek Revival rendered very simply with flat brick arches over the windows and a large lintel over the doorway. The foundation has been rebuilt. The front porch is not original and the building has been sandblasted. The addition on the back is not original, although such a structure is characteristic. Typical as a farmhouse, the building is entered on the National Register of Historic Places and is open to the public in the summer.

Continue south out of the forest preserve to Dean Street. Turn left (east) on Dean Street to Randall Road. Turn right (south) on Randall Road 1.2 miles to Route 38,

GENEVA

GENEVA

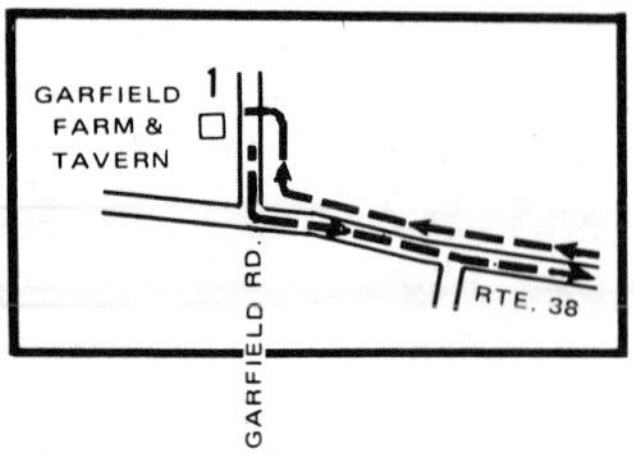

GARFIELD
FARM &
TAVERN   1

GARFIELD RD.

RTE. 38

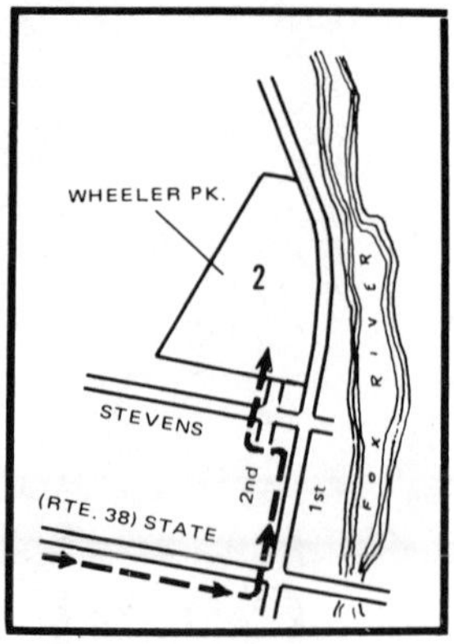

WHEELER PK.   2

STEVENS

2nd   1st

(RTE. 38) STATE

FOX RIVER

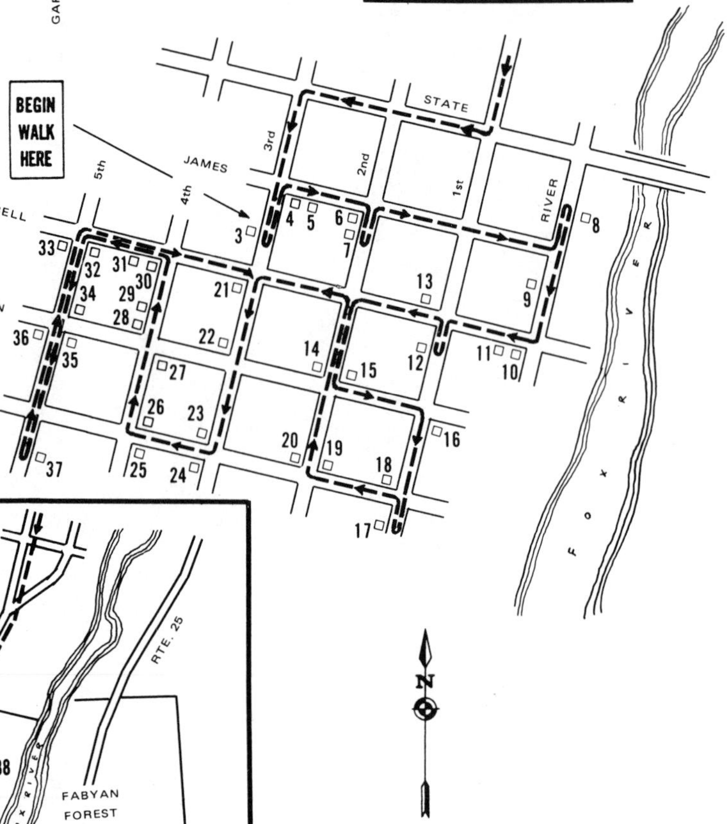

BEGIN
WALK
HERE

STATE

5th   JAMES   3rd   2nd   1st   RIVER

CAMPBELL   4th

3   4 5   6
7   8

33   31   30   13
32   29   21   9
34   28
FRANKLIN   22   14   11 12
36   35   15   10
FULTON   27   23   16
26
37   25   24   20 19   18

17

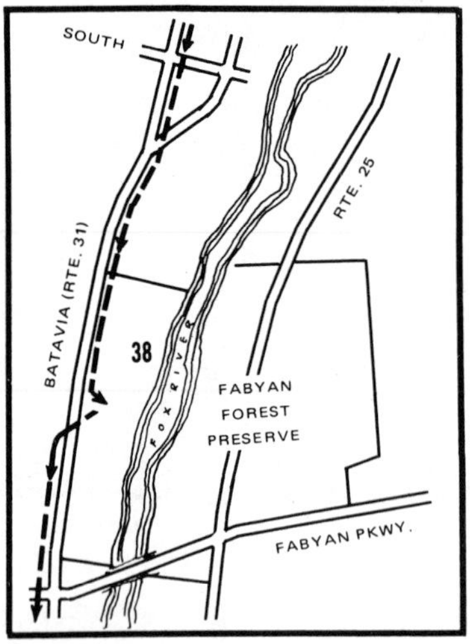

SOUTH

BATAVIA (RTE. 31)   RTE. 25

38   FABYAN
FOREST
PRESERVE

FOX RIVER

FABYAN PKWY.

N

FOX RIVER

Turn right (west) on Route 38, 3.3 miles to Garfield Road. (Garfield is presently an unmarked, paved, private road extending north from Route 38.) Turn right (north) on Garfield Road. Just past and across from the cemetery, on your left, is

1. GARFIELD FARM AND TAVERN—1842

This farm, originally founded in 1842, contains early structures from its first development. Dominant among them is the two-story Greek Revival farmhouse, which at times was also used as an inn. Projecting to the south is a one-and-one-half-story clapboard addition. Note, on the brick structure, the especially generous front entrance with transom and sidelights, and on the second story, the small panes of glass: twelve in the upper sash, eight in the lower. Notice also the wood sills and the flat brick arches for all of the openings. Directly west of the farmhouse is a small outhouse, a "four seater."

Several barns on the property are from a very early date; the one directly west of the house is from 1842; the one to the southwest is from 1849. Both provide particularly fine examples of braced frame construction, a type of construction eventually outmoded by the introduction of power-driven saws which produced accurately sized, dimension-cut lumber. These buildings use hand-hewn lumber and carefully made custom pieces fitted into one another and secured with pegs. These outbuildings are presently being restored.

The farm, which has several different fields, is displayed as a period working farm. It is listed on the National Register of Historic Places.

Turn right (south) on Garfield Road, returning to Route 38. Turn left (east) and continue 5.6 miles into Geneva. Turn left (north) on First Street (Route 31) 4 blocks to Stevens Street. Turn left (west). Then follow the signs to the Geneva Historical Society in Wheeler Park on your right.

2. GENEVA HISTORICAL SOCIETY

Most of the items in the museum once belonged to residents of Geneva. Of special interest are industrial collections, one of irons and the other of shoes, produced locally. Also of interest is the Swedish collection; Swedes were the second influx of immigrants to settle in Geneva, in the 1850s. The museum boasts an hundred-year-old organ, piano, and portable organ. Wednesdays, Saturdays, and Sundays: 2:00 p.m.-4:30 p.m.

1. Garfield Farm
and Tavern

Leaving Wheeler Park turn left (east) on Stevens Street, 2 blocks. Turn right (south) on First Street (Route 31) 4 blocks to State Street. Turn right (west) on State Street to Third Street, then turn left (south) on Third Street 1½ blocks to the Kane County Courthouse. Stop.

About a dozen antique stores and several dozen interesting shops greet the visitor. Pamphlets, which include orientation maps, are available in most shops.

GENEVA WALKING TOUR

On the west side of Third Street between James and Campbell streets is

3. KANE COUNTY COURTHOUSE—1891

This massive brick building, designed by Edbrooke and Burnham, was built in the Romanesque Revival style in 1891 on the site of the courthouse which burned the year before. The main entrance to the major block of the building is on the east, through great stone arches set into the lower level of the projecting front. On the end of each wing, a single arch serves as an entrance. At the center of the building, under the square dome covered in copper, is a dramatic balcony-lined space, richly decorated with a colorful stencil pattern and scenes representing the landscape of the area.

Cross to the east side of Third Street and walk north. On the SE corner of Third and James streets is

4. 101 S. THIRD STREET—c. 1870

This white clapboard building with a second story porch was built about 1870.

Walk east on James Street. The first house on your right is

5. 220 JAMES STREET—1861

This 1861, frame structure is covered in clapboards and has window surrounds that recall the Greek Revival. The cornice, with its simple brackets, indicates an enrichment of that form in the direction of the Italianate but with traces of the Gothic Revival. The front porch has Italianate brackets and a typical, Gothic Revival, arch rib spanning between the posts and from the posts to the wall.

Continue east on James Street. The next building on your right, on the SW corner of Second and James streets, is

6.   102 S. SECOND STREET
Unitarian Church—1843

This simple, straightforward, white structure was built in 1843 and gives clear evidence of the New England source of Geneva's first settlers. The main body of the pitched roof church is possibly built of riverstone and has a stucco coat with thin lines drafted into it to represent masonry. On the front facade, the cornice has been extended across the gable to represent a pediment and the wall has been moved forward on each outer end to represent pilasters. Pilasters are also seen equally spaced in the center of the facade; projecting from them is a small wooden entrance porch and above, in the center, is a stout flat-topped tower. The porch and tower are constructed from wood but the detail is in the classical style, based upon New England prototypes. Notice the generous size of the windows; the breadth and flat tops indicate that the classical, not the Gothic, is the ultimate source of this design.

Walk south on Second Street. The second house on your right is

7.   124 S. SECOND STREET—1857

This tall, two-story, brick structure was built in 1857 and displays characteristics of two normally incompatible styles: the classical and the Gothic. The classical is evident in the windows with their large stone lintels and thin sills, the proportions of which are those of the Greek Revival, at that time drawing to a close; the front entrance, with transom and sidelights, is also that style. The porch is a later addition. The Gothic is represented by the steep pitch of the roofs and by the equally steeply pitched gable, rising to face the street, in which is a circular window, lined with a complete circle of riverstone.

Backtrack north to James Street. Turn right (east) 2 blocks until it ends at River Street. Turn left (north). The brick, industrial-looking building on the east side of the street is

8. 21 S. RIVER LANE
Creamery Building—c.1874

This industrial building, along the river, with its neat rows of windows from the original construction, portrays quite clearly the surviving traces of the classical revival styles previously used for domestic architecture. This is the first structure we have encountered in Geneva built of riverstone; more will be seen later. This stone was easily extracted in bedding planes from the river. It could then be dried for use as seen here, or it could be trimmed into dressed stone as seen here in the lintels and sills of the building. The walls show a cruder use of the material than would be tolerated in residences.

The conservative character of the design is appropriate for the date, about 1874. The layer of brick across the top of the building is a more recent addition and probably is a substitution for an original pitched roof.

Stretching north along the river is a series of industrial buildings, most of which have been abandoned. Many have collapsed, and others have disappeared. This marked the original industrial area of this independent town far west of Chicago which rose with the Chicago and Northwestern Railroad in the middle of the nineteenth century.

Backtrack south on River Lane past James Street. The third house on your right (west side of the street), with a hand pump in front, is

9. 118 S. RIVER LANE—1843

This building, built in 1843, is an excellent example of the riverstone construction indigenous to the area. The basic configuration of this L-shaped, one-and-one-half-story structure is given by the Greek Revival. The use of riverstone produces a particularly interesting character for that style. Notice that the walls are made of rather crude, flat layers of the stone but that larger stones, more carefully worked, are placed at the corners and much larger neatly dressed stones are used for the sills and lintels. On the wing projecting to the south, in the second story, notice the small windows under the eaves, lighting the rooms tucked into the second story. The porch and carport are recent additions.

Continue south. On the SW corner of Campbell Street and River Lane is

9. 118 S. River Lane

10.   208 S. RIVER LANE—c.1859

Built about 1859, this white clapboard house has very low proportions and very simple forms.

Walk west on Campbell Street. The first house on your left is

11.   18 CAMPBELL STREET—1843

This 1843, frame, clapboard house is unusual because it faces the long, rather than the short, side of its Greek Revival mass toward the street. One-and-one-half-stories high, the second story windows are visible as openings in the cornice. The entrance is elaborate, with pilasters on the outer edges of the projecting structure, and the gable is treated as a full pediment with a very high entablature. There is no room for the transom but the sidelights, characteristic of the style, are present. The addition on the east is later, and the cupola base atop it is a quite unique feature.

Continue west on Campbell Street to the corner. Turn left (south) on First Street. The second house on your right (west side of the street) is

12.   208 S. FIRST STREET—1844

This 1844, stone, Greek Revival residence also turns its long side to the street (like Geneva #11). It lacks the small windows to light the second story. Especially nice is the extreme simplicity of the wooden cornice. The riverstone landscaped terrace and porches on the front are later additions.

Backtrack to Campbell Street. Turn left (west). The first house on your right is

13.   115 CAMPBELL STREET—1852

Now in adaptive reuse as the Geneva Clinic, this 1852 frame structure is an especially elegant example of the archaeologically oriented, Greek Revival style. Notice the care with which the top element on the entrance entablature, and those on the window frames, have been given a slight pitch to suggest the pitch of the pediment. Notice also the care with which the entablature at the top of the structure has been defined as the architrave, the frieze, and the cornice. In the pediment field, notice that the boards have been laid parallel to the raking cornice, and the care with which the lower element of the raking cornice exactly reproduces the cornice of the entablature. The frame wing on the south and the brick wing on the north are both later additions.

Continue west on Campbell Street to Second Street. Turn left (south). On the NW corner of Franklin and Second streets is

14.   228 S. SECOND STREET—1853

This white clapboard structure either grew to its present configuration through accretion or, in 1853 when it was begun, was built as an extremely irregular, but interesting, collection of then-current styles. The windows are grouped and topped by long cornices; the porches, each with a different kind of post, all represent different styles of carpentry from that found on the wing projecting to the south, where the window surrounds are much simpler. This structure is typical of domestic architecture, departing from strict norms when built by people of more humble means.

On the NE corner of Franklin and Second streets is

15.   227 S. SECOND STREET—1854

The original kernel of this clapboard cottage dates from 1854.

Turn left (east) on Franklin Street, 1 block. On the SE corner of Franklin and First streets is

16.   301 S. FIRST STREET—1855

This riverstone structure, built in 1855, has the characteristic features of the Greek Revival rendered in the Geneva vernacular. It stretches higher than others already seen by including nearly two full stories before the pitched roof is reached. Another interesting feature is a slight recess into which the doorway is placed. This doorway lacks sidelights, but has a transom.

Walk south on First Street 1 block. Just past Fulton Street, on your right, is

17.   416 S. FIRST STREET—1851 and 1865

The northern section of this stone house dates from 1851 and shows traces of its original Greek Revival massing. Notice on this section, the relative roughness with which the stone has been cut. In 1865 the octagonal addition to the south was added and a new roof was placed over the entire structure with the present Italianate cornice, featuring its heavy modeled brackets. Notice on the addition, the stone is cut much more carefully and the lintels are more carefully finished, with moldings, unlike the lintels on the older section. Also from this period is the one-story polygonal projection to the south which features rope moldings around the extensive openings; more a conservatory than a bay, this was an extremely popular feature during the latter part of the nineteenth century.

Backtrack to Fulton Street and turn left (west). The first house on your right is

18. 113 FULTON STREET—1855

The central section and the western projection of this frame, clapboard house date from 1855. Notice the relatively simple brackets under the eaves. Added at a later date, perhaps in the 1870s, was the wing to the east, ending in a projecting polygonal bay rising through both stories. It has more elaborate brackets under its eaves. Also dating from this time are the two porches, one on the east end the other on the west, providing verandas that look out over the grounds. The two periods make a very nice accommodation to one another.

Continue west. On the NE corner of Fulton and Second streets is

19. 327 S. SECOND STREET—1870s

This structure is not characteristic of Geneva, but is like many found in other parts of the suburban area. It is a cubic block, topped by a hipped roof with a polygonal projection on the south side and a stout square porch on the west. The windows on both stories are topped by low pediments with cut-out forms suggestive of a foliate pattern. The paired brackets under the eaves and the general mass of the house suggest a date between 1870 and 1880. The two-story projection, toward the back on the north side, and the shed roof extension beyond are recent construction.

On the NW corner of Fulton and Second streets is

20. 328 S. SECOND STREET—1876

This white clapboard frame structure from 1876 shares the general configuration of the one at 327 S. Second Street (Geneva #19), but is more elaborate. Clear indications of the builder's knowledge of the Eastern Stick style are evident in the treatment of the sides, the gable of the dormer, and of the area between the first and second floor, both of which have diagonal siding; the belt course also has rosettes nailed into it. Also characteristic of the Stick style is the elaborate porch with scroll-cut brackets and diagonal struts, and cut-out knees arranged between the tops of the posts and the shed roof. The bib of the porch extends beyond the roof to form a large veranda, lined by turned balusters. The one-story projection on the north, with the cornice matching the main block, is original but the slightly lower insertion in the reentrant angle is a later addition.

Walk north on Second Street, 2 blocks to Campbell Street. Turn left (west) 1 block. On the SW corner of Campbell and Third streets is

21.   200 S. THIRD STREET—1850 and 1870
This clapboard, frame, farm house was built in 1850 with an 1870 addition. The extensive alterations on the east side, which include rebuilding the windows and enclosing the porch to turn it into a shop, have detracted from its quality.

Walk south on Third Street. On the NW corner of Franklin and Third streets is

22.   220 S. THIRD STREET—1850
The finest early house in Geneva, this structure is one of the premier Greek Revival residences in the Chicago area. It was built in 1850. The original, major block comes very close to imitating a Greek temple, adapted to use as a residence. The four great Doric columns, properly lacking their bases, are careful copies of the Doric order as used at the Parthenon in Athens. The entablature above, however, lacks the triglyphs and metopes that are canonic in the order. Attached to the front wall are large pilasters, reflecting the columns in front, but lacking the flutes; between them are the windows with proper shoulder blocks on the upper side and sills extending below the outer frame, as is appropriate in the Greek Revival. On the north side of the ground floor is the recessed entrance with smaller piers flanking it and holding a lintel which is carved to suggest the pediment above.
   At a slightly later date a wing was extended to the west, terminating in what originally was an open porch formed by columns like those on the

22. 220 S. Third Street

front. Notice that the capitals are just slightly different from those on the front, and the windows on this wing (on the second story) are different from those on the main section of the structure, indicating that a different carpenter made them.

In adapting this structure to its present use as shops, certain changes were made. For example: the addition of the small covered columnar porch on the wing, and the enclosing of the porch at the north end of the wing. The balustrade on the second story of the porch is probably original.

Continue south 1 block. On the NW corner of Fulton and Third streets is

23. 328 S. THIRD STREET—1869

This tall, frame structure on an L-plan is a perfect antithesis to the Greek Revival grandeur of the structure at 220 S. Third Street (Geneva #22). This is a fine example of the Gothic Revival and was built in 1869. Notice the steep pitch of the roof and the division of the building into tall, thin sections. The front gable, the gable of the wall dormer, and the north gable have bargeboards with various cut-out, Gothic forms and pendants at their peaks. The porch is sustained by octagonal columns that swell into capitals supporting the porch roof which itself is sustained by a Gothic cut-out pattern simulating a low, pointed arch. Behind it is the double-door of the entrance, topped by a transom with an arch that approaches the ogive form. Projecting from the front wing, on the ground floor, is a polygonal bay with carpentry work tracing another Gothic pattern. Viewing the building from the southeast corner, one sees that the south facade is a repetition of the east facade, but the porch is lacking; the oblique angle helps to produce the vivid impression of the asymmetrical breaking up of forms, characteristic of the Gothic Revival. Also notice, in the gable, the triangular window with its cut-out trifoil.

On the SW corner of Fulton and Third streets is

24. 404 S. THIRD STREET—1862

The original block of this 1862 Italianate structure has a hipped roof rising to a widow's walk and a front porch, both displaying the robust forms of the Italianate. It has expanded considerably, more recently.

Walk west on Fulton 1 block. On the SE corner of Fulton and Fourth streets is

23.   328 S. Third Street

25.   403 S. FOURTH STREET—1851

Built in 1851, this clapboard house in the Federal style was later moved to
this location. Although a frame structure, it has the full-bodied pretension
usually found in masonry structures. Notice that the cornice extends across
the front to define a complete pediment above the two-story block. The
small windows in the pediment indicate the attic was used. Also part of this
greater pretense are the wings on either side, which invest the house with the
characteristics of the formal Palladian villa, which provided an important
source for Federal architects.

On the NE corner of Fulton and Fourth streets is

26.   327 S. Fourth Street—1854

This 1854 clapboard house is an unpretentious example of the Greek Revival.

Walk north on Fourth Street. On the SE corner of Franklin and Fourth streets is

27.   St. Mark's Episcopal Church—1868

This tall but thin riverstone church, built in 1868, shows very clear allegiance to the Gothic Revival style. Carefully dressed riverstone is used to define the pointed arches and the canted stringcourses above the first and second stories of the tower. The third story of the tower is topped by a cross-gable roof. The openings in the tower become smaller with each story. The middle story is closed and has Gothic moldings in its woodwork, to define a triple lancet blind window.

On the NW corner of Franklin and Fourth streets is

28.   401 Franklin Street—1854

This 1854 house later received a wing stretching to the west and at that time, most likely, it was shingled. From a date close to its original construction comes the iron fence in front, an especially fine example of something too often lost.

Continue north on Fourth Street. The first house on your left is

29.   218 S. Fourth Street—1870

Built in 1870, and moved to this location in 1890, this small frame structure covered in clapboards presents its broad side to the street and quite unusually has only two windows on the second floor, placed near the outer walls. The porch and the corbels on top are quite large and robust and portray the vigorous style of the early Italianate period.

Continue north on Fourth Street. On the SW corner of Campbell and Fourth streets is

30. 200 S. FOURTH STREET—1857

This stone house, begun in 1857, has an unusual cross-shaped plan with two-story wings projecting north, east, south, and west. The areas flanking the central projection on the east side form porches with very early carpentry work sustaining the roof. The second story of that projection is frame and clapboard as is the complementary projection to the west.

Walk west on Campbell Street. The next building on your left is

31. 410 CAMPBELL STREET
Disciples of Christ Meeting House—1857

Unmarked, mid-block on the south side of the street, the northern-most section of this one-story riverstone structure, with a low slope to its pitched roof, was built in 1857. It shows an extremely simplified version of the then-current Greek Revival style.

Continue west to the corner. On the SE corner of Campbell and Fifth streets is

32. 207 S. FIFTH STREET—1850s

The stone section of this house is a very early riverstone structure which dates from the early 1850s. Notice the extremely thin cornice and eaves, the tall narrow windows, and the flat stone arches above the openings which betray the early date.

On the SW corner of Campbell and Fifth streets is

33. 212 S. FIFTH STREET—1853 and 1890

The original construction of this house occurred in 1853 and produced the two windows on the ground floor and the two on the second floor on the north side of the front facade. Their small size and their placement indicates the Greek Revival origin of that part of the structure. A new third floor and roof, a wing stretching to the south, and the front porch were added in 1890 in the Queen Anne style. The later date of this construction is indicated by the larger size of the windows and by the elaborate board textures in the gable with scalloped shingles and patterned boards below the attic windows. The bosses and grooves in the gable rafters, and the spindles and turned posts of the porch, also are part of that style. On the north facade, the smaller windows belong to the earlier construction but the polygonal bay window belongs to the later period.

Walk south on Fifth street. On the NE corner of Franklin and Fifth streets is

34.   227 S. FIFTH STREET—c.1848

It is possible that the stucco on this structure dates from the original design and construction, about 1848. It is a blocky, hipped-roofed structure. Its squarish windows are set well in from the corners, a characteristic of the Federal style, as is the simple porch sustained by piers with pilasters at the walls and a simple, flat entablature and roof. The extension to the north is a recent addition.

Continue south. The second house on your left is

35.   315 S. FIFTH STREET—1863

The back of this structure, with a two-story wing, fronts the street. The original structure, built in 1863, contains details characteristic of the early Italianate, but the massing preserves the blocky shapes of the Greek Revival, except the roof is hipped, again characteristic of the Italianate.

Across the street, on the west side, is

36.   316 S. FIFTH STREET—1906

Frank Lloyd Wright designed this house in the Prairie style in 1906. The broad, low, hipped roof with very thin eaves is sustained at the corners by strong piers, which have boards on their stucco surfaces, wrapped around the corner to define their solidity. The second-story casement windows are tucked under the stuccoed soffits of the eaves and are aligned with the ground floor windows by boards. The strong horizontality characteristic of the Prairie School is achieved by having a series of horizontals in the design, produced by the thin line of the eaves, the thicker lines of the boards set in the stucco, and the strips of windows. The entrance porch and the pargola at the front wall have been extensively reworked.

Continue south on Fifth Street. In the next block, on your left, set back from the street, is

37. 415 S. FIFTH STREET—1857

This 1857 building is a stunning example of the local riverstone used to produce a structure incorporating stylistic features from several periods. The main mass of the house indicates the Italianate with its two-story blocky form, hipped roof, the cupola with segmental windows, broad pilasters, and double-scrolled brackets supporting the hipped roof. The Greek Revival remains evident in the shape and construction of the windows. They are square and have heavy, smooth-faced, riverstone lintels. Within the openings, however, are frames derived from the Gothic Revival. Note that the tops of the windows on the second floor have hood moldings which drop down on either side to bulbous finials.

The ground floor shows some reconstruction. The window on the north side of the door has many small panes, characteristic of the Queen Anne from the 1890s, as does the broad diamond-paned window opening to the south of the doorway. The doorway, and the porch with its single-bottled balusters and its square posts topped by cannon balls, suggest the neo-Classical styles of the turn of the century. The variety of stylistic features provides an extremely attractive and harmonious ensemble. The two-story, thin clapboard addition to the north, and the garage beyond, are from fairly recent times.

Backtrack north on Fifth Street 2 blocks. Turn right (east) on Campbell Street 2 blocks.

This concludes the Geneva Walking Tour.

Drive south on Third Street, which merges into Route 31 (Batavia Avenue) in 6 blocks. 5 blocks further south on your left (east side of the street) is the Fabyan Forest Preserve. Turn left into the second driveway on your left.

38. THE FABYAN FOREST PRESERVE
1923 Batavia Avenue—1905

This complex began in 1905 as the Riverbank Estate of a curious couple, Colonel George and Nelle Fabyan, and was maintained as their home until their deaths, his in 1939. Now 245 acres, at its peak it had about 600 acres and a variety of activities. There were extensive gardens, including a carefully tended Japanese garden, and greenhouses to provide flowers for the home and for sale in Chicago. In several areas there were pens and ponds for a variety of wild and semi-wild animals ranging from alligators and monkeys to bears and wolves. The Colonel (the title was honorifically conferred by the Governor of Illinois) also kept 500 pigeons and herds of prize cattle, raised chickens to provide eggs for the market and sheep to mow the grass.

The estate housed from 60 to 100 people during its heyday. Three of its many structures survive and provide special interest. One is on the island, connected by a bridge that Fabyan built with special permission of the federal government which had to protect the navigation requirements of the Fox River. It is a wooden windmill originally built sometime in the middle of the nineteenth century and moved to this site in 1914–1915. Its sail power drove wooden gears, axles, and a train of equipment to mill a variety of grains reportedly because the Colonel liked fresh bread from specially milled flours. This structure is listed on the National Register of Historic Places.

Another structure is outside the present forest preserve on a section of the original estate on the west side of Route 31. It is the Riverbank Laboratories which include the Sabine Accoustical Laboratory, now operated by the Illinois Institute of Technology Research Institute. From it has come material and ideas used in such structures as the House and Senate Chambers in the U.S. Capitol and in Radio City Music Hall in Rockefeller Center, New York City. The structure grew from 1918 onward and housed the Colonel's personnel who carried on research in three of his favorite topics. One was to prove that Francis Bacon was the author of the works of Shakespeare. Another was the development of an anti-gravitational device that allowed levitation by the vibration of violin-like strings. The third was in cryptography. This work bore important fruits, for this was the only location where the government could find specialists in coding and decoding their own and enemies' messages when needed on an emergency basis at the beginning of both world wars.

The third structure is Fabyan's house. Called the Villa, Frank Lloyd Wright made sketches for it in 1906, but after a falling out, Fabyan completed it to his own design. Note the wide eaves and the Prairie style surfaces of stucco and boards. The relatively small structure contains a collection of materials Fabyan received as gifts from his many visitors from throughout the world; Fabyan seldom traveled but enjoyed having the exotic brought to him. Other items perhaps originated from his hobby. To pursue it he had an entire structure built, complete with a railroad siding. He bought unclaimed railroad freight merely to discover what was in the packages.

BATAVIA

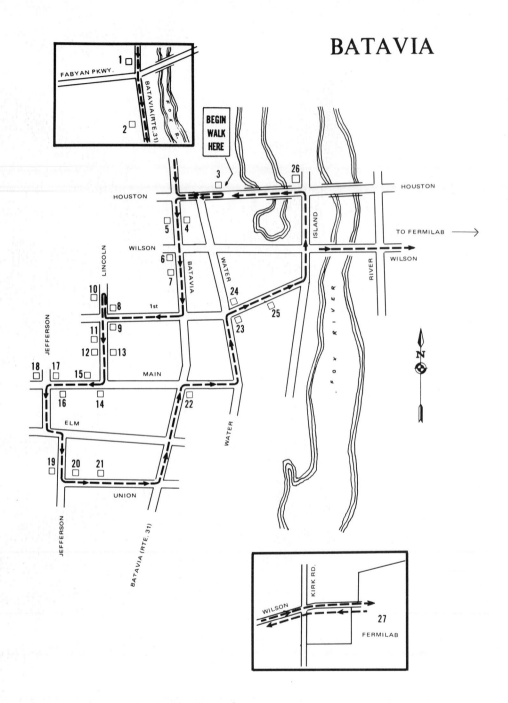

BATAVIA

FABYAN PKWY.

BATAVIA (RTE. 31)

FOX R.

1

2

BEGIN
WALK
HERE

3

26

HOUSTON

HOUSTON

TO FERMILAB →

LINCOLN

WILSON

5 4

6

7

BATAVIA

WATER

ISLAND

FOX RIVER

RIVER

WILSON

10

8

1st

24

25

23

JEFFERSON

11

9

12 13

18 17 15

MAIN

16 14

22

WATER

ELM

FOX RIVER

19 20 21

UNION

JEFFERSON

BATAVIA (RTE. 31)

N

WILSON

KIRK RD.

27

FERMILAB

Leaving Fabyan Forest Preserve turn left (south) on Route 31. Turn right (west) into the first driveway.

1. CAMPANA FACTORY
Batavia Avenue—1936-37

This important early monument of the International Style, built in 1936-37 and designed by the Chicago firm of Childs and Smith with Frank Chase, shows the use of the European-developed style in a factory building, built to exploit the success of a line of fine cosmetics developed during the Depression, and hence is one of the few major structures built during that very inactive decade. The International Style stressed the machine-made appearance of buildings, as is evident here with glass block used as windows in long strips on the first and second floors and a slightly smaller strip on the third floor, separated by lines of yellow and green glazed brick. The tower in the center provides a strong vertical accent. It offsets the horizontality of the lower section, and rises to the brand name "Campana" repeated at the top of the tower, as it is above the stainless steel entrance set into a black polished marble which contrasts strongly with the shiny stainless steel. The one-story wings on either end, added in the late 1940s, are done in careful harmony with the original design. It is among the first air conditioned industrial buildings and so could be designed with windows that do not open. The basis of the prosperity of the company was Campana Italian Balm, a hand lotion that was promoted extensively through radio advertising, one of the early uses of that medium. The company wanted an "ultra-modern building" that would reveal the company's progressive character. The structure is listed on the National Register of Historic Places.

Leaving Campana Corporation, turn right (south) on Batavia Avenue (Route 31) .3 miles. On your right is

2. 637 N. BATAVIA AVENUE—1906

This Prairie style house, designed by Frank Lloyd Wright in 1906, is frame and stucco and has massive chimneys. It shows the characteristics of the style almost fully developed. The horizontals, extending out to the podia at either end of the front porch, dominate the broad landscape. Beyond the front veranda rises the house, with a low pitched roof and casement windows tucked into the thin eaves. The sill line of the second story windows is carried as a belt course around the entire house. The windows on the ground floor are wrapped around or tucked into corners, and are again defined by broad horizontals. To the south is an open porch, again covered by a low pitched roof with broad dominant overhangs.

BATAVIA WALKING TOUR

Continue south on Batavia Avenue .6 miles. Turn left (east) on Houston Street. Just east of Water Street, on your left, is

3. BATAVIA DEPOT MUSEUM
Chicago, Burlington and Quincy Railroad Depot
155 Houston Street—1854

This former railroad station, built in 1854, portrays the oversized characteristics of the Greek Revival. This was considered appropriate for a public structure (such as a railroad depot) in a small community (such as Batavia) at that time. On both the river and the track side, the facade breaks into a very steep gable. The pitched roof of the structure is supported by heavy molded brackets. The windows, pointed on the second floor and flat on the ground floor, are covered by heavy wood molding. The sides are sheathed in board and battens which rise to a top board, cut to represent pointed arch terminations for the battens. On the south end of the building, between the first and second stories in the section where the battens are discontinuous, the building originally carried a sign with the station's name. The one-story extension on the north end dates from 1868.

In 1973 it was moved to its present location to preserve it from destruction. It was the first depot of its type to be built by the railroad and therefore is a little more carefully detailed than the later ones. In the basement is a warming house for ice skaters on the lagoon. It is listed on the National Register of Historic Places.

Walk west on Houston Street 1 block to Batavia Avenue. Turn left (south). The church on your left (east side of the street) is

4. 8 N. BATAVIA AVENUE
Methodist Church—1887

This rugged Romanesque church was designed in 1887 by Solon S. Beman, the designer of Pullman. It displays in full force the vigor of Romanesque masonry, with rubblestone walls using large stones laid in a seemingly random manner, but with larger stones at the corners to give additional strength. Openings are trimmed with oversized stone of a lighter color.

4. Methodist Church
8 N. Batavia Avenue

The mammoth arch for the entrance is reflected in nearly equal size arches for the tiny windows in the next level of the tower and on the far flanks on either side. Near the top of the tower is a Palladian window with its large arch supported by columns that appear too small, introducing a sense of whimsy within this otherwise grave structure. The pyramidal roof of the tower, like the planes of the hipped roofs farthest back, curve over the arches as if the roof has been pushed down on the structure. The gravity of the exterior is also relieved by the tiny diamond panes of the windows on the curved sections next to the towers, the paneling on the front doors, and the stained glass in the sidelights and transom. The interior is beautifully paneled with wood and contains excellent examples of Romanesque Revival carpentry.

Directly across the street, on the west side of Batavia Avenue, is

5.   11 N. Batavia Avenue
Batavia Library—1878

This delightful structure was built as a residence in 1878, of cream colored brick and limestone. It is a very early example of the Queen Anne style, which is evident in its variety of shapes and materials, and broken silhouette. It is still close to the Gothic Revival (seen by the thin brackets) and the Stick style (seen in the carpentry work under the pointed polygonal roof of the eastern projection). The interior is especially delightful with rich ornamentation in wood, fine hardware, and remaining original glass.

Continue south. On the SW corner of Batavia Avenue and Wilson Street is

6.   9 S. Batavia Avenue—1886

This 1886 structure shows the Queen Anne style in full flower. It is a wooden structure, giving an opportunity to show off the variety of textures, projections, and patterns that make the style extraordinary. The spindles and turned posts of the porch are complemented by the tricky carpentry of the porch balustrade, which survives from the original construction. The gable on the north has undercut soffits and exuberant detailing. A bell dome covering the polygonal tower on the opposite side introduces variety and the style's required asymmetry. Note the finial surviving atop the bell dome.

Continue south. The next building on your right is

7. 21 S. Batavia Avenue
The Congregational Church—1856

This 1856 structure is based on New England prototypes, with a broad pitched roof covering a classically detailed sanctuary, and a tall spire rising from the center in the front. The classical detailing has been considerably reduced so the expected capitals and bases for the pilasters are lacking, and the structure as a whole lacks adornment in the stone. This type of stone, which would not be suitable for fine carving, is laid in very precisely cut ashlar blocks with neatly finished arches, sills, and entablatures.

The carpentry work within the openings is characteristic of the mid-nineteenth century and has the heavy, fully round moldings often associated with the Italianate style. It is especially well done in the trifoil openings, in the arched area above the central doorway, in the double arched window above the doorway, and in the quatrefoil near the top of the masonry section of the tower. The section above the masonry on the tower is a recent sheet metal replacement of an earlier wooden structure, although the character of this design is excellently adapted to the rest of the building.

Continue south to the corner. Turn right (west) on First Street. On the NE corner of First and Lincoln streets is

8. 355 First Street—1852

This rugged 1852 building originally housed the Methodist church. The porch is a recent addition. Within it is the name of the church and the date. The transom and sidelights reproduce the original configuration of the entrance as do the stout piers and lintel framing the doorway. That entrance is appropriate to the rugged walls which form the basement of the structure. On top are the broad pilasters that reproduce the character of a Doric temple. The pilasters rise to extremely simple, block capitals which sustain the broad, unadorned wood forming the canonic architrave, frieze, and cornice of the Doric order. The raking cornice of the pitched roof defines the pediment of this temple of worship. Between 1886 and 1976, the building was used as a schoolhouse by the Batavia school system. It is now adapted to yet another use, housing professional offices.

On the SE corner of First and Lincoln streets is

9. 356 First Street—c. 1850

Built about 1850, this extremely simple, frame, clapboard-covered house

8. 355 First Street

has the general lines of the Greek Revival, rendered with great simplicity. Later additions have enlarged it with the large dormer on the east side and the one-story extension to the south.

Walk north on Lincoln Street. The first house on your left is

10. 33 S. LINCOLN STREET—1850

This 1850 Greek Revival house has a fine, formal simplicity which arises from its length; it is a bit longer than is usual for its type. This allows for the use of other variations on the standard design: a pair of windows in each floor, one pair on each side of the entrance; a broad flank between those windows on the second floor; the central window; and, near the drain pipe, the greater than usual height of the entablature, which still maintains the canonic architrave, frieze, and cornice of the Greek Revival. That style also provided the corner pilasters. Disturbances to the original structure are seen in the curved pediment above the front door, the siding on the ground floor, and in the window frames, which probably originally would have been like those on the second story.

Backtrack south on Lincoln Street, past First Street. Then, the second house on your right is

11.   111 S. LINCOLN STREET—c. 1850
Although the addition of metal siding has obscured the authentic character of this structure, which dates from about 1850, it is still worth noting because the severe cubic block portrays an aspect of the Greek Revival from the early part of the nineteenth century, an aspect which is reinforced by severity of the window surrounds and the door details. The door has stout pilasters supporting a broad entablature that swells to sustain a cornice, peaked slightly to suggest a pediment.

Continue south. The second house on your right is

12.   125 S. LINCOLN STREET—1852
This 1852 house, in the Greek Revival style, shows the result of trying to put more space inside the formal envelope of the style than the style was meant to allow, but it also shows the skill with which the disruption of the requirements of the style were handled in compensation. The central section describes the temple with a pilaster on either side rising to a pediment which is indicated only by the returns of the entablature above corner pilasters. On the south side a one-story wing projects, with stout piers with chamfered corners, to act as an entrance. A full two-story addition has been built on the north side, but to allow sufficient room on the second floor, large wall dormers were built, intersecting the generous cornice and topped by arches for the windows, which wear small pitched roofs as if they were hats. The result is a succession of broad and generous classical elements outlining a constricted, tightly confined design.

Directly across, on the east side of Lincoln Street, is

13.   359 W. Main Street
stable—1850s

This utilitarian structure is an excellent example of the handling of the local stone. The side walls are the rugged stone easily extracted from the river, but in front the stone is more carefully dressed. The openings are covered by lintels, topped by thin curved moldings. The central door has a huge lintel, probably brought to this site and put in its place with great difficulty. The structure probably dates from the middle of the nineteenth century. (Notice, at this writing, the roof beam projects to accommodate the fork and the tackle for hoisting the hay into the upper story.)

Continue south to the corner. On the south side of Main Street at Lincoln Street is

14.   360 Main Street—1855

This structure shows the waning of the Greek Revival and the beginning of the Italianate growing out of the Gothic Revival. The Greek Revival is very clear in the simple massing and the clapboard sheathing, and especially in the window frames where the upper member is treated as if it were a Greek lintel. The approaching Italianate is clear in the very simple, scroll-cut, paired brackets and the hipped roof. The close alliance between the Italianate and the Gothic Revival at the middle of the nineteenth century (the house was built in 1855) is evident in the thin members bunched to form porch posts and the arches traced by curved strips between those posts. The amalgam of those sources makes for an especially delightful structure.

Walk west on Main Street. The second house on your right is

15.   415 Main Street—1860

Built in 1860, this house has Italianate features added to a basically Gothic Revival mass, seen in the height and the prominence of the pitched roof. The Italianate features dominate, however, as seen in the scroll-cut paired brackets (notice how they have been cut to correspond to the roof pitch), the segmental arches over the windows, and the heavy forms on the double door entrance. Notice that the door is larger than the windows, but that is compensated by the small ventilating window set in the gable. Beyond the formal front facade are the informal aspects characteristic of the Italianate, a polygonal bay on the east side and two wings, each with its own gable on the west.

Cross to the south side of the street and continue west. The third house on your left is

16.   432 MAIN STREET—c.1850

This Greek Revival house was built about 1850. Although the front porch may not be original, it still reproduces an original design which lends the building a formality befitting its broad proportions.

On the NE corner of Main and Jefferson streets is

17.   433 W. MAIN STREET—1850

This 1850, L-shaped, Greek Revival house shows a generosity of form in all of its elements, reflecting early prosperity. The reverse-curve brackets under the eaves and across the gables are matched by smaller brackets supporting the projecting entablatures and cornices on both the first and second floors. The entrance, with its pediment projecting beyond the face of the building and supported by fluted piers, makes an especially grand entrance to an otherwise small structure. The one-story projection to the east, and the brick and wrought iron front porch, are very recent.

On the NW corner of Main and Jefferson streets is

18.   505 MAIN STREET—1858

This 1858 house is in the Swiss style. The second story balcony, which rises into the steep gable, is a special delight. It has a peacock feather motif described by scroll-cut boards nailed to a backing, supported by long tubes produced on a lathe. Below them, at the corners, are trifoils set in circles to fill another area of a gable. On the left side, the area under the extension of the roof contains incised ornaments suggesting tall thistle-like plants. On the east side of the building a brick porch has been added, probably about 1910, with the clear indication of knowledge of the way brick was used by Prairie School architects.

Walk south on Jefferson Street. Jog left, then right, continuing south on Jefferson Street. The second building on your right is

19.   333 S. JEFFERSON STREET
Batavia Institute, Bellevue Mental Hospital—1853
This 1853 Italianate structure is on the National Register of Historic Places

19. Batavia Institute,
Bellevue Mental Hospital
333 S. Jefferson Street

in part because at one time, following the assassination of her husband, it was the residence of Mary Todd Lincoln. The structure commands the highest piece of ground in the area and was built to present an image of utter formality. The central section breaks forward from the main block and has prominent quoins on each side; it rises into a pediment above a high entablature; below, on the third floor, is a pair of arched windows; and below that, a triplet of windows, the sidelights thinner than on the central one. On the ground floor an ornamental porch stretches forward beyond the steps as a protective cover for arriving carriages. The original building projects to large pediments on each end and is built of carefully dressed ashlar stone quarried at the Fox River. The projecting flat front bays, on the first two stories on each side of the central tower, are probably original.

Projecting on each end are two-story wings with Mansard roofs containing a third story, built of a cruder masonry than the original structure and probably added within fifteen years of the original construction. The additions, by their strict symmetry and by being set back from the main face and kept well below the original construction, help to reinforce the symmetry that lent the original structure its imposing monumentality.

Turn left (east) on Union Street. The first house on your left is

20.   419 UNION STREET—1863

Built in 1863, this house shows the picturesque potentials of the informal compositions of the Italianate style. Notice that on the right, the building erupts through both stories to a broad bay window and opposite it, projecting from the roof, is a cupola. The Italianate style is also visible in the great height of the windows, in the prominent quoins on the corners, and the heavy brackets under the eaves of the hipped roof. Additional character is added by the multiple curved brackets for the cupola and by contrasting the heavy stone quoins of the corners with a smoother stucco. The west wall still shows original grooves placed in the wet stucco to suggest the character of fine cut ashlar. This indicates that the walls under the stucco are a very crude and coarse riverstone. It would not have been out of keeping with this style to have tinted each of the sections in the stucco with a slightly different tint of gray, in order to suggest a more colorful and picturesque pattern for the masonry. The character of this structure is disrupted somewhat by the New Orleans style porch and by obscuring the broad transomed window at the front of the bay with a window containing much smaller panes.

Continue east on Union Street. The second house on your left is

21.   345 Union Street—1870

This 1870 building shows the Italianate style used in a formal composition
with a central projection containing the entrance and a large window on the
second floor. The other windows have winged segmental pediments at the
tops of their ample window frames. The whole building is topped by a
French Mansard roof ending, as it should, in a prominent curb. The top of
the tower still retains its cast iron cresting. Note the delicacy of the blacksmith's art exhibited on the corners of that cresting. The wrought iron porch
posts are new.

*Continue east on Union Street to the corner. Turn left (north) on Batavia
Avenue. On the SE corner of Main Street and Batavia Avenue is*

22.   222 Main Street
Calvary Episcopal Church—1880

This 1880 building is in the "American Gothic" style. Its assertive Gothic
forms show it was part of an Episcopalian revolt against "paganism" suggested by the classical forms used by English churches during the previous
two centuries. The pointed windows, hood moldings, wall piers, and the
tower set at the corner acting as an entrance show that its sources are in the
1840s movement in England, which led to the High Victorian Gothic. That
English movement was based upon the belief that the Gothic style was English and that it was the only proper style for English places of worship. This
much later structure shows the American style that had interceded in the
meantime, most prominent in the heavy squareish forms in the tower, the
double pitched roof for the spire with bosses and discs set in the zone between the two levels, and the little dormers projecting from the lower roof up
into the upper one, all done in sheet metal.

*Turn right (east) on Main Street, 1 block. Turn left (north) on Water Street,
1 block. On the SE corner of First and Water streets is*

23.   140 First Street—c.1864

This limestone building, built about 1864, contained the largest paper mill in
the Midwest. Note the broad low-pitched roof which is not uncommon in
early industrial structures. The brick arches that cover the openings are a

22. Calvary Episcopal Church
222 Main Street

departure from the standard building techniques of this region. Atop that low pitched roof is a monitor roof containing sky-lights that could be opened to provide the ventilation required when chemicals were used in processing or on other buildings, when ventilation was required as a result of metal working.

On the NE corner of First and Water streets is

24.   143 First Street—c. 1863

This limestone industrial building dates from about 1863. Its west facade has the brick arches observed on the structure across the street (Batavia #23) and a cruder quality of masonry than is seen on the south facade, which also has carefully cut stone arches, showing that this was considered the front face of the building. At the north end is a tall tower, probably originally holding a water tank, providing the necessary room for pulleys and other equipment requiring a great ceiling height.

Walk east on First Street. The first building on your right is

25.   120 First Street—1882

The 1882 limestone building, now entered through a brick addition, was once a paper bag company. It is in adaptive reuse as a bowling alley and lounge.

Continue east to the corner. Turn left (north) on Island Avenue, 2 blocks to Houston Street. The building on your left (west) is

26.   101 N. Island Avenue
Batavia Municipal Building—1895

This broad riverstone structure was originally a factory and stretches a considerable distance to the north. The low-pitched roof, layers of stone projecting at the top of the south walls, and the carefully cut ashlar stone give it a particular dignity. Its adaptive use as a muncipal building helps to tie the roots of this community to its present. The building sits in the area which originally was an island between two branches of the river. One branch has now been filled in. The fall of the river here provided water power and the ease of reaching it with the railroad conspired to make this an early industrial center. The construction of this building was facilitated by the ease with which the riverstone could be extracted from the banks while leveling the land to build the structure.

Walk west on Houston Street to the Batavia Depot Museum on your right.

This concludes the Batavia Walking Tour.

Drive east on Houston, turning right to Island Avenue, to Wilson Street. Turn left (east) on Wilson Street 1.6 miles to the entrance to Fermilab, at Kirk Road. Continue east on Wilson into the Fermilab grounds.

27.   FERMI NATIONAL ACCELORATOR LABORATORY

Fermilab offers both guided and self-guided tours. There are also many interesting things to see, among them a herd of buffalo. Yellow booklets, outlining self-guided tours, are available at the reception desk inside the front doors of the central laboratory building.

Leaving Fermilab from the west, drive west on Wilson 1.8 miles to Batavia Avenue (Route 31). Turn left (south).

AURORA

AURORA

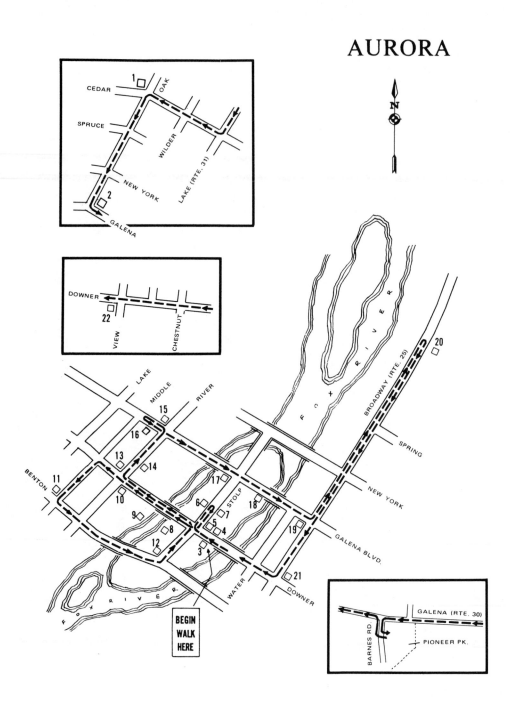

CEDAR
1
OAK
SPRUCE
WILDER
NEW YORK
2
LAKE (RTE. 31)
GALENA

DOWNER
22
VIEW
CHESTNUT

N

FOX RIVER

BROADWAY (RTE. 25)
20
SPRING
NEW YORK

LAKE
MIDDLE
RIVER
15
16
13
14
17
BENTON
11
STOLP
10
18
6
7
9
5
8
4
19
12
3
GALENA BLVD.
21
DOWNER

FOX RIVER

WATER

BEGIN
WALK
HERE

GALENA (RTE. 30)
BARNES RD.
PIONEER PK.

Drive south on Route 31, 6½ miles to Cedar Street in Aurora. Turn right (west) 2 blocks. On the NW corner of Cedar Street and Oak Avenue is

1. AURORA HISTORICAL MUSEUM
304 Oak Avenue and
305 Cedar Street—1856–57

Built on a slight rise above the surrounding land, this brick structure, dating from 1856–57, sits high on a limestone basement. It displays the formal characteristics of the Italianate style, built in brick. It has a cross-shaped plan with the entrance from a porch facing east. The porch (following a later design) rises to an octagonal cupola in the center. The roof overhang is ample and is supported by angle brackets with turned pendants, a motif repeated on the roofs above the ground floor windows. Those windows are slightly more elaborate than the one above, but like the ones on the second floor above the entrance door. They have a pedimented lintel supported by corbels and holding cast iron anthemions. The entrance is through a very wide opening with sidelights and a transom.

On the southwest is an entrance porch with square posts, large capitals, and scroll-cut knee brackets. It is probably a reduced version of the original front porch. The structure is listed on the National Register of Historic Places and is also known as the William A. Tanner House.

The museum features a Victorian parlor, complete with the original gas lights in the ceiling; a music room with an Aurora piano, music boxes, and a victrola; a dining room with a hanging kerosene lamp, and a glassware collection; a watch room; a ladies' fashions room, with 1880s clothes, toys, and dolls. There are also collections of Indian artifacts and a carriage house with many antique vehicles. Wednesdays and Sundays: 2:00 P.M.-4:30 P.M.

Drive south on Oak Avenue 3 blocks. On the NE corner of Oak Avenue and Galena Boulevard is

2. FIRST BAPTIST CHURCH—1887

Built in 1887, this large structure is a delightful combination of the Romanesque Revival and the Queen Anne. The basement, the porch posts, the window trim, and the stringcourses are all done in heavy rusticated stone, while the walls are built of a complementary color of brick. The windows on the ends of the cross-shaped plan describe a Palladian motif, except at this large scale, the openings are broken into a variety of different shapes and the side windows are arched instead of flat-topped. The architect took the opportunity to decorate various blocks with a foliate ornament characteristic of the Romanesque Revival. From the Queen Anne comes the extensive surface decoration: the shingle pattern in the various left-over areas on the south facade, the spindles under the porch lintel, and the foliate decoration in the gable of the porch which contains the name and date plate. Also characteristic are the complementary shapes of the gabled porch and the half-round end of the projection on the other side of the south facade. Note also the blind windows in each gable, topped with Romanesque arches but with the slimness characteristic of the Queen Anne.

Drive east on Galena Boulevard, across the river to Broadway. Turn right (south) 1 block to Downer Place. Turn right (west) across the bridge. Stop.

AURORA WALKING TOUR

On the left (south) side of Downer Place, just east of the river, is

3.   G.A.R. HALL
23 E. Downer Place—1877

Erected in 1877, this building stood as a tribute to veterans of the Civil War ("Grand Army of the Republic") and is now a memorial to veterans of all wars. The prototypes of the structure are quite clear: one is a memorial chapel with a cross-shaped plan topped by an octagonal cupola with a dedicatory figure on top, in this case a Union soldier; the other is a castle, appropriate to armies, which is the square structure on the west side (a slightly later addition), complete with a bulging oriel and a crenellated top. The martial character at the chapel is conveyed by the two cannons on the porch podia. The rusticated ashlar used for the structure is characteristic both of chapels and of castles. An interesting feature is the memorial bench from 1938 in cast concrete with cannonballs on each corner, which perhaps reproduces an earlier bench, contemporaneous with the building, which would have been done in cast iron reproducing the forms of logs and other parts of the forest. They are extremely rare survivors, hence the replication here.

Across the street, on the north side of Downer Place, is

4. 18 E. DOWNER PLACE
Aurora Herald Building—1866

When built in 1866, this structure overwhelmed the scale of the one- and two-story, wood, frame buildings that made up most of downtown at that time. Note the "eye" of the public press at the cornice which watched the goings-on at the city hall across the street.

The Italianate forms of this structure are quite clear, although the brick parapet replaces the original structure in that zone, which probably was a sheet metal cornice. Notice that the facade is composed of thin slabs of limestone, covering the brick, a common form of construction at that time. The limestone is called Athenian marble although it was not from Athens, but from Lemont south of Aurora, near Ottawa, an important source of limestone for construction in the Chicago region. The brick, segmental hooded arches above the windows also replace earlier construction. The original lintels may have been more elaborate carved versions of the same limestone facing, but they probably weathered away and had to be replaced.

Visible on the west side, facing the alley, are original features of the building. Most notable are the segmental arches in stone above the windows and paired wooden brackets supporting the eaves.

Walk west on Downer Place. On the NE corner of Downer Place and Stolp Avenue is

5. 6 E. DOWNER PLACE
Aurora Silver Plate Building—1871

This 1871 structure is typical of New England buildings early in the Industrial Revolution, with large arched windows for light and air. (Traces of similar windows are still visible along the ground floor.) The corner has stone quoins to give structural stability to that part of the building. The present parapet is a replacement. The building was angled to sit next to the millrace (power source) that ran along the length of the west side of the building.

Turn right (north) on Stolp Avenue. The fourth building on your left is

6. 33 N. STOLP AVENUE
Graham Building—1926

This building was designed by George Grant Elmslie in 1924 and built in

1926. William Grant, contractor for Elmslie buildings in Aurora, selected that architect when he built this structure which he owned. The building has decorative terra-cotta, and the overall design is typical of its architect, who also designed the building facing it. (See further description as part of Aurora #7, below.)

Across the street, on the east side of Stolp Avenue, is

7.   24–36 N. STOLP AVENUE
Keystone Building—1922–23

This structure, built in 1922–23, was designed by George Grant Elmslie. It delights in its proportion, quality of exterior detail, and resolution of site constraints. It is on the National Register of Historic Places.

This building and the Graham Building (Aurora #6) are extraordinary examples of the use of the Prairie style for commercial office structures. A third example will be seen later (Aurora #13). The architect was a draftsman for Louis Sullivan, who after the turn of the century set up his own office and here exhibits a rare example of the Prairie style's use for commercial structures.

Normally associated with the horizontality of Prairie houses, there is a balance between the horizontal emphasis and the vertical emphasis. The horizontality is emphasized through the stringcourses above the first floor and above the fourth floor, while the verticality is stressed by the structural members rising through the pairs of windows. The relationships of the sizes and of the materials produce an excellent sense of proportion.

Certain elements of the building are elaborated with extensive polychroming terra-cotta, and they, in typical Prairie School fashion, call attention to the structural aspects of the building. Note on the ground floor the large piers are topped by richly decorated, foliated terra-cotta, and the bottom and the top of the great band that crosses the ground floor is decorated with a small scale terra-cotta ornament. A similar treatment occurs across the very top of the building and across the top and bottoms of the horizontal members between the windows, but those members are intersected by undecorated piers.

Another important aspect of the building's design is the entrance, where the opening is decorated by an arched-topped, terra-cotta decoration and flanked by shops which are set farther within the building than the next two along the street. Notice that the undersections of the central shop's entrances have terra-cotta ornament like the soffits of the windows above.

7. Keystone Building
24–36 N. Stolp Avenue

Extremely rare in their survival are the Luxifer prisms above the plate glass windows of the shop fronts. The Luxifer prism was invented and produced in Chicago in the middle of the 1890s. They were installed in order to refract light into the depth of the shop at a time when merchandising was being developed as a science and when it was recognized that the more light shed on the goods, the more likely the goods were to be bought. The only disturbance to the original character of this building is the loss of the glass globes which once surrounded the light bulbs on the bronze light fixtures between each shop.

Backtrack south to Downer Place. Turn right (west). Cross to the south side of the street. Immediately before the river is a foot bridge running to

8.   20 W. DOWNER PLACE
Aurora Woolen Mills, Dye House—c.1858

This charming little brick building sits on a limestone basement. Located on the riverside, it survives from its construction about 1858, when this area was filled with mills, subsequently replaced by the present commercial structures.

On the west side of the river, what appears to be one massive building is actually two. Of interest is the part on the left which is

9.   E. & A. WOODWORTH BUILDING—1857

If one looks carefully, the brick cornice and blocked-up windows of this typical 1857 New England mill-style building can be discerned. Note the brick cornice surviving on the original north facade.

Return to Downer Place. Walk west across the bridge 1 block. On the SE corner of Downer Place and River Street is

10.   52-54 W. DOWNER PLACE—1880?

This structure, built by Mr. Frazier, contains two sections. The western one, facing River Street, is apparently from 1880. Note the difficulty of reading the date stone. Three stories high, it has tall windows on the third floor and broad, arched windows on the ground floor. The shops on the ground floor replace the original construction. This combination of retail and commercial space is typical of the period. The second floor windows are quite interesting: the inner and outer circles, defining the brick for the arches, have different centers which make the arch bigger at the center than it is at the base. That variety in shapes as well as the texture of the brick in the parapet at the top, and the other slight departures from absolute plainness in the facade, suggest the decorative style of the Queen Anne.

Added perhaps as soon as one year later is a structure to the north which turns the corner and presents a conspicuous facade to Downer Place. Its ground floor has also been rebuilt, and the windows in the second floor have been replaced, but the masonry survives very much intact. Again the name Frazier can be read, now with elements of plant life acting as a back-

ground for the neat letters. The combination of brick and terra-cotta with a
sheet metal cornice is a richer example of the Queen Anne style. Notice the
pediments, two on River Street, one on Downer Place, which are centered
above piers rather than above windows as is usual. This structure also contains a combination of retail and commercial space. As a whole, this structure expresses confidence and permanence in precise and elaborate brickwork with the company name worked into it as part of the design.

*Continue west on Downer Place, 1 block. Turn left (south) on Middle
Avenue. On the NW corner of Benton Street and Middle Avenue is*

11. HOLBROOK MILL—c. 1840

Built about 1840 as a saw mill, this is probably the oldest building still standing in downtown Aurora. The texture of the irregular ashlar used for the
walls indicates the quality of building stone available from the Fox River at
this point. Comparison with the similar riverstone buildings in St. Charles is
instructive. This stone did not weather well. It was, however, laid up with a
precision appropriate to a saw mill; it was more important to finish the saw
mill than to produce a fine example of masonry. The lintels, for the broad
front door and the other openings, use stone taken from a different quarry
and have weathered much better.

*Turn left (east) on Benton Street 2 blocks. On the NW corner of Benton
Street and Stolp Avenue is*

12. 705 BENTON STREET
Elks Lodge—1926

The design was undertaken in 1926 by William Carbys Zimmerman, an important early Chicago architect, following his visit to the recently discovered
and uncovered Aztec and Mayan ruins in Central America. This structure
may be unique in the entire region. It shows the taste of the period for historical styles.

The stone is decorated with very sensitively done versions of the typical
Mayan decorations found on temples and other structures with vigorous
faces with abstracted features, intermixed with masks and decorative forms
derived from vegetables, and patterns and forms abstracted from sources
difficult to identify. The brickwork is done to suggest both the ruinous character of the area when the architect visited it and also the character of origi-

nal brickwork in the Mayan construction which did not use the neat, square-cut bricks we use, but much more irregular ones. Even the block-like composition of the massive building resembles the block-like composition of Mayan temples. Setting back slightly at the top, and having broad linteled windows, the identity of the building as the Elks Club is made by having the initials of the Benevolent and Protective Order of Elks in the decoration for the lintel of the main portal, and by putting elks heads on the pushplates of the front doors. The structure is listed on the National Register of Historic Places.

Walk north on Stolp Avenue, 1 block. Turn left (west) 1 block. On the NW corner of River Street and Downer Place is

13. 37 RIVER STREET
Old Second National Bank—1924

This 1924 building is another of the very important Prairie style buildings designed by George Grant Elmslie. It reflects some of the best features of the Prairie School, particularly the care with which the masonry is handled, the elaboration of openings with precise terra-cotta ornaments, and the incorporation into the design of sculpture, here emblematic of the uses and purposes of the bank.

The composition of the building is quite unusual. It rises through a high banking floor revealed by the entrance wings flanked by the piers, to two stories above (indicated by rows of windows) each with a balcony in front (the balcony for the second floor is the roof of the projecting entrance), to a gabled roof with a pointed, linteled light in the gable, filled as are other windows with very nicely done stained glass in the Prairie style.

As you enter the bank, notice in small letters immediately above the front door, the name of the sculptor, Emil Zettler, and of the architect. Inside, the general configuration of the original space is visible, but the counters and ceiling have been altered. The walls have been divided into squares, with a piece of colored ceramic tile set in each corner, which form a part of the original Prairie School style interior. The large murals, showing early life of the settlement close to the river that grew into Aurora, provide an impressive decorative feature. It is listed on the National Register of Historic Places.

Across the street, on the east side of River Street, the fourth building north of Downer Place is

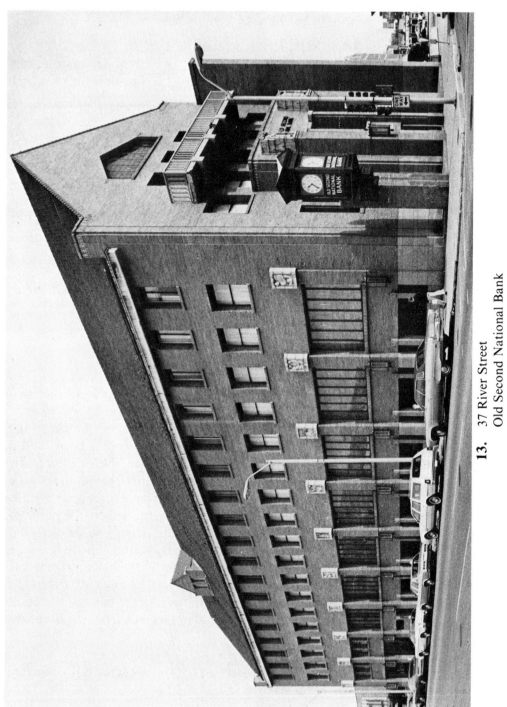

13. 37 River Street
Old Second National Bank

14.   34 N. River Street—c.1840

The core of this structure was built about 1840. The original riverstone may be viewed from the alley from the north, but the facades are twentieth century.

Continue north. On the NW corner of Galena Boulevard and River Street is

15.   2 N. River Street—c.1895

Built about 1895, this building is characteristic of the emerging masonry and iron skeletal construction that preceded the true skeletal forms used in the first Chicago skyscrapers. It has a masonry shell with arched windows, fine detail in the brickwork, and exotic corner bays with an oriel at the corner rising into an onion dome at the cornice over the entrance.

Walk west on Galena Boulevard. In the middle of the block, on your left, at the alley, is

16.   116 W. Galena Boulevard
Galena Hotel—1862

This 1862 building provides a rather grand example of the blocky form of the classical revival, for example Greek or Federal styles, rendered originally with Italianate details. It has a stepped cornice on the ends and rows of windows with a different window head on each floor: simple lintels on the ground floor, and abstracted hood-moldings on the second floor, and a segmental hooded arch on the third. On the front facade, the location of the original paired brackets may still be seen in the discolored brick. In the attic were additional rooms lit by dormer windows which have since been rebuilt.

The central entrance is the largest opening. It originally had a porch of some sort which probably had a balcony on its roof which could be entered through doors where the present projecting bay is located. Above it can be seen a pair of narrow windows and the traces of where the balcony for it was attached to the wall. Most likely, the entrance was a two-story columnar structure. It is also interesting to note that the two street facades are brick from top to bottom whereas those that would not be seen from the street are of riverstone through the first floor.

Backtrack east on Galena Boulevard, across the river. On the SW corner of Galena Boulevard and Stolp Avenue is

17. 7 S. STOLP AVENUE
The Leland Towers—1928

This 1928 building was designed as a modern adaptation of the Italian Romanesque style. The bottom several floors, done in terra-cotta, show the small round arches and tall windows with simplified foliate decoration of the capitals, characteristic of that style. Above it, and reaching a total height of nineteen stories, can be seen a continuation of the style with the zig-zag pattern followed by a bias-cut cornice projecting above brick corbels to form the top of the building, and standing above the arches, flanked projecting brick to produce the rough brick surfaces, are also characteristic of that style. The building represents both the grand aspirations of Aurora in the 1920s and the adaptation of historical to modern needs characteristic of American architecture in that period.

Continue east on Galena Boulevard. At the next bridge, on your right, is

18. PARAMOUNT ARTS CENTRE—1931

This 1931 building is a monument to the popularity of the film industry, which began building magnificent movie palaces for itself in 1921, with the Chicago Theatre designed by C. W. and George Rapp, who a decade later designed this structure. Earlier movie structures had depended more heavily on historical styles: for example, the court of Louix XIV in Versailles, or the Moorish castles of Spain conquered by El Cid.

This building comes toward the end of the era of the great movie structure and shows the streamlining as highly stylized forms which became popular just before the Depression. Inside, the fluid and geometric forms of clouds, prisms, leaves, birds, American Indian symbols, and decorative borrowings from the Prairie School are typical of the Art-Deco period, with which this building is identified. Outside, the polychromatic terra-cotta with extensive foliage, and the sloped roof done in tile, suggest the survival of Moorish and Baroque styles.

The long walls flanking the riverbank are done in careful brick work to give those walls character and to help decorate, in a quite simple manner, the river banks. They also reveal the interior configuration of the space, with the deep lobby, followed by a stairhall serving the interior spaces, the auditorium itself, and finally the fly gallery above the stage (indicating that the structure could be used for vaudeville and theater as well as for movies). The structure is listed on the National Register of Historic Places and has been

18. Paramount Arts Centre

extensively refurbished to recall its original grandeur. Its restoration was supervised by the ELSF Design Group of New York City. Originally seating 2,125 people, as a part of its recent (1976–78) restoration, the seating was rearranged and reduced to 1,885. It contains a full stage and can accommodate any type of theatrical presentation. It now is an arts center with a regional appeal.

Take a look around on the river side of the building, then continue east on Galena Boulevard. On the SW corner of Broadway and Galena Boulevard is

19. 1 S. BROADWAY—c.1925

Built as a bank, and designed by George Grant Elmslie about 1925, this structure has undergone several alterations at the first floor level. The south facade originally served as an entrance with a stylized eagle on the silhouette proclaiming the use of the building. The long north facade has a frieze between the first and second floor windows with a highly stylized, geometric, terra-cotta, Prairie School frieze. Similar Prairie School decoration appears at the top of the building, above the second and third floor windows, and framing the panel that separates the ground floor from the second floor.

Walk north on Broadway 3 blocks. On your right is

20. CHICAGO, BURLINGTON, AND QUINCY ROUNDHOUSE AND LOCOMOTIVE SHOP
1850s and later

This early industrial site is one of the most significant areas of the entire Chicago region because it was the central headquarters and machine shops of the Chicago, Burlington, and Quincy Railroad from the time of its foundation in the great age of railroads beginning in the 1850s. The oldest structure is the one farthest south and the western part of that is the oldest. Note the cut of the irregular ashlar. The round structure (actually polygonal), is built of rough-cut, smooth-faced rubblestone with clear-cut lintels above the large windows. Its northern extension shows a more refined masonry and the expansion of the original roundhouse. The next structure north is built of irregular ashlar riverstone. The next, the last of the series surviving from the 1880s, is a brick structure with round arches in some portions and wrought iron lintels for others.

Note the monitor roof on the southern end. This was the blacksmith

20. Chicago, Burlington, & Quincy. Roundhouse and Locomotive Shop

shop and the machine shop for the locomotives that were made here. Elsewhere on the grounds were other structures containing additional parts of this large complex. Fragments of other original buildings may be seen by inspecting the ground.

Inside the roundhouse may be seen vigorous and simple construction of these early industrial buildings including arches and timbers to support the timber roofs. The original turntable for the locomotives has long since disappeared. On the roof are vents which let smoke escape. The structures are listed on the National Register of Historic Places.

Backtrack south on Broadway 4 blocks. On the NE corner of Downer Place and Broadway is

21.   34 S. BROADWAY
Coulter Opera House—1874

In the late 1960s, Merchants National Bank redecorated the upper floors of this historic building with aluminum work which obliterates the building's significant visual identity. (The ground floor was obliterated by an earlier alteration, probably in the 1920s.) In 1874, this building was opened as Aurora's cultural center, but by the early 1890s, it was remodeled into offices and stores. (Many communities which have similar grilles obscuring older buildings have found magnificent old buildings under them when the grillework was removed.)

Walk west on Downer Place, across the bridge, to G.A.R. Hall on your left.

This concludes the Aurora Walking Tour.

Drive west on Downer Place .6 miles. On the SW corner of Downer Place and View Street is

22.   506 W. DOWNER PLACE—1870s

This is a particularly fine example of the Italianate style from the 1870s. The brick box is cubic and rises two stories to a hipped roof topped by a prominent cupola with broad eaves supported by very large brackets. The main block's cornice has paired brackets at the center and on the cornice with a single one between. Heavy moldings define panels placed in the cornice between the brackets. The window lintels have pediments and are supported by brackets. They are almost large enough to suggest that they are little windows over the windows. The windows have segmental arched tops. The front porch and the side porch (facing east on the back of the building) have square posts and large brackets. A small pediment on the front porch indicates the center of the composition; a similar, pedimented, heavily bracketed device is placed on the southeast corner of the main block, providing a flat-fronted bay. A two-story, polygonal, brick bay extends to the west on the ground floor. The ample grounds indicate a grandeur for this homestead, appropriate for the grandeur of the forms of the building.

Continue west on Downer Place 1.8 miles until it ends at Edgelawn Drive. Turn right (north) 1 block to Galena Boulevard. Turn left (west) 1.7 miles. Turn left (south) on Barnes Road to the third driveway on your left. Turn left into

PIONEER PARK
Pioneer Park is run by the Aurora Park District. It features the lifestyle of early settlers.*

Leaving Pioneer Park, turn right (north) on Barnes Road to the corner. Turn left (west) on Route 30 (Galena Boulevard) 1.2 miles to Route 56 East. Turn right and follow Route 56 to Route 5 East. Take Route 5 east to the Eisenhower Expressway, into Chicago.

*You are now as close as the route takes you to the world-famous Farnsworth House. (See pages 57-61.) The house is not accessible to the public and not visible from public roads, but its international significance merits its mention in this book.

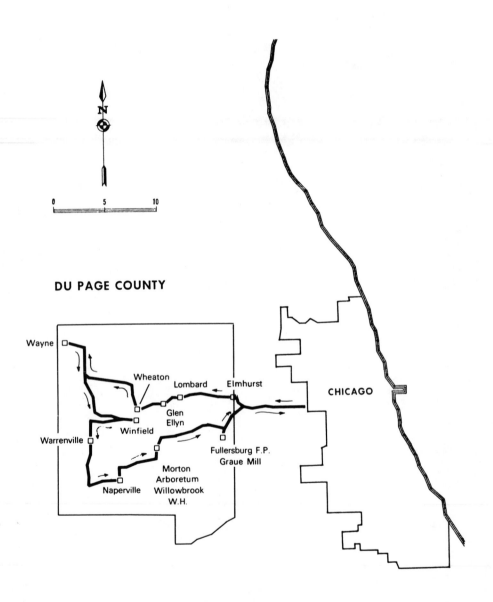

DuPage County

ELMHURST

ELMHURST

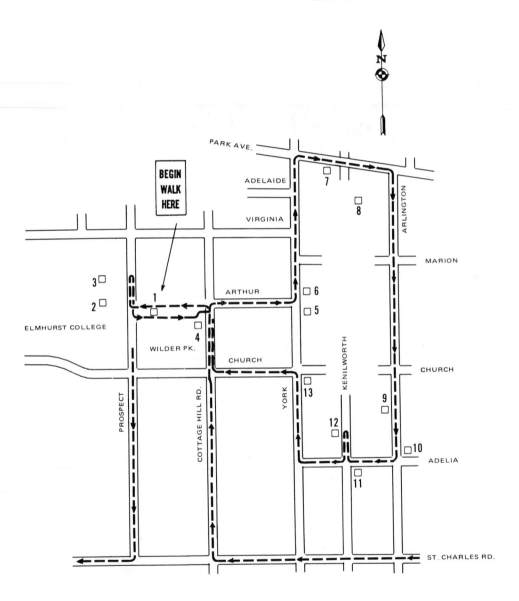

Follow the Eisenhower Expressway west to Route 290 (to Rockford). Continue 2 miles on Route 290 to St. Charles Road. Exit at St. Charles Road West, then continue west 1½ miles to Cottage Hill Road. Turn right (north) on Cottage Hill 1 very long block, past Church Street. On your left is Wilder Park. Turn left (west) into the driveway (at Arthur Street). Stop.

ELMHURST WALKING TOUR

At the west end of Wilder Park is

1. ELMHURST PUBLIC LIBRARY—1868

This two-story structure with a hipped roof started in 1868 as a large Italianate house. Note the distinctive paired brackets and the hipped segmental arches with prominent keystones on the tall windows. The slightly lower wings, set back on either side, may be early additions to the original structure. The entrance on the north side of the building dates from very recently whereas the magnificent temple front, rising two stories on the front facade, was placed there sometime after the 1893 World's Columbian Exposition held in Chicago, which made such correct classicism the only acceptable style for important buildings of this sort.

The order of the temple front is Tuscan, with slightly slim proportions popular during this revival period. The low base is followed by the shaft's base composed of a torus, cavetto, and astragal and then follows the shaft to an astragal necking ring topped by the standard Doric capital with an echinus and abacus. Notice, at the west end, the lengthy extension (built during the last generation), that a conscientious attempt has been made to render the character of the Italianate block and of the temple front in contemporary materials and forms. The painted brick on the front of the original block is rendered here as a white glazed brick and the wooden brackets and cornice have been rendered in simplified forms in cast concrete. The temple front here is much more abstracted and perhaps less successful.

Walk west, past the library, through the park to the west side of Prospect Road. This is the Elmhurst College campus. Across from the library is

2. OLD MAIN
Elmhurst College
190 Prospect Road—1878

This large brick building constituted the original structure of the college.

Built in 1878, it was originally called the Hauptgebäude. The main front of this square, blocky building has a tower rising from the center of the tall two-story mass. The tower has crenelations above the third story and a steeply pointed roof on a square plan with gables on each face atop the fourth story. The hipped roofs have hipped roofed dormers. The ends project to form pavilions and the entrance also projects to add additional dignity and formality to the overall composition.

The building is given elaboration by a very economical means, that of using two different colors of brick, a light colored brick (now rather dirty) for the main mass and red brick to outline the segmental arches, the stringcourses at the level of the sills, at the spring points of the window arches, and to form the corbelled cornice. Note the larger corbels at the third level of the tower. A slightly greater amount was expended in constructing the arch on the second floor above the entrance, where limestone is used in conjunction with brick, a combination which developed in England in the middle of the nineteenth century and is sometimes derisively called the "streaky-bacon style." The two colors of brick are a less expensive way of extending that form across the entire design. The building is listed on the National Register of Historic Places.

Walk north on Prospect Road. The first building on your left (after the next driveway) is

3.   KRANZ HALL
Elmhurst College—1873

This structure, built in 1873 as the first permanent building for the college founded by German Protestant churches, has the general massing and character of the classical styles prevalent during the earlier part of the nineteenth century and used for monumental buildings. Above the rough ashlar foundation are the two main stories with a high hipped pitched roof containing the third story; facing east is a gable shingled with square-cut and scalloped shingles and a pair of windows lighting the full third story. The segmental arched windows, with an arched upper sash and four-over-four configuration, are regularly placed and work well with the projecting brick (between the first and second floors) describing the stringcourse, which corresponds to the formality of the composition given by the quoins at the corners. Note that the third floor windows on the east and west facades have been reduced to tiny openings crammed under the eaves.

Walk east through the park, passing the library. At the east end of Wilder Park is

4. LIZZADRO MUSEUM OF LAPIDARY ART
220 Cottage Hill Road

This museum was founded to house and display gems, minerals, and objects of art made of gem material; to promote interest in the lapidary arts; and to the study and collecting of minerals and fossils. Lectures on earth science are given on the second and fourth Saturdays of the month at 2:00 P.M. from September through May. Adults: 50¢; children: 25¢. Free on Fridays. Tours by appointment.

Leaving Wilder Park from the east end, walk east on Arthur Street 1 block to York Road. To your right, across the street is

5. 203 S. YORK ROAD—1880s

This blocky, red brick building from the 1880s conveys the character of the styles popular in Germany at that time. The level of the stringcourse atop the mud sill, the stringcourse at the window sills on both the first and second floors, and the third floor in the northwest corner tower are brownstone. Also of brownstone are the segmental arches on the ground floor and the lintels on the second floor on the facades which are visible from the street.

The corners step forward. The one on the south side of the front facade terminates in a gable. The one on the north side rises to a pointed tower atop which is a closed, pointed lantern. It has wall dormers and extensions of the tower's hipped roof. Dormers also appear in the centers of the other facades covered, like the main roof, with a hipped configuration. The slate on the roof is in particularly good condition, with sheet metal accoutrements which include the ridges and the finials.

The graveness of the building is enlivened a bit by the wooden porch with its turned posts and attenuated brackets. Notice the particularly fine brick work throughout the building with very thin mortar courses and with an inset reveal at the corners of the tower of the second floor. On the south side, in the center, is a projecting polygonal bay which rises to a steep gable that projects over the splayed corners and has a half-circular window, punctured and pushed apart by a chimney rising above the gable. A complementary chimney is corbelled from near the top of the ground floor to the west. Again, exquisite brick work adds interest. Visible from the south side are the secondary porches with their finely done and very well preserved spindle work and other carpentry features. The sheet metal cornice with simple, closely spaced brackets is in excellent condition, rather than being rusted and poorly repaired (or not repaired at all) as is too often the case.

Walk north on York Road. The next house on your right is

6.   185 S. YORK ROAD—1905

This clapboard Victorian house was built in 1905. It conveys a marvelous compromise between Queen Anne and the more formal classicism popular at the time. The octagonal tower rising through the blocky hipped roof mass on the south side of the front facade, topped with its pyramidal roof and sheet metal finial, is Queen Anne; but the overall blocky massiveness and the finely detailed composite capitals on the four robust porch columns (the center ones supplemented by brackets holding a pediment) convey the more subdued refinement of the classical revival. Note that in the back, the fine coach house with the scalloped shingles and steeply pointed roofs still conveys the Queen Anne style.

Continue north on York Road, 2 blocks, to Park Avenue. Turn right (east). The second building on your right is

7.   ELMHURST HISTORICAL MUSEUM
120 E. Park Avenue
Glos Mansion—1892

Now in adaptive reuse as city offices, courthouse, and a museum, this 1892 limestone mansion originally contained eighteen rooms. The inside features beautiful woodwork and several exhibits of historic artifacts which are changed throughout the year.

The blocky building is constructed from random sized, quarry-faced ashlar with smoothed stone used for stringcourses (for example, above the windows and at the sill line). The north facade has a great gable above the porte-cochere and the main facade features, in addition to the columnar porch, a copper dormer with interesting strap-work decoration in the gable and a round tower topped with a flared conical roof rising to an urn-like finial. It is an impressive, solid structure now unfortunately facing over a roadway viaduct rather than across the broad lawns that such a massive mansion deserves. Tuesdays and Thursdays: 1:00 P.M.-5:00 P.M.; Saturdays: 10:00 A.M.-5:00 P.M. Free.

Continue east on Park Avenue, over the overpass. In the park on your right is

8. GLOS MAUSOLEUM—1894

Originally part of the Glos Mansion grounds, the 1894 mausoleum is now separated from its mansion by a road. Circular and octagonal mausolea have been popular as commemorative burial places since antiquity. This one is octagonal and has a very carefully rendered classical system with a pier arcade juxtaposed against a colonnade composed of half columns rising to a high frieze with reeds and garlands. Above it, in the parapet, is the highly stylized anthemia fronting on the ribs which run through the dome to the final finial. The finely done grates over the windows represent the prison, which is death, but the large sheets of glass behind them represent the liberation of the soul from the body through death.

Continue east on Park Avenue to Arlington Avenue. Turn right (south) past Church Street. The fourth house on your right is

9. 248 ARLINGTON AVENUE—1910

This 1910, Prairie School style house was designed by Walter Burley Griffin (a disciple of Frank Lloyd Wright), who won the international competition for the design of a new capital city for Australia and emigrated there to build Canberra. He is responsible for the dissemination of the Prairie style to Australia and eventually also to India.

   This structure is typical of his simpler style, with a broad horizontal, covered by a long hipped roof running parallel to the street, and a square hipped-roof projection rising in the middle. Both roofs have stuccoed soffits extending the eaves beyond the roof plane and, on the second story, boards articulating the stucco surface. Notice the symmetrically designed glass divisions in the casement windows, a common and typical Prairie School device. Notice also the planters, one of which carries the house number, that are designed in the same general style as the house. They help to convey tne horizontal design of the building across the landscape even on a relativ₀ly small city or suburban lot.

Continue south on Arlington Avenue. On the NE corner of Arlington Avenue and Adelia Street is

10.　281 ARLINGTON AVENUE—1901

This 1901 Prairie style house of half-timber and stucco was also designed by Walter Burley Griffin. This earlier design shows the close liaison between the Prairie style and the Tudor style, although this structure is distinctly Prairie.

　　The ground floor is brick and rises at each corner to form pylons, enclosing the corners of the upper story, and strong masonry masses. The second story is quite high and has a strip of casement windows under the eaves, framed by continuous strips of boards. On the end walls, these boards line the entire stucco field and also enclose a strip of casement windows. The pitched roof projects farther at the ridge than at the eaves and the eaves are turned out horizontally both on the main roof and on the porte-cochere entrance facing west which extends from the facade at the north end.

Walk west on Adelia 1 block. On the SE corner of Adelia and Kenilworth Avenue is

11.　301 S. KENILWORTH AVENUE—1901

This Frank Lloyd Wright house, of half-timber and stucco, was built in 1901. The building is superbly designed for its corner site. The entrance projects to the north while, in the opposite corner of the design, a one-story projection extends to the west. The broad hipped roof, ending at sharp eaves with a copper rain gutter worked into the design, extends from the entrance across the west facade as a pent roof and then moves westward as a broad hip over the flattened polygonal projection. Above rises the foursquare second story with its ridged hipped roof and a chimney, exactly centered, indicating the location of the all-important hearth in the center of the family spaces, the place that was "the home" in Frank Lloyd Wright's philosophy. The windows are arranged in horizontal and vertical segments within boards that line the stucco and are precisely integrated with the triangular-ended sections by coming together at a smaller scale of design. The glass here is particularly nice.

Turn right (north) on Kenilworth Avenue, then the second house on your left is

12. 284 S. Kenilworth Avenue—1889

This 1889 house displays all of the characteristics of the Queen Anne style: elaborate pitched roofs providing a broken silhouette, a round turret projecting from the rounded corner and topped by a conical roof ending in a finial, saw tooth shingles above the roof line, and a gable with a wavy shingle pattern below a scalloped shingle pattern. The gable is closed by a pent roof above the dentil frieze, which courses around the entire building beneath the eaves. Below that, a rounded corner projection takes up only half of the space under the gable roof; the opposite corner is sustained by a square post that could not resist inserting a small column into it. A dentil pattern shingle layer is between the first and second floors, and between the foundation and the ground floor window sill level is vertical grooved siding. The front porch, hipped at the south side and rounded at the north, is sustained by turned posts with brackets and a balustrade (hidden by shrubbery), which now has new balusters. The ground floor is given additional interest by having a multi-paned window on the rounded corner and a double door with a half-circular split-open pattern in the middle frame.

Backtrack south to Adelia. Turn right (west) 1 block. Turn right (north) on York road. On the SE corner of Church and York roads is

13. 245 York Road
Old St. Mary's Rectory—1876

This 1876, two-story, pitched roofed, clapboard house is typical of its period. It retains its original siding and window frames (including a neat, completely circular window) but has new porch elements that probably reproduce the original construction. The building is a simple vernacular reduction of the Greek Revival style, extended to a greater height than the Greek Revival to provide the additional room needed or desired by the family, an extension sanctioned by the intervening Gothic Revival.

Walk west on Church Street, 1 block, to Cottage Hill Road. Turn right (north) 1 block to Wilder Park on your left. Turn left (west) into the driveway.

This concludes the Elmhurst Walking Tour.

Leaving Wilder Park from the west, drive left (south) on Prospect Road until it ends at St. Charles Road. Turn right (west) on St. Charles Road.

LOMBARD

LOMBARD

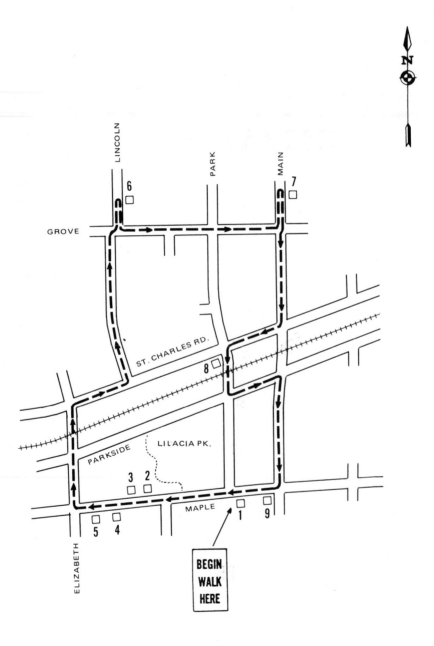

*Continue west on St. Charles Road 3.5 miles. Turn left (south) on Grace
Street, 2 blocks to Maple Street. Turn right (west) 7 blocks to Park Avenue.
Stop.*

LOMBARD WALKING TOUR

On the south side of Maple Street at Park Avenue is

1. LOMBARD HISTORICAL MUSEUM
23 W. Maple Street—c.1875

This clapboard house was built about 1875. The metal siding detracts, but
the simple, plain, and robust porch, which contrasts with the delicate window heads, survives. The museum is furnished with displays from the 1870s.
Wednesdays and Sundays: 1:00 P.M.-4:00 P.M.

*Walk west on the north side of Maple Street, past the library. The third
house on your right is*

2. 206 W. MAPLE STREET—1891

This simple two-story house covered with a pitched roof is constructed according to the general lineaments of the Greek Revival style, but without the
cornice of that period, and shows the very long survival of that classical
house type. The walls are made of brick produced in the local Hammerschmidt brickyards and have limestone lintels and sills. The porch has slightly chamfered square posts and scroll-cut knee fillets. The railing is not
original.

Continue west on Maple Street. The next house on your right is

3. 216 W. MAPLE STREET—c.1891

This frame structure could also have been built in 1891 and is more representative of that period than 206 Maple Street (Lombard #2). Clad in clapboards, it rises through two stories to a hipped roof with gables projecting
over portions of each face. The front gable has a scalloped shingle field
surrounding the heavy double windows that light the attic. The porch begins
at the projection toward the back on the east side, continues to and across
the front, where it extends to the west to form a porte-cochere. The turned

posts bulge, are grooved, and have very simple scalloped-cut shoulders for the lintel.

Cross to the south side of the street and continue west. The first house on your left is

4.   219 W. MAPLE STREET—1870

This frame house, built in 1870, is covered in clapboards and has broad pitched roofs over the attic, which on the west has a dormer with pilasters flanking the thin double-hung windows and is topped by a pediment. The gable facing the street (above the main section of the house) has a pair of circular-headed windows and an extended, segmental arched cornice which has the extensive projection similar to that of the dormer pediment and like that of the cornices above the other windows. The porch extending to the east is an addition from the turn of the century, as are (most likely) the canonic Tuscan columns supporting the porch roof, which otherwise is probably original.

Continue west on Maple Street. The second house on your left is

5.   241 W. MAPLE STREET—1868

This two-story frame house has the general massing of the Greek Revival style, with a relatively low pitched roof and relatively small windows topped by straight cornices with a number of moldings. The remnants of the Greek Revival can also be observed in the board below the eaves following the gable pitch. The L-shaped plan provides accommodation for the porch which runs across the west and north. The porch has posts, spindles, and brackets characteristic of its date of construction, 1868, rather than of the Greek Revival massing of the building as a whole. Especially nice here are the rope moldings underneath the lintels between the brackets. Projecting to the east is a two-story polygonal bay beyond which is a service porch.

Continue west to the corner. Turn right (north) on Elizabeth Street, across the railroad tracks. Turn right (east) on St. Charles Road 1 block, then turn left (north) on Lincoln Street, which jags to the right then left at Grove Street. The third house on your right is

6.   121 N. LINCOLN STREET—1872

This clapboard farm house features a sunset motif on its pediment and later additions to the original core, which dates from 1872.

5. 241 W. Maple Street

Backtrack south on Lincoln to Grove Street. Turn left (east) 2 blocks to Main Street. Turn left (north). The second house on your right is

7.   119 N. MAIN STREET—1881

This Italianate mansion was built in 1881. It was the home of Dr. William LeRoy, maker of artificial limbs after the Civil War. Later, it belonged to Harold Gray, cartoonist and originator of Little Orphan Annie. The metal siding detracts a little from the otherwise excellent representation of the classic Italian Villa style, with a three-story tower rising between the pitched roof that runs parallel to the street and another which comes forward to form a gable. The tower rises through a curved-sided hip to a flat top that still carries its cast iron cresting and corner finials in a palmette design. The brackets under the eaves are repeated as pairs under the gables, are grooved, and hold pendant knobs. The windows are sometimes single, sometimes paired and have a pedimented top and a rosette. The porches have chamfered posts supporting segmental arches with quatrefoils squeezed into the spandrels, and incised keystones. The service porch on the north is simpler than the main porch with its broad arched opening and original balusters surviving.

Backtrack south on Main Street to St. Charles Road. Turn right (west) 1 block. On the SW corner of Park Avenue and St. Charles Road is

8.   4 S. PARK AVENUE and
101 ST. CHARLES ROAD—1858

This 1858 limestone building with Federal influence was originally the Babcock's Grove house, later the Lombard Hotel. It must originally have been a very impressive place to stay, at the crossroads in this distant suburb. The original configuration has been disturbed by the addition (sometime before the turn of the century) of the shopfronts but traces of the original construction can be seen on the St. Charles Road side, where the smooth face of the lintels and the new blocks of quarry-faced ashlar, that replace the windows, can easily be discerned. On the east facade, immediately north of the center line, was another door like the one that still exists. Those two entrances were originally covered by a porch, probably flat-topped and supported by robust posts. The second floor has much larger windows than the third floor in order to honor the characteristics of the classical revival styles. The classical revival viewed the second story as being a *piano nobile* or "noble floor" which required that the third floor be diminished in size. The extensive cornice above is in proportion to the entire block of the building, suggesting that the distant model in the mind of the designer was an Italian Renaissance palazzo. On the St. Charles Road side of the building, below the mud sill, can be seen nicely wrought or hammered "S" anchors that tie the interior structure to the outer walls. Note, inside the corner store, the nicely preserved tin ceiling.

Walk south on Park Avenue, across the railroad tracks. Turn left (east) on Parkside Avenue 1 block. Turn right (south) on Main Street 1 block. On the SW corner of Maple and Main streets is

9. 220 S. MAIN STREET
First Church of Lombard—1870

This wooden, Gothic church was opened in 1870 and is a superb example of the Gothic Revival style popularized in the 1840s and rendered with extreme simplicity of means. The body of the structure is encased in board and battens and rises in a central steeple to a belfry with very steep gables and a serrated spire. The belfry corners are marked by simple pilaster frames while the corners of the sanctuary have pier buttresses terminating in gabled spires that are diminutive versions of the main spire. Flanking the building on each side are porches; the one on the west extends with a straight pitched roof to square cross-section carpentry pieces; the one on the east does the same, but has been pushed back into the body of the church to form a gable sequence. The windows have pointed arches and heavy moldings. Especially nice is the one in the tower which has two lancets within the single pointed arch; above it, in the next story, is a circular blind window; and related to it, below, on either side are triple-radius blind windows. This building is listed on the National Register of Historic Places.

Walk west on Maple Street ½ block to the Lombard Historical Museum on your left.

This concludes the Lombard Walking Tour.

If you have time at the end of the Walking Tour, kitty-corner from the museum, is

LILACIA PARK
Especially beautiful in the springtime, this lovely collection of lilacs include 1,200 hybrids in 275 varieties.

Leaving the Lombard Historical Museum, drive north on Park Avenue, across the railroad tracks to St. Charles Road. Turn left (west).

GLEN ELLYN

GLEN ELLYN

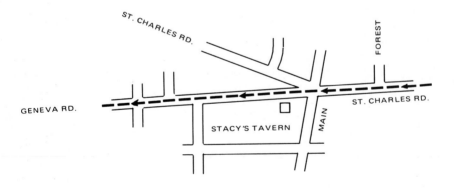

Drive west on St. Charles Road, 2½ miles. When St. Charles Road forks to the right and Geneva Road begins to the left, bear left on Geneva Road. On your left is Stacy's Tavern.

1. STACY'S TAVERN—1846

Because this 1846 wooden building was originally an inn for travelers, it is a larger structure than the usual Greek Revival configuration allowed. The main section conforms to the Greek Revival pattern but added a long wing set back from the front face in order not to detract from the main section. A wing is not unusual but one that matches the size of the main structure, as this one does, is unusual. Especially noteworthy is the excellent detailing in the building. Note the careful cyma molding under the eaves and gable, and the very nicely detailed capitals for the pilasters flanking the sidelighted doorways, which support an equally nicely detailed entablature with the canonic architrave, frieze, and cornice. The six-over-six, double-hung windows used throughout the building are typical of the period; but unusual is the very nice attic ventilator, which follows the lines of the gable but contains fan spokes derived from the attic fanlight of the Federal style. Notice the irregularity of the clapboards, a result of the relatively crude woodworking equipment available at the time. The corner boards have a three-quarter round edge set out from deep reveals, a detail encountered in high quality masonry that corresponds to the care noticeable in the other details of the finished carpentry work here.

Inside, a section of the wall has been removed in order to expose the interior construction. Note here the machine-cut studs with the brick nogging placed between the studs. The nogging adds insulation and dampens sound transmission through the walls, as well as prevents mice and other vermin from traveling within the building. The machine-cut studs indicate that the structure is built according to the balloon frame construction technique.

The interior is furnished with authentic period pieces, although these pieces came from various other sources. Friendly, knowledgeable, authentically costumed guides conduct tours. Stacy's Tavern is on the National Register of Historic Places. December-March: Wednesdays and Sundays: 1:30 P.M.-4:30 P.M. April-November: Wednesdays, Fridays, and Sundays: 1:30 P.M.-4:30 P.M.

Leaving Stacy's Tavern, turn left (west) on Geneva Road.

WHEATON

WHEATON

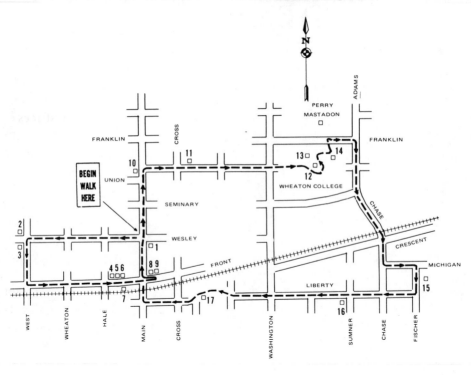

Drive west on Geneva Road, 2.2 miles. Turn left (south) on Main Street, 1.6 miles to Wesley Street. Stop.

WHEATON WALKING TOUR

On the SE corner of Wesley and Main streets is

1. DuPage County Historical Museum
102 E. Wesley Street—1890

Built as a library in 1890 and designed by Charles Frost, this structure exhibits the Romanesque style popularized during the previous decade for use in designing major civic monuments. The two-story limestone mass rises to a great hipped roof (which originally would have been slate) which has gables extending the second floor ceilings on each face. The gables have a modified form of Palladian window with the voussoirs of the central arch in stones of alternating colors. The yellow is the same as the limestone used for the walls while the tawney color is used for the lintels, sills, stringcourses, and coping stones. The entrance facing north has the heavy stone voussoirs, characteristic of the Romanesque style, and includes richly carved ornament on the inner and outer chords. Next to it, on the ground floor, a bow window bulges forth. At the eastern end of the building, a turret rises to a conical roof set above the eaves of the main roof. The building is a good example of the picturesque and massive effects which can be achieved in the Romanesque style.

The interior survives virtually intact and conveys the refined character the period demanded of important civic buildings such as this. Especially notable are the pilasters and other detailing around the librarian's desk, and the hall on the second floor with wood paneling extending across the broad curves of the cross-vaulted ceiling.

Walk west on Wesley Street, past the post office, to West Street. On the NW corner of West and Wesley streets is

2.   208 N. West Street—c.1875

This mansion, built about 1875, is in adaptive reuse as law offices. It is about as good an example of the Shingle style as will be found in the Midwest. Notice that the surfaces above the ground floor are clad in this material, which is edged by very slightly projecting moldings, one of which describes a large pediment for the gable that faces the front of the building. Within it is a Palladian window with very simple moldings. On the second story, the shingle surface is cut into with an arch to allow an opening for a balcony, tucked within the outer surface of the building. Shingles are also used to enclose the porch and for the pediment that marks the entrance to the porch. The brick foundation and clapboard ground floor, as well as the asymmetrical composition of the structure, indicate the Queen Anne characteristics which were also fashionable at that time. Originally the shingles would have been stained a dark brown color; the present coating of paint unfortunately disguises the Shingle style origins of the design.

On the SW corner of West and Wesley streets is

3.   130 N. WEST STREET
Trinity Episcopal Church—1881–82

This exquisite chapel was built in 1881–82 and designed by Henry Dann Compton. It is a frame structure covered in grooved, horizontal siding. It displays the careful art of the Gothic Revival carpenter who built it. The steeply pitched roof has (on the east end) shields in the gable top and bottom, the latter being held by curved brackets between which is a trifoil. On the south side is a gabled porch with brackets holding pointed, arched bargeboards that end in a cut-out; the far end has a similar porch. Notice also that the siding is intersected by verticals, diagonals, and quadrants of circles to represent structural shapes on the surface.

The inside is entirely paneled with deep brown, nicely finished wood. Note the ceiling, which has two different slopes and is sustained by four, king-pin, triple-chord arches with the suggestion of pendants at the second chord. The pews are original and exhibit the character of the Eastlake style, which is prominent in the stunning stained glass windows in the chancel and at the opposite end. These windows correspond perfectly to the original style of the Gothic Revival architecture. The other windows are either quite simple (these are the original windows) or memorial windows added at a later time including one in the style of Tiffany and one as recent as 1975. The building is an excellent example of the Gothic Revival architecture that accompanied the ecclesiastical reforms of the middle of the century in England as they were rendered in wood by American craftsmen and carpenters. It is on the National Register of Historic Places.

3. Trinity Episcopal Church
130 N. West Street

Walk south on West Street 1 block. Turn left (east) on Front Street 2 blocks. On the NE corner of Front and Hale streets is

4. 133 W. FRONT STREET—c. 1870

The upper story of this building is a very good representation of the Eastlake style as it merged with the "U.S. Grant" style as used for Main Street buildings in the years around 1870. The limestone lintels have incised Eastlake decoration. The cornice with its brackets and rosettes is sheet metal and in the "U.S. Grant" style, although now discontinuous (its central section probably originally projected as a pediment).

Continue east. The next building on your left is

5.   129 W. Front Street—1860s

Projecting beyond the buildings on either side of it, this building has lower floor levels and the half-circular arched windows with exaggerated keystones, characteristic of the Italianate style. It is a slightly older structure than the one next to it (Wheaton #4), probably dating from the 1860s, and had a cornice that would have projected beyond the panel formed by the raised bricks at the top of the present facade.

Continue east. The next building on your left is

6.   123–127 W. Front Street—1875 and later

This structure is particularly interesting because five different layers of construction are visible and they combine to produce an effective design. The oldest layer, from 1875, is the red brick wall on the second story which sits on the yellow limestone cornice immediately above the ground floor shops. This section established the original configuration of the building, with three windows grouped at each end in a pavilion projecting slightly from the wall and related visually to the single window in a similarly projecting section in the center, where the original entrance would have been found.

The second layer is found in the sills and arches of the second floor. These are made from a composition stone first produced sometime after 1910. Note that the delicate forms of the arches are out of character with the Italianate style which determined the compositional principles for that second story. Also from the same modernization is the copper cornice which has similar, thin forms. The third layer is visible on the west half of the building and dates from the late 1920s. Refined, smooth-face limestone has been used to line the shopfronts, and the intersections of the horizontals and verticals are marked by five-petal rosettes. The fourth layer is on the east end of the building and reveals the styles of the 1950s. Here composition stone is used to produce a very spare frame for the windows and the door. The fifth layer is represented by the plastic signs identifying the drugstore and the dress store.

Directly across the street, on the south side of Front Street, is

7.   134 W. Front Street
Railroad Station—1911

This railroad station, built in 1911, is in adaptive reuse as a boutique. It is almost a textbook example of the conservatism of railroad architects as they attempted to operate within the context of current domestic designs. The oversized corbels, which hold the gable rafters at each end, suggest the Italianate style of some of the earliest railroad stations, for example the one in Batavia (Batavia #3). But the choice of rough-faced brick, the way it is laid, and its combination with stucco in the gable ends (characteristics now obscured by the paint) suggest the Tudor style which was becoming very popular in the first decade of the twentieth century. Also characteristic of the older railroad station style are the square chamfered posts between the station and the rails, which supported the roof to protect passengers from inclement weather; however, they are made from cast iron, which is used to render forms normally made from wood and is a material that had gone out of fashion with builders by the turn of the century. To continue the mélange of references, note the hoods over all of the windows, probably added in conjunction with its adaptive use to a boutique. The small-scale, fussy ornament on the long sides of the building is particularly inappropriate for the robustness of the original design. The hoods apparently are meant to suggest awnings, which could have been used in the original building.

Continue east to Main Street. On the NE corner of Main and Front streets is

8.   101 E. FRONT STREET and
103 N. MAIN STREET—1885

This two-story brick structure proudly displays its date, 1885, and its original use as a bank. It has a formal front made of stone with a pilaster-flanked entrance and a broad, arched window to lend it monumentality; but above, simple brick walls with limestone lintels and sills, and a sheet metal cornice produce a characteristic commercial structure of the period. The building is an excellent representation of typical small-town banks of the period.

Continue east. The next building on your left is

9.   103 E. FRONT STREET—c. 1870

This building dating from about 1870 has Eastlake decoration. Notice the central lintel, with the segmental arched top and incised ornament, which dresses up the building, as does the eared motif with an incised cross on the top of the ends of the party walls enclosing the building's facade.

The building was very tastefully modernized about 1940. That accounts for the delicately detailed Mansard cornice sloping down from the top silhouette; for the grille-work balcony fronts added below the windows; for the nine-over-nine window sash in the double hung windows; and for the shop-front, which has black glass sills, brass and copper sashes (now unfortunately tarnished), and original hardware on the door.

Backtrack west to Main Street. Turn right (north) 3 blocks. On the NW corner of Main Street and Union Avenue is

10.   404 N. MAIN STREET—c. 1870

This Victorian house from about 1870, with extensive gingerbread trim on both the front and sides, has a very steeply pitched roof. It features numerous Tiffany windows; a curved pediment roof, sliding down over the gable, in the very steep front roof pitch; a porch on the ground floor, with two broad arches and spindles above with another porch for the balcony, above the gabled section of the lower porch; and extensive displays of the potential of shingles for producing patterns on the surface. Note the chimney, which is treated plastically by arranging the bricks in even more decorative patterns or additional decorative manners.

From the front of the building, cross the street and walk east on Union Avenue. Past Cross Street, the second house on your left is

11.   213 E. UNION AVENUE—1887.

This frame house was built in 1887. Among the features are square nails and rough-hewn lumber. The proportions are very high, allowing for two full stories and a nearly complete third story in the attic of the front section. The two porches, indicating a double house configuration, have fine turned posts and a simple spindle lintel.

Continue east on Union Avenue 1½ blocks. At Washington Street continue east through the gates leading to Wheaton College. The limestone building directly in front of you is

12.   BLANCHARD HALL
Wheaton College—1858–1927

This complex and imposing limestone structure capping the brow of a hill was built in many different stages which worked together to produce a unified design but with noticeable differences in the details. Buried in the exact center (and just barely visible) is the original, 1858, two-story, pedimented structure. Added in front of it in 1871 was the polygonal tower rising nearly eighty feet from the ground to a considerable distance above the original pediment. This was followed two years later (1873) by the entire west wing, but the wing balancing it followed in 1890 and only reached the site where the end pavilion would eventually be built. That occurred in 1927, when the far eastern terminus was added to correspond to the appearance of a structure at the other end that was, by then, more than fifty years old.

The result is a structure with a general configuration following the standard pattern of the Italianate style, with end pavilions connected by long wings to the central section, but with major and distinctive departures in the fenestration of some parts and curious juxtapositions in others. Note that within the central polygonal projection is a double-curve staircase running up the building to provide a magnificent spatial design. Note also on the exterior the heavy brackets in the cornice, the long thin windows in the main body of the building (with their double-curved upper sash), and the crenelations along the silhouette of the east wing. The building is listed on the National Register of Historic Places.

Behind it (to the north) is

13. WHEATON COLLEGE BOOKSTORE—1898
This brick building from 1898 shows the formal composition of the Classical Revival of the late nineteenth century with the central section projecting forward to carry an extremely large and steeply pitched pediment. Otherwise, the building is quite plain, touched up only by quoins on the ground floor and let-in panels below the arched windows on the second floor.

Walk east past the student center. The massive, red brick building is

14. WILLISTON HALL
Wheaton College—1895
This red brick Romanesque Revival residence hall was built in 1895. It features variegated brick, rounded projecting corners, a plythora of gables, and a clear central entrance under the most massive of the gables.

Walk due north, across the street, to the Science Building. In the wing on your left is

THE PERRY MASTODON

There is a taped presentation on the habits of this fascinating prehistoric animal. This specimen, found nearby, is behind a show window.

Leaving the Science Building, turn left (east) on Franklin Avenue ½ block to Adams Street. Turn right (south) on Adams 2 blocks to the end. Bear left on Chase Street, across the railroad tracks, to Michigan Street. Turn left (east) on Michigan 1 block to Fischer Street. Turn right (south). The first house on your left is

15.　808 MICHIGAN STREET—1876

This structure, which sits on a high piece of ground, began in 1876 as a frame Italianate building, characterized by the cubic form with the low hipped roof on top and a lower wing stretching to the east. Especially nice are the curved upper corners of the windows and the small attic windows, acknowledged by the dip of the cornice molding to frame them. Sometime in the 1890s a gabled dormer was added on the north facade with circular-cut shingles and a window which suggests the Palladian motif, but without the arch in the center window. The porch, with pairs of columns extending from the front door, was added slightly later; it extends to the east to form a pleasant spot in the reentrant angle on that side.

Continue south on Fischer Street to Liberty Drive. Turn right (west). On the SW corner of Sumner Street and Liberty Drive is

16.　528 E. LIBERTY DRIVE—1880s

This simple, unpretentious structure has the general massing of a one-and-one-half-story Greek Revival building, but was built in the 1880s. It uses elements on the front facade normally found in much more elaborate buildings. Notice the textured shingle pattern in the gable and the oversized window with heavy carpentry work and colored glass enframing the upper sash, a motif repeated in the transom and sidelights of the front entrance and in the upper sash of the pair of windows on the front porch. The porch posts are replacements of what were probably heavy and robust porch posts, which would have matched the oversized moldings on the half-pedimental ends.

Continue west on Liberty Drive to the Old Courthouse (with the clock tower), which is behind the new courthouse straight ahead of you. Walk to the right, around the new courthouse, to

17. DuPage County Courthouse
201 Reber Street—1896

This magnificently designed, massive, Romanesque Revival structure is built of smooth-faced brick with smooth-finished brownstone for lintles, stringcourses, and various decorative areas. Designed by Mifflin E. Bell in 1896, it has the formal composition characteristic of civic monuments and government buildings of the late nineteenth century. Heavily German in detailing, it has extensive foliate ornament in the pediments of the arched window dormers and projecting turrets on each corner of the pyramid-topped central tower. Particularly nice are the strings of arches, supported both by lintels and columns, in the top story of the tower; the broad arch serving as the entrance, set within a buttressed frame that contains foliate limestone ornament in the spandrel; and the two smooth-faced columns set within. Unfortunately the original doorway has been replaced by one of aluminum and glass and a few windows have been altered, but the building survives in excellent condition to convey the character of the style at its monumental best. The building is listed on the National Register of Historic Places.

With your back to the front of the courthouse, walk forward and you will be walking west on Liberty Street. Walk 2 blocks to Main Street. Turn right (north), across the railroad tracks to Wesley Street.

This concludes the Wheaton Walking Tour.

Leaving the DuPage County Historical Museum, drive north on Main Street 2.7 miles to Route 64. Turn left (west) 5.7 miles to Route 59.

17.　DuPage County Courthouse

WAYNE

WAYNE

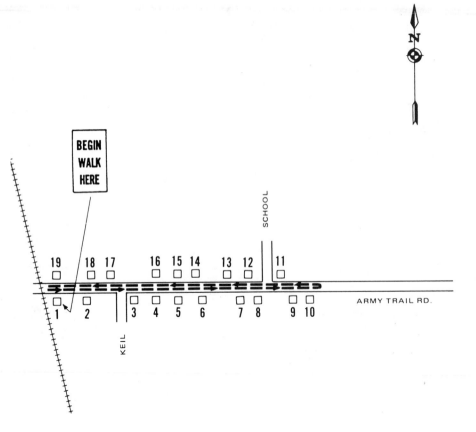

Turn right (north) on Route 59, 2.3 miles to Army Trail Road. Turn left (west) past one railroad crossing, a total of 2.2 miles, to the second railroad crossing. Stop.

The Village of Wayne is listed as a district on the National Register of Historic Places not because it contains outstanding architecture but because it is a good survivor of the kind of village found in the six-county area that has now, elsewhere, been swallowed by the expanding suburbs. Many people in Wayne were connected with the horse farm farther to the west.* Notice that the town is stretched along a road from the railroad at one end to a crossroad at the other and is little more than that one street in depth. It lacks sidewalks, curbs, and other "improvements" that disturb the ease with which buildings sit on their land and that land extends outward across the landscape. Notice also the large number of outbuildings beyond the houses; we now make do with little more than a garage and perhaps a tool shed; earlier periods needed more.

WAYNE WALKING TOUR

On the south side of the road is

1.   32 W 273 ARMY TRAIL ROAD
James Campbell Hardware Store—c. 1880–85

This frame structure, built in the early 1880s, stands at the location where the town and the railroad had long met. It is a typical, heavy, commercial structure dealing in hardware and probably had a blacksmith shop attached to it; most recently it has been used as a gasoline station. It has the typical cornice projected upward in the center to form a gable, below which is a small sunburst that grows into a full burst motif in a panel in the center of the second floor. It is an impressive structure appropriate for its location next to the railroad.

Walk east on Army Trail Road. The first house on your right is

* The Village of Wayne is partly in Kane County. At the end of the Wayne Walking Tour, you may choose to drive west 1 mile on Army Trail Road. (See pages 265-68 in Kane County.)

2.   32 W 245 ARMY TRAIL ROAD—c.1855–60

This small frame structure, from the late 1850s, is set well back on a large lot. It is typical of the simple structures built by the early settlers soon after the railroad arrived. Its only elaboration comes with the carefully detailed classical frames around the windows, enlarged and made slightly more grand for the entrance, but special interest is given to this one-and-one-half-story house by the projection from the northwest corner of a low, fully glazed polygonal projection.

Continue east. The second house on your right is

3.   32 W 215 ARMY TRAIL ROAD
—1852 with later alterations

This 1852 house belonged to Solomon Dunham, the first settler in the vicinity and the founder of the community. He was also the station master of Wayne Station who helped as a surveyor and civil engineer in building the railroad here, the first railroad built from Chicago, and the only major railroad built by Chicagoans. The original structure is visible in the central section as a simple Greek Revival building with a central doorway and two windows above. Subsequent alterations have included the extension on both sides of the house (wings which carry a roof slightly lower and extending at the same slope as the original one), the addition of the front porch which projects from the original house, and the replacement of the original siding with the broad lapped siding of a later form of construction.

Continue east. The next house on your right is

4.   32 W 185 ARMY TRAIL ROAD—c.1885

This small, L-shaped building dates from about 1885. It has a low wing projecting east. The two-story gable building on the west side has a bay window on the ground floor and a pair of small vertical windows above it in the center of the facade. The porch enclosure across the front dates from the turn of the century, but the building is a good representative of the early buildings of the settlement.

Behind it is a board and batten stable with a pair of doors on the ground floor and a small upper door to serve the hayloft. This structure is typical of barns of the period even from before 1850 to 1900. Buildings of this sort have usually disappeared but were originally parts of any town, village, or even city.

Continue east. The first house on your right is

5. 32 W 167 Army Trail Road—c.1880

Built on a quarry-faced, regular ashlar, limestone foundation, this simple gable-front house dates from about 1880. It has a fine porch across the entire front with turned posts, scroll-cut knee brackets, and a spindle lintel.

Continue east. The next house on your right is

6. 32 W 141 Army Trail Road—1893

This 1893 frame house shows the Queen Anne style in full but subdued flower. The gable facing the front has a window set well back in its shingle field with scalloped shingles above, plain shingles at either side, and sawtooth shingles across the bottom. Across the entire front is a porch with turned posts, a projecting pediment marking the entrance and containing a cut-out motif, a spindle lintel and spindle balusters forming the balustrade.

Continue east. The second house on your right is

7. 32 W 115 Army Trail Road—c.1885-90

This simple, gable front house dates from the late 1880s. It has a stubby wing of full height toward the back on the west side and a one-story wing projecting farther on the west. The entrance next to the chimney on the west side is sheltered and enclosed. The building shows the conservatism of the village architecture in general by retaining the overall lines of the Greek Revival style.

Continue east. The next house on your right is

8. 32 W 101 Army Trail Road—c.1910

This is one of the newer houses in the village and shows the same basic pattern as the previous house but now enlarged and broadened, indicating the greater prosperity at the beginning of the twentieth century. The pent roof serving the porch and the areas below it are of recent construction.

Continue east. The second house on your right is

9. 32 W 057 Army Trail Road—c.1885

Originally a farmhouse located outside the settlement, it was moved here soon after it was constructed and before 1890. A trace of the Gothic Revival style is visible in the steep pitch of the roof but the classical continues to dominate, as indicated by the cornice above the windows and the full pediment with the pilasters dressing the entrance.

Continue east. The next house on your right is

10.   32 W 035 ARMY TRAIL ROAD
—c. 1862 with later alterations

The central kernel of this structure was the first school building in Wayne which originally stood on the other side of the street several houses to the west. It dates from about 1862. At some later date it was moved here and converted to a residence. Perhaps in the 1890s it received the scalloped and diamond-patterned shingle field in the gable and the front porch which is representative of the turn-of-the-century styles. Notice, in the back, a surviving board and batten stable.

Cross to the north side of the road and backtrack west. On the NE corner of School Street and Army Trail Road is

11.   32 W 080 ARMY TRAIL ROAD
Congregational Church Parsonage—1889

This fine corner structure illustrates the lingering Eastlake style worked into a decorative style, known as the "U.S. Grant" style. The 1889 building has a very high pitched roof with a number of gables extending into it to protect projections on the two-story mass. On the southeast corner, set diagonally, is a square tower rising to a tall pyramidal roof with flared lower sections. It is marked off by flattened diamonds in a frame attached to the clapboard walls. On the south facade is a projecting bay window with a clipped, scalloped shingle roof and fine stained glass in the transom and sidelights. The front facade, facing School Street to the west, has a porch with heavy keyhole elements next to punched out patterns forming the lintel space supported by robust turned posts. Note in the peaks of the larger gables more scroll-cut fillets.

On the NW corner of School Street and Army Trail Road is

12.   32 W 112 ARMY TRAIL ROAD—1883
The peculiar composition of this 1883 structure may be explained by the fact

it was the house of Dr. William L. Guild, a doctor who probably practiced here, perhaps in one of the equally prominent sections of the house projecting at each end of the porch nestled between them. One projection has a two-story, flat-fronted bay window; the other projection has a one-story polygonal window; both have incised brackets (Italianate in origin) while the window in the center of the building, extending into a wall dormer, is topped by a typical "U.S. Grant" style lintel. The final touch of dignity is given the structure by the carefully detailed, but sharply reduced, classical elements around the two windows and central door within the sheltered porch.

Continue west. The next structure on your right is

13. 32 W 128 ARMY TRAIL ROAD
Now United Church of Christ, originally the
Wayne Congregational Church—1871

The structure was built at the time the church was organized in 1871 and is a fine example of the Italianate forms, relatively rare for a church, used very simply to produce a dignified structure. The belfry on top (note that the bell is clearly visible) has a pedimented spire with a prominent cornice supported by simple paired brackets. The entrance projects with a gable following the angle of the main gable of the building and its transom is half-circular with five circular-headed windows fanning out, a motif repeated with four circular windows fanned out. On the sanctuary are tall, slim, round-headed windows with the same prominent upper cornice projection found over the central doorway. The clapboard-covered structure survives in an excellent state of preservation.

Continue west. The second house on your right is

14. 32 W 150 ARMY TRAIL ROAD—c. 1875–80

The original structure is the one-and-one-half-story gable front building with two windows above and two windows below as well as the entrance, which dates from the late 1870s. Added at some later time was the columnar porch protecting the entrance and the shed-roofed extension on the west side. Notice the board and batten garage in the back, extensively restored but containing traces of the original stable from which it was made.

Continue west. The next structure on your right is

15.   32 W 164 ARMY TRAIL ROAD—pre-1874

The central kernel of this structure apparently pre-dates 1874 but the wings extending on each side are more recent. The western one probably replaces an entrance extension of some sort, which was originally on that side. This may have been one of the more "correct" Greek Revival buildings in the early years of Wayne.

Continue west. The next house on your right is

16.   32 W 180 ARMY TRAIL ROAD
pre-1874 with later alterations

The original, central section (its clapboard siding is still visible on the side) was a Greek Revival structure from before 1874. It had its long side facing the street, an unusual configuration for that style. It has been considerably altered.

Continue west. The third house on your right is

17.   32 W 236 ARMY TRAIL ROAD
—c.1860 with later alterations

Originally located across Army Trail Road, the central section of this structure dates from about 1860. It still shows its Greek Revival origins.

Continue west. The next structure on your right is

18.   32 W 242 ARMY TRAIL ROAD—c.1860

Now a residence and considerably altered from its original construction about 1860, this building was originally a boot and shoe store.

Continue west. The second structure on your right is

19.   32 W 270 ARMY TRAIL ROAD—1904

Located at the intersection of the railroad and the village's street, this 1904 store is typical of the period, a store with general merchandise. The building runs back to a considerable depth and has three walls of brick. The front is enclosed in a manner typical of the period which survives here in very good condition. Cast iron elements hold large plate glass windows with an entrance in the center section, and they support a wrought iron lintel holding the brick section above. This is topped with a sheet metal cornice. Its Italianate forms were barely in style at the date given in its pediment, but they were still considered serviceable. The front, the windows, and townspeople lingering at the store would be shielded from the sun and weather by a shed-roofed porch. Note the foundry name and its location cast into the cast iron threshold bib, now well worn by the store's customers.

This concludes the Wayne Walking Tour.*

Continue east on Army Trail Road 2.2 miles to Route 59. Turn right (south). Drive 6.3 miles to Route 38 (Roosevelt Road). (Circle around to the right, to drive east on Route 38.)

* Dunham Castle is one mile west on Army Trail Road. (See Kane County, pages 265-68.)

WINFIELD

WINFIELD

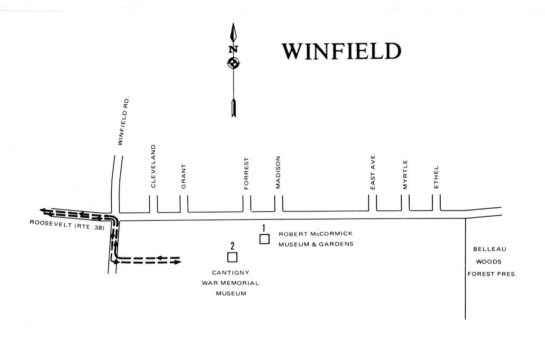

N

WINFIELD RD.

CLEVELAND

GRANT

FORREST

MADISON

EAST AVE.

MYRTLE

ETHEL

ROOSEVELT (RTE. 38)

1
☐ ROBERT McCORMICK
MUSEUM & GARDENS

2
☐
CANTIGNY
WAR MEMORIAL
MUSEUM

BELLEAU
WOODS
FOREST PRES.

Drive east on Roosevelt Road 1.9 miles to Winfield Road. Turn right (south) on Winfield Road about 1 block. Turn left (east) into the entrance of

CANTIGNY MUSEUM AND GARDENS

This privately maintained 500-acre estate belonged to the late Colonel Robert R. McCormick and his grandfather, Joseph Medill. Included on the grounds are the McCormick Museum and Gardens, and the First Division Museum.

1. McCORMICK MUSEUM—1896

This 1896 Georgian residence was built by C.A. Coolidge, designer (with the Boston firm of Shepley, Rutan and Coolidge) of the Art Institute of Chicago and the Chicago Public Library. The middle section, which faces north, is the 1896 section. It was later enlarged and remodeled, beginning in 1932. Based on the classical revival, it has beautifully detailed composite columns supporting a pediment that contains a lowered arch fanlight. Within is a two-story entrance structure with sidelights and another fanlight. The oval windows on either side are characteristic of the refinement associated with the Federal style, which provided some of the sources used in this characteristic Georgian Revival design. It is patterned after Thomas Jefferson's portico at Monticello (compare it with the building on the nickel) which is one of many sources drawn on by Coolidge in this design.

The wing on the east was added in 1936 and faces over a formal allée, defined by two rows of cedar trees. The allée extends across the expansive grounds open to a prospect of a water spout in a square pond at the bottom of a terraced, sodded hillside. At the head of that axis stands a Tuscan temple front with a fanlight modeled on Jefferson's state capitol in Richmond, Virginia, which in turn was modeled on the ancient Roman Maison Carré at Nimes in the south of France. The large porch is reached by a split circular staircase with very fine wrought iron hand rails. Inside the portico is a heavy door frame with Adamesque details including a swan's-neck pediment.

A similar portico is found on the south facade overlooking a broad garden punctuated with various deciduous trees and containing a square, grade-level pond. Here the columns are set farther apart but are still in the Tuscan order, and a fanlight again graces the pediment. The doorway within has a broad fanlight and sidelights within the pediment. This, too, is Jeffersonian in inspiration, perhaps based on his design at Montpellier, and the columns are of stone.

There are many Oriental works of art, including silk screens and hand-painted wallpaper. The largest room is twenty-two-feet high with a concealed Art Deco bar. The estate was originally named Red Oaks. After World War I, McCormick renamed it Cantigny, honoring a town outside Paris that had been leveled by artillery and then rebuilt.

Ten acres of gardens are divided into seventeen groups, each self-contained, focusing on various garden functions and groupings of trees, shrubs, and flowers. There is a well-marked trail for hiking.

There are Sunday afternoon concerts, mostly chamber music, held in the library of the McCormick Museum at 3:00 P.M. Reservations are recommended. Art exhibits are presented in the Long Corridor of the McCormick Museum. Documentary movies are shown regularly in summer (and by arrangement with groups in the winter) in the Gold Theater of the McCormick Museum.

2.   FIRST DIVISION MUSEUM

The museum displays authentic details of famous military campaigns from World War I, World War II, and Viet Nam. In front of the museum are six tanks from World War II, Korea, and Viet Nam. Children are allowed to climb on them.

Leaving Cantigny, turn right (north) and backtrack to Roosevelt Road. Turn left (west) on Roosevelt (Route 38) 1.7 miles to Route 59. At signs to Route 59 South, turn right, then left (south) on Route 59 (S. Neltnor Boulevard). Follow Route 59 south 2.4 miles to Batavia Road.*

* Fermilab crosses the county line with Kane County. (See pages 265-68 in Kane County.) If you want to go there now, turn right (west) on Batavia Road.

WARRENVILLE

WARRENVILLE

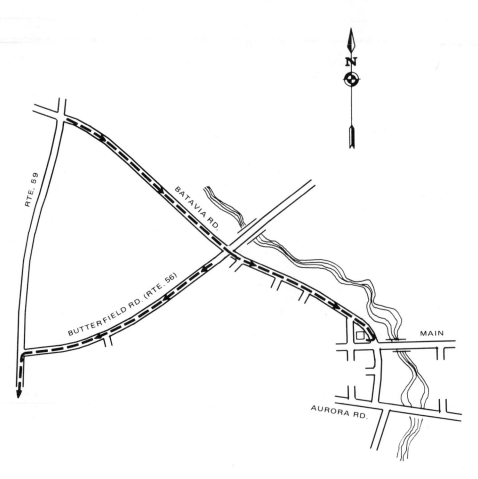

From the intersection of Route 59 and Batavia Road, drive southeast on Batavia Road 1.7 miles. On the NW corner of Batavia Road and Main Street is

1. 28 W 310 MAIN STREET
Julius Warren House—1832–34

This is probably the oldest extant structure in DuPage County, and one of the oldest in the six-county area. It was begun in 1832 by one of the area's first settlers who promoted various improvements in the county which he helped form and occasionally represented in the state legislature. The original structure is an excellent example of the small but well-finished Greek Revival houses of the earliest leading settlers. It rises one-and-one-half-stories with two openings in the upper section and three in the lower. Especially finely done are the clear cyma molding in the cornice of the split pediment and the delicate capitals of the fluted pilasters flanking the sidelighted entrance. The shed-roofed extension on the north was added about 1842; other additions followed, including the recent metal siding over the original clapboards.

Backtrack on Batavia Road ½ mile to Butterfield Road (Route 56). Turn left (west) 1¼ miles. Turn left (south) on Route 59.

NAPERVILLE

NAPERVILLE

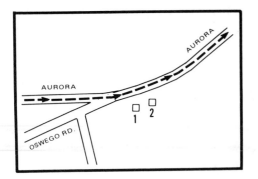

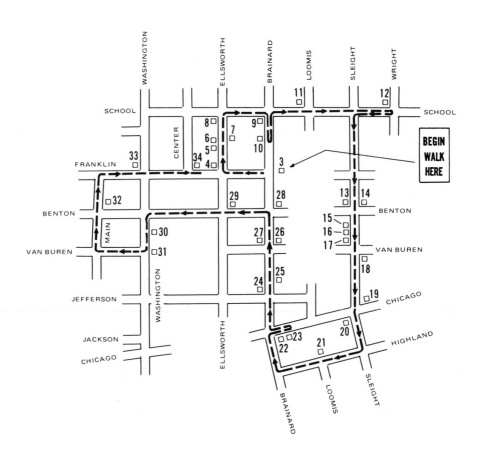

Continue south on Route 59, past the East-West Tollway (Route 5) 4.1 miles to Aurora Avenue. Turn left (east) on Aurora Avenue 2.8 miles. Just past the Naperville Central High School is

NAPER SETTLEMENT

Naper Settlement is an exhibit of life in a small northern Illinois town during the period 1830-1870. On the grounds are a log cabin, a reconstruction of Fort Payne used during the Blackhawk Indian War, the village green with its bandstand, modest and elaborate homes, a church, and business buildings typical of the era.

1. CAROLINE MARTIN-MITCHELL MUSEUM
Pine Craig—1883

This 1883 building is a good example of a smallish yet grand, later, Gothic Revival structure dominating the high ground on which it stands and complemented by the numerous large trees. The two-story brick structure has a high hipped roof topped by cast iron cresting and finials. The front has a gable, with end returns for the cornice, which has quite thick brackets. Notice the egg and leaf molding just below the brackets in the middle zone of the cornice. The chimney with its numerous vents is an especially attractive piece of bricklaying. Projecting toward the street is the front entrance porch, protected by a polygonal bay on the north side and containing a porte-cochere with forms remodeled on the east porch. The brackets are repeated and small quadrant fillets stand between the lintel and the oversized capitals for the chamfered porch posts. The slate roof is notable for having both flat-cut and scalloped-cut slates; the former is bluish-grey slate color, the latter has a slightly lighter hue. Textured polychromatic slate roofs of this type were formerly quite common but few have survived in such excellent condition. To the southwest is a board and batten carriage house with nice carpentry work in the gable. Pine Craig is listed on the National Register of Historic Places. Wednesdays and Sundays: 1:30 P.M.-4:30 P.M. Adults: $2.50; children: $1.00.

East of the house is

2. THE CENTURY MEMORIAL CHAPEL—1864

Built in 1864 and relocated on this site in 1970, this is a fine example of board and batten construction used for the Gothic Revival. Note the steeply

1. Pine Craig

pitched roof over the sanctuary, echoed by the gable protecting the enclosed porch which projects in front. Notice also the pointed window with trifoils inserted in each of the three sections defined by the window tracery. The battens run up to a scroll-cut board that imitates the corbel course used in masonry construction of the early Gothic period. The plan is that of the standard Latin cross, with transepts projecting at the end of the sanctuary which extends beyond the transepts into the area called the choir. It has an apsidal end which provides a picturesque addition on the back of the church. Note the thin, pointed, arched wall dormers that project into the pitched roofs. The stained glass is especially noteworthy.

Leaving Naper Settlement, turn right (east) on Aurora Avenue. Follow Aurora until it ends at Washington Street. Turn left (north) 5 blocks to Franklin Avenue. Turn right (east) 3 blocks to Brainard Street. Stop.

NAPERVILLE WALKING TOUR

All of the area included in the Naperville Walking Tour is included in the Naperville Historic District (roughly bounded by Julian, Hyland, Chicago, Jackson, Eagle, and 5th streets), which is listed on the National Register of Historic Places.

On the east side of Brainard Street at Franklin Street is

3. OLD MAIN
North Central College—1870

This is slightly more than half of the design that was begun in 1870. It is built of limestone used in a manner characteristic of this period and in a composition characteristic of the Italianate style, as used for monumental structures. The wing and outbuilding complementary to the one on the south of the main building were never constructed.

The center of the main building is marked by a tower rising above the four-story building. The tower's fifth story is a belfry, and above that it erupts into a magnificent copper-sheathed roof that swoops quite high into an oversized finial. A dormer is placed in each of the four faces. The block, like the end structure, is topped by a Mansard roof with a quite large curb on top and with broad double window dormers set into the slate face (the slate survives only on the southern structure). The brackets, quite large and

3. Old Main
North Central College

paired in the center and at the corners, complete the Italianate elements at that level. The building materials are vaguely related to the ones used in a more finished way in more sophisticated examples of the styles then current. Also characteristic of the Italianate are the round-headed windows, but note how they are grouped into triplets, with small ones flanking a larger central one in the tower, and how they are paired under a single arch in the wing connecting the outer and central sections. The wing may be a later addition that corresponds to that original intention.

Walk west on Franklin Avenue. On the NW corner of Franklin Avenue and Ellsworth Street is

4. 105 N. ELLSWORTH STREET—1874

This clapboard farmhouse, built in 1874, has the massing and details reminiscent of the Greek Revival, but with pedimented window heads characteristic of the 1870s date. Added at the turn of the century was the porch with its four, standard, Tuscan columns. The west end of the building has a porch from the same construction campaign and columns selected from the same catalogue, but with slightly different proportions.

Walk north on Ellsworth Street. The fourth house on your left is

5. 125 N. ELLSWORTH STREET—c. 1870

This frame house was built about four years earlier than 105 N. Ellsworth Street (Naperville #4) and is slightly grander. Notice that the pedimented windows are larger, its pedimented window heads are slightly grander, and the porch (which here is original) has brackets above the posts that stand on high podia. On the south end is a flat-fronted projection with its own hipped roof. The porch railing is not original.

Continue north. The next house on your left is

6. 129 N. ELLSWORTH STREET—1866

This clapboard house was built in 1866 and has had few modifications.

Directly across the street, on the east side of Ellsworth Street, is

7. 130 N. ELLSWORTH STREET—1870s

The front section of this red brick, Italianate building dates from the 1870s. Note the round-headed windows with round-headed upper sashes and the keystones in limestone, the same material used for the foundation. Note also the half-circular window in the gable and the fine scroll-cut pendant brackets under the eaves.

In 1903 an addition was built on the south. Notice that it has larger windows and segmental arches. The porch columns are especially interesting. They are modeled on the most elegant example of the Ionic order ever produced by the Greeks, the order used for the Eructheum on the Acropolis in Athens. They are, of course, catalogue items. The capitals are made from a composition material; the rest is made of wood.

Continue north to the corner. On the SW corner of School and Ellsworth streets is

8. 151 N. ELLSWORTH STREET—1896

This tall, frame, T-plan structure was built in 1896. It has clapboard up to the top of the second floor windows but the gable facing east has a layer of shingles, then a sunburst motif split apart by the attic window. The handsome structure suffers from the inappropriate alteration to the front window (it should be a large sheet of glass with a transom on top, instead of the many small panes that suggest Williamsburg, Virginia) and by the heavy, split shingles used as the roofing material.

Walk east on School Street 1 block. On the SW corner of School and Brainard streets is

9. 153 N. BRAINARD STREET—1872

This simple clapboard house, with turned porch posts, was built in 1872.

Walk south on Brainard Street. The third house on your right is

10. 133–135 N. BRAINARD STREET—1870s

Although the original porch is missing, this is a good example of a cubic, Italianate building from the 1870s. Especially notable are the window surrounds which have feet and shoulders and nice incising in the upper parts and in the keystone.

Backtrack on Brainard Street to School Street. Turn right (east). On the NW corner of School and Loomis streets is

11. 321 E. SCHOOL STREET—1912

This 1912 brick building, based on the Tudor style, was once a church. It is now in adaptive reuse as the Student Service Center for the Evangelical Theological Seminary.

Continue east. On the NW corner of Wright and School streets is

12. 529 E. SCHOOL STREET and
205 N. WRIGHT STREET—c.1875

This frame Italianate structure displays a number of finely executed details typical of the mid-1870s. The window surrounds have feet, shoulders, and prominent keystones with incised Eastlake decoration. In the conspicuous cornice is an unusual but impressive alternation of modillions and brackets with gouged sides and pendant knobs. The porch toward the rear on the south side has punctured quatrefoils in the spandrels of the wooden tracery arches, springing from the chamfered posts.

Backtrack west on School Street to Sleight Street. Turn left (south) 2 blocks. On the NW corner of Sleight Street and Benton Avenue is

13. 5 N. SLEIGHT STREET—1880s

This frame, clapboard-covered house from the 1880s has pedimented cornices above the windows. On the south facade a polygonal bay projects on the ground floor. On the east facade, a porch with Tuscan columns was added just after the turn of the century.

On the NE corner of Benton Avenue and Sleight Street is

14. 8 N. SLEIGHT STREET—1880s

This frame structure from the late 1880s has clapboards up to the gable, where saw-tooth shingles take over. Those are followed by a sunburst motif, in front of which stands intersecting turned elements to decorate the top of the gable. The entrance is in a recess on the north side; the north slope of the pitched roof extends out over it to project beyond the limit of the south side of the pitched roof. The porch has turned posts and a spindle lintel which carries a fragment of a Mansard roof. Within the porch is a window characteristic of the style with a transom divided, like the windows below, into a broad central section and two narrower sections (one on each side) containing double-hung sashes.

Continue south on Sleight Street. The second house on your right is

15.   15 S. SLEIGHT STREET—1883

This 1883 frame structure has clapboard on the ground floor and various shingle patterns on the second floor, a hipped roof, and a front-facing gable with eave returns. The top of the gable has one full and two half sunburst motifs and the porch has square posts with let-in panels and details that suggest the Tuscan order. A tower, similar to the one at the next house (Naperville #16), was removed.

Continue south on Sleight Street. The next house on your right is

16.   21 S. SLEIGHT STREET—c.1884

Differing only a little from the previous structure (Naperville #15), this house was probably built in the next year. This has the same features and, in addition, a tower (a similar one was removed from 15 S. Sleight Street) which stands out at the southeast corner and, on the ground floor, is cut on a bias and has a roof that slopes into a steep truncated hip. The porch has turned posts and a variety of carpentry work enlivening the lintel.

Continue south. The next house on your right, on the NW corner of Sleight Street and Van Buren Avenue, is

17.   29 S. SLEIGHT STREET—c.1890

This frame structure, clad in clapboards, has two distinctive motifs not often encountered. One is on the south half where the roof slides down in a continuous plane to cover the porch. The other is the gable which, above the flared base, has a circular-cut shingle pattern that is seldom found. It was probably built around 1890.

Kitty corner, on the SE corner of Sleight Street and Van Buren Avenue, is

18.   110 S. SLEIGHT STREET—1892

This elaborate Queen Anne structure is from 1892 and exhibits the full exuberance of the style. It has a variety of shingle patterns; the roof is broken by a tall cone over the rounded quadrant corner, and, at the crossing of the hipped roofs, a small dormer is topped by its own hipped roofs. The porch, which slides across the front to run down the other street side, has slightly bulging, turned posts and a lintel elaborated by a square checkerboard pattern interspersed with wheels of two different sizes.

Continue south on Sleight Street 1 block. On the NE corner of Sleight Street and Chicago Avenue is

19.   144 S. SLEIGHT STREET—1917

This Prairie School brick residence, of stucco and half-timber, was built in 1917 and designed by Harry Robinson. Robinson was important in the office of Frank Lloyd Wright for the decade before World War I. The Prairie style motifs are contained within a relatively conventional, box-like, pitched roof configuration. But note that the pitched roof is lower than most and that the corners of the box and the ground floor have simple rough-textured brick framing the half-timbering, which holds strips of windows with the characteristic, rectangular, Prairie style motif.

On the SW corner of Sleight Street and Chicago Avenue is

20.   432 CHICAGO AVENUE—c.1892

This large Queen Anne structure, from about 1892, successfully occupies its corner position on a slight rise of land. A broad pitched roof, forming a gable in the front, faces the main street; the corner is turned by a round turret that rises to a finial atop its conical roof. Here, as is often the case with pitched roofs, the bottom part is flared. The gable formed by the pitched roof has a cornice across the bottom which, like the rest of the eaves, has modillions attached underneath it. The projection within the gable contains triple windows. The turret on the ground floor becomes polygonal; the sweeping circular corner of the porch fans out from it to cross almost the entire front, then returns to the south until it intersects the projecting wing, topped by a gable front much like the one facing the street on the north facade. The porch has bulging columns with oversized capitals and a lintel, with very small spindles that run around between the capitals and the decorative knee fillets with bead-like pendants. The balusters for the porch are of normal size. Notice the variety of shingle textures, diamond-cut, scallop-cut, and flat-cut courses, used for the second story in the gables.

Continue south on Sleight Street 1 more block. Turn right (west) on Highland Avenue ½ block. On your right, opposite Loomis Street, is

21. 401 HIGHLAND AVENUE—1917

This 1917 brick house was also designed by Harry Robinson. The Prairie School roots of the house are clear in the broad, hipped roofs with flat soffits; the grouping of casement windows, which are divided in the distinctive Prairie style manner; and in the projections out from the main mass of the building, on the east with a one-story enclosed porch, and on the west with an entry porch from the driveway. A distinctive element in this structure is found on either side of the central projection, on the south facade on the ground floor, where thermal windows containing Prairie glass are introduced. This may be unique in the Prairie School repertoire.

Continue west on Highland Avenue to Brainard Street. Turn right (north) 1 block. On the SE corner of Chicago Avenue and Brainard Street is

22. 308 CHICAGO AVENUE—1890s

Rare among the neo-classical revival styles of the 1890s is this house, a revival of the Federal style. The main clues to its sources are in the half-circular window in the pediment and in the sidelighted, fanlighted entrance. The slightly heavy-handed details, with a bit too much archaeological rigor, betray the revivalist tendencies of the design.

Walk east on Chicago Avenue. The next house on your right is

23. 320 CHICAGO AVENUE—c.1890

This tall Queen Anne house, from about 1890, bears an interesting comparison to the earlier one at 432 Chicago Avenue (Naperville #20). It too has a front porch which sweeps around to the side, there justified by being on a corner lot. Here the turret is placed opposite the circular sweep of the porch. Other variations from the earlier structure include fewer changes in the textures of the shingles and a curious (if not unique) handling of the porch elements, in which a squat column rests between the lower and upper posts. Notice the foliate decoration in the top of the front-facing gable.

Backtrack west on Chicago Avenue to Brainard Street. Turn right (north) 1 block. On the NW corner of Brainard Street and Jefferson Avenue is

24. 227 E. JEFFERSON AVENUE—1866

This 1866 house is now the May Watts Society. The front of the house reveals the general massing of the Greek Revival but it has been heightened slightly. The windows are larger, although not wider, and the window frames with their segmental cornices are distinctively Italianate, as is the front door with its double doors and transom and generous segmental molding. Notice, on the east side of the house, a broad porch overlooking the side yard.

Continue north on Brainard Street. The first house on your right is

25.   122 S. BRAINARD STREET—1874
This 1874 Italianate house was occupied for many years by the Hammerschmidt family, prominent in the local quarrying business. Ironically a frame structure, it has the heavy and robust forms that the Italianate style handled so well. Note the shoulder moldings with extensive incising and, on the ground floor, the projecting flat-fronted bay with its large pilasters and large, elaborate brackets.

Continue north on Brainard Street. On the NE corner of Brainard Street and Van Buren Avenue is

26.   30 S. BRAINARD STREET—1870
This Italianate house was built in 1870. More subdued than the earlier example at 122 S. Brainard Street (Naperville #25), it has quite simple round-headed windows on the second floor and segmental arches suggested by the ground floor frames; note the foot and shoulder motif for these window frames. The porch, set in the reentrant angle of the L-shaped plan, is a turn-of-the-century addition but works well with the overall design of the house.

On the NW corner of Brainard Street and Van Buren Avenue is

27.   31 S. BRAINARD STREET—c.1871
This frame house was built about 1871. It forms an instructive contrast to the building it faces (Naperville #26): the massing is that of the Classical Revival of the earlier period; the window heads have pedimental cornices that correspond to that massing; but it has a massiveness characteristic of the Italianate. Unfortunately the original front porch has been replaced.

Continue north on Brainard Street. On the NE corner of Brainard Street and Benton Avenue is

28. 6 N. BRAINARD STREET
North Central College Library—c.1900

This relatively small but quite massive structure shows that, at North Central College, the library was a serious place. It has pairs of Ionic columns flanking the doorway and supporting the pediment which is made of sheet metal, as is the cornice. In the block to which that frontispiece is attached are pairs of arched windows with the extrados of the arch traced in limestone, corresponding to the frontispiece and to the quoins and mud sill of the brick structure.

Walk west on Benton Avenue. On the NE corner of Benton Avenue and Ellsworth Street is

29. 6 N. ELLSWORTH STREET—1925

This neo-Gothic church, finished in 1925, replaced a structure destroyed by fire in 1922. Its west facade is asymmetrical with a very tall, spire-topped tower sitting on the southwest corner and a much lower spire above a projection on the north face, set behind the front facade to balance it. Note the gargoyles on the taller tower, which extend dramatically beyond the face where the steep gables meet. Below them are finials in limestone and below that, the tower becomes less open and changes in each floor. The triple arched entrance is characteristic of Gothic basilicas. Above the central portal is a large window lighting the nave; and above that, where one would expect to find a window, is a flat field of masonry enclosed by a multi-lobe frame. This field is apparently still awaiting a carver to produce a religious sculpture.

Continue west on Benton Street to Washington Avenue. Turn left (south). The third building on your left is

30. 12 S. WASHINGTON AVENUE—1899

This 1899 limestone church is in adaptive reuse as the Naperville Woman's Club. The small building forms an interesting comparison to the great cathedral-type church at 6 N. Ellsworth Street (Naperville #29). This is a parish church type and is built in the simpler forms with a small sanctuary lit by a pointed arched window under an unornamented gable with a simple coping. In the southwest corner is a stout, foursquare tower whose pointed roof reaches only slightly higher than the ridge of the sanctuary roof. The simple ornament is enriched by the care with which the masonry is handled and by the stepped corner pier buttresses.

Walk south on Washington Avenue. The third building on your left, across from Van Buren Avenue, is

31. 110 S. WASHINGTON AVENUE
Nichols Library—1897

Designed by M.E. Bell in the Romanesque Revival style, but considerably tamed from the usual heaviness that that style had, this 1897 building has a rectangular base with a ridged, hipped roof on the west facade. The central section is stepped forward slightly and topped by a gable. The gable has large knobs at its base and top and is lined, as is the projection, by quarry-faced limestone in alternating thin and thick courses. That limestone is also found on the corner quoins and as the basement, which rises into a broad arch within which is set the front entrance. Similar limestone is used as lintels and sills for the windows. The modillions are broad and unelaborated. The wing, set back from the face and extending to the south, is from 1962.

Walk west on Van Buren 1 block to Main Street. Turn right (north) 1 block. The first house on your right past Benton Street is

32. 10 and 12 N. MAIN STREET—1846

This Greek Revival house was built in 1846. It originally stood on Washington Avenue and was moved to its present site in 1898. It is one of the earliest temple-fronted, Greek Revival, residential structures in Northern Illinois. Instead of columns, piers are used and the simple moldings indicate the Doric order. The entablature with its architrave, frieze, and cornice closely follows the required canonic proportions. The pediment is carried quite nicely by the posts. Within the porch, formed by the frontispiece on the second floor, are three windows; on the ground floor are two small windows and a massive entrance with pilasters, holding a high, complete entablature. Note the sidelights and transom, and the very simple porch balusters, which appear more like attenuated nine pins used in bowling than like the bottle baluster types common since the Renaissance. The wings extending on either side are later but, set well back from the front, do not detract from the grandeur of this early structure.

*Continue north on Main Street to Franklin Avenue. Turn right (east) 1
short block. On the NW corner of Washington and Franklin avenues is*

33.   101 N. WASHINGTON AVENUE—1867

This red brick Italianate house was built in 1867. Its massing and the character, disposition, and proportions of its openings are characteristic of the
style but are handled in a unique manner. On the main (east) facade are four
irregularly spaced openings, although the ones on the second floor are in line
with the ones on the ground floor. The second opening from the north is the
entrance. It is not quite centered under the elongated cupola at the top of the
building. A similar irregularity occurs on the south facade, where there are
three openings (including an entrance) which are shoved slightly to the west
of center.

The veranda is a display of the art made possible by the power-driven
scroll saw, with elaborate patterns cut out of thin boards to produce a rich
result. The designer has very carefully aligned one of the arches of the porch
with the front entrance and provided a broader arch for each of the two
windows to the south. He almost succeeded in aligning the one at the far
northern end with the window but he missed slightly and was forced to insert
a smaller one. Especially notable is the clerestory cupola with its paired
brackets surviving and the larger paired brackets in the cornice.

Projecting to the west is a lower service wing. Its general character follows the design of this large structure which sits on a high piece of ground on
one of the main roads serving Naperville. It is possible that the limestone
slabs now serving as retaining walls for the yard originally were paving
stones for the walks around the house or on its grounds.

*Continue east on Franklin Avenue. On the NE corner of Center Street and
Franklin Avenue is*

34.   108 N. CENTER STREET—c. 1870

This clapboard Italianate house on a limestone foundation was built about
1870. It contains all of the distinctive characteristics of the style in excellent
repair. It has scroll-cut cornices, incised with stars and containing knobbed
pendants with the panels between the brackets in the cornice and dentils
above. The generous window frames have both feet and shoulders. A segmental cornice, above, has slightly rounded corner boards.

On the wing projecting to the south, on the ground floor, is a projecting polygonal bay. The slightly lower service wing that projects to the east has the original metal roof, although it is now covered with tar. Added sometime in the second decade of the twentieth century was the porch set across the west and south facades. It has cast concrete blocks, imitating quarry-faced ashlar, forming pedestals for cast concrete columns. These are in the Tuscan order with flutes and egg and leaf molding in the echinus, a distinctive form of the order that derived from Renaissance pattern books popular during this period. The use of cast concrete for such an element is an important factor in the development of early twentieth-century building technology.

Continue east on Franklin Avenue 2 blocks.

This concludes the Naperville Walking Tour.

Drive north on Brainard Street 1 block to School Avenue. Turn left (west) 3 blocks to Washington. Turn right (north) on Washington Street, ½ mile to Ogden Avenue (Route 34).

LISLE

MORTON ARBORETUM

WILLOWBROOK
Forest Preserve

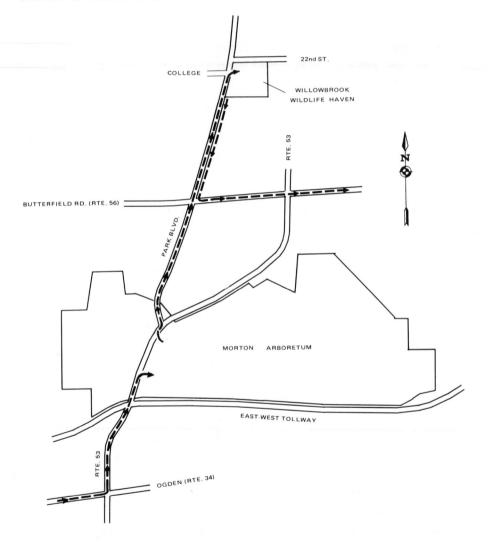

Turn right (east) on Route 34, 3.9 miles to Route 53 North. Turn right, then left onto Route 53, under the tollway a total of 1 mile to the entrance of the Morton Arboretum. Turn right (east) into the

Morton Arboretum

The Morton Arboretum's resources include 1,500 acres devoted to cultivated plants and natural vegetation, a visitor center, an administration building, and a conference center. There are numerous trails to enjoy and picnic tables are provided. Hours: 9:00 A.M. to sunset.

Leaving the Morton Arboretum, turn right (east) on Route 53. Then, almost immediately, turn left (north) on Park Boulevard 1.9 miles to College Street. Turn right (east) into the entrance of

Willowbrook Forest Preserve, Wild Life Haven

This unique forest preserve is a haven for wild animals that have been injured or wounded. About 3,000 animals a year enter this refuge and about 2,700 are cured and released. Animals include coyotes, eagles, many species of birds, a skunk, badgers, and turtles. Most are temporary visitors, but there are several permanent residents that make this spot worthwhile.

Leaving Willowbrook Wild Life Haven, turn left (south) on Park Boulevard .9 miles to Butterfield Road (Route 56). Turn left (east) 5 miles to Route 83. Turn right (south) 1 mile (across the tollway) to 31st Street (Oakbrook Road). Exit right, then turn left (east) onto 31st Street, ½ mile to Spring Road.

OAK BROOK

FULLERSBURG
Forest Preserve

GRAUE MILL

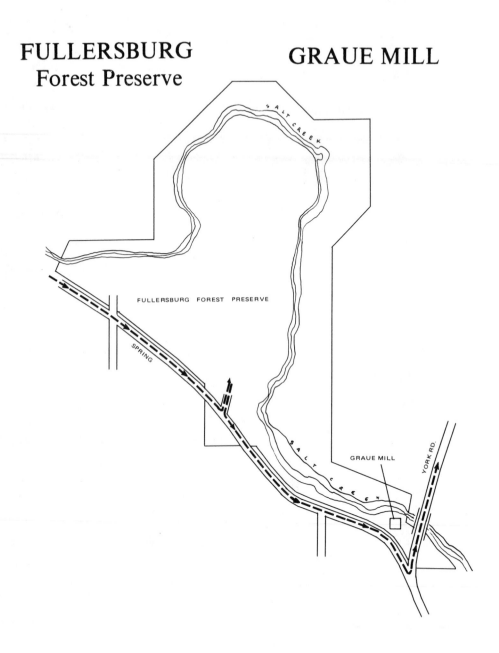

FULLERSBURG FOREST PRESERVE

SPRING

SALT CREEK

GRAUE MILL

YORK RD.

Turn right (south) on Spring Road .9 miles. Turn left (east) into the entrance of Fullersburg Woods Nature Preserve.

FULLERSBURG WOODS NATURE PRESERVE

This unique forest preserve, along with such traditional offerings as woodland trails and prairie restoration, features an environmental center. The center includes a theater which presents a twenty minute slide and sound show highlighting DuPage's five major ecosystems. There are several ecology exhibits as well as a nature art show and a nature photography exhibition, which features some of the finest artists in the Midwest.

With regular headphone rental, groups of fifteen or more may make arrangements for additional presentations tailored to the age and interest of the group. A special outdoor education program is offered from November–March for grades 3–5. The environmental center is open from 9:00 A.M. to 5:30 P.M. throughout the year, except holidays and on winter weekends from Halloween to February 15th.

Leaving Fullersburg Woods, turn left on Spring Road .3 miles. On your left is

GRAUE MILL—1852

This Federal Style structure stands on a high limestone foundation made from irregular ashlar and rises through three stories to a low pitched roof which, on the stream side and the opposite side, has eave returns indicating the classical revival origin. In the gable of the entrance side is a half-circular window, split apart by a chimney that rises through the roof at that point, but the link between the two sides is indicated by brick, layed with the butt end out, tying the two quadrants together. The sills and lintels throughout the building, except on the side facing the stream, are low segmental arches. The three-story height and the simplicity of the eave and gable detailing indicate the departure from the standard massing of this style and make clear the utilitarian purpose for which it was built. Twelve-over-twelve double-hung windows are common to the period and appear in most parts of the building. The undershoot waterwheel was originally driven by the water impounded by the weir now visible in simulation on the river side of the building. Also visible at this point are the regularly placed anchor plates tying the interior wooden structure, exemplary of braced-frame construction, and machinery to the exterior brick walls. The entrance, away from the river, is very wide to accommodate the loads that passed in and out. The floor level is considerably above grade in order to make transfering the loads, from wagon to mill and back again, easier.

This 1852 mill is on the National Register of Historic Places and is the only waterwheel grist mill still operating in the state. Due to a fall in the river, the wheel is now turned by electricity. Stoneground yellow corn meal is produced during visiting hours and sold in souvenir bags. With each grinding operation, the miller on duty explains the process. The second and third floors of the mill have been turned into a museum reflecting farm life in the community a century ago. Spinning and weaving demonstrations may be arranged. Open 10:00 A.M.-5:00 P.M. seven days a week from early May to late October. Adults: 50¢; children under 14: 25¢.

Leaving Graue Mill, continue on Spring Road until it ends at York Road. Turn left (north) on York Road 2.8 miles to Route 38 (Roosevelt Road). Turn right onto Route 38 East, then bear left immediately onto Route 290 East (Eisenhower Expressway) into Chicago.

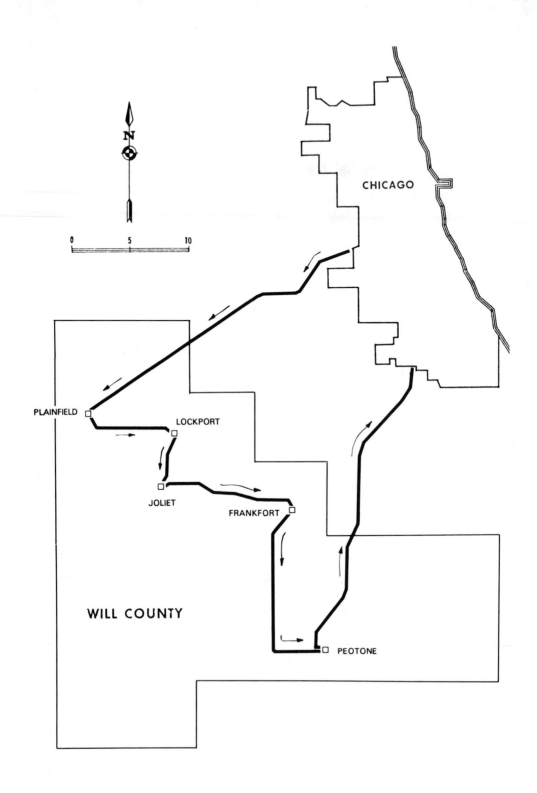

N

0   5   10

CHICAGO

PLAINFIELD

LOCKPORT

JOLIET

FRANKFORT

WILL COUNTY

PEOTONE

Will
County

PLAINFIELD

PLAINFIELD

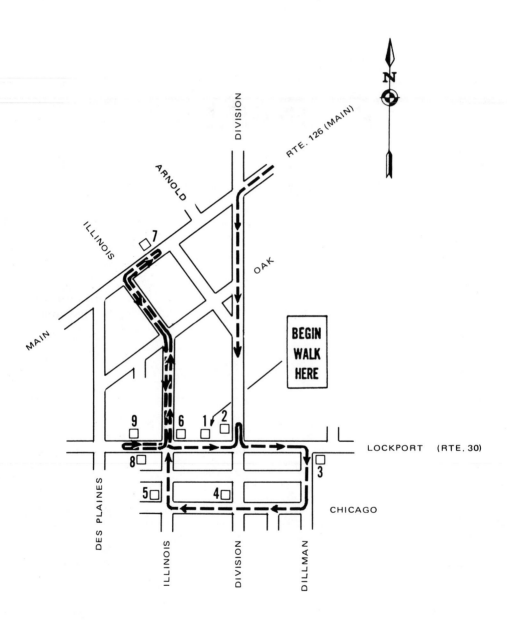

From Chicago take Route 55 to Route 126 West. Drive west 2.8 miles. (Route 126 becomes Main Street as you get into town.) Turn left (south) on Division Street 2 blocks to Lockport Street. Turn right (west) on Lockport Street ½ block. Stop.

PLAINFIELD WALKING TOUR

On the north side of Lockport Street, between Division and Illinois streets, is

1. THE SANCTUARY—1868

This 1868 building was originally the Universalist Church. The simple, frame, clapboard-covered structure has a great elegance. The sanctuary is enclosed under a pitched roof and lit by pointed windows with fine stained glass. The entrance is through a tower standing against the front (south) facade; the top of the tower is above the pitched roof and rises at first gently, then steeply into a multi-faceted pyramidal top. The greater length of the tower is taken up by a great window with a circle at its top and two arched openings in the frame below. The entrance is topped by a broad pointed-arched tympanum filled with arched tracery and a trifoil with fine stained glass. The building has undergone extensive renovation and is in adaptive reuse as a restaurant. The downstairs room has photographs of Plainfield in bygone days lining the walls.

Walk around the corner on Division Street to your left. In the same cluster of buildings, on your left, is

2. 704 DIVISION STREET—pre-1890

This house, probably dating from before 1890, has been restored and is in adaptive reuse. It is a typical, frame and clapboard, two-story, pitched roof block of the period with a one-and-one-half-story wing projecting to one side and a porch along the east side of the wing. The simple scroll-cut, incised brackets above the porch posts add a restrained elegance.

Backtrack south to Lockport Street. Turn left (east) to Dillman Street. On the SE corner of Dillman and Lockport streets is

3.   SHARON UNITED METHODIST CHURCH—1855

The clapboard, meeting-house-type building was built in 1855. It forms an interesting comparison to the 1868 Universalist Church (Plainfield #1). Here, the roof pitch is lower and the windows have square tops, with additions on the corners of pilasters, all indicating its Greek Revival sources. The tower on the north face, which contains the entrance, is square instead of rectangular and has an arched entrance. The pair of arched windows above is topped by a circle forming a blind window that is not enclosed within the frame of the windows below. It is quite clear that the builder of the Universalist Church had this one in mind when he built his church, but that he altered its classical forms to suggest the Gothic forms which had become fashionable in the 1860s.

Walk south on Dillman Street 1 block to Chicago Street. Turn right (west) 1 block. On the NW corner of Chicago and Division streets is

4.   602 DIVISION—1888

This two-story, frame structure covered in thin clapboards is an extraordinarily fine example of a rare building type. Basically Italianate, it is topped by a Mansard roof. The plan is quite traditional, with a cubic block facing the front and a one-and-one-half-story wing projecting to the rear. The way that basic type is handled shows how two styles could be very pleasantly combined into a single design. One style is that of the Italianate, with paired scroll-cut incised brackets under the eaves of both the main and the service block and on the bay window projecting to the side; the other style is the Stick which is relatively rare in the six-county area. It is seen in the decorative treatment given the wall surface by the manipulation of small pieces of wood and under the cornice. There is a broad band of grooved sticks placed on an angle. The cornice around the southeast corner, which is cut on a bias, is sustained by panels with incising and bosses. The bay window, projecting on the ground floor on that angled corner, has diagonal siding placed between the window frame, a motif repeated on the polygonal bay farther to the rear. Note the material used on the Mansard roof: square panels of cement asbestos board laid in 45° courses to produce a pattern to complement the Stick style features. The west side of the front facade has a very simple shed porch held by very simple brackets.

Continue west on Chicago Street 1 block. On the NW corner of Chicago and Illinois streets is

4. 602 Division Street

5. UNITED METHODIST CHURCH—1866

This church from 1866 (the date indicated in the name and date stone in the gable on the east end) has a main sanctuary like the ones at the previous two churches (Plainfield #1 and #3), but it is limestone instead of frame and has the tower set at the corner instead of at the end of the sanctuary. The forms here are Romanesque instead of Gothic or classical, as can be noted by the buttresses in the east wall at the corners of the tower and in the round arches above the thin windows. Interesting to note: on the east end of the sanctuary is the same double window observed earlier with a large circle above it, but here the entire motif is set within the masonry wall. The general configuration of the spire (atop the tower with a steep gable on its face, and a thin hexagonal spire rising to a point) follows the original construction, but the original one probably had more elaborate carpentry work than the present sheet metal replacement displays. Twentieth century additions, on the north side and projecting to the west, have been designed to work well with the original structure.

Walk north on Illinois 1 block to Lockport Street. On the NE corner of Illinois and Lockport streets is

6. CONGREGATIONAL CHURCH—1850

This elegant, clapboard, Federal Revival church was built in 1850. It has an elegance and finish quite unusual on the prairie frontier at this early date. The broad pediment with its triple window has large scale moldings giving clear definition to that classical element. Below it are well-detailed pilasters. The center of the front facade opens to a porch and contains two slim, fluted, Ionic capitals with their characteristic volutes in the capitals, and richly worked bases below the shafts of the columns. Above the entrance is a tower rising to a pointed spire (a replacement for an earlier one); a tower similar to this would have been characteristic of this period and style. Within the porch is the elegant pedimented entrance to the church. At the back of the building, on the west side, is a polygonal projection; on the east side is a wing as high as that of the sanctuary. The stained glass within the simply framed windows is a later addition from closer to the turn of the century.

Continue north on Illinois 2 blocks to Main Street. Turn right (east) ½ block. On your left (north side of street) is

6. Congregational
Church

7. 503 MAIN STREET
Halfway House—1834 with later additions

This clapboard farmhouse was Arnold Tavern, the first government franchised post office in Will County (1834–1845), home of Dr. E. G. Wight, one of the first physicians in Northern Illinois (1836). The post office was for the passengers of the Frink & Walder stage lines operating between Chicago and Ottawa from 1836–1886. This is also known as the "Halfway House," because of its location between Chicago and Ottawa. Much of the upstairs was once a large ballroom.

This structure was built in several stages, the first two in 1834–1836. That early construction is visible in the main block of the building in the faint, thin, Greek Revival reminiscences in the gabled roof and corner pilasters, the very thin simple unornamented windows visible behind the present storm windows, and especially in the irregularity of the walnut siding. The entrance, with pilasters flanking the sidelights, is also characteristic of this early period of construction and of the building's use (it was for a utilitarian purpose, and it was built very early in the settlement of this area). The structure is listed on the National Register of Historic Places.

Backtrack west on Main to Illinois. Turn left (south) on Illinois 2 blocks to Lockport Street. Turn right (west).

Lockport Street between Illinois and Des Plaines streets is very historical. There were fires on either side of the street in the 1890s.

On your left is

8. 503 LOCKPORT STREET—1876
Built in 1876, this building survived the fire, but the ground floor has been subsequently mutilated. On the second floor, the windows have been reduced in size and a new parapet has been added. But notice the keystones in the arches with an "S," an ampersand, and an "R" giving the initials of the original owner.

Across the street is

9. 508 LOCKPORT STREET—1876
This is a row of brick shops, one of which has a circular pediment with the

name Sonntag. This row is characteristic of the period, and the Sonntag building from 1876 survives in excellent condition showing the simple cast iron columns and lintels (the lintels decorated with bosses) and the plate glass with a large panel below and two smaller panels in the transom. The sheet metal cornice with knobs on either end and the pediment above it are also characteristic of the period.

Notice next to it, at **510 LOCKPORT STREET**, the triangular pediment. The structures to the west have variations on the same sheet metal cornice and surviving traces of the original cast iron shopfronts. They also display a variety of treatment used between the cast iron and the sheet metal, although they have always lacked projections above that cornice line.

Backtrack east on Lockport Street to The Sanctuary on your left.

This concludes the Plainfield Walking Tour.

Drive west on Lockport Street ½ block to Illinois Street. Turn left (south) 1 block. Turn left (east) on Chicago Street, 1 block. Turn right (south) on Division Street, 2 blocks to the left fork, Lincoln Highway (Route 30). Continue southeast on Route 30, 1.1 miles to Renwick Road. Turn left (east) 6 miles to Route 53.

LOCKPORT

LOCKPORT

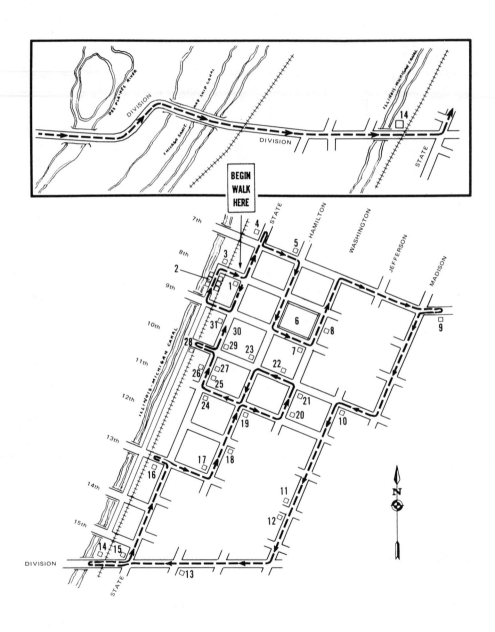

Turn right (south) on Route 53, .9 miles to Division Street. Turn left (east).

You will cross a single lane bridge. The next bridge is a rare example of a nineteenth century "swing bridge." Instead of being raised to allow boats to pass, the swing bridge pivots in the channel, allowing boats on either side. The third bridge crosses to the south of the first lock on the canal.

THE ILLINOIS AND MICHIGAN CANAL

This is one of the most historic waterways in the midwest. The desire to construct it, and the early history of its construction, accounts for the founding of Chicago as a city and its growth as a commercial center. In order to build this link between the Great Lakes water system (which was by this time linked to the Atlantic Ocean by the Erie Canal) and the Gulf of Mexico by way of the Illinois River and the Mississippi River, it was necessary to dig a canal across the intervening watershed divide. The Indians had to be cleared from the area, which was accomplished by a treaty negotiated in 1833. It also required that construction funds be raised. This was accomplished by bond issues underwritten by the state of Illinois and by the sale of federal lands granted to the state to raise revenue for construction. Chicago, for example, was built on such canal land which was first sold in 1834.

The construction of the canal began soon after Chicago was chartered as a town in 1833, but construction proceeded very slowly and the canal was not opened until 1848. Subsequently, the original canal has been increased in size, changed in location, and given a competitor (the railroad) which stunted the growth of canal traffic and eventually caused the canal to be abandoned. The Calumet (Sag) Canal is the present waterway between the two great waterways that made Chicago possible. The Calumet (Sag) Canal is in some stretches also the Chicago Sanitary and Ship Canal.

Continue east (now on Division Street) 1 block to State Street (Route 171). Turn left (north) 8 blocks. Stop.

LOCKPORT WALKING TOUR

On your left (west side of State Street just before Eighth Street) is

1. WILL COUNTY HISTORICAL SOCIETY
803 S. State Street
Illinois and Michigan Canal Museum
1837 and 1876

The one-story, clapboard, meeting-house style wing was built in 1837 as the headquarters for the canal. The two-story Italianate addition was constructed in 1876, and windows similar in form to the Italianate structure were added to the older building at that time. About 1890 the porch, with delightful scalloped gables and spindle work on the ground floor, was added to provide additional dignity to the structure. This structure contained the home of the canal commissioners. The entire building is on the National Register of Historic Places. It is now a museum and has many period displays. Exhibits include a Victorian bedroom, a surgeon's office, and Indian artifacts. Daily: 1:00 P.M.-4:00 P.M. Free.

Walk south on State Street 1 block to Ninth Street. Turn right (west). (Notice the limestone building on your right: 18 W. Ninth Street.) Cross the tracks, then turn immediately right into the driveway.

2. NORTH PUBLIC LANDING
On this site is a cluster of buildings, some of which have been relocated here by the Will County Historical Society. The log cabin, built in 1830 and said to be the oldest known building in Will County, originally stood in Reed's Grove. Originally the canal was wider at this point allowing for a loading basin; note the lower level of the ground and fragments of the original canal wall which formed a dock.

Walk north to

3. CANAL WORKS
later G. B. Martin Elevator and Gaylord Store,
later the Hyland Building—1837, 1858, 1895

The oldest part of this structure is the oldest industrial building connected with the Illinois and Michigan Canal. It is the two-story limestone section nearest the canal where two great arches allowed equipment and materials used in constructing the canal to be stored and serviced, and it dates from 1837 when work on the canal began in earnest. The section between it and the railroad tracks was added in 1858 to extend the building, now serving as a grain elevator, to the tracks. The building now provided a convenient transloading facility between the canal and railroad which had reached this point a few years earlier. The facade facing south is a three bay, three-story design with classical grandeur and careful masonry giving that part of the building a dignity suitable to the role played by commerce. The brick structure atop the older section was added in 1895.

Walk east, across the tracks on the pedestrian crosswalk, to State Street. Turn left (north). The first house on your left, past Seventh Street, is

4.   613 S. STATE STREET—1840s
This Greek Revival house, with returns on the eaves to suggest a pediment, was built in carefully cut local limestone. It contains a half-circular or "bull's-eye" window in the pediment area. The cornice and the front porch are not original and the south section of the building, with the Mansard roof, is a recent addition. The structure dates from the 1840s.

Backtrack south on State Street to Seventh Street. Turn left (east) 1 block. On the NW corner of Hamilton and Seventh streets is

5.   128 HAMILTON STREET—1894
This two-story frame structure is a quite late example of the Italianate style. It has a wing projecting on one side to produce a porch containing exactly the same features as the front porch which shelters the double door entrance. These porches have Mansard roofs and terminate in excellent cast iron crestings. Such cresting also originally appeared along the top of the hipped roof. Notice the simple paired brackets with turned pendants and the suggestion of a pediment on the window lintels on the ground floor.

Turn right (south) on Hamilton Street, 1 block. In the block between Eighth and Ninth streets, on your left, is

6.   OLD CENTRAL GRADE SCHOOL—1890
This school, built in 1890 in the local limestone and recently renovated, is a very fine example of the typical schoolhouse design of the period, displaying the Romanesque Revival typical of this period's school buildings. The plan of the south section is typical with one classroom in each corner and a cross-shaped hallway system on the inside. The front (south facade) has the grand-

est treatment with Palladian windows in the gable, and below that is an easy swell of the bow with a slight pattern in the bulging area above the second floor windows. The entrance in that facade is made conspicuous by a vigorous arch between the two projecting wings. In the equivalent space, in the east, is a stairway; opposite is a side entrance. The two-story mass is topped by a great hipped roof with gables on each side of each facade. The building's shapes are strongly outlined by the large blocks of stone, and the demarcation between the basement and the first floor is established by a strong stringcourse containing the largest stones used in the construction.

Continue south on Hamilton Street. Turn left (east) on Ninth Street. On the SW corner of Ninth and Washington streets is

7.   CONGREGATIONAL CHURCH—1840

This Gothic, limestone building with stained glass windows is now in adaptive reuse as the Lockport Youth Center. Built in 1840, it is claimed to be the oldest stone building in Northern Illinois. Especially interesting are a few features to support that early date. The front portal is made of many fewer pieces of stone than would be common later. In a later period the pointed arch would have been made of a series of voussoirs rather than just a few pieces cut to have the inner surface describe the pointed arch as occurs here. Another early feature is visible from the side of the building; note that only the front face of the tower is limestone while the area behind it is frame construction, making it unnecessary to carry heavy stone construction through the building from the foundations except at the front facade. Also interesting is the series of slanted coping stones along the gable, an expediency that facilitated the construction process but, nonetheless, produced an interesting effect.

Walk north on Washington Street. The fourth house on your right is

8.   814 WASHINGTON STREET—c. 1850

This early residence is built of local limestone and contains the characteristics of the Greek Revival style. It is a very simple one-and-one-half-story structure with the opening for the door only slightly wider than those for the windows. Its narrowness prevents the use of the sidelights common in the style. The building is given an elegance, beyond that suggested by the simple masonry, by its richly worked wooden cornice with eave returns suggesting a pediment. The chimney on the north is a modern addition.

7. Congregational
Church

Continue north past Eighth Street, then veer right (east) onto Seventh Street. (Notice the lovely ravine, lined in some places with limestone, on your left.) Continue east on Seventh Street. The second house on your right, past Madison Street, is

9. 535 E. SEVENTH STREET—1842

The Erastus Newton and later Robert Milne house was built in 1842 with a front porch and back wing from just before 1873. It originally had a parapet around the base of the roof which was removed in the late 1940s. The builder and early owners of the house were associated with the construction on the Illinois and Michigan Canal. This house was built to face the town Milne

9. 535 E. Seventh Street

(detail)

hoped would develop in this direction ("East Lockporte") and the farm he operated which ran in the opposite direction. The wing was later placed on that side of the house. The building is listed on the National Register of Historic Places.

The one-and-one-half-story, square, limestone structure is covered with a low roof rising to a pair of chimneys. It faces away from the street, and its simple, 1873 square porch has posts. The ground floor windows are very tall but the second story windows are very low. Especially interesting is the use of large and simple limestone blocks to describe the cornice. Beyond the modern addition to the east, an early limestone outbuilding can be seen.

Backtrack on Seventh Street to Madison Street. Turn left (south) on Madison Street to Tenth Street. Turn right (west) on Tenth Street. On the SE corner of Tenth and Jefferson streets is

10.   1006 JEFFERSON STREET—c.1850

This limestone house, built about 1850, shows excellent care in its proportions and its use of materials. The basic block of the building is characteristic of the mid-century with the cubic mass and two lower wings projecting from it. The limestone blocks are very carefully cut and the large lintels for the windows and door have precisely turned moldings. The front door is a grand one and has sidelights and a transom and large corbels supporting the door lintel within the masonry reveal. The roof of this structure is not original but does date from an earlier period and is made of asbestos cement sheets laid in a diagonal pattern, an early artificial roofing material which works quite well with the structure. Its location on high ground and the careful finish of the design indicate a care associated with the prosperity of early successful settlers.

Walk south on Jefferson Street to Thirteenth Street. On the NW corner of Thirteenth and Jefferson streets is

11.   1229 JEFFERSON STREET—1850s

This clapboard Greek Revival house, on a limestone foundation, was built prior to the Civil War. The metal siding detracts from the original character, but the characteristic proportions from the original period are still visible.

On the SW corner of Jefferson and Thirteenth streets is

12.   1305 JEFFERSON STREET—1850s

This frame, Greek Revival house, on a limestone foundation, was also built prior to the Civil War. It features a sunset motif on the pediment. Again, artificial siding detracts from the building, but the greater elegance of this building (relative to Lockport #11) is visible in the fanlight, the more elaborately treated corner pilasters, and the octagonal columns with their quite large capitals framing the pediment of the front door. The cornice and the eave returns are original.

Continue south on Jefferson Street 2 blocks to Division Street. Turn right (west). On the SE corner of Division and Hamilton streets is

13.   1514 HAMILTON STREET—c. 1870

This two-story, cubic, frame, clapboard-covered house (with a wing that has received an additional story) has retained excellent, scroll-cut products typical of the Italianate, particularly in the paired brackets under the eaves and, more interestingly, in the cut-out decoration attached to the pedimented window lintels and front door lintel. These produce an elegance through very economical means. The structure was perhaps built with the funds resulting from the prosperity of the post-Civil War period.

Continue east on Division Street past State Street. On your right is

14.   LOCK NO. 1—c. 1845

This lock, probably the first one constructed on the Illinois and Michigan Canal, was built about 1845 and had a ten-foot lift. The stone was locally quarried and the hydraulic cement used as mortar was locally produced.

Backtrack west on Division Street to State Street. Turn left (north). The first house on your left is

15.   1513 S. STATE STREET—1848

This humble, clapboard, Greek Revival cottage was built in 1848 for use by the lockkeeper of Lock No. 1.

Continue north on State Street to Thirteenth Street. Turn left (west). At the railroad tracks on your left is

16. Chicago and Alton Railroad Station—1870s

This station, built in the 1870s, is unique because it is built in the local lime-stone. Notice the care with which it uses projecting quoins on the corners and, for the openings, a limestone from a different quarry that allowed for a very smooth surface. The overhanging eaves are supported by large curved eave brackets, scroll-cut and gouged on the outer face. The result is a nicely finished but strictly utilitarian structure. Facing the railroad tracks is a large door for the baggage and a smaller opening for the waiting room.

Walk east on Thirteenth Street. On top of the hill, on the NW corner of Hamilton and Thirteenth streets, is

17. 1225 Hamilton Street—c. 1850

This Italianate house was built about 1850 in limestone, an unusual material for this style, just as the date is also early in this area for this style. Note the especially tall windows on the ground floor.

Walk north on Hamilton Street. On the SE corner of Hamilton and Twelfth streets is

18. St. Dennis Church—1870 and 1897

This imposing limestone structure was begun in 1870 in the Gothic style. It has a very steeply pitched gabled roof which runs into a buttressed corner tower that rises through three stories to reach the height of the gable. The entrance, protected by a gabled roof, is in the center of the facade. The arched entrance has tracery work of pointed arches and stained glass.

In 1897, the top story of the tower was added. Lest anyone mistake the new structure for the old, the date was placed at the bottom of the string-course of the addition. Here the style is classical, its Tuscan columns and pilasters having an exaggerated enthasis. Atop the columnar opening is the final parapet which returns to the Gothic style by having a very simple cop-ing and a slight gable suggestion before the pointed spire is reached. The large pointed-arched opening above the front entrance has recently been filled.

Continue north on Hamilton Street. On the SE corner of Hamilton and Eleventh streets is

19. 1104 HAMILTON STREET
Old Norton Home—1870s

This mansion has been altered, but its basic massing with its Mansard roof with great dormers and their window surrounds and the distinctive cast iron fence remain visible. It dates from the 1870s.

Turn right (east) on Eleventh Street. On the NE corner of Washington and Eleventh streets is

20. ST. JOHN'S EPISCOPAL CHURCH—1873

This 1873 limestone building has been described as one of the finest examples of English Gothic architecture in the Midwest. Support for that claim can be noticed in the extremely fine use of stone within a very well proportioned massing. The front door has a very large keystone and voussoirs, rough-faced on the outer face and smoother on the intrados of the arch. The gable above that pointed arch has thin slabs used as coping stones which terminate in very large, rough-faced blocks undercut in a semicircle. The masonry blocks used for the walls are random ashlar and graded from larger blocks on the bottom to the smaller ones above. The only alteration to the original design appears to be the replacement of the circular window lighting the interior sanctuary, required perhaps by the deterioration of the stones in the area.

Walk north on Washington Street. On the SE corner of Washington and Tenth streets is

21. METHODIST CHURCH—1855

This fine, Greek Revival, 1855 structure is set on a high basement that contains the entrance. The Greek temple above is clearly portrayed by the pilasters built from rough-faced stones which contrast with the smoother stones between. The smoother masonry is also used for the pediment. The windows have been altered (originally in each opening there probably was one small, square-topped window instead of the present two), and the original wooden cornice has been lost. Nonetheless, the building is a striking example of an almost literal translation of an ancient Greek prototype for American uses.

Turn left (west) on Tenth Street. The second house on your right is

22. 224 E. TENTH STREET—1880s

This simple structure from the 1880s rises two stories to a hipped roof, a gabled roof projection in the front, and an additional projection (the square tower with a tall hipped roof) dominating the front. Along the side is a porch with porch posts turning into half arches and lined with a bead molding on each corner. The union between the first and second floors is flared and contains two rows of scalloped shingles above plain shingles. The overall effect is impressive, subdued, and simple.

Continue west on Tenth Street. On the NW corner of Tenth and Hamilton streets is

23. PILGRIM HALL—c.1850, adapted 1896

This Greek Revival, clapboard hall was built as a church. Its steeple is gone, and its entrance was originally under the full pediment facing the side street (south), supported by pilasters with large capitals. It is characteristic of frame churches of about 1850. In 1896 it was converted to a hall called Pilgrim Hall. It is now in adaptive reuse as a furniture and an antique store. Visible along the west facade are the original window frames, although the windows have disappeared and been replaced by clapboard.

Walk south on Hamilton Street 1 block. Turn right (west) on Eleventh Street 1 block. On the SE corner of Eleventh and State streets is

24. 1100 S. STATE STREET
Adelmann Block—1891 and 1895

This structure, built in two stages, began as a livery stable with a cast iron ground floor allowing for large windows and a large central doorway. Above were apartments behind a limestone wall with six large, double-hung windows topped by lintels extended to the corners to describe the stringcourses. Above that is a rich sheet metal cornice typical of the date it bears.

In 1895 the structure extended to the corner. Here, Moorish arches stand above the double windows. The stained glass survives in some of the windows. The cast iron elements of the ground floor are similar to those of the earlier construction but present a slightly different pattern. On the corner in the second story, which is open on a diagonal to the street, is a sheet metal oriel topped by a bell roof and terminating in a knobbed finial.

Most of State Street, from Eighth to Eleventh streets and extending to the canal, constitutes the Lockport Historic District listed on the National Register of Historic Places.

Walk north on State Street ½ block. On your right is

25.   1020 STATE STREET—1848

This small, wooden, two-story structure with a pedimented gable facing the street originally served as a stage coach stop and retains its Greek Revival character. This is clearly portrayed by the pilasters on the inner wall on the second story and the inner wall of the ground floor. At some later date, perhaps at the turn of the century, the front section was rebuilt but follows closely the construction it replaced and retains much of its original material. Even more recently, metal siding has been placed on the building and the cornice of the pediment and the cornice along the side have been replaced. The overall character of the building, however, is visible as representative of the commercial structures found along this main street of Lockport as it grew with the Illinois and Michigan Canal.

Cross to the west side of State Street and continue north. On your left is

26.   1011 and 1015 STATE STREET—1886 and 1880s

These buildings form an interesting pair. They are both the same building type with a shop on the ground floor and an entrance to the upstairs apartment at the outer edge. They both have a typical sheet metal cornice, the one at 1011 State Street with the bulging forms associated with the "U.S. Grant" style but quite late, dating from 1886. The one at 1015 State Street has the large brackets and peacock tail motif of a slightly earlier period. 1011 State Street has stone segmental arches with pedimented tops but flat faces for its window heads, whereas 1015 State Street has cast iron lintels carried on small brackets and a small half-circular device set in the center. The ground floors of both have been substantially altered.

Cross back to the east side of the street and continue north. On your right is

27.   1006 STATE STREET—1895

This brick building has stained glass windows and a stone archway in heavy rusticated stone. Above, in brick of a complementary color, are the same forms topped by a thin ledge of rough-faced stone. At the top is a sheet metal cornice bearing the date, 1895. Notable here is a form of shop formerly very common and now extremely rare: a below-grade shop, entered by steps leading off the sidewalk parallel to the building and lit by windows opening from the steps. Such an arrangement requires that the "ground floor" shop be raised several steps above the sidewalk level.

Walk west on Tenth Street. At the railroad tracks, on your left, is

28. NORTON WAREHOUSE AND STORE—1848
This massive, limestone building was built the year the Illinois and Michigan Canal was opened for traffic between Lake Michigan and the Illinois River, and hence the Mississippi, in 1848. It is in adaptive reuse as the Lockport Iron Works. Only the loss of the original penthouse and the new materials suggesting a pediment detract substantially from the original construction. The brackets immediately under that carry through the motif of the Greek Revival turning in the direction of the Italianate.

The division of the massive structure into two sections, one for warehousing and one for display, is seen on the east end of the north facade. Two bays are defined by rustic projecting stones with a rough face which suggest pilaster pairs. These hold standard windows on the second and third floor and small windows in the top floor. Small windows are also found on the main, unfenestrated block (they have been bricked in); their size and form suggest the window type often found lighting the attic of a Greek Revival house. They originally lit the dormitories used by bargemen and others who worked the canal. The openings, if small, have smooth-faced lintels but if larger have an arch. The corners are trimmed by smooth-faced pilasters. Notice on the north and west facades the rows of anchor ends, used to attach the inner timber framework holding the floors to the masonry walls that support them around the perimeter; they help keep the walls from bulging.

Backtrack east on Tenth Street. On the NE corner of State and Tenth streets is

29. 938 STATE STREET
Norton Store—1878
This limestone building was built in 1878 to contain Norton's expanded business which could no longer be held by his earlier building, Lockport #28.

28. Norton Warehouse and Store

It was untouched by the fire in 1895 that destroyed the rest of this block. It is in adaptive reuse as Miller Ace Hardware.

Two features are especially notable here. One is the ground floor which uses massive blocks of stone supplemented with large wooden posts, rather than cast iron columns, to support the spaces between the windows. The other is in the cornice which has very simple forms indicating an early date. The outer third of its length is set forward relative to the middle third, a suggestion of the formal composition associated with the Second Empire, a style prominent elsewhere at the time the structure was built.

Look at the east side of State Street between Ninth and Tenth streets.

30. COMMERCIAL ROW—1895 and later
Almost all of this block was burned in a fire in 1895 and these buildings were built soon after. Note the dates on many of them and the fine sheet metal cornices at the tops of the buildings and the many cast iron store fronts.

Across the street from Commercial Row, the second building south of Ninth Street (on the west side of State Street) is

31. 903 STATE STREET—1876
This 1876 brick storefront has massively scaled segmental arches and corbels. It is in adaptive reuse as Century 21 Realtors. Note the very thin cast iron columns on its ground floor.

Continue north on State Street 1 block to the Historical Society on your left.

This concludes the Lockport Walking Tour.

Drive south on State Street (Route 171).

JOLIET

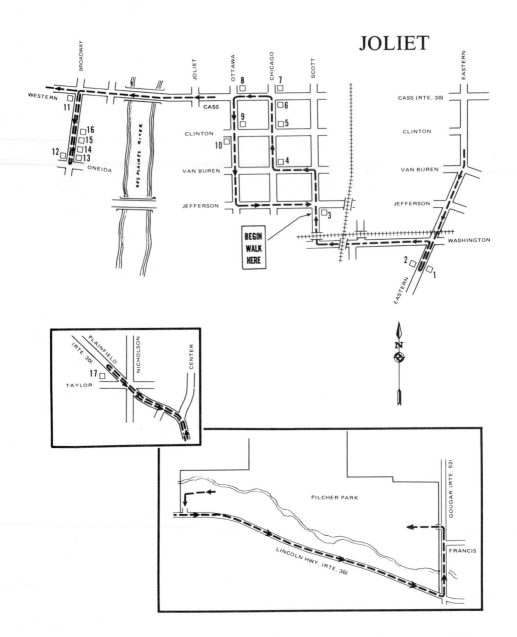

Drive south on State Street (Route 171) 4½ miles (Route 171 becomes Collins Street as you get into Joliet) to Cass Street. Turn right (west) on Cass Street, 2 blocks. Turn left (south) on Eastern Avenue 4½ blocks. On your left is

1. VICTORIAN MANOR
Jacob A. Henry Mansion
20 S. Eastern Avenue—1873

This 1873 mansion contains over forty rooms. It cost $70,000 and, at the time of completion in 1876, was the most expensive home built in Will County. The structure is a superb combination of three basic styles prominent during the third quarter of the nineteenth century. Archaeological exactitude based upon Italian Renaissance elements is visible in the columnar detailing, in the treatment of the windows on the wing extending to the east, and on the second and third floors of the tower, except that the keystones (normally worked more closely into the shape of the arch) are exaggerated in their size. The Second Empire provided the overall composition of the main mass with the very large, curved Mansard roofs covering the third floor. Notice here the combination of polygonal and square-cut slates producing an interesting texture. The top of the Mansard roof is crowned by a corbeled cornice characteristic of the Italian Renaissance rather than of the Second Empire. Finally, the Italianate is evident in the general composition with its insertion of the tower on the front facade terminating in a quite conspicuous roof. That roof, like those above the dormer windows in the Mansard, has a split segmental pediment above its cornice, and set within that opening is a dormer, itself with a split segmental pediment. Also characteristic of the Italianate is the collection of paired windows into redstone projections set into the brick mass of the main bulk of the building. A similar stone is used for the extensively detailed porch, and for the curved corner and curved bow projecting on the south. Note that it has a copper cornice and is topped by a copper onion dome, an unusual feature. Characteristic of this period is the use of sheet metal to produce the elaborate detailing in the cornices and windows above the top of the second story. Notice that the lawn is fronted by an original cast iron fence which survives in very good condition. Across the street the ground slopes away indicating that originally this building commanded a view over Joliet and was itself a prominent feature on the skyline from the downtown area. The structure is on the National Register of Historic Places and forms part of a National Register district encompass-

1.   20 S. Eastern Avenue
Henry Mansion

ing several blocks in the surrounding area, originally the "silk stocking" district of Joliet. Wednesdays-Sundays: 1:00 P.M.-5:00 P.M.

The surrounding neighborhood has wonderful nineteenth-century homes ranging from very simple to very elaborate. Although the buildings are in various states of disrepair, they are worth a short walk.

Across the street, on the west side of Eastern Avenue, is

2. 15 S. EASTERN AVENUE—1887

This structure, originally the Dr. Salter home, dates from 1887. It shows how the same forms (as those used in Joliet #1) could be used to produce a much less expensive structure. Here turned elements characteristic of the Italianate style are used to provide a long veranda that extends around three sides of the brick building that rises to a Mansard roof which has wood framed dormers and cornices similar to the sheet metal ones on Joliet #1. The brick block has paired windows like the Henry Mansion, but notice that its stone, hooded, segmental arches are extremely simple.

Drive north (backtrack) on Eastern Avenue to the corner. Turn left (west) on Washington Street under two underpasses. Then turn right (north) under another underpass. Stop.

JOLIET WALKING TOUR

On the SE corner of Jefferson and Scott streets is

3. UNION STATION
50 E. Jefferson Street—1909–1912

This structure, opened in 1912, is on the National Register of Historic Places. Its architect was Jarvis Hunt, an important Chicago architect who used his personal interpretation of the classical style to produce prominent structures. The form of this station was determined by the oblique angle formed by the intersection of the tracks of the four major trunk lines, two belt lines, and an outer belt line, all serving Joliet. These were consolidated and elevated as a part of an urban redevelopment project from 1909. The result was the regular polygon plan of the main waiting room area with two wings projecting at each side parallel with the tracks between the waiting room and the extensive train platforms. Across the lower level is a walkway with a terrace walkway above. The basement level is treated with deeply grooved masonry to provide the appearance of strength. It is punctured by large arches, the central one serving as an entrance. The three arches are replicated in the waiting room above by very high windows with carved-out frames. The top of the building has a balustraded parapet. The structure is being rehabilitated; extensive alterations planned for the interior should bring to light the great vaulted roof above the upper level waiting room.

There originally was an ample carriage and streetcar forecourt area which now is filled by an unfortunate, smaller, later structure.

From the Union Station, walk north on Scott Street 1½ blocks to Van Buren Street. Turn left (west). Observe the building on your right, then turn right (north) on Chicago Street. On your right is

4.   RUBENS RIALTO SQUARE THEATRE BUILDING
102 N. Chicago Street and
5-25 Van Buren Street—1926

This spectacular theatre, designed by Rapp and Rapp and featuring sculpture by Eugene Romeo, was modeled after the great Baroque palace at Versailles. It opened in 1926 and since being listed on the National Register of Historic Places is in the process of being restored. Ballets and musical programs are regularly presented on the full proscenium stage. The structure is a multi-use facility built to bring a new vitality to Joliet's downtown at a time it was beginning to wane. It therefore combines a spectacular theatre with offices and shops. The shops on the second floor in the south section were exclusive specialty shops while the ones on the ground floor, as is typical, had a more plebian appeal. The building itself, one of the earliest air conditioned theatres in the country, is a spectacular fantasy land with a very carefully worked out circulation plan.

The entrance from Chicago Street is marked by a pair of great freestanding columns backed by an aedicula rising to a great hemisphere which breaks through the foliate cornice atop the rest of the block. The hemisphere has polychromatic terra-cotta (some of it with gold in the glaze to cause it to sparkle) and electric lights worked into the design. Beyond the entrance is a large mirrored hall that penetrates through the office block to an oval, domed area with stairways rising to the balcony level. Originally in its center was a fountain, and above it remains a large crystal chandelier. The water and lights in the fountain and other lights in this area were coordinated with the large pipe organ so that a sound and light show could be produced during intermission or to entertain those who were awaiting admission to the hall. The hall itself is a dazzling display of the movie palace genre. After viewing the film the patrons would exit by continuing to the east, then turn to the south and find themselves out in the street. This exit has subsequently been converted to a shop, but at 15 Van Buren Street you can notice that the shop front is like the one at 5 Van Buren Street which serves as an entrance

4.   Rubens Rialto Square Theatre

(detail)

into the south wing of the theatre block. The original exit from the theatre was at 15 Van Buren Street. Within the entrance at 5 Van Buren Street is a set of stairs which originally led downstairs to a billiard hall and bowling alley with a cafeteria, all part of this early Joliet revitalization project.

Walk north on Chicago Street 1 block. On the NE corner of Chicago and Clinton streets is

5. 156 N. CHICAGO STREET—1891

This limestone building, designed by Julian Barnes, dates from 1891 and has always housed the Universalist Church. The church is surrounded by professional offices and, on the ground floor, by commercial uses. A trace of the original storefront survives immediately under the point where the limestone begins on the corner store. One can imagine the heavy Joliet limestone above a relatively thin cast iron storefront. The limestone walls are given a rough-face on their irregular ashlar and around the windows that rise through two stories to a rounded stringcourse that runs around the top of the arches. The Chicago Street facade bulges slightly in three bows. The middle one extends all the way to the silhouette, providing a counterpart to the oriel on the corner. The oriel rises through the third and attic story; in the second it is supported by a stout column with a polished granite shaft. Under it is an arched opening leading to an interior auditorium. On Clinton Street is an arcaded entrance with similar granite shafts leading to the church, which is indicated by the row of ecclesiastical-type windows above.

Continue north. On the SE corner of Chicago and Cass streets is

6. 174–182 N. CHICAGO STREET—1880s

This building was built in two phases the second of which was in 1886, the first probably only a few years earlier. The joint between the sections can be seen between the second and third windows on the second floors facing Chicago Street on the west facade. The cornice that originally topped the building has been lost, but traces of the original ground floor are still visible under the southern section. Note that the fascia, between the shops and the brick, is cast iron and has the same design in both sections. That fascia runs north to the soffit of the corner oriel, which originally would have been supported by a single cast iron shaft on the corner of the oriel. Notice that the segmental arches on the second floor are constructed in a flat plane for the straight walls and around a curve for the oriel.

On the Cass Street facade, on the second story, are two sheet metal bays. At the far east end, a stairway with very heavy cast iron stair rails rises to a porch on the second story running across the east end of the building.

On the NE corner of Chicago and Cass streets is

7. 1 CASS STREET—1880s

This structure was originally a very elaborate one built sometime before 1890, probably in the mid-1880s. Originally facing Cass Street was a series of shopfronts with cast iron elements; the lintel is still visible immediately below the masonry. On the ground floor facing Chicago Street is a Joliet limestone facade, the northern end of which has three arches; the central and the northern ones still contain their elaborate cut glass. This was perhaps originally an entrance to a hotel in the upper two stories of the building. Notice, in the center of that facade, an original fire escape with cast iron balconies. The two upper stories combine brick and stone into a vigorous Romanesque effect with quarry-face limestone for sills, lintels, and arch moldings and for a stringcourse that also acts as the spring blocks for the third story arches. At the corner is an oriel. Notice, in the top level, the remains of cast iron elements which serve as a visual anchor for what was originally a flagpole projecting above the silhouette; a trace of it may be seen in the very top layer of the sheet metal cornice. Elsewhere, across the rest of the silhouette, are curve-sided protrusions. The Bedford limestone columnar entrance facing Cass Street is a later addition, perhaps from a time when the hotel was abandoned and the upper stories converted to professional offices.

Walk west on Cass Street 1 block. On the NE corner of Cass and Ottawa streets is

8. METHODIST EPISCOPAL CHURCH
19 W. Cass Street—1909

This 1909 church is in the full-blooded Renaissance Revival style. It is a brick block trimmed with limestone to produce a proper classicism that differentiates the two zones of the church. Facing Ottawa Street is the entrance to the porch leading to the sanctuary. The pediment stands above an entablature carrying the inscription "For The Glory of God" and borne by two Ionic columns. Along Cass Street is a similar entrance with a smaller recess leading to the fellowship areas and labeled "For The Good of Man." The fellowship area interior spaces are indicated by the size of the windows while the volume of the sanctuary is shown by the great segmental arched windows that rise the full two stories.

Walk south on Ottawa Street 1 block. On the NE corner of Clinton and Ottawa streets is

9.   JOLIET PUBLIC LIBRARY
150 N. Ottawa Street—1903

This stone building, designed by Daniel Burnham and built in 1903, is in the process of restoration. Look inside, particularly at the second floor which has a stunning window. The L-shaped plan allows a small public plaza to appear at the corner. The entrance is indicated by the tower set at the reentrant angle of the "L." The Collegiate Gothic style chosen for this structure allows associations with the medieval bookwork to be stimulated in the imagination of the visitor. It also gives an opportunity to produce a picturesque design. Its steeply pitched roofs produce high gables. On the end facades of the two wings are projections, one a polygonal bay on the second floor of the Clinton Street facade, the other a bow on the ground floor of the Ottawa Street facade. The style also allows for the variety of the structure's window treatments. Normally such structures would be built of brick with limestone. Here the local Joliet limestone is used with the grey or blue Bedford limestone used to trim the openings, the basement, the copings, and quoins.

On the SW corner of Clinton and Ottawa streets is

10.   ST. MARY'S CATHOLIC CHURCH
113 N. Ottawa Street—1882

This Gothic, limestone church was built in 1882 and survives in excellent condition except for the reconstruction of the front steps and its ample open porch. The plan is a standard one with a pitched roof over the nave, but the central tower rising in its octagonal plan lends it an uncommon dignity. Note the pier buttresses on the lower levels of the tower. The smooth-faced pointed arches surrounding the windows and smooth face used for the stone on various other parts of the structure contrast with the quarry-faced ashlar of the walls and the composition roofing material, an early example of the use of this material.

Continue south on Ottawa Street 2 blocks. Turn left (east) on Jefferson Street 2 blocks to Union Station.

This concludes the Joliet Walking Tour.

Drive north on Scott Street, 3 blocks. Turn left (west) on Cass Street (which becomes Western Avenue after you cross the bridge) .4 miles (5 blocks) to Broadway. Turn left. Stop.

On the SW corner of Broadway and Western Avenue is

11. 225 N. BROADWAY STREET—1850s

This simple, two-story, Joliet limestone, Greek Revival house is elegantly finished and survives in very good repair. It dates from the 1850s. The limestone blocks are carefully cut ashlar and have lintels over the five windows on the east facade. There is a neatly cut, half-circular, bull's-eye window in the gable. The entrance, under a cornice-topped lintel, has sidelights and transoms. Note that the side wall of the structure (on the south, away from the street) is of a less carefully finished Joliet limestone.

The contrast between the small Greek Revival structure at the bottom of the hill (Joliet #11) and the elegant large structure at the top of the hill (Joliet #12) pays eloquent testimony to the varying levels in prosperity brought to this area by the opening of the canal and the railroad which linked it with the developing industrial center at Chicago.

Walk south on Broadway 1 block. On the NW corner of Broadway and Oneida streets is

12. 201 N. BROADWAY STREET—1850, later additions

On the highest piece of land in the area is a large, two-story, frame structure topped with what is apparently a later Mansard roof with three arched dormers in its east facade. This structure is now unfortunately covered in asbestos siding but the original woodwork remains and indicates the pretense that this house, from 1850, has always displayed. Notice the rope molding around all of the openings in this structure. The porch across the ground floor stands high above the basement and has four tapered piers that support oversized, scroll-cut brackets which have knee braces and attached, cut-out, filagree molding. Projecting to the south is a polygonal bay window rising through two stories.

Directly across the street is

13.   200 N. Broadway Street
Wilsonia—c.1905

This is an elegant turn-of-the-century four-flat with precise brick work and neat Bedford limestone trim. It indicates that the high land value called for a multi-family structure and that, by the turn of the century, such structures were accepted by people who wished to live in an area which probably still contained some elegance of the earlier period.

Walk north on Broadway. The first house on your right is

14.   206 N. Broadway Street—1870s

This Italianate structure with a Mansard roof dates from the 1870s or very early 1880s. A brick structure, it has a wooden cornice with very simple brackets interspersed with disk bosses, and it uses Joliet limestone for the windows with a semicircular center protrusion and quarter circles cut from the corners. Both lintels and sills are supported on simple corbels. The lintels are incised with Eastlake designs which are especially prominent on the entrance lintel under the three-story tower that rises to a fourth story where the tall Mansard has dormers in each face and ends in cast iron cresting. The building dominates the large grounds and extends into them, on the south side with a wooden porch and on the north side with a square brick bay on the ground floor.

Continue north. The next house on your right is

15.   210 N. Broadway Street—c.1870

Contemporary with Joliet #14, this structure shows a reduction of that more august example, with a tower indicated only by the very low Mansard. A motif repeated on the south side of the ground floor over the double windows and the porch is also more subdued than that of its grander neighbor. It survives in excellent repair except for the parging of the brick with a thin coat of stucco and the replacement of the original porch balusters.

Continue north. The next structure on your right (east) is

16.   216 N. Broadway Street
Broadway Nursing Home—c.1900

This turn-of-the-century structure was originally a school. The large blocks of quarry-faced ashlar and the blocky configuration of the masonry mass are characteristic of the Romanesque Revival. But a date later than the one suggested by the style is suggested by other aspects: the use of rectangular linteled windows instead of arched ones, a small arch instead of a very large one as the entrance, and the hipped roof with its simple central dormer. It must have formed an attractive and appropriate element in what was originally a quite elegant street.

Continue north to the corner. Turn left (west) on Western Avenue (Route 30). Drive west 2 blocks following Route 30. Turn right (north) on Center Street. Continue .4 miles, following Route 30, onto Plainfield Avenue. (From Broadway Street to Taylor Street is ½ mile.) On your left, just past Taylor Street, is

17. St. Francis Convent
520 Plainfield Avenue—c.1870

Occupying a high piece of ground and facing over a broad lawn is the monumental convent built of Joliet limestone probably about 1870, very much in the style of William W. Boyington, who at that time was constructing the prison in Joliet. Its massing is Italianate, but its detailing is meant to suggest the Norman style. Subsequent additions have followed the design of the original structure which remains the most prominent part. Its facade steps forward at each end to form pavilions topped by stepped gables. In the center is a tower splitting apart a stepped gable. The tower is four stories high. On the first floor above the high basement (reached by steps that are later replacements but most likely follow the original design) is a doorway sheltered by a pointed arch and a steep gable containing insignia of the order that built this structure. At the third story is a statue of St. Francis. The tower is topped by a canted roof with scalloped slates and a dormer set in each of the four faces. Its cornice is topped by quite high cast iron fret work with the finials still intact. Atop the roof is a lantern containing a bell, atop which is an octagonal steeple topped by a cross. Note throughout the building the simplicity of the limestone treatment with simple pilasters set at the corners that rise to support the slight projection following the stepped pattern of the gables. Note also the pedimental shape given the lintels over the windows. The window sash contains double pointed arches in the upper sash, a pattern found in the masonry only in the gable field. Flanking them are three-centered windows. The pitched roof has three dormers on each side and these too have pointed windows. On the back face of the building is a broad, multi-story porch with heavy woodwork which formally looked out over the broad convent grounds.

Backtrack on Plainfield Road (Route 30) which becomes southbound Center Street. Follow the signs to Interstate 80, a total of 1.6 miles, bearing left onto Route 80 East. Drive 2.9 miles. Exit at Briggs Street. Turn left (north) on Briggs Street 1.6 miles until it ends at Route 30. Turn right (east) on Route 30, 1½ miles to Gouger Road. Turn left (north) .3 miles. On your left, just past Francis Road, is

18.   JOLIET PARK DISTRICT CONSERVATORY—1926

The original section of this enchanting greenhouse was built in 1926, and designed by Lord and Burnham. It has the lighthearted neo-classicism characteristic of the 1920s and a design for the entire structure which calls to mind the conservatories of the great nineteenth century English country houses. The outside grounds feature elaborate formal gardens during the warmer months. Inside the greenhouse are several displays including one with tropical plants, one with cacti, and an exhibit that changes seasonally. It is open every day of the year. There is also a bird haven behind the conservatory.

Continue north on Gougar Road .3 miles to the entrance of Pilcher Park. Turn left (west) ¼ mile. On your left is

FLOWING WELL

This artesian well attracts people from far away to sample its pure water.

Continue, following the arrows, to

19.   PILCHER PARK NATURE CENTER AND MUSEUM

This museum is geared towards children, with excellent educational exhibits that are fun. Behind the museum is a small zoo with several animals, including a coyote, a fox, a turkey, and a racoon. Also near the zoo area are a sensory trail and a forty minute nature walk.

Leaving the Nature Center, turn right .3 miles to

WILHELMS LANDING

Here one may stop to enjoy a restaurant, paddleboat rides, a petting zoo, pony rides, stagecoach rides, train rides, bicycle and canoe rentals, and a ferry boat to an island.

Continue on Highland Park Drive through the park, ¾ miles, until the road ends at Route 30. Turn left (east).

FRANKFORT

FRANKFORT

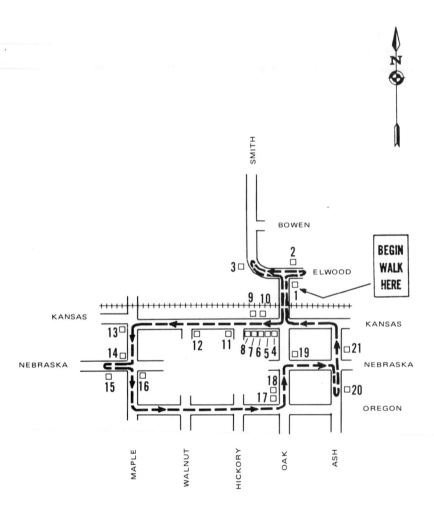

Continue east on Route 30, 10.4 miles to Route 45. Turn right (south) on Route 45, then immediately veer left on White Street to Elwood Street. Turn right (west) on Elwood Street to Oak Street. Stop.

FRANKFORT WALKING TOUR

On the SE corner of Elwood and Oak streets is

1. THE GRAINERY
This large, wooden building, once the lumbershed and feedstore of the Frankfort Grain Company, is in adaptive reuse with more than thirty shops in an 1890s atmosphere. The Grainery has combined old paving bricks, old-time street lights, and wooden sidewalks to produce an interpretation of a charming city street of days past.

Across the street, at the end of Oak Street and on the north side of Elwood Street, is

2. 41 ELWOOD STREET
Jurres House—c.1900
This turn-of-the-century house was built by Mr. Jurres, who was in the lumber business. This may account for the high quality of the woodwork both inside and out. The simple frame house with a pitched roof above the second story has small paired brackets under the eaves and medallions containing circles set in the eave peak above the half-circular, round, saw-tooth motif in that zone. It frames a half-round-headed window which has a dentil frieze wrapping over it, which repeats the dentil molding above all of the windows and along the lintel of the porch. The turned posts have scroll-cut knees, and the porch railing combines square and thin turned elements to produce a rich pattern.

Walk west on Elwood Street 1 block. On the NW corner of Smith and Elwood streets is

3. 12 SMITH STREET
Village Blacksmith Shoppes—1870s
Built over one hundred years ago and altered from time to time since then,

this building was originally used as a machine and farm implement shop. Today it is in adaptive reuse with boutiques and a restaurant. The boards nailed onto the surface are completely spurious, but below them is stamped metal reproducing the pattern of brick, a common late nineteenth century building material which is seldom encountered now.

Backtrack east on Elwood Street to Oak Street. Turn right (south) 1 block. Cross the tracks.

Kansas Street comprises the main portion of the Frankfort Historic District, which is on the National Register of Historic Places.

On the SW corner of Kansas and Oak streets is

4.   100 KANSAS STREET—1866 and later

The eastern half of this clapboard building was built in 1866 and operated as a general store and post office. The addition is also from the nineteenth century, and the porch was probably added at that time. Note the cut-out corner of the original structure, with its turned post and the triangular pieces inserted in the corners with tiny spindles. That helped to give character to this otherwise quite simple structure.

Walk west on Kansas Street. The second building on your left is

5.   112 KANSAS STREET—1856

This frame building, now in adaptive reuse as law offices, was originally a harness shop built in 1856. Although the actual pieces on the two-story porch in the front are new, they probably reproduce the original form.

Continue west. The next building on your left is

6.   114 KANSAS STREET—1883

This stone building with leaded glass and Greek Revival columns and pediment was built in 1883 as the State Bank. It presents a curious interpretation of proper classical elements; we see a combination of prototypes that are not normally forced into a conjunction, yet the combination becomes the most august building on the main street, as is appropriate for a bank. Note that the pediment bears no relationship to the columns below and that the third

6. 114 Kansas Street

column is not placed in the middle of the composition nor matched by a fourth column in a similar location on the right; such a column would have interfered with the window. The window is not a feature associated with the temple-front motif from which the overall scheme derives, but the entranceway on the side does belong to the type of design that might have had such a window.

Continue west. The next building on your left is

7. 116 KANSAS STREET—1863
This commercial structure from 1863 was originally a meat market. The

ground floor is an excellent example of the use of cast iron columns and a wrought iron beam to produce a field for large plate glass windows, here amplified by the larger size of plate glass that became available later. Because an entrance is required for the stairway leading to the second floor, the shopfront is off center relative to the second floor. The second floor is brick trimmed with limestone and rises in the center to produce a formal character for the building. Added to it (to the west, but not much later) was another storefront with a second story that is almost, but not quite, the same. This addition was the first bank in Frankfort. Like the rest of the structure, it is now in adaptive reuse.

Continue west. The next building, on the SE corner of Hickory and Kansas streets, is

8.   122 KANSAS STREET—1850s

This 1850s building was originally operated as a hotel. The second story, including the broad pediment, contains original construction with chamfered square posts and single-bottle balusters providing an indication of the simplicity with which the Italianate style was rendered in this small farming community.

Cross to the north side of the street and walk east. The first building on your left, east of the Village Hall, is

9.   119 KANSAS STREET—1870

This structure, built in 1870, was originally used as a general store and also served as a post office. It is in adaptive reuse as an antique shop. The front and the walls have been altered but the metal roof could very well be original.

Continue east. The next building on your left is

10.   113 KANSAS STREET—1855

This 1855 structure retains the false front with the paired scroll-cut brackets that gave an otherwise very simple structure great dignity in its time, but the wall surfaces have been covered with modern synthetic materials.

Walk west on Kansas Street. On the SW corner of Hickory and Kansas streets is

11. **130 Kansas Street** and **14 S. Hickory Street**
Frankfort Historical Society Museum

The exhibits here are changed regularly. They feature authentic period displays of furniture and costumes in life-like settings.

Continue west on Kansas Street. On the SE corner of Kansas and Walnut streets is

12. **144 Kansas Street—1869**

This yellow, clapboard, frame house was built in 1869. It is very modest with very simple frames around the openings and under the eaves. The one-story enclosed porch, tucked within the "L" of the plan, is modern.

Continue west. The house at the end of Kansas Street, on the west side of Maple Street, is

13. **10 Maple Street—1855**

This charming house began in 1855 as a simple structure covered in clapboards with the ground floor corners cut out on a bias and the overhangs supported by very simple brackets. The only surviving original windows are the six-over-six windows on the second floor on the south side. The porch is new, as is the one-story extension on the south toward the rear.

Walk south on Maple Street. On the NW corner of Maple and Nebraska streets is

14. **231 W. Nebraska Street** and
30 Maple Street—1904

This relatively large corner house from just after the turn of the century has a broad porch set close to it, running along the two street sides, with the entrance marked by a pediment and simple Ionic columns. The west section of the front facade on both floors bulges out into a broad polygonal projection which produces overhangs for the gable above; these are exploited by the flare of the gables of the roof projecting from the hipped roof that covers the bulk of the house.

Cross to the south side of Nebraska Street and walk west. The second house on your left is

15.　236 W. Nebraska Street—1868

Little now visible indicates the 1868 origin of this house. The entranceway has been subsequently aggrandized and the ground floor windows have been enlarged. An interesting feature is the curb stone at the foot of the walk with its inscription from 1885.

Backtrack east to Maple Street. On the SE corner of Maple and Nebraska streets is

16.　220 W. Nebraska—c. 1900

This small, cross-gabled, pitched roof structure has a porch crossing the west and north sides supported by Tuscan columns and carrying a lintel with rectangular indentations. It is very simply ornamented in the gables with an attached strut running under the eaves.

Especially interesting is the surface used for the walls. The rich pattern is produced by using artificial shingles stamped or molded to imitate wood shingles. This is representative of the early twentieth-century experiments with the use of technology to facilitate the construction industry.

Walk south on Maple Street. Turn left (east) on Oregon. Continue east 3 blocks to Oak Street. On the NW corner of Oak Street and Oregon is

17.　120 Oak Street—1867

This clapboard covered, frame house was built in 1867 and moved to this site in 1882. The basic configuration of the building is a survivor from the classical revival of the earlier period. The Italianate style is indicated by the paired brackets and by the ample window frames with feet and shoulders, and segmental arches and keystones with Eastlake incising. The polygonal bay on the south side is also Italianate; it appears as an intrusion into the simple massing from the earlier period but works very well with the amplification of that simplicity by the Italianate trappings.

Walk north on Oak Street. The first house on your left is

18.　112 Oak Street—1890s

This very tall frame structure, covered in clapboards, forms an interesting comparison with its neighbor (Frankfort #17). Note that the clapboards here are much thinner, the proportions of this building much higher, and the

17. 120 Oak Street

details produced on a lathe are combined into intricate patterns characteristic of the period following the Italianate. It dates from just before the turn of the century.

Continue north on Oak Street to the corner. On the NE corner of Oak and Nebraska streets is

19.   39 NEBRASKA STREET—c.1865 (maybe earlier)

This tall frame structure, covered in clapboards, rises to a pitched roof with quarter round paired corbels under the eaves and along the gables. The original two-story structure was built around the end of the Civil War, although it may date from 1855. Later one-story additions include a garage and a small addition extending to the east. Especially nice on the Oak Street facade are the unusual round-headed windows with window frames having both shoulders and feet. Also nice are the curiously shaped windows in the upper section of the double door. At one time a porch wrapped around the south and west faces providing a veranda, popularly called a piazza.

Walk east on Nebraska Street. Turn right (south) on Ash Street. The third building on your left is

20.   111 ASH STREET—1857

This 1857 frame, clapboard-covered structure was a harness shop until the early 1900s. The basic framework of its design is that of the Greek Revival, but the ground floor has characteristic features of shopfronts of the period. Notice the anachronistic mixture of the Tuscan pilasters on the shopfronts (characteristic of the Italianate style) and the quatrefoil in the circular window in the gable (which belongs to the Gothic Revival, current at the same time).

Backtrack north on Ash Street past Nebraska Street. The second building on your right is

21.   25 ASH STREET—1870s

This structure forms an instructive contrast to the previous building (Frankfort #20). It, too, was probably originally built as a shop but it has the roof pitches parallel with the street rather than facing the gable ends to the street. This allowed for the broad porch to be added, which is decorated with the carpenters' art including turned posts, saw-tooth boards under the lintel terminating in turned spindles, and punched-out quarter-round knees. Atop the turned posts are volute-like brackets, and, in the center, a pediment marks both the center of the building and its entrance. It is characteristic of the styles of the 1870s.

Continue north to the corner. Turn left (west) on Kansas Street 1 block to Oak Street. Turn right (north) 1 block to Elwood Street.

This concludes the Frankfort Walking Tour.

Drive south on Oak Street, across the tracks, 1 block. Turn right (west) on Kansas Street. When Kansas Street ends, turn left (south) 1 block to Maple Street. Turn right (west) on Nebraska Street .4 miles to Route 45. Turn left (south) on Route 45, 10½ miles to the intersection with Route 52 West. Turn left (east) on the road opposite Route 52 West.

PEOTONE

PEOTONE

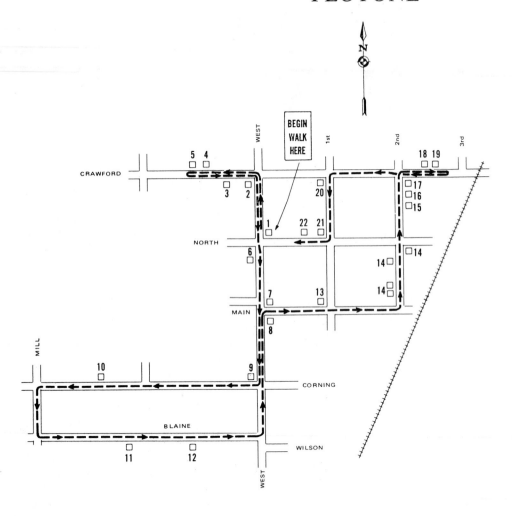

Drive east, a total of 6 miles (you will cross over Route 57). The road winds and becomes West Street as you get into Peotone. Continue to the intersection of West and North streets. Stop.

PEOTONE WALKING TOUR

On the NE corner of West and North streets is

1. PEOTONE PUBLIC LIBRARY
213 W. North Street
Peotone Historical Museum—1899

This 1899, former First Evangelical United Brethren Church building has been beautifully restored. The L-shaped plan is characteristic of the later Gothic Revival style as it had grown into the Stick style and then simplified for use in smaller communities such as this. A tower, reaching only as high as the ridges of the pitched roof, stands at the corner and contains the entrance. The wing ends are marked by pointed arched windows, both large and small, and the gable ends contain scalloped shingles and struts at the top of the gable. The stained glass, Gothic windows are especially lovely when viewed from the interior.

Inside the library, note the elegant wood paneling. Various objects from the nineteenth century are exhibited. In the basement are many unusual collections which are part of the Peotone Historical Museum's exhibits.

Walk north on West Street 1 block. On the SW corner of West and Crawford streets is

2. 304 CRAWFORD STREET—c.1860

The original, gable front, one-and-one-half-story, frame structure is from about 1860 and has segmental arched cornices topping the segmental arched windows. The double valve door with its transom is a larger version of the same opening design. In the gable are thin paired brackets. These features indicate an early date for this quite subdued structure. On the north side a new entrance porch, with a second story covered open porch, was added shortly before the turn of the century.

Walk west on Crawford Street. The next house on your left is

3.   308 CRAWFORD STREET—c.1900

This is the first of several structures that will be encountered in Peotone constructed with concrete blocks made by a patented machine that appeared on the market in the late nineteenth century. It produced blocks that imitated quarry-cut ashlar. The material was used to produce buildings that are vaguely related to the more finished versions of the sophisticated styles current during the period. This one, for example, combines certain aspects of the Italianate and of the Classical Revival but in a manner that is unique and born of its singular creator. The stout classical columns, with their oversize abaci, were perhaps specially made for this installation. The roofs are poorly coordinated with the massing below, which suggests something about the amateur skills that went into this construction.

Cross to the north side of the street and continue west. The second house on your right is

4.   317 and 319 CRAWFORD STREET—1903

This 1903 structure forms an extremely interesting comparison to the previous house (Peotone #3), built by the same man. Here the blocks were made with a different mold but on the same machine and laid up in a slightly more regular fashion. The result is a double house with one complete unit on the second story and another on the ground floor. The slate roof and the slate surfaces in the gables are original.

Especially notable is the assemblage that produced the porch. Precast concrete pieces have been assembled in a manner that resembles no other example among the classical vocabulary of forms. Note that only a limited number of molds were used to produce the great number of pieces found in the three porch columns and the ornament next to the steps. The products of a single mold serve as base and capitals; the base is simply the capital turned upside down. Above the base and below the capital is another piece doubled to produce rings. Between them is a single column drum; a normal column shaft would have six or eight of these to reach the distance which, on this porch, would stretch from the floor to the ceiling. The ornament next to the porch also has been made with one piece, upside down for the base and right side up for the capital, and one ring in between, the assemblage then topped with a ball.

Continue west. The next house on your right is

4. 317 and 319 Crawford Street

5.   321 CRAWFORD STREET—1904

This structure from 1904, and again by the same builder, is the simplest of the three. Note that once again the same building blocks as those used in Peotone #3 occur but the pattern in which they are placed is one of extreme simplicity, a pattern that produces what is sometimes called the "grandmother's" type of house. It is characterized by a block covered by a hipped roof and with the front crossed by a broad porch supported by, in this case, pillars.

Backtrack east on Crawford Street to West Street. Turn right (south) past North Street. The third house on your right is

6.   106 WEST STREET—1905

This simple rectangular structure from 1905 stands on a quarry-faced ashlar foundation with common brick side walls and a pressed brick front facade rising, in the second story, to a steeply pitched roof. The double window on the second story and the single windows on the ground floor are covered by segmental brick arches. On the facade can be seen the outline of the original porch. It was replaced by a new porch which is a small version of the house. The difference between the size of the mortar courses used in earlier and more recent construction can be observed quite clearly by comparing the walls of the house with those of the porch.

Continue south to the corner. On the NE corner of West and Main streets is

7.   UNITED METHODIST CHURCH
105 N. West Street—1906

This simple 1906 church was built in brick and designed by Turnbull and Jones. It has suggestions of the Gothic style in the pointed arches over the openings with their hood moldings simply traced in raised brick, and in the pattern of the windows which contain elaborate stained glass. The top of the tower has been reconstructed.

On the SE corner of Main and West streets is

8.   216 W. MAIN STREET—c.1900

This turn-of-the-century clapboard house has a sunrise motif on the north gable with the window set into it. That same motif, without the window, appears in the pediment of the porch which is set diagonally at the junction of the porch that is attached to the west and north faces of the wing extending to the north. A stunning contrast is formed by the relative delicacy of the carpentry work with its tight clapboards and small elements forming the body of the house and, on the other hand, the crude, cast concrete elements from which the porch has been constructed. Here each column is made from five vermiculated tori, two at the bottom, one between the two drums, and two below the capital.

Continue south on West Street 1 block. On the NW corner of Corning Avenue and West Street is

9. IMMANUEL CHURCH
311 Corning Avenue—1904

This large, 1904, red brick church has the cross plan characteristic of this period. It gains considerable distinction by using limestone to form the pointed arches and other elements within the framing of the openings, and by the extension of slate roofs into pyramids at the corner tower and the octagonal cupola in the center. The tall tower that rises in the southeast corner is very prominent. In the upper level it has round elements rising into the roof topped by cones and constructed from quarry-faced brick to form a textural contrast with the rest of the structure.

Walk west on Corning Avenue 1½ blocks. The mill on your right is

10. RATHJE MILL—1870s

This windmill was built in the 1870s and is one of the fewer than ten wind mills remaining in the state of Illinois. It was placed on high ground that faced over the prairie in every direction in order to catch the full blast of whatever wind might exist. The rough stone foundation is built on an octagonal plan. The wooden structure rises through a slow curve to an overhang approximately a third the way up the structure where the smooth, curved face begins again. On the top is the cap set on a large circular structure and covered with an oblong dome. The shingle covering on this structure is used because the shingles could easily be wrapped around the surfaces. The blades and the outriggers, which braced the mill against the wind that drove the blades, have largely disappeared although remnants appear in the cap. Originally the outriggers would have reached the ground where rollers al-

10. Rathje Mill

lowed the cap to be rotated to face the blades into the wind. At some later date the brick structure to the north was built to contain steam machinery that replaced the wind power of the mill. The chimney is the most prominent feature indicating the function of this later addition.

Continue west to the corner. Turn left (south) on Mill Street. Turn left (east) on Blaine. The ninth house on your right is

11.   328 BLAINE—1880s

This charming clapboard house, built in the 1880s, was moved to its present site. In pristine condition, it exhibits a characteristic plan with a stubby gabled projection facing the street and a pedimented porch in the reentrant angle leading to a small vestibule. Note the halving of a turned post attached as a half column at the point where the open porch meets the wall.

Continue east. The fifth house on your right is

12.   308 BLAINE—1880s

This 1880s clapboard house sits on a limestone foundation of relatively large blocks. It has an extension to the rear, but the part nearest the street is characteristic of the one-and-one-half-story frame structures built following the Greek Revival and that continued to have Greek Revival aspects. Here the pitched roof, rather than the gable, is turned to the street. The entrance, in the gable end, is a protected porch with turned columns and a small pent roof crossing the pediment.

Continue east to the corner. Turn left (north) on West Street 2 blocks. Turn right (east) on Main Street. On the NW corner of First and Main streets is

13.   201 MAIN STREET—c.1905

The ashlar-producing masonry machine has again provided the materials for a two-story house that follows styles popular during the decade after the turn of the century. Rough-faced blocks were used for the quoins and for the porch piers, but smooth-faced blocks were used for the rest of the structure. The style it follows is the one that evolved from the Queen Anne in the direction of the Tudor as is indicated by the bay window and its roof projecting on the east and the other hipped roofs which follow the outline of the plan. Notice, on the south facade on the ground floor, the three windows with their upper sashes containing diagonally placed panes. The equivalent windows on the second story have three vertical panes in the upper sashes.

Continue east on Main Street 1 block to Second Street. Turn left (north).

14.   SECOND STREET BETWEEN NORTH AND MAIN STREETS

Almost every building on this block is quite old, although none can be dated specifically. The east side of the street dates from the 1890s while the west side dates from the first decade of the twentieth century.

Of interest is **106 SECOND STREET**. Its second story is covered in pressed metal which reproduces the character of quarry-faced limestone. The cornice is also sheet metal and has Italianate details.

The building to its left (probably **104 SECOND STREET**) uses the same material and produces a similar effect on the second story and in the cornice. This metal-faced construction is characteristic of the period and earlier, especially in southern Illinois. Its appearance this far north is somewhat rare and its survival even rarer.

The structure on the southeast corner of Second and North streets was originally the Peotone Opera House. It was built prior to 1900.

Also notable because it survives in such excellent condition is **116 SECOND STREET**. Notice the below-grade shops entered by stairs that parallel the face of the building, and note the large plates of glass set in the cast iron framing elements on the ground floor. The entrance to that shop is slightly off center relative to the second story in order to make room for the entrance to the second story. The center of the second story is stressed by doubling the windows there. The sheet metal cornice is topped by a brick parapet which itself has a sheet metal coping with a dentil frieze between the parapet terminations. Originally the entire street front had a character similar to the one portrayed by this structure.

Walk north on Second Street. The fourth house on your right past North Street is

15.   207 SECOND STREET—1880

By disregarding the shutters and the projecting plastic signs, one can see the brick cottage from 1880 with a relatively rare configuration: a full attic story above a single story sitting directly on the ground rather than on a basement. The window openings are topped by segmental brick arches. Notice that those on the ground floor, which must carry a heavier load, have two rows of bricks while the one in the attic (which has very little weight above it) has but a single row of bricks.

Continue north. The next building on your right is

16. 209 SECOND STREET—c. 1900

The second story of this structure has panels of pressed metal like those seen earlier on Second Street, although here the pattern is entirely different. The cornice has highly stylized anthemions but the panels between the windows contain Renaissance motifs composed of a candelabra with dolphins flanking its lower section. The candelabra rises to a basin above which are more fish-like forms. The pattern from top to bottom is elaborated by various swags and garlands. One normally encounters this type of Renaissance festive decoration in stone work, so clearly it was the intent here to reproduce in pressed metal the much more expensive stone decoration of elaborate commercial structures.

Continue north on Second Street. On the SE corner of Second and Crawford streets is

17. 213 SECOND STREET—1880s

This block of a building, built in brick in the 1880s, rises to a hipped roof and, on the front facade, has a steeply pitched roof gable with scalloped shingles. The present porch is a replacement, but its configuration reproduces two-thirds of what was probably there originally. Note in the back (east) face, the pent roof and the almost spindle-like porch posts for the ground floor porch. The second story porch is a later addition.

Turn right (east) on Crawford Street. The third house on your left (north side of the street) is

18. 117 E. CRAWFORD STREET—c. 1860

This clapboard cottage is the oldest building still standing in Peotone. Built about 1860, it was the second house built in the town. Its very simple forms around the openings, eaves, and gable indicate the early date, as does the one-story configuration. The porch is an addition from the turn of the century.

Continue east. The next house on your left is

19.   121 E. CRAWFORD STREET—1860s

This 1860s brick cottage has a frame addition. The quoins suggest the masonry origin of the style, which is neither Federal nor Greek Revival but suggests the Italianate grandeur that was becoming prominent at this time. The double window is most likely a replacement for the original window which was placed under the broad segmental arch.

Backtrack west on Crawford Street to First Street. On the SW corner of First and Crawford streets is

20.   FIRST UNITED PRESBYTERIAN CHURCH—1871

This fine, simple, Stick style, frame church was built in 1871. Especially nice is the projection of the upper gables in the eaves beyond the hips and the matching element near the entrance of the wall dormer on the east facade. It has a trifoil window with a small gable-topped window above it and, on the north face, a double window rising into the wall dormer in a complementary manner. Next to that dormer is a three-story tower. The second story is marked by a pent roof beyond which is the muscular open grill-work of the bell house. The pyramidal tower has hipped roof dormers and, at the top, a sheet metal finial. The windows on the north face of the cross projection are tall and narrow and rise into segmental-arched tops covered by gabled frames. Notice also the fine stained glass in all of the windows.

Walk south on First Street. On the NW corner of First and North streets is

21.   206 FIRST STREET—1887

This clapboard Italianate mansion was built in 1887, except for the porch which replaces the original one. Especially nice is the flared Mansard roof which rises into a thin curb and, at the base, has a rain curb which allows the water to be directed into downspouts within the building. Also prominent on the east face is the polygonal projection which rises through a flared polygonal tower to a point higher than the top of the Mansard roof. Projecting to the south is a flat-fronted bay topped by a gable that rises out of the Mansard. The paired, scroll-cut, incised brackets are complemented by the window heads which have embossed disks, and by the flat surfaces and rectangular frames of the panels in the cornice of the building and in the cornice of the ground floor of the eastern bay.

Walk west on North Street. The first house on your right is

22.   209 North Street—c. 1900

This turn-of-the-century, clapboard-covered house was originally the parsonage of the First Evangelical United Church, which is now the Peotone Public Library (Peotone #1). The ample gables above the second floor have scalloped shingles introducing a rich pattern which is reinforced by their radial arrangement in the peak of the gable. A similar scalloped shingle field appears between the first and second floors and in the pediment of the porch in front of the entrance. The present porch posts and porch railings are later additions; an indication of the original porch columns is given by the half columns attached to the building at the point where the porch meets it. Note the polygonal bay projecting beyond the gable on the east facade.

The next building west is the Peotone Library.

This concludes the Peotone Walking Tour.

Drive south on West Street until it ends at Wilmington Road. Turn right (west) 1¼ miles to Route 57. Turn right on Route 57 North, to Chicago.

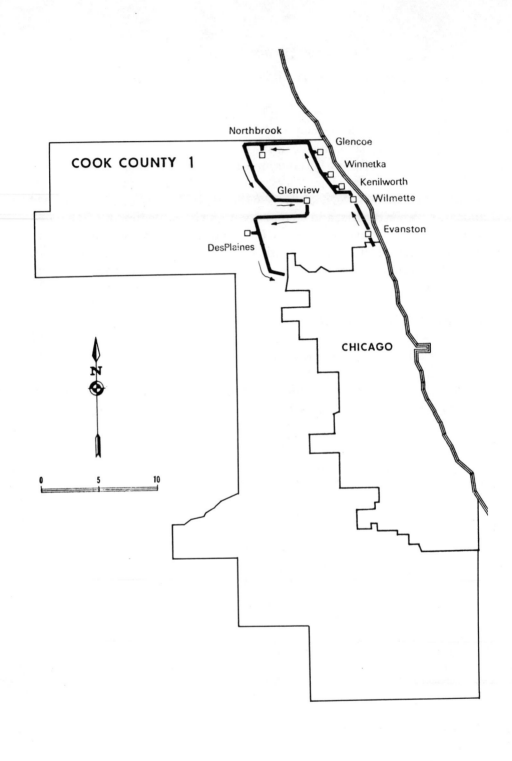

COOK COUNTY 1

Northbrook

Glencoe

Winnetka

Kenilworth

Wilmette

Glenview

Evanston

DesPlaines

CHICAGO

N

0   5   10

Cook
County 1

EVANSTON

EVANSTON

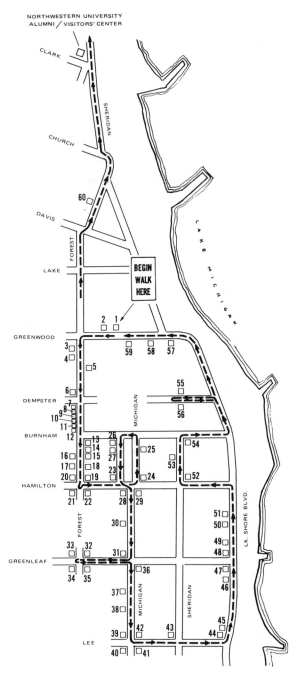

NORTHWESTERN UNIVERSITY
ALUMNI / VISITORS' CENTER

CLARK

SHERIDAN

CHURCH

DAVIS

FOREST

LAKE

BEGIN WALK HERE

LAKE MICHIGAN

GREENWOOD

MICHIGAN

DEMPSTER

BURNHAM

HAMILTON

FOREST

GREENLEAF

MICHIGAN

SHERIDAN

L.K. SHORE BLVD.

LEE

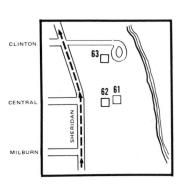

CLINTON

CENTRAL

MILBURN

SHERIDAN

From Chicago, take the Outer Drive north, until it ends at Hollywood. Turn right (north) on Sheridan Road. Continue north a total of 4.7 miles, following Sheridan Road (as it turns). After you have turned west on Burnham Place in Evanston, turn right (north) again, continuing on Forest Avenue. Continue north 2 blocks to Greenwood Street. Turn right (east) to the third house on your left. Stop.

All of the area on the Evanston Walking Tour is included in the Evanston Lakeshore Historic District listed on the National Register of Historic Places. You may wish to explore other parts of this district which is bounded, roughly, by Northwestern University on the north, Lake Michigan on the east, Calvery Cemetery on the south, and, on the west, by Chicago Avenue.

One of the aspects of the district that does not appear in the individual building descriptions is the general character of the area. Note the large lots, generally deep setbacks, and, especially, the street lighting fixtures which were designed in 1930 by Thomas Tallmadge, an Evanston resident who with his partner Vernon Watson designed some of the houses on the walk.

EVANSTON WALKING TOUR

On your left, on the north side of Greenwood Street, is

1. CHARLES GATES DAWES MANSION
225 Greenwood Street—1894

This massive structure is probably the best example of the Chateauesque style in the six-county area. Built in 1894, it is sited on a large piece of land overlooking the lake. It presents an impressive entrance to the street and, along the east facade, a terrace fronting on a loggia overlooking the lake. The basic block of the building is a square. On the south facade two great round tourelles project from each corner, each with a conical roof rising to the same height as the hipped roof over the main block. A central dormer is in a deep brown sandstone, the same material used for the window frames and for the zone on the ground floor between the projecting tourelles. In that section is the broad arch enclosing a recessed porch with a large doorway. Set to one side, the entrance introduces the only asymmetry in the design. Next to it is a balcony carried by a series of corbelled arches. The forms in

1. Charles Gates Dawes Mansion
   225 Greenwood Street

that central area, in the double window on the second story, in the dormer, and elsewhere on the structure are typical of the combination of late medieval and early Renaissance elements brought into the graceful yet fortresslike composition of the chateaux of the period of Francis I. Unusual in this building is the use of a warm orange brick instead of the expected limestone. The building is a National Historic Landmark and was built in 1894 to the design of the New York architect Henry Edwards Ficken. It was bought by Charles Gates Dawes, vice-president in Calvin Coolidge's administration.

The remarkable building is furnished and maintained in lavish style, much as it appeared during Dawes' residency. The library, with its stunning cherry paneling, is one of the main attractions; the two-story dining room, with a musicians' balcony, is equally impressive. Also on exhibit are antique toys, costumes, and a room full of artifacts about the Dawes family. The Evanston Historical Society has its offices on the second floor. Mondays, Tuesdays, Thursdays, and Fridays: 1:00-5:00 P.M. Adults: 50¢; seniors and students: 25¢; families: $1.00. Free on Fridays.

Walk west on Greenwood Street. The first house on your right is

2. 235 GREENWOOD STREET—1892

This masonry building by Joseph Lyman Silsbee from 1892 begins as a simple cubic block with a hipped roof carrying two dormers but extends itself to the west and the east with a porte-cochere and an octagonal pyramidal-roofed projection. In the middle is a bay window projecting next to the entrance porch which is carved out of the interior of the building. The cream-colored brick of the walls is complemented with pale limestone used as window dressings around the ground floor, as piers for the porte-cochere, and as pilasters and entablature on the second story. Decorative interest is added by the wreathed cartouches in the dormer gables and by the art glass in some of the windows as well as by the care with which the stone carving has been executed. The building is typical of Silsbee's blending of many different sources into a coherent whole (for example aspects of the Queen Anne, the Colonial Revival, and the Chateauesque are all evident), but each has been so transformed that a new synthesis emerges.

Continue west to the corner. Turn left (south) on Forest Avenue. The second house on your right (on the west side of Forest Avenue) is

3.   1324 FOREST AVENUE—1898

This structure, designed by Barfield and Hubbell in 1898, shows the imposition of classical rigor on a Queen Anne armature. The basic block, topped by the hipped roof with a prominent dormer, is brick on the ground floor and stucco above. A porch supported by piers at the ends with columns, some in pairs, crosses the entire front. The entrance is slightly to the north of center and is marked by prominent podia in the limestone basement. Its eccentric position is balanced by the bay window in the second story at the south end between a pair of squat pilasters. These are matched on the other side and contain, between them, a smaller window than the others on the second story. It is a prime example of the merging of the classical tendencies of the late 1890s with the waning Queen Anne.

Continue south. The next house on your right is

4.   1318 FOREST AVENUE—1911

This is the first of many Tudor designs by Ernest Mayo encountered in this walk. Mayo was an extremely prolific and gifted local architect. The brick ground floor of this 1911 house contains the entrance on the north end and two flat-fronted bay windows with a sunporch closing the composition on the south end (the windows are modern). The second story has a projecting mid-section covered by three gables topping a wall-dormer-type rise between the flared pitched roof on either side. The half-timbering, complete with molded stucco plaques between the second and third story windows, is very well executed with spiral colonettes featured around the attic windows. Notice also how the scuppers and collectors for the drain pipes are worked into the pattern of the half-timbering.

Cross to the east side of the street and continue south. The first house on your left is

5.   1315 FOREST AVENUE—1907

This Prairie style house, the Linthicum house, was designed by Tallmadge and Watson in 1907. It is one of the prime monuments of the Prairie School and shows that partnership's distinctive style. It is a broad, horizontally composed block built of cream-colored brick edged with limestone. The full porch crossing the front is supported by four piers, the end piers rising to geometrically ornamented caps each with a broad squat urn. The windows on the second story are the familiar Chicago windows with a wide central window flanked on each side by narrower ones. The block is topped by a high frieze which in the center turns through a half circle to produce a conspicuous hood. The entablature here is especially rich with the geometric, foliate ornament introduced by Louis Sullivan and very popular among the Prairie School architects. The broad, hipped roof with a truncated ridge provides an appropriate horizontal cap for the building. Projecting to the north is a porte-cochere with a room above. Its center also contains the hood motif calling attention to the formal relationship between this projection and the main block.

Cross back to the west side of the street and continue south. On the NW corner of Forest Avenue and Dempster Street is

6. 1304 FOREST AVENUE—1894

Once again we encounter the merging of the classicising tendencies of the 1890s with the Queen Anne. The basic cube of the 1894 building designed by John Turner Long, a local architect, is edged by pilasters rising to abstracted Ionic capitals under the entablature. The block is enlarged by extending a porch across the entire front with a porte-cochere on the north and, on the south, a curved sweep of the veranda which then continues down to the west projection. The porch is supported by evenly spaced Ionic columns. The openings on the second story provide a marked symmetry which is reinforced by the prominent dormer featuring a Palladian motif merged with the gable form and featuring a steeply pitched pediment matching the steep pitch of the untruncated hipped roof. Separating the roof from the block below is a thin, widely projecting cornice above a frieze level with strung-out garlands sitting above the architrave, which is stone.

On the SW corner of Forest Avenue and Dempster Street is

7. 1246 FOREST AVENUE—1895

This 1895 building, by A. W. Buckley, is a prime example of the Queen Anne style featuring a heavy, random ashlar, rough-faced ground story for the turret that contrasts nicely with the heavy shake sheathing on the turret's next two floors. The porch facing east swells outward from the turret and is supported by clusters of colonettes. On the second story, on the side opposite the turret, a polygonal bay window erupts, carrying the cornice outward with it. The steeply pitched roof, above, has a large dormer above the bay window and a smaller one marking the entrance within the porch. On the north facade the gable projects beyond the face of the wall, which itself projects with an enclosure for the stairhall which is sheathed in vertical siding calling attention to that particular interior space. Certain of the details here (for example the ornamental frieze atop the porch lintel and the hooded window moldings on the second story of the turret) indicate the increasing interest in the examples of English Tudor architecture which soon will pervade the design of buildings more thoroughly than is seen here.

Continue south. The next house on your right is

8.   1244 Forest Avenue—c. 1870

This is an excellent example, in a fine state of preservation, of the speculative houses built by Luther Greenleaf, an important early Evanston developer, immediately after the 1871 Chicago Fire. He built to provide residences for those fleeing a city that burned from time to time. It is a simple T-shaped plan with the stem of the "T" facing the street and projecting on the ground floor with a polygonal bay with fine carpentry work. Tucked in the northern reentrant angle is the entrance porch, and projecting from the southern one in front of another projecting bay is a large veranda. The segmental cornice above the second story window, the bracketed forms of the parapets, and the carpentry details on the porches betray the Italianate style, but the general configuration and proportions of the house extend back to the Gothic Revival period. There are many structures like this in Evanston but none is as well preserved.

Continue south. The next house on your right is

9.   1240 Forest Avenue—c. 1890

This house, from about 1890, shows an interesting composition with a large veranda on the ground floor covered by a second story that projects out to its limits beyond the interior core of the building on both the east and south facades. A further projection is provided in the center of the conspicuous three bay composition on the second story where the design is enlivened by a flare at its base.

Continue south. The next building on your right is

10. 1236 FOREST AVENUE—1909

This simple 1909 structure by H.J. Schlacks shows the use of the Tudor style in diluted form on a simple block with a porch, originally open, projecting on the ground story and with a side entrance. Especially interesting is the gable story; it has a peaked beam at the base of the gable, its projection supported by small wooden corbels. The gable rafters terminate in flares and, at the top, meet at a pendant.

Continue south. The next building on your right is

11. 1230 and 1232 FOREST AVENUE—pre-1894

This clapboard covered structure is a double house, a common type of building in the more exclusive suburban areas such as this part of Evanston which resisted the construction of multi-family residences as long as possible. Built before 1894, the ground floor and the gables are sheathed by very tightly packed thin clapboards. The second and attic stories are within a gambrel roof which on the north half carries on its second story an extension of the polygonal bay which begins on the ground floor. This feature is balanced on the south half by a pair of dormers that begin in the lower section of the gambrel and extend into the upper one. Notice that each porch is handled differently to give each unit a distinct individuality.

Continue south. The next house on your right is

12. 1228 FOREST AVENUE—1897

This building, designed in 1897 by the firm headed by Franklin Burnham, sits on a large lot and makes good use of its ample site. The front of the site is defined by an excellent wrought iron fence with the entrance marked by an especially well done gateway. The structure itself has an intersecting gambrel roof enclosing the second and full attic stories above a cream-colored brick ground floor. It extends out beyond the ground floor to cover the ample veranda which extends to the north as a porte-cochere and is supported by richly detailed Ionic columns and a fine single-bottle balustrade. The entrance is marked by a curving segmental pediment within which is a radiant scallop motif. The gables are shingled (notice the saw-tooth edging on some of the shingle courses) and the windows are as rich as the entrance motif with segmental pediments containing a scallop shell on the second story and a Palladian window on the third story. This residence was lived in briefly by the brother of Vice-President Dawes.

Cross to the east side of the street. On the SE corner of Forest Avenue and Burnham Place is

13.   1225 FOREST AVENUE—1899

This 1899 house, one of the earlier designs by Ernest Mayo, shows his use of the Dutch Colonial merged with Queen Anne composition. Prominent on the west facade in the dormer is a broken gable form. Below it on the second story a bow window swells out from the masonry mass; here, as in all of the windows, the opening is spanned by rough-faced redstone lintels. Below that bow is a large polygonal porch, originally open, to form a veranda supported by stout octagonal columns. On the south end of the veranda these are clustered on either side of the entrance to indicate the location of the front door. Notice that on the north facade (which faces the side street) a chimney with multiple vents suggested on the face rises well above the projecting three-story polygonal bay, balanced by another chimney to the east.

Continue south. The next house on your left is

14.   1221 FOREST AVENUE—c.1895

This is a simplified version of buildings already encountered with the mass of a simple masonry block amplified by a veranda, here supported by piers, across the front and down the south side. The second story moves forward gently with polygonal bays kept within the confines of the hipped roof's cornice. The southern bay projects down to the ground floor, but the northern one terminates to provide for the entrance and its neighboring window. It was built about 1895.

Continue south. The next house on your left is

15.   1217 FOREST AVENUE—1907

This 1907 house is another fine example of the Tudor Revival by Ernest Mayo rendered here in masonry. The basic block is broken open on the ground floor on the south side to provide a deep porch with typical Tudor forms around the entrance; these are echoed above on the second story by the diminutive pilasters with their small Ionic capitals. A similar pilaster appears on the north end on the second story. Notice that the entablature is not continued as a complete form but only as a cornice (this is a typical Tudor motif). On the north half of the front face the polygonal bays, built in limestone, move through the first two stories and are topped in the attic by a steeply rising gable with a half-round terminus.

Cross to the west side of the street, to

16. 1218 FOREST AVENUE—c.1871

This is another Luther Greenleaf cottage from immediately after the 1871 Chicago Fire. It has the same asymmetrical T-shaped plan as Evanston #8 and with the same bay window on the ground floor, but this one has a better preserved example of the typical second-story window on the front stem. The porch, however, comes from a turn-of-the-century renovation.

Continue south. The second building on your right is

17. 1210 FOREST AVENUE—1910

This 1910 house is another Tudor structure by Ernest Mayo. It has a masonry ground floor that uses classical elements rather correctly to mark the entrance along the north side. On the second story is stucco and wooden construction with a strip of windows in the center, framed by typical Tudor carpentry. A double gable appears in the attic level with half circles running along the gable rafter to a flared, cusped terminus. Notice the spiral colonettes set into each corner and the dormers with a different kind of gable rafter projecting from the side roofs.

Across the street, on the east side of Forest Avenue, is

18. 1215 FOREST AVENUE—1902

This 1902 house by Ernest Mayo is a rather heavily detailed Colonial Revival design with a basically Tudor plan arranged on a cross, a combination which produces great dignity. The uncovered veranda, stretching across the entire front, is marked by single-bottle balusters in limestone punctuated by brick piers. Limestone also appears in the keystoned lintels and in the Palladian motif in the front-facing gable which has large consoles and a split-bottom cornice supported by corner quoins. The entrance is deftly tucked into the northwestern reentrant angle and is balanced on the other side by a porch which originally was open.

Continue south. The next building on your left, on the NE corner of Forest Avenue and Hamilton Street, is

19.   1203 Forest Avenue—1905

This building, also by Ernest Mayo, shows his use of a brick ground floor and a half-timbered upper story. The reentrant angle in the slight, L-shaped plan is marked by a massive chimney. The entrance is on the south facade, protected by a complete masonry porch. Especially nice here is the repetition of the gable from the north end of the west facade in smaller scale as the dormer toward the south end of the longer wing. Also nice are the quatrefoils in the lower level of the second story which become thin or fat depending upon the breadth of the bays defined by the vertical boards.

On the NW corner of Hamilton Street and Forest Avenue is

20.   1200 Forest Avenue—1913

This corner building was built for circus magnate P.T. Barnum and designed by the Milwaukee architect A.C. Clas in 1913. In the back are large grounds and a large coachhouse where Barnum liked to keep an elephant which could be brought into the house to entertain guests at his numerous parties. The house's floors are designed to carry such a load. The building itself is a fine revival style of mixed origin with some Tudor and some Dutch. It does an especially nice job of acknowledging its corner site by placing its entrance on the western side, marking it by a classically correct Tuscan portico which contrasts with the relatively blank wall along the south facade next to the porch. Notice the broad segmental arches over the groupings of windows on the east facade; these are marked by limestone blocks in the brick arch, a material also used elsewhere to enliven the design. Additional richness comes from the richly sculpted and punctured bargeboard along the gable facing the side street on the south. Also quite fine is the wrought iron fence enclosing the property along the sidewalks.

On the SW corner of Hamilton Street and Forest Avenue is

21.   1140 Forest Avenue—1899

This 1899 structure by the important early Prairie School architect Myron Hunt shows the combination of the Tudor and the Prairie style. Typical of the Tudor is the combination of masonry and stucco visible on the west end, the molding of the ends of the beams forming the porch, the polygonal bay within the porch with its diamond-paned glass, and the double gable in the central projection facing to the north. Combined with that is the broad horizontality and general abstraction typical of the developing Prairie School style.

On the SE corner of Forest Avenue and Hamilton Street is

22. 1143 FOREST AVENUE—1893

This building by Stephen A. Jennings from 1893 is a fine example, beautifully cared for, of the Queen Anne style. A broad veranda crosses the ground floor and sweeps in a great curve around the corner facing the street intersection. It is supported by pairs of Tuscan columns standing on high, rough-faced limestone piers which are connected by tightly spaced, thin spindles. Within that curve is a polygonal turret rising through two-and-one-half stories to a flared pyramidal roof, the top of which is just short of reaching the ridge of the structure's main pitched roof. On the west face, a polygonal dormer with a similar roof stands above a polygonal bay window on the second story. On the north face, the eastern pitch of the roof extends to form a gable containing a Palladian window with curved sides in the shingle field; its recession allows the columns to stand free and produce a balcony. This gable projects beyond the face of the second story, a projection emphasized by its curved corners. The asymmetrical placement of the windows situated on the eastern end of the north face helps to balance the placement of the corner polygonal turret. The ground floor is a russet-colored brick. The entrance, which faces the side street, is marked by a nicely curved parapet constructed from the same tawny-colored limestone as the veranda pedestals and the foundation.

Walk east on Hamilton Street. On the NW corner of Hamilton Street and Michigan Avenue is

23. 225 HAMILTON STREET—1894

This excellent design by the important partnership of Pond and Pond, two brothers involved in Chicago social issues who assisted Jane Addams in her work, was designed in 1894 for an important Evanston lawyer and Illinois jurist. It is a classicising Queen Anne design with the discipline associated with the Shingle style. The ground floor and end walls are tawny brick and the upper stories are shingled as was the original roof. The composition is balanced by a screened porch on the east and a lower wing on the west, the central motif of which echoes the central motif of the main block which rises

23. 225 Hamilton Street

through two stories and into a full attic. The balance is emphasized by having the polygonal projection on the ground floor of the main block enlarged both horizontally and vertically when used on the western wing. Especially delightful in this design is the repetition within strict limits of the Palladian motif. The motif is most clear in the window above the entrance. The variation in the attic level of the central projection of the main block lacks the lintel and substitutes a fan motif for the window in the central arch. The variation in the dormers has the central arch shingled and the side windows replaced by the shingles of the dormer walls. The Palladian motif found in the main wing is repeated almost line for line on the west wing's dormer, but here it is above the polygonal projection which can be read as a downward extension of the same Palladian motif. (See Oak Park #20.)

On the NE corner of Hamilton Street and Michigan Avenue is

24. 1201–1213 MICHIGAN AVENUE and 205–207 HAMILTON STREET—1901

This multi-unit apartment building has four entrances facing the greensward at Michigan Avenue and another facing the side street. It was designed in 1901 by Wilmore Alloway in the sophisticated urban style associated with Henri IV of France who introduced the Renaissance styles into the urban architecture of the bourgeoisie in Paris with buildings detailed much like this one. Notice that it combines into an, at times, curious mixture of remnants of the Romanesque with the svelte polish of the Italian Renaissance. The entranceways are marked by broad, fully rounded arches supported by piers with curious vegetable capitals, but the sidelights and fanlight have thin, elegant patterns. The ground floor is treated as a basement with two sections, one in limestone the other in coursed masonry, terminated by a prominent entablature which provides the base for the second and third stories. These have single terra-cotta pilasters dividing the composition and near the corners. They are supported by corbels rising from the frieze and cornice level of the ground floor entablature. The entablature they sustain, with its very low architrave and high blank frieze and prominent modillions, is typical of the style of Henri IV. That architrave acts as the window head for the third story windows; the second story windows are covered by either lintels or arches or, above the larger entrances, by a combination of the two. The swelling bows have nothing to do with Henri IV but instead with Chicago apartments of the period. They were required by tenants and helped to expand the space within the apartment.

Walk north on Michigan Avenue. The first house on your right is

25. 1217 MICHIGAN AVENUE—1894

Although a large dormer originally on the south side of the roof has been removed, the overall character of this 1894 design by J.C. Lane can still be appreciated. It has a broad porch supported by Tuscan columns crossing the entire front and a pair of wall dormers with steep roofs on the north side of the front face. A projecting section of wall with a garland plaque appears between the windows on the south side of the second story. This area is shingled while the ground floor, which was probably originally clapboard, is now stucco.

Continue north to the corner. On the SW corner of Michigan Avenue and Burnham Place is

26. 222 BURNHAM PLACE—c.1890

This clapboard-clad house by Baumann and Cady was built about 1890. It rises two stories to a steeply pitched roof that is pulled down over the second story. It has (on its north face) two large dormers and (on the east face) another dormer with an even more steeply pitched roof with flared sides (originally the entire roof was shingled in wood). The tautness of the clapboard cladding is emphasized by being pushed out in the polygonal bay on the southeast corner. The porch, constructed in 1911, is supported by broad boards with curved fillets rather than by the posts or columns of the original porch. Notice, on the northwest corner of the house, the use of large rubble-stone to form the foundation for the projection at that point. This structure was the residence, in the late part of the nineteenth century and early part of the twentieth century, of one of the early supporters of various women's rights issues including the sponsoring of the distribution of birth control information.

Backtrack south on Michigan Avenue. The second house on your right is

27. 1210 MICHIGAN AVENUE—1880s

This building, started in the 1880s, grew over time by adding sections to the back or west. It is a simple, clapboard farm house. It has an especially nice, if simple, veranda across the front with groups of struts in the lintel, which is supported by thin turned posts.

Continue south to the corner. On the SW corner of Hamilton Street and Michigan Avenue is

28. 1144 MICHIGAN AVENUE—1890

This design from 1890 by Enoch Turnoch, an important architect who produced several large commercial and apartment buildings in Chicago, is an excellent example of the independence of the area's major architects from the strict stylistic precedents of east coast trend-setters in architectural fashion. It could perhaps be said that the building combines the best features of the Queen Anne and Shingle styles and suggests the approach of the Tudor Revival style. A large, complex, gambrel-like roof with various dormers covers the upper story and full attic, and large timbers have been crafted to stand above the heavy stone basement and porch parapet to hold it and to enclose the porch and porte-cochere projecting to the north. Especially fine is the combination of timber, clapboard, and glass along the north wall used in rising windows to reveal the location of the interior stairhall. Within the porch is a recessed entrance with curved sides, a further reiteration, now in small scale, of variations of a standard set of elements that here show the fine talents of this gifted architect.

On the SE corner of Michigan Avenue and Hamilton Street is

29. 208 HAMILTON STREET—1913

This is a modest 1913 design by Chatten and Hammond that shows the Prairie style merging with the Tudor style. The Prairie provided the groupings of the windows and simplicity of the carpentry work, whereas the Tudor provided the overall, simplified configuration and the placement of the entrance in a projecting section balanced by a series of dormers.

Continue south on Michigan Avenue. The fourth house on your right is

30. 1122 MICHIGAN AVENUE—1890s

This building was constructed in the 1890s. In 1916 a two-story porch was extended on the left and a new front porch was built to replace the original veranda, but the work was done so well it is hardly noticeable. Especially fine here is the variation in levels of the siding with clapboard, then shingle, then clapboard, and then shingles in the two stories and attic zone. The building gains great dignity from the turret that rises into the roof level in the very center of the present composition.

Continue south. The third house on your right, on the NW corner of Michigan Avenue and Greenleaf Street, is

31.   1104 MICHIGAN AVENUE—1895

This fine 1895 design by W.K. Johnson shows the Queen Anne adapted to a corner site. Its broad veranda sweeps across the front and curves around both the north and south ends, supported by paired Ionic columns. They, in turn, support a broad lintel with nice, applied cut-out work in its upper level. The main mass of the house erupts on the ground floor at the northeast corner with a circular bay and, on the second story of the southeast corner, with a similar circular oriel that has a bell roof atop it, supported by pairs of very squat, seemingly Corinthian columns. The main face of the building has a gable with a balcony carved out of it with a parapet swelling forward in its shingled face. Another bow and a small two-faced projection occur within the projecting lip of that gable. Adding character to the design are the porch columns, pedestals and entrance podia in redstone, and the tightly ranked spindles forming the porch balustrade.

Walk west on Greenleaf Street. On the NE corner of Forest Avenue and Greenleaf Street is

32.   1101 FOREST AVENUE—1896

This large masonry structure was designed in 1896 by Beers, Clay, and Dutton. It was built for the son of the man who lived across the street. A vigorous design, it has a porch across the entire front and a gambrel roof intersected at each end on the front facade by a masonry wall dormer with pilasters on the sides rising into a volute-shaped gable extending into the upper level of the slate gambrel. Between those two projections is a pair of straightforward tabernacle dormers. The strength of the design is amplified by the careful masonry detailing visible in the oval windows in the volute gables, in the quoins at the corners, and in the frames given the windows. Notice the projecting, two-story, wooden, polygonal bay at the southeast corner; the porte-cochere on the north end; and the redressing of the front's balance by the slightly asymmetrical placement of the entrance. Note also the coachhouse at the back.

On the NW corner of Forest Avenue and Greenleaf Street is

33.   1100 FOREST AVENUE—1896 and 1930

The original design of this building dates from 1896 and was by Beers, Clay, and Dutton. Its character is still visible, in part, in the coachhouse which sits to the northwest of the major building. In 1930 Mayo and Mayo subjected the building to extensive modifications which gave it an entirely new character. The present design represents the slickness and smoothness to which the historical precedents of the revival style in the period were subjected at that time. Notice that the site extends back for the entire block to the next street and that it is enclosed on three sides by an excellent wrought iron fence obtained at the 1893 Chicago World's Fair. The building is now in adaptive reuse as the Cove School.

On the SW corner of Forest Avenue and Greenleaf Street is

34.   1048 FOREST AVENUE—1887 and 1941

Designed in 1887 by J.T.W. Jennings the building, unfortunately, has had inappropriate metal siding added to it but it is locally referred to as the "Longfellow House" because it follows in its general design and in many of its specific details the New England house of the famous poet. Its original mass was also an excellent example of the earlier phase of the Colonial Revival with somewhat small scale and fussy detail closer in spirit to the Queen Anne used above the windows, in the balustrade around the semicircular porch, in the gable that emphasizes the location of the entrance, and in the upper sash of the second story double-hung windows. The porte-cochere is original but the south end, with the second story set back from the face to acknowledge the porte-cochere, was added in 1941 by H. Ring Clauson.

On the SE corner of Greenleaf Street and Forest Avenue is

35.   1047 FOREST AVENUE—1897

This 1897 building, designed by Harvey L. Page and Company, is one of the most august reflections in suburban architecture of the grandeur that swept over design following the World's Columbian Exposition held in Chicago in 1893. Its architect had a short practice in Chicago (he came from Washington, D.C. and soon moved farther west). He produced a frame structure, clad in clapboard, forming a cube with prominent pilasters at each corner. Attached to its front is a large, two-story frontispiece with four Corinthian columns with oversized capitals that work well with the high entablature of the pediment and its richly detailed cornice. Notice how, on the second story, the windows are shoved into the entablature level, somewhat disturbing the correctness expected in such a design.

Backtrack east on Greenleaf Street. On the SE corner of Greenleaf Street and Michigan Avenue is

36. 1049 MICHIGAN AVENUE—1910

Designed and built by C.H. Thompson, an important local Evanston developer who designed many of the houses he built, the importance of the Prairie style in the region is quite evident here. The 1910 design began as a basic block with a hipped roof. It was given a more fashionable appearance by attaching an entrance on the north side with a typical Prairie hood, a motif repeated in the face of the west hip pitch to form a large dormer. Below the dormer a porch projects with an emphatic horizontality. The second story and the north face of the entrance structure, with their boards with stucco surfaces, are indebted to the examples of the Prairie School as is the detailing of the brick with simple geometric patterns produced by changing the way the brick is laid rather than by adding extensive detailing or additional pieces to produce decoration.

Walk south on Michigan Avenue. The third house on your right is

37. 1032 and 1034 MICHIGAN AVENUE—1899

Another double house, this one was designed by Myron Hunt in 1899, shortly before he left the area to take up a practice in the Los Angeles region. Here each of the two dwelling units is given a distinctive treatment. The northern one has a projecting porch and a two-story polygonal bay; the southern one has a recessed porch and a Palladian window. The units are tied together by the gable, the cornice of which provides the top for the northern section's polygonal bay. The gable contains a group of four double-hung windows and, like the rest of the building, is shingled.

Continue south. The second building on your right is

38. 1026 MICHIGAN AVENUE—1915

This excellent Prairie style house by John Van Bergen, designed in 1915, shows the horizontality that can be produced, even in a three-story structure, by manipulating the Prairie School vocabulary. The entrance, on the south side, is protected by a thin plane cantilevered from the side of the building to provide a porch roof. The base of the structure is buff brick up to the sill level of the second story windows. Projecting to the east in the front is a porch (originally open) with the wide, soffited eaves of its hipped roof providing a horizontality that is repeated for the roof above the second story and above the third. The third story is tucked within the hipped roof. The entire composition is brought into balance by having a massive chimney project on the north side opposite the entrance on the south.

Continue south. The fourth house on your right, on the NW corner of Lee Street and Michigan Avenue, is

39. 1010 MICHIGAN AVENUE—1911
This massive mansion originally sat on a large corner lot; it recently received a new neighbor on what originally was its north lawn. The building portrays the Tudor style at its masonry best and was designed in 1911 by Ernest Mayo. Its entrance is stressed by a nicely detailed classical motif between a large chimney and a projection of the main mass. The Lee Street facade has a gable in its third story similar to the one facing to the east onto Michigan Avenue. Porches, bows, gables, chimneys, and groups of windows with varying designs complete this complex composition.

On the SW corner of Michigan Avenue and Lee Street is

40. 940–950 MICHIGAN AVENUE—1927
Lee Street marked a boundary in Evanston's early zoning ordinance with multi-family residences forbidden to the north and allowed to the south. This interesting design by Frank W. Cauley from 1927 shows the attempt made by apartment building architects to produce buildings in Evanston that worked well with the single family residential character of the suburb. This is a square building with the corner opened to an interior sunken court leading to the apartment tiers. The style is the sophisticated Georgian style popular during the period. It features delicate wrought iron work in front of the French windows, and it has bulbous urns marking various important parts of the composition. Broad segmental arches cover groups of windows in various sections, and the combination of brick and limestone provide further demarcation within the structural and compositional sections.

On the SE corner of Michigan Avenue and Lee Street is

41. 999 MICHIGAN AVENUE and
200 LEE STREET—1927

This apartment building was constructed in 1927 to the designs of McNally and Quinn who designed many of Chicago's tall, lakeshore apartments. This one provides an example of the Tudor style for a building similar to the one across the street (Evanston #40) which also uses a combination of limestone and brick. The roof, visible here and there, is slate. The design is picturesque: the windows are of varying sizes and groupings; the wall planes and silhouette are broken; the corners are enriched with buttresses; and the entrances are integrated with the projecting limestone bases of polygonal projections or with richly carved limestone Tudor frames.

On the NE corner of Michigan Avenue and Lee Street is

42. 1005 MICHIGAN AVENUE—1913

This very subdued and highly sophisticated design from 1913 is by the prominent North Shore society architect Howard Van Doren Shaw (although there is some evidence that it is instead by Ernest Woodyat). Its point of departure was the Colonial Revival, but liberties were taken with that model. It has a slate, truncated pitched roof with three flat-roofed dormers above a two-story, light colored, brick base. The facade has five openings per floor; the middle one on the second story has a wrought iron balcony face matched by the ground floor's broad arched opening which holds a delicate fanlight above the double door entrance. The main mass is enclosed by a chimney which projects above the roof truncation, but its symmetry is broken on the south end by a low, projecting, two-story, flat-roofed extension originally with an open porch on the upper level and an enclosed one on the ground floor.

Walk east on Lee Street. On the NW corner of Lee Street and Sheridan Road is

43. 1000 SHERIDAN ROAD—1919

This building by Ernest Mayo dating from 1919 is an example of the architect's exploration of the English Cottage style, although the two-story, rough-stuccoed block has suggestions of the Georgian style's refinement

41. 999 Michigan Avenue
and 200 Lee Street

combined with the sophistication of the English country houses being built at the turn of the century by a famous group of architects especially around Lake Windemere. Their designs were important sources for many of Mayo's and Shaw's buildings. Here the sources are modified considerably to suggest the more rustic country character, for example the hipped roof which suggests thatch, in the exposed brick around the entrance, and in the porch tucked under the hipped roof's extension on the eastern end.

Continue east on Lee Street until it ends. On the NW corner of Lake Shore Boulevard and Lee Street is

44. 1000 LAKE SHORE BOULEVARD—1911

This fine house by Tallmadge and Watson from 1911 shows the close conjunction of the Tudor and Prairie styles. The L-shaped plan with polygonal projections, dormers, and the combination of stucco and boards is very close to the Tudor style. The detailing, however, is geometric and almost abstract, and the masses are clear-cut and distinctive which are characteristics of the Prairie style discipline.

Walk north on Lake Shore Boulevard. The first house on your left is

45.   1012 LAKE SHORE BOULEVARD—1894

Designed by Robert Spencer, Jr. (when in the partnership of Spencer and Kendall) in 1894, this is an early example of the work of a man who later became prominent in the Prairie School. It is also perhaps the earliest full-fledged, correctly detailed Tudor design in the six-county area. Rising two stories to a high pitched roof enclosing a complete third story, the building has a brick ground floor beyond a full width front veranda which has heavy Tudor timbers carrying the half-timbered upper structure. The gable, with its group of four windows, projects beyond the second story which has a pair of broad polygonal bays kept within the overhang. The entrance is down the northern side; it is clearly located by its own small gable which covers a beautifully carved doorway. The nearly full-height wing beyond it provides a background for the entrance and the brick chimney rising next to it also helps to mark the entrance. Notice the size of the wooden members and the careful carving of the various corbels which carry those timbers.

Continue north. The fifth house on your left is

46.   1040 LAKE SHORE BOULEVARD—1895

Designed in 1895 by John Turner Long, an important early Evanston architect, this is a fine example of a subdued masonry Queen Anne design. It has a block covered by a steeply hipped roof made asymmetrical by a large round corner turret that rises through three stories to a tall conical roof rising higher than the main roof's peak. Like the main roof, it is slate and has a flared base. The dormer in the main roof has a group of three windows separated by half columns and an additional half column set at each corner of the copper facing. The porch across the front has pairs of columns at either end but a singular column in the center. A porte-cochere projects in the middle of the north face. Notice the three different widths of the masonry blocks with high and low courses alternating on the second story and an even higher smooth course serving as the cornice for the main block which is extended where it acts as a rough lintel and stringcourse for the turret.

Continue north. The next house on your left, on the SW corner of Greenleaf Street and Lake Shore Boulevard, is

47. 1044 LAKE SHORE BOULEVARD—1906

Designed in 1906 by C.W. Rapp who, with his brother George, later designed the Chicago Theatre, this building makes very good use of the Dutch Revival style and of its corner lot. Its basic block is disrupted by having wall dormers in each street face of the hipped roof, the northern one flanked by two small ones. The north face of the block is disrupted by the central projecting porch with side stairways. Next to the entrance is a window (whose position between the first and second stories is clearly marked by having its arch formed by an extension upward of the stringcourse at the sill level) which lights the stairhall within. The facade facing the lake has large windows on its south end to provide views over Lake Michigan.

On the NW corner of Greenleaf Street and Lake Shore Boulevard is

48. 101 GREENLEAF STREET—1913

Designed by Ernest Mayo in 1913, this house was built by the brother of Vice-President Dawes. It is basically a rather small house that is given grandeur and the impression of increased size by the manipulation of its forms. The Georgian block has large quoins at the corners which support the tiled hipped roof. In its south facade, three dormers are placed between the five openings on each of the two stories below. The Doric order provides dignity at the central entrance. Projecting to the west is a low service wing and to the east an open ground floor porch with its flat roof supported by carefully detailed Doric columns. Notice on the main block facing the lake, a projecting chimney has a split pediment attached at the cornice level to carry through the cornice line yet acknowledge the existence of that chimney. Furthermore, in order not to disrupt the rhythm of the fenestration, a window like the others on that floor is set into the face of that chimney, a quite unusual motif but typical of Mayo's inventiveness.

Continue north on Lake Shore Boulevard. The next house on your left is

49. 1114 LAKE SHORE BOULEVARD—1909

Designed by Tallmadge and Watson in 1909, this building shows the simple Prairie box rendered with strict horizontality and with clear evidence of the Tudor background of the Prairie style. The basic box is covered by a hipped roof, truncated to emphasize the horizontality which is also stressed by the smooth, soffited eaves. On the half-timbered second story are flat-fronted projections reaching halfway out into those eaves: the one on the north has a pair of windows, the one on the south a triplet of windows, a difference giving the first evidence of the asymmetry of the block. The doorway, within a porch set inside the arched opening on the brick ground floor, is slightly to the north of the center line. The ground floor window on the north side is smaller than the Chicago window type on the south side; the side windows have fine Prairie glass and the jambs have Prairie capitals. The disbalance of the asymmetry is corrected by the projection of a ground floor porch slightly to the front and extensively to the east; it was originally open and sustained by pairs of piers whose forms follow those of the window jambs.

Continue north. The second house on your left is

50.   1130 LAKE SHORE BOULEVARD—1911

This is one of the finer and more sophisticated Georgian Revival designs in the area. It was apparently designed by Charles Hodgkins and Charles Coolidge of Shepley, Rutan, and Coolidge, the successor firm of Richardson's office in Boston, the architects for the Chicago Public Library Cultural Center and the Art Institute of Chicago. This design is quite formal. The basic block with its four windows on each story has a lacy parapet hiding the third story which contains the ballroom. Projecting to the south is an open porch; more prominent on the north is a projection which contains the entrance with a transom and sidelights and, beyond the parapet on the second floor, a broad Palladian window with a segmental arch tying together the outer jambs of the side windows. The design is formally placed on its site against a parterre defined by a brick wall with large, single-bottle balusters set well back from the sidewalk.

Continue north. The next house on your left is

51.   1136 LAKE SHORE BOULEVARD—1909 and 1920s

The original design from 1909 and the alterations from the 1920s are all by Tallmadge and Watson. Especially nice is the Prairie style glass in the second story of the central wing and the careful detailing of the brick work which provides both horizontal and vertical articulation for the walls.

Continue north to the corner. Turn left (west) on Hamilton Street. On the NE corner of Hamilton Street and Sheridan Road is

52. 1201 SHERIDAN ROAD—1912

This large building, designed in 1912 by Robert Spencer, Jr. (when in the partnership of Spencer and Powers), originally sat on ample grounds stretching eastward to Lake Shore Boulevard and might properly be termed a Prairie villa. It has a long block stretching north and south with a projecting, battered-walled entrance covered by a pitched roof. South of the entrance is a massive chimney; immediately to its north is a projection that extends upward into the roof zone to carry a half-timbered top. That design is repeated as the end wall of the projection at the north end of the main block. Between those two can be seen four windows, their sills stepping upward to follow the interior stairs, which contain fine Prairie glass, a style of glass repeated in other windows elsewhere on the building. The brickwork is very simple and is highlighted by a minimal use of stone for the window sills and around the entrance. The grounds are beautifully landscaped and provide an attractive setting for this house.

Cross to the west side of the street and walk north on Sheridan Road. The second house on your left is

53. 1218 SHERIDAN ROAD—1901

This Tudor design by Ernest Mayo from 1901 shows the highly decorative pattern that could be produced with the half-timbering of that style. The long building has gables of unequal size at either end, each with fine gable rafters, and two dormers and a multi-vented chimney projecting from the slate roof. Between the pair of dormers is a projecting window, and below that is the entrance which extends to the north in its projection under an abstracted quatrefoil cut-out in the half-timbered upper zone of that entrance projection. The ground floor is brick and moves forward on the south end to provide a low hipped-roofed porch.

Cross to the east side of the street. On the SE corner of Sheridan Road and Burnham Place is

54. 1225 SHERIDAN ROAD—1902

This 1902 structure is probably the largest Tudor house designed by Ernest Mayo and is one of the finest examples of the style in the six-county area. Its basic composition is like that of Evanston #53, but everything here is enlarged and enriched. The entrance, between the two gables, projects forward into a broad, stilted, segmental arch with alternating brick and redstone

54. 1225 Sheridan Road

voussoirs. The brick ground floor swells forward on either side in slight bow windows (appropriately, in Boston they are called "swell windows") with prominent redstone lintels. The second story is built from beautifully carved and worked Tudor half-timbering with the ends marked by pilasters carried by heavy corbels, the projections further supported by consoles. The pairs of windows are flanked by beautifully carved colonettes attached to the window jambs. Broken pedimental tabernacle windows are in the gables. The roof between the two gables has a large dormer. The pitched roof swoops down to the south through the second story and across a glazed porch projecting from within it. On the north facade, facing the side street, the projecting second story and gable motif is repeated, this time without the broken pediment in the gable; between it and the massive chimney on the ground floor is a small projecting bay.

Walk east on Burnham Place.

The entire tract of land on your left, now a subdivision with large homes dating over a number of years in the post World War II period, was originally the estate of Daniel H. Burnham, the important city planner and architect in Chicago. The wall that you will pass was the retaining wall of that estate. The balustraded parapet survives on the far east end.

Turn left (north) on Lake Shore Boulevard, 1 block. Turn left (west) on Dempster Street. The third house on your right is

55. 147 DEMPSTER STREET—1914

Designed by Chatten and Hammond in 1914, this is a variation on the Tudor Revival style which nearly merges with some of the formal aspects of the Georgian. The two-story, dark brown building rises to a pitched slate roof and has forward projections on both the east and west ends; the west one is smaller but has larger windows. The entrance is placed centrally between them. It has a gable over its projection and, in the second story, a strip of five windows set within carefully detailed masonry frames. The building is beautifully sited; the porch takes up the entire area between the wings and extends outward as a brick walk to the sidewalk, with lawns stretching on either side.

Directly across the street is

56.   200 DEMPSTER STREET—1941

This building was designed by William Deknatel, a student of Frank Lloyd Wright. It represents the extension of the Prairie style into the later parts of the twentieth century. The ground floor is brick; the upper section, beginning at the window lintel level, is broad, dark boards; the windows are metal casement windows; the roofs are flat. The composition is a series of cubic shapes, some open, some enclosed, connected by a trellis, by a linear pattern, and by a repetition in the fenestration. A similar geometric ordering of rectangular shapes extends outward from the building across the grounds and toward the sidewalk in the form of planters.

Backtrack east on Dempster Street. Turn left (north) and walk 1 block until it ends at Greenwood Street. Turn left (west). The second house on your left is

57.   144 GREENWOOD STREET—1915

Notice the rubblestone wall that stretches across this and the next two properties. It is the fence of the original estate grounds surrounding the next structure. This building, built by the treasurer of Carson Pirie Scott and Company, was designed by Ernest Mayo in 1915. It is a fine example of the Tudor style. It takes full advantage of a slight rise in the topography with its L-shaped plan, masonry walls, dormers, chimneys, half-timbered gables, and porch with a lip extended outward over the driveway as a reduced form of a porte-cochere oriented to produce the best picturesque effect to a person approaching along the driveway.

Continue west. The next house on your left is

58.   202 GREENWOOD STREET—1889 and 1897

Designed in 1889 (note the date in huge numbers in the chimney set toward the east end) by Joseph Lyman Silsbee, this is an excellent example of the originality of this architect, who combined many sources into his own quite original designs. A freestone lower section gives way to tightly laid clapboards for the ground floor. Projecting beyond its face is the great gambrel roof with a row of four pedimented dormers on the lower plane lighting the second story and a low dormer with a Palladian window in the upper plane. On the west end, a porch is carved out of the ground floor. Its entrance is marked by an ornamented circular pediment carried on corbels arranged in two planes and carried on stone columns. The additions to the south, from 1897, are also by Silsbee.

58. 202 Greenwood Street

Continue west. The next house on your left is

59.   214 Greenwood Street—between 1894 and 1916
Shrouded in ambiguity, this building has a coherence in appearance that
belies the incoherence of the information about it which includes references
to Harvey L. Page and to George S. Kingsley as architects and dates ranging
from 1894 to 1916 for parts that cannot be identified. The result is a restrained Tudor design with an especially rich entrance in the brick ground
floor; the entrance has a pilaster frame with beautifully detailed Tudor
forms. The second story has a highly stylized half-timbering, and the chimney on the north face is random rubblestone rising as high as the broken
hipped roof.

Across the street is the Dawes Mansion.

This concludes the Evanston Walking Tour.

*Drive west on Greenwood Street to the corner. Turn right (north) on Forest
Avenue, as it winds and becomes Forest Place, ¼ mile. On your left, on the
west side of Forest Place, is*

60.   1616 Sheridan Road
(actually, 1616 Forest Place)—1902
This large frame structure, designed by George L. Harvey in 1902, represents the palatial grandeur of the ante-bellum mansions of aristocratic southern cities. It features a pitched roof faced toward the street supported by six
tall Ionic columns sustaining a correct entablature which crosses each end of
the building to complete the gable design on each side elevation. Beyond the
columns is a deep porch with an opening centered beyond each intercolum-
niation. The central one, on the ground floor, frames a slightly projecting
entrance vestibule with a carefully detailed Serlian door frame topped by a
swan's-neck pediment which assists in supporting the balcony on the second
story, which is also sustained by consoles projecting from the wall. The window heads on the ground floor, like the entrance details, are richly and
classically correct. The final finish for this design is provided by the tall
balustrade on the roof above the entablature. The house is important as a
fine example of southern ante-bellum styles and also as one of the settings
used in D.W. Griffith's epic 1915 movie "Birth of a Nation," the first film to
demonstrate that movies could be art.

*Continue north, now on Sheridan Road, 1½ blocks. On the NW corner of
Sheridan Road and Clark Street is*

THE NORTHWESTERN UNIVERSITY ALUMNI/
VISITOR'S CENTER—1800 Sheridan Road

Here information on Northwestern University campus tours is available.*
Some of the highlights include:

UNIVERSITY HALL
1897 Sheridan Road—1869

This 1869, brick and stone, Gothic building is the oldest on the campus.

MUSIC ADMINISTRATION BUILDING
711 Elgin Road—1873

This 1873 Victorian structure originally housed the Evanston College for
Ladies.

ANNIE MAY SWIFT HALL
2029 Sheridan Road—1895

This 1895 building is now the administrative offices for the School of Speech
and the Radio and TV Film Department.

FISK HALL
1845 Sheridan Road—1899

This 1899 building now houses the Medill School of Journalism.

DEARBORN OBSERVATORY
2131 Sheridan Road

On Fridays, April through October, at 9:00 P.M. or 10:00 P.M. there are
public viewings through the eighteen-and-one-half-inch telescope. There are
also a slide show and lecture. If the weather doesn't permit a viewing, there is
a film showing what one would have seen.

LINDHEIMER ASTRONOMICAL
RESEARCH CENTER—1966

On Saturdays, April through October, from 2:00 P.M.-4:00 P.M. there are
public viewings through the telescopes.

* An alternate reference would be to see Walk #30 in *Chicago On Foot* by
this author, 3rd edition, 1977, published by Rand McNally.

Continue north on Sheridan Road 1.2 miles to Central Street. On your right is Grosse Pointe Lighthouse Park.

61.　Grosse Pointe Lighthouse
2535 Sheridan Road—1873

Grosse Pointe Lighthouse is a landmark in the original sense of the word because it marks the land from the sea (here in the form of Lake Michigan). It rises as a tapering column to a catwalk supported on robust but simple Italianate brackets and is topped by a polygonal glass lantern within which is the prismatic lense that focuses the light and sends it as a beacon across the water. The entrance into the lighthouse is from a small attached structure on its western side. This is a simple rectangular structure in brick on a limestone base covered with a pitched, jerkin-head roof and with brackets along the eaves. It is listed on the National Register of Historic Places.

Just west of the lighthouse is

62.　Nature Center—1870s

This 1870s brick structure is the lighthouse keepers' house. It, too, is a brick structure on a limestone base covered with a hipped roof with jerkin-heads and a pair of entrances on both the west and the east facades. The west facade (facing the street) is the more finished one with shouldered arches over the doors which are set in the gabled, jerkin-headed projection and with segmental arches over the pairs of segmental headed windows on each side on each floor. Projecting to the south is a small porch with Italianate posts, lintels, and brackets. There are indoor and outdoor exhibits from May-October, Saturdays and Sundays 2:00 P.M.-5:00 P.M.

Continue north on Sheridan Road. The next driveway on your right is

63.　Evanston Arts Center—1920s

This 1920s building houses an art and a photography gallery. Exhibits change monthly. Free.

Continue north on Sheridan Road.

61. Grosse Pointe Lighthouse
2535 Sheridan Road

WILMETTE

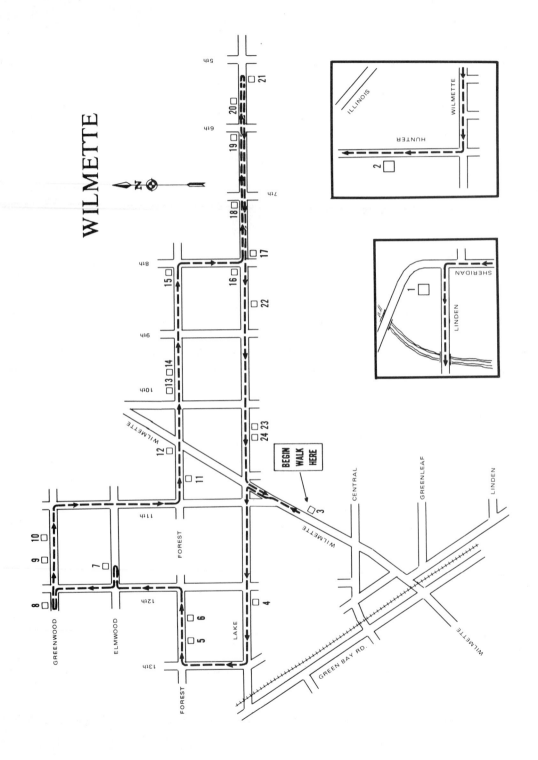

WILMETTE

Drive north on Sheridan Road .9 miles to Linden Avenue. Turn left (west).
On your right, on the NW corner of Linden Avenue and Sheridan Road is

1. BAHA'I HOUSE OF WORSHIP
100 Linden Avenue—1931

Planning for this spectacular temple began in 1903, although it was not fully
built until 1953. The building is on the National Register of Historic Places.
Built on one of the sites in the world considered sacred to this religion, this
temple is in the shape of a large polygon with each angle marked by a long,
curved, concrete element rising to a central point to enclose a domical shape.
The webs between these members are filled with perforated, glazed webs to
fill the interior with a lacy display of light. The striking structure is set on a
broad, landscaped site that is terraced down towards Lake Michigan where,
across Sheridan Road, is a beautiful and well-kept garden and the residence
lived in by the architect, Louis Bourgeois, while he supervised the construction of his design. The auditorium contains 1,200 seats and the dome is 138
feet high. Down the stairway, below the auditorium, is the Visitors Center
where slide presentations can be activated at all times. Be sure to tour the
lovely landscaped gardens surrounding the temple. Open daily 10:00 A.M.-
5:00 P.M., October 15-May 14 and 10:00 A.M.-10:00 P.M., May 15-October
14. Free.

Drive west 1.3 miles on Linden Avenue, over the tracks, and then 1 more
block to Park Avenue. Turn right (north) on Park Avenue 1 block to
Wilmette Avenue. Turn left (west) on Wilmette Avenue, 1.2 miles to Hunter
Road. Turn right (north) 1¾ blocks. On your left, on the west side of Hunter
Road, is

2. WILMETTE HISTORICAL SOCIETY
565 Hunter Road

The historical society has revolving exhibits that focus on the history of both
the area and the town. They are well executed and include maps, old tele-
phones, daguerreotypes, and other artifacts. There is also a costume exhibit.
Tuesdays-Thursdays: 9:30 A.M.-noon and 1:30 P.M.-4:00 P.M.; Sundays: 2:00
P.M.-5:00 P.M. Free.

Drive north on Hunter Road 3 blocks. Turn right (east) on Lake Avenue 1.5
miles to 11th Street. Turn right on 11th Street and immediately right again
on Wilmette Avenue to the railroad depot on your left. Stop.

WILMETTE WALKING TOUR

3. CHICAGO & NORTHWESTERN RAILROAD DEPOT
1135 Wilmette Avenue—1873

This pale brick building, moved to this site by the Wilmette Historical Society, is a typical suburban train station built in 1873. The original track side faces the street where a wooden bay window projects for the station master and a long porch protected the awaiting passengers. On each end is a stepped corbel course under the gable and long curved brackets to support the roof overhang. The segmental arched windows are covered by shouldered pediments constructed from the same brick as the rest of the structure. The structure is listed on the National Register of Historic Places.

Walk northeast on Wilmette Avenue to Lake Avenue. Turn left (west), past 12th Street, then the first house on your left is

4. 1215 LAKE AVENUE—1890s

This very tall, one-and-one-half-story house from just before the turn of the century has a front gable, the upper section of which is shingled with alternating flat-cut and scalloped shingles producing a rich textured field. It is topped in the gable by a criss-cross of knobbed, turned spindles intersecting one another within a scroll-cut, abstracted, foliated ornament. The porch, spanning the entire front, reinforces the massing of the gable, spreading it as a welcoming shelter before the house.

Continue west to 13th Street. Turn right (north) 1 block to Forest Avenue. Turn right (east). The third house on your right is

5. 1231 FOREST AVENUE—1898

This simple, 1898, clapboard house rises two stories to a flared, hipped roof which establishes the character for the simple design. Projecting on each side and in the front is a complementary hipped roof dormer. The front porch is also hipped and crosses the entire house. Within the porch a broad polygonal bay projects balancing the pair of openings, one for the door, the other for the vestibule window.

Continue east. The third house on your right is

6. 1215 FOREST AVENUE—c.1909

This cubic, two-story house is built of dressed ashlar. It has a flared hipped

6. 1215 Forest Avenue

roof and, projecting in the front, a steeply pitched pediment with a broken cornice at the bottom which contains a false balcony for the fully rounded attic window establishing a strong center line for the extremely formal composition. In the second story, in the center, a slightly projecting bay with a pair of windows between a pilaster stands above the entrance which is sheltered by a large porch. The door has a massive limestone lintel like the large lintels above the openings on the side of the building. The center of the porch is marked by a projecting pediment with an arc rising into it. The pediment is sustained by a masonry pier with two squat columns next to it. They have an exaggerated entasis. Note that the foundation is given an additional sense of solidity by being constructed from drafted regular ashlar. It was built about 1909.

Continue east on Forest Avenue to 12th Street. Turn left (north) 1 block to Elmwood Avenue. Turn right (east). The first house on your left is

7.   1134 ELMWOOD AVENUE—1873

This tall Italianate villa, built in 1873, is an excellent example of the type, marred only slightly by the addition of metal siding. The emphasis in the design is on the massing, the window framings, and roof detailing. The L-shaped plan, covered by a pitched roof with flat eaves, presents a gable to the front with paired brackets and large dentils. The same cornice is repeated under the eaves of the wing projecting to the east. In the reentrant angle a tower rises two stories higher than the two-story mass below with a pair of windows in the third story and a tall Mansard roof in the fourth, crowned by cast iron cresting with its corner finials intact. The elongated horseshoe window above the fully rounded break in the cornice adds a very rich touch to this feature. Note the typical Eastlake incising in the panel in that cornice, in the pediment of the segmental window on the second floor of the tower, across the lintel of the porch, and above the transom above the double entry door, a motif popularized in America by the publication in 1872 of Charles Locke Eastlake's book on furniture. The other windows, paired and pedimented on the front wing and single with a lintel on the side wing, have the typical elongated proportions of the Italianate, just as the porch fronting on the wing has the heavy carpentry elements typical of that style. Projecting to the east and west are polygonal bays. The next three houses (Wilmette #8, #9, and #10) were built by the same developer.

Backtrack to 12th Street. Turn right (north) 1 block to Greenwood Avenue. Turn left (west). The second house on your right is

7.   1134 Elmwood Avenue

8.   1210 GREENWOOD AVENUE—1873
greatly altered

The original 1873 proportions of this building are still visible. Note the projecting polygonal bays under the broad eaves of the hipped roof and the tall proportions of the windows with their disposition in the front marking the center line of the facade. When the house was about forty years old, it was completely modernized to conform to the Prairie style. The eave soffits and walls were covered in a continuous stucco sheet, and a porch matching the one above was added in the front with a projection to the side to provide a new entrance to the building. It is a handsome example of the combining of two styles, one superimposed on the other.

Backtrack east on Greenwood Avenue. The third house on your left (past 12th Street) is

9.   1128 GREENWOOD AVENUE—1873
greatly altered

Although the core of this house apparently dates from 1873, what is visible now represents the Augustan age of Rome popular during the first decades of the present century in domestic architecture. Great, carefully detailed Corinthian columns sustain a slightly too steeply pitched pediment set against the projecting wings with the slopes of their roofs backing up the frontispiece. From the second story, within the porch, projects a balcony sustained by long corbels with very thin balusters introducing a delicacy matched only by the small-scale glass divisions in the stilted round-headed windows in the pediment. In the reentrant angle on the west side is the entrance porch sustained by very carefully detailed Ionic columns providing a pleasant counterpart to the impressive front facade.

Continue east. The second house on your left is

10.   1112 GREENWOOD AVENUE—1873
greatly altered

This is the third example of a modernization to a building which, like the previous two (Wilmette #8 and #9), began as an Italianate structure in 1873. The original Italianate mass may still be perceived in the broad, gabled, front facade with the very high windows on the ground floor. The additions have been numerous and introduced periodically. The polygonal projection on the west toward the back is probably from about the turn of the century, the nicely detailed Federal columnar entrance with the fanlight and side-lights is probably from the 1920s. The metal siding and the false, wrought iron balconies across the ground floor are more recent alterations. (Keep this house in mind when you look at the next one.)

Continue east to 11th Street. Turn right (south) 2 blocks to Forest Avenue. Turn left (east). The third house on your right is

11. 1041 FOREST AVENUE—1873
Despite the artificial siding, the recent front porch, and canopy over the doorway, the basic configuration of the 1873 Italianate building can still be seen. The tall windows with segmental hoods on the ground floor are answered by only a single paired window on the second floor but a small square window appears in the attic.

Continue east to the corner. On the NW corner of Forest and Wilmette avenues is

12. COMMUNITY CHURCH OF WILMETTE—1920
This 1920 building is notable as a fine example of how a large building type can be fitted nicely into a residential neighborhood without disturbing its character. Set well back from the street, it has simple massing composed of large rubble ashlar walls with broad arches and a porch that extends as a welcoming projection from the building.

Continue east on Forest Avenue 1 block. On the NE corner of Forest Avenue and 10th Street is

13. 932 FOREST AVENUE—1890s
This tall two-story house with a tall hipped roof portrays the simple massing of the Classical Revival of the 1890s. Especially notable are the large Ionic pilasters at each corner including the corners of the projecting central section which contains the broken pediment, supported by pilasters, sheltering the entrance.

Continue east on Forest Avenue. The second house on your left is

14. 922 FOREST AVENUE—pre-1873 and c.1900

This building presents a curious reconstruction of an Italianate structure
predating 1873. The oldest elements are the pedimented windows on both
side facades and the cornice with its paired brackets in the front and single
brackets along the side. At some point, most likely around the turn of the
century, the building was reconstructed. From that time come the present
gables with their adaptation of Palladian windows and the front facade with
its broad bow that includes pieces taken from the older building. The front
porches at the entrance and on the east side are both more recent.

*Continue east on Forest Avenue. On the NW corner of Forest Avenue and
8th Street is*

15. 804 FOREST AVENUE—1906

This is a typical and fine example of a modest version of a type of Prairie
house perfected by George Washington Maher, built in 1906. A porch, with
large piers at either end and solid looking square piers with square capitals
flanking the stairs, leads to a slightly projecting section containing the entrance. Above the flat-roofed porch, on the second story in the center, is a
small square window with two leaded glass casements surrounded by a frieze
repeated as a broad swelling sill beneath. It features squares and circles subjected to variations arising from geometric manipulations. Above it is a high
hooded dormer, a motif repeated on each side of the high hipped roof. The
single broad window, on each side of the center line on each floor, reinforces
the geometric clarity of this basic, stuccoed cubic mass.

*Turn right (south) on 8th Street 1 block. On the NW corner of 8th Street
and Lake Avenue is*

16. 802 LAKE AVENUE—1871

This frame clapboard house from 1871 is an excellent example of the suburban houses built in the early period of this suburban settlement. A tall one-
and-one-half stories, it has a gable facing south containing a broad window,
formerly a double window, with a segmental pediment. On the ground floor
are three tall linteled windows. The porch across the front, which returns
down the east side to the entrance, has a beautifully preserved and maintained scroll-cut balustrade, scroll-cut posts, and knees for the lintel, all of
which are made from thin boards rather than from stouter elements. The

service porch at the back of the east side repeats the front porch motifs in more modest dimensions.

On the SE corner of 8th Street and Lake Avenue is

17.　729 Lake Avenue—1871

This frame, clapboard-covered house was also built in 1871 and manages to gain interior space by pushing out in various directions from the tight confines of its cross-shaped plan. One notable projection is the wall dormer on the west side of the wing facing north, where the pitch of the roof suddenly becomes less than the rest of the steeply pitched roof to accommodate a window lighting the room in that upper half story. Another projection is at the reentrant angle on the east side beyond the modern entrance. It is a tower covered with a steep pointed roof.

Walk east on Lake Avenue. On the NW corner of Lake Avenue and 7th Street is

18.　704 Lake Avenue—c.1916

This fine masonry structure on a corner site portrays the dynamic balance achieved by Prairie School architects. This house was designed by Thomas Tallmadge around World War I. On the western side a slight projection appears on both floors, balanced on the east by a greater projection for a one-story sun porch. The center contains the entrance and is marked by a gable set into the slight hipped roof containing a tripartite frontispiece on the upper story with stained glass in the attic windows, terminated by a broad blank panel supported by two massive corbels above the corbels flanking the front entrance. Broad plain stringcourses strengthen the horizontals and the fenestration maintains the simplicity of the entire design by featuring a Chicago window on each floor on each side of the entrance. The only ornament comes from the patterns produced by the careful laying of the brick and the manipulation of the wooden elements in the frontispiece and the flat soffited eaves.

Continue east. On the NW corner of Lake Avenue and 6th Street is

19.　602 Lake Avenue—c.1900

This late, simply massed, Shingle style, Queen Anne house is from the turn

18. 704 Lake Avenue

of the century. It accommodates itself to the corner very nicely by having a broad porch face both streets behind which rises the two-story clapboard-clad frame structure with a broad flared gable divided into two sections, the lower one with octagonal shingles and a triplet of Queen Anne windows, the upper one with scalloped shingles. Facing the side street is a polygonal bay topped by a polygonal hipped roof.

Continue east. The second house on your left is

20. 524 LAKE AVENUE—1904

This massive building from 1904 features the gambrel roof as its dominant element. The west side has a magnificent rubblestone chimney rising to the roof peak level. The east side has an extension of the upper slope projecting outward to form the porte-cochere sustained at its ends by single, rather thin columns supported on massive rubblestone pedestals. The entrance is within a semicircular porch with properly proportioned Tuscan columns and tight-ly ranked, square-section balusters. The roofs are covered with metal shin-gles and trimmed at the bottom by a pent roof that runs in front of the chimney to join the roof of the porch. The only disruption in this fine design is in the replacement of original carpentry work with modern wrought iron.

Cross to the other side of the street and continue east. The second house on your right is

21. 507 LAKE AVENUE—1909

This 1909 Prairie School house was designed by Frank Lloyd Wright. It satisfies all the conditions of that style, with the broad, low, hipped roofs rising one behind the other as long wings stretching to the west, with the higher one turning at the east end to move forward as a wing to the north projecting to the street. The windows are extended, horizontally-placed, diamond-shaped, leaded glass set in the same simple plain boards that act as caps to the mudsills and to the walls and as fascias for the roof. The entrance is set on the west wing, next to the higher projecting north wing, and is framed by flat sections of the stucco walls to give a sense of the shelter that this internationally famous architect believed should be at an entrance. The structure is listed on the National Register of Historic Places.

Backtrack west on Lake Avenue. The fourth house on your left, past 8th Street, is

22. 825 LAKE AVENUE—c. 1870

This frame, clapboard-covered house from about 1870 displays a typical T-shaped plan with the leg of the "T" projecting north toward the street and covered on all three sides by a porch sustained by very thin turned posts. Within the porch, on the front of the wing, is a polygonal bay; above it a small hood roof sustained by small corbels stands in the front face; above that is a gable finial of which only the pendant appears; behind it can be seen a small square window which originally would have ventilated the attic.

Continue west on Lake Avenue. The second house on your left, past 10th Street, is

23. 1007 LAKE AVENUE—1873, later alterations

This small frame house reveals three periods of construction. It started in 1873 as a single story farm house with its roof pitches facing the street and containing a full attic story. Some twenty years later it received Queen Anne modifications, visible in the top of the gable where a textured shingle field appears, and at the front, where the half-circular extension was placed on the east. This necessitated re-siding the house which was done with the narrow clapboards typical of the Queen Anne, which probably replaced wider ones typical of the earlier period. Vertical siding was placed below the sill level of the ground floor windows, a motif of the style not often encountered. The slight projection for the entrance and the slight, one-story projection to the west (with a pediment containing a textured shingle field) also date from this time.

The third period of construction involved raising the roof to enlarge the attic rooms producing the flat-roofed, flat-fronted element across the front. Note that the windows here are quite different in proportion from the Queen Anne ones and that the window lintel has a slightly different molding pattern which indicate the later date. Apparently at this time the frames around the entrance and the front porch were placed on the building.

Continue west. The next house on your left is

24. 1011 LAKE AVENUE—c. 1873, later alterations

This frame, stucco-covered house has a T-shaped plan, which may be from an original construction of about 1873. Sometime around the turn of the century the frame house received the stucco, and (on the second story) the half-timbering and the decorative bargeboards, the polygonal window, and (on the ground floor) the present porch which is a very simple rendition of the Tudor style.

Continue west to the corner. Turn left on Wilmette Avenue ½ block to the railroad depot on your left.

This concludes the Wilmette Walking Tour.

Drive southwest on Wilmette Avenue across the tracks. Turn right (north) on Green Bay Road.

KENILWORTH

KENILWORTH

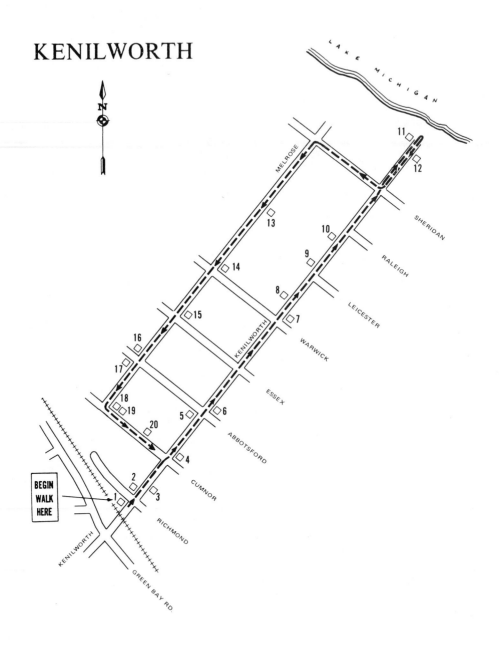

Drive north on Green Bay Road .9 miles. Turn right (east) on Kenilworth Avenue and cross the tracks. Stop.

KENILWORTH WALKING TOUR

On the north side of Kenilworth Avenue between the railroad tracks and Richmond Road is

1. KENILWORTH RAILROAD DEPOT—1891

This small commuter station by Edbrooke and Burnham is a superb example of the merging of the Romanesque Revival style and of the Queen Anne. The enclosed structure is quite small, composed of a shingled, wood vaulted waiting room with original vertical wainscoting, set within the veranda which circumambulates, except for the projecting station master's office, the entire building. The Queen Anne touches are seen in the shingles, in the diamond glass in the upper sections of the waiting room windows, and in the delicate modeling beneath the lintels of the stone structure around the building. The stone structure recalls the Romanesque with battered buttress-like piers on the north and south faces and on the north end where broad arches springing from a low point support the pitched roof which originally was slate covered. The random quarry-faced ashlar walls support lintels with segmental bottoms containing a fat bead and reel molding along the cord and a small reel molding along the top which runs over the small capitals atop the piers. Especially noteworthy is the identifying sign for the station on the track side with its fine wrought iron strap work and highly stylized letters. On the west side of the tracks is a small platform shed. The three northern-most posts are original and show an interesting construction technique of the 1890s: large cast iron posts support large square wooden members which are framed and extend to form the supports for the roof. Of similar interest are the kingpost trusses in the north and south sections of the waiting room veranda.

Walk east on Kenilworth Avenue. On the NE corner of Kenilworth Avenue and Richmond Road is

2. KENILWORTH HISTORICAL SOCIETY
Stuart Memorial Building

This small organization has a great deal of information on Kenilworth's

1. Kenilworth Railroad Depot

older homes. It also features changing exhibits made up of Kenilworth artifacts, including antique postcards, toys, costumes, and furniture. Mondays only 1:00 P.M.-3:00 P.M. Free.

Across the street, on the south side of Kenilworth Avenue, is

3. KENILWORTH CLUB
410 Kenilworth Avenue—1906

George Washington Maher designed this stucco and half-timber Prairie building in 1906. Originally an open porch, roofed with a trellis, connected the large section which holds an assembly room to the smaller section with service and smaller rooms, dominated by a large chimney, that balances the composition. The broad, low hipped roofs originally had striated patterns in the shingles emphasizing the broad horizontality of the design. The stucco walls are articulated with patterned boards and the windows have a similar decorative pattern; the pattern combines the thistle, one of Maher's favorite motifs, with Kenilworth's logo. The structure is listed on the National Register of Historic Places.

Walk east on Kenilworth Avenue. On the SE corner of Kenilworth Avenue and Cumnor Road is

4. 354 KENILWORTH AVENUE—1891

This excellent, large, and conspicuous Queen Anne house, the first residence in the village, was built in 1891 and designed by Edbrooke and Burnham. The quarry-faced random ashlar on the ground floor rises in the center to enframe the triple windows on the second floor and then into a chimney reaching the peak of the roof. The entrance, topped by an arch with large stone voussoirs, is framed by a sharply and precisely turned wooden door frame. Note the wrought iron tie rod anchor on the chimney face. Above the windows (which are modern casement windows) is a steeply pitched gable with an elongated oval window and coved sides under the eaves. This surface is shingled as are all of the wooden parts above the ground floor.

Flanking it on either side are gable-topped sections that intersect the broad pitched roof which displays an eaveless gable on either end with a slight flare above the gutter. The group of four windows at both ends are gables which are set behind a curved jamb and topped by a flared head. The original effect has been disturbed by replacing the original wooden shingles with asphalt roofing and painting the shingle walls yellow rather than allowing them to retain their original dark brown stain. The original effect would have been that of groups of wooden surfaces molded and cut in geometric shapes enfolding themselves around and atop the massive stone supports below.

Continue east. On the NW corner of Abbotsford Road and Kenilworth Avenue is

5. 339 KENILWORTH AVENUE—1891

This limestone and stucco house was the second residence in the village, also built in 1891. The stucco replaced the original surfaces which were almost certainly shingles. One must restore in his mind the original Queen Anne character of the building.

On the SE corner of Abbotsford Road and Kenilworth Avenue is

6. 322 KENILWORTH AVENUE—1892

This 1892, frame, clapboard-covered corner house sits on a high random ashlar, quarry-faced foundation. It shows the lessons of classical restraint beginning to be absorbed by the Queen Anne style. The basic block of the house, topped by a tall hipped roof, breaks forward at the northeast corner with a fully rounded bay and on the ground floor proceeds to the west slightly. In the center of the composition is a carefully detailed classical doorway with a broad fanlight and transoms on either side. To its east is a two-story motif with windows on the first and second floors and between them an elaborate relief, foliate panel. Similar relief is found in the pilasters separating the windows on the second floor and forming the corners of the several dormers in the roof. A garland is strung along the cornice.

Continue east 2 blocks. On the SE corner of Warwick Road and Kenilworth Avenue is

7. CHURCH OF THE HOLY COMFORTER
222 Kenilworth Avenue—1903

The original 1903 section of this boldly massed stone church is the L-shaped plan section with the tower standing away from it and the parish halls to the south. The tower is in the form of a Norman keep with an oriel projecting at a corner on the second story rising beyond the crenelated top. On the ground floor are entrances in the two prominent faces protected by slate-covered timber structured porches, flanked on either side by pier buttresses. The rough-faced random ashlar is controlled by the smooth-faced limestone that is used for the buttress copings, for the belt courses, and for the jambs framing the pointed arched openings. The extensions to the east are modern construction but form excellent complements to the original design.

Continue east. The church on your left is

8. KENILWORTH UNION CHURCH
211 Kenilworth Avenue—1892

This Gothic church is based upon a later style of English architecture than the previous building. Its entrance is again through a tower but the tower is set next to the nave which has a large, pointed, arched window in its end facing the street to the south. At the north end is an extension with rusticated arches forming its windows, which are smaller and in sharp contrast to the neatly dressed tracery and jambs of the sanctuary window. The tower rises to a pyramidal roof with a copper finial and crockets along each edge and is buttressed at the base by a 45° angle battered pier buttress. On the opposite side (to the west) is a pointed arch arcade extending out to the street. At the northwest corner of the sanctuary rises an extremely impressive fleche built in copper and exhibiting a marvelous display of crocketed finials and a very steep, octagonal, pyramidal roof ascending to a weathervane, a cross, and a lightning rod. The original structure is from 1892; the arcade and the copper fleche are from the early 1950s, as is the extension to the east, all of which complement the original design.

Continue east. The first house on your left, across from Leicester Road, is

9. 165 KENILWORTH AVENUE—1890s

This building, the oldest rental house in Kenilworth, was built in the 1890s. It has a broad base built of brick that features, near its center, a broad segmental shouldered arch. The brick base, now unfortunately painted, holds a gambrel roof with two hipped dormers in the east section and a full gambrel gable at the east end which includes a window on the second story capped by a small roof. This gable is similar to the gambrel gables at the east and west ends.

Continue east. The second house on your left is

### 10.	149 KENILWORTH AVENUE—1890s

This Colonial Revival mansion from the later 1890s is in the finest correct style. Fluted pilasters, with slightly undersized Ionic capitals, frame the corners of the cubic mass and the slight projection that contains the entrance. The entrance projection is capped by a pediment with a deeply recessed tympanum that contains a circular window flanked by richly modeled foliate decoration. Large modillions appear beneath the properly detailed cornices. The entrance is under a semi-circular porch sustained by svelte columns of the Composite order. On each side is a broad, double-hung window with eight panes in the upper sash. The ground floor windows are topped by an entablature panel. Dormers containing a Palladian window appear on the east and west sides.

Continue east past Sheridan Road. The fourth house on your left, and the last house on Kenilworth Avenue, is

### 11.	37 KENILWORTH AVENUE—1891

This Queen Anne, limestone and shingle house was built in 1891, the same year as the railroad station (Kenilworth #1) which is at the extreme end of this street, as if it is the beginning and this is the termination. Both were designed in the same year by Edbrooke and Burnham. That notion is reinforced by the resemblance between the porches at either end with their battered piers. Above the rough-faced random ashlar ground floor is a great gambrel roof intersected twice by nearly full gambrel gables on each side. The front gable has a neatly precise Palladian window with a tall keystone barely penetrating the arch above it. On the second story a broad incised paneled section separates a pair of windows from the projecting polygonal bay from which a view from the lake could be attained. Here is a rare example of the survival of wooden shingles providing a glimpse of the original character of such shingle style designs. Note how the walls and roofs merge into an harmonious ensemble because the same color and texture is maintained across all surfaces.

Cross to the south side of the street and backtrack west. The second house from the lake, on your left, is

### 12.	42 KENILWORTH AVENUE—1892

This Colonial Revival house from 1892 still retains a Queen Anne feature,

11.　37 Kenilworth Avenue

the great bow on the east side of the house to provide a large bay that contrasts sharply with the small scaled semicircular porch with its Ionic capitals and, above, slim columns immediately to the west. The broken pediment gables set in the hipped roof are evenly placed relative to the very high and quite proper cornice, but the eastern dormer is not quite in line with the window grouping on the second story. Similar dormers appear at the east and west ends. The cubic mass is framed by plain-faced Ionic pilasters on each corner and is extended on the eastern side by a one-story porch (originally open) supported by Ionic columns.

12.   42 Kenilworth Avenue

Continue west to Sheridan Road. Turn right (north) 1 block to Melrose Avenue. Turn left (west). The fifth house on your left is

13.   158 MELROSE AVENUE—1892

This Queen Anne house from 1892 is a rather more restrained version than is usual in the style in that the projecting elements are kept within the main silhouette. The central gable set in the center has at its side a circular tower that rises only through the second floor and then receives its conical roof. It, like the ground floor, is of rough-faced random ashlar in the creamy yellow stone used throughout the suburb but has darker stone used for the lintels. That turret is answered on the east side by a wall dormer. Notable here is the Tudor detailing in the second story and the gable, an early instance of the use of this historical style which became more common as the decade progressed.

Continue west over the bridge, then, the first house on your left, on the SE corner of Melrose Avenue and Warwick Road, is

14. 220 MELROSE AVENUE—1893

This Queen Anne house from 1893 very nearly becomes Tudor Revival. The stone along the ground floor supports two stories, the second in half-timbered stucco ending in a frieze, the third within the roof. The frieze is ornamented with garlands, ribbons, and rosettes while two of the panels in the projecting bay window on the eastern side have cartouches and sprigs of foliage. The gable, which covers much of the front, has a similar cartouche with a strap-work frame beneath the triplet of windows set beneath the richly carved, rosette-studded gable rafter. To the west is a smaller version of the same gable serving as a dormer; at the west end the gable follows the basic pattern established on the front. A porch stretches from the bay across most of the front to wrap in a semicircle around the west corner. It has a deep lintel supported by paired Tuscan columns that follow very closely the pattern books originating in early sixteenth-century Italy. Such snippets of Italian Renaissance classicism were extremely popular in the court of Henry VIII of England where the basic style emulated in this fine building originated.

Continue west. On the SE corner of Melrose Avenue and Essex Road is

15. 258 MELROSE AVENUE—1895

This fine, simple structure from 1895 has a gambrel roofed second and third floor flaring over the ground floor, all covered in dark stained shingles swelling out toward the corner at the northwest with a large circular projection. It contains the porch on the ground floor and a strip of windows, separated by squat Ionic capitals and covered by a square low conical roof on the second. Along the north facade are three hipped roof dormers opening to the second story below which on the ground floor swells a bowed window. The underside of the gambrel roof describes a line that becomes the lintel, supported by the squat columns of the porch. The building illustrates the plasticity of the Shingle style and provides an excellent representation of it.

Continue west. On the NE corner of Melrose Avenue and Abbotsford Road is

16.   321 MELROSE AVENUE—1893

This classic Queen Anne house was built in 1893. It takes full advantage of its corner site which is lined by a very fine wrought iron fence with special posts for the driveway and the entrance walkway to the house. It displays the full picturesque potential that the Queen Anne was especially adept at promoting. The ground floor is lined with thin clapboards, the second floor and gables with various shapes to produce rich texture fields. Projecting to the east at the corner is a polygonal bay. Beyond that are two flat-fronted bays on the south facade. A wall dormer rises above the glazed polygonal entry vestibule under the porch with its paneled piers holding shouldered balustrades. On the opposite side of the south facade the bottom two floors are polygonal with a steeply pitched gable with a flared base. Here also is a polygonal window in the lower section of the gable and a small oval topped by scroll-cut foliate decoration flanking a spire. Additional motifs appear on the west facade where the steeply pitched roof slides down at a slightly lessened pitch to provide an awning-like extension supported by broad curved brackets. Next to it is a polygonal bay rising to a very high polygonal hipped roof supporting, in one field, a hipped roof dormer like the one above the awning-like projection next to it. Below that projection is a sun-porch (now enclosed) overlooking the broad side yard. Notable also are the chimneys with patterned brick work erupting through the roof from place to place.

On the NW corner of Melrose Avenue and Abbotsford Road is

17.   337 MELROSE AVENUE—1894

This building from 1894 displays the use Queen Anne architects could make of the gambrel roof. The building is disturbed only by the loss of the original porch and its replacement by a shrub-laden terrace. The gambrel here is extremely steeply pitched, and both its gables and roof planes are covered in slate. The pair of windows with the oversized garlands in the oversized entablature frieze, appearing in the south gable, is repeated three times on the south face and twice on the east face as dormers. Between them on the east rises a chimney which, because of its extreme height, requires a wrought iron tie rod anchored on the outer face with a whirligig pattern in cast iron. The brilliant roof sits atop a brick base made of thin, long, cream-

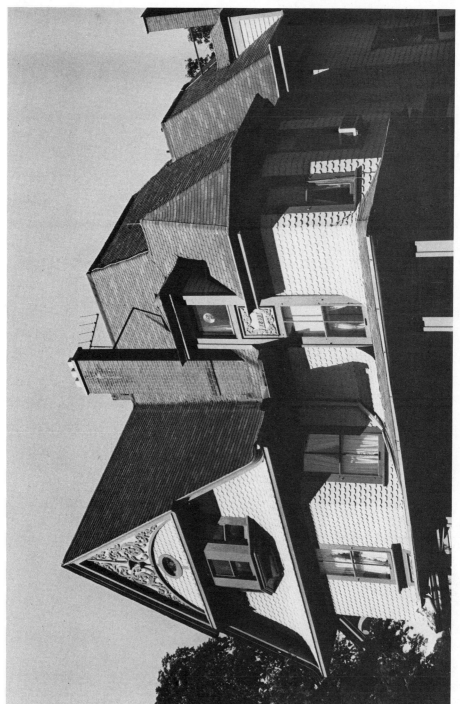

16. 321 Melrose Avenue

17. 337 Melrose Avenue

colored brick, a Roman brick type soon popularized by Prairie School architects. The area on the ground floor beneath the gambrel gable projects as a broad bow window topped by a plain parapet.

Continue west on Melrose Avenue until it ends. Turn left (south) on Cumnor Road. The first house on your left is

18.   433 CUMNOR ROAD—1893

This building, built in 1893 in the Tudor style, is a fine example of the early use of that historical revival style. The full impact of its design is lessened by painting the half-timbered members grey and the stucco white which reduces the contrast that is an essential element in the style. The plan is basically T-shaped, with the leg extending west to the street. It has a projecting bay on the ground floor with rain spouts at the corners of the parapets and four windows grouped above. These are matched by four smaller windows in the attic, two of which are now roof ventilators. On the north side of the entrance is a hooded roof for the porch, carried by corbels; on the opposite side is a trellised porch which originally was open.

Continue south. The next house on your left is

19.   423 CUMNOR ROAD—1890s

This simple frame structure, probably built soon after 1895, is very effective because it uses the gambrel roof well to enclose the great shingled mass of the second and third floors, which sits atop the clapboard-covered ground floor, edged at the corners by Ionic pilasters. The north and south faces of the roof are punctuated by dormers with decorative motifs in the pediments and small Ionic capitals at their sides. The top of the gambrel gable contains a late steamboat Gothic version of the Palladian windows complete with the attenuated keystone extending well above the arch.

Across the street, on the left side of the front lawn of 416 Cumnor Road, is an Indian marker tree.

Continue south. The second house on your left is

20.   415 CUMNOR ROAD—1893

Built in 1893, this building presents a variation on the gambrel roof type. The slopes now face the street, the lower one curving outward to enclose the porch, its top containing dormers lighting the second story.

Continue south to Kenilworth Avenue. Turn right (west) on Kenilworth Avenue 1½ blocks.

This concludes the Kenilworth Walking Tour.

Drive west on Kenilworth Avenue, across the tracks. Turn right (north) on Green Bay Road.

WINNETKA

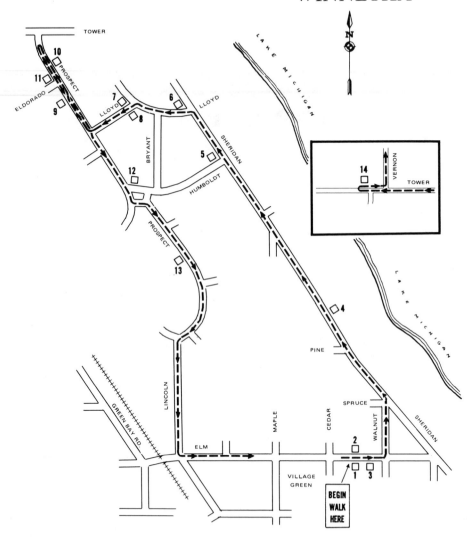

WINNETKA

N

TOWER

10

PROSPECT

11

ELDORADO

9

7

LLOYD

8

6

LLOYD

BRYANT

5

SHERIDAN

HUMBOLDT

12

PROSPECT

LAKE MICHIGAN

VERNON

14

TOWER

13

LAKE MICHIGAN

4

PINE

SPRUCE

LINCOLN

GREEN BAY RD

MAPLE

CEDAR

WALNUT

SHERIDAN

ELM

2

1 3

VILLAGE GREEN

BEGIN
WALK
HERE

Drive north on Green Bay Road 1.7 miles to Elm Street. Turn right (east), over the bridge, 2 blocks to Maple Street. On your right is the Village Green. Stop.

WINNETKA WALKING TOUR

Walk east on the south side of Elm Street. The second house on your right is

1.   608 ELM STREET—1840s and 1870s

This house is set far back from the street and is the site of an early homestead from the 1840s. What is visible now of the present house is considerably newer and is for the most part from the late 1870s. It is a rare type, having a high shingled Mansard as the second floor. (Mansards usually appear on the third floor.) The entrance, set well back on the east side, has classical details in its carpentry work which match the original two windows on the front facade with linteled heads and large modillions under the flared lower curve of the Mansard. Notable here is the fence with acorns atop the posts which are finished with moldings from the Italianate period and fence rails in between stiles, half of which reach only half the distance to the upper rail; these, too, are topped by small versions of acorns.

Directly across the street is

2.   603 ELM STREET—c.1870

This one-and-one-half-story Gothic cottage has an addition on the west side that extends a gambrel down the original pitched roof but otherwise is a fine representation of a typical North Shore building type very popular at the time of the Chicago Fire. Facing south and toward the street on the ground floor is a polygonal bay, above it a pair of windows topped in the gable by diamond-shaped shingles. On the eastern side is a porch with a fine turned balustrade.

Cross back to the south side of Elm Street and continue east. The next house on your right is

3.   594 ELM STREET—1872

This frame, clapboard-clad house was built in 1872. It has a pitched roof with the lower slope characteristic of the classical revival styles, but all else about it is an excellent example of the Carpenter Gothic style. Notice how it exploited the power driven scroll saw to produce decorative work to lend a sense of magnificence to an otherwise humble structure. The center of the building is marked by a small gable, breaking the roof plane, supported by curved brackets. Below it is a window, and below that window is a gabled porch flanked on either side by extensions of its gable field. The lintels are filled with scroll-cut work featuring stars, roundels, and abstracted foliate designs. Variations on those motifs appear in the porch and stair railing among single bottle balusters supporting the very broad bannister characteristic of the Italianate style. Additional scroll-cut abstracted foliate ornament appears in the gable tops. The window-heads throughout the building are especially interesting. On the eastern side facing the side street is a special treat: a polygonal bay window with the outer face topped by its own pediment filled by its own scroll-cut ornament.

Turn left (north) on Walnut Street until it merges with Sheridan Road. Turn left on Sheridan Road and continue north 1½ blocks. Just before the iron fence on your right is

4.   645 SHERIDAN ROAD—1902

This 1902 structure illustrates the formality of gracious lakefront living. The broad front of the frame clapboard-covered structure has a projecting front section containing a Palladian window on the second floor. A pediment, above, stands behind a porch extending across the middle half of the facade. It projects outward over the entrance with coupled columns on the front face. These have especially fine Italian Renaissance Doric columns with an egg and leaf molding in the echinus. Projecting to the south is a porch, originally open, supported by pairs of the same columns. The cornice with an egg and leaf molding below the dentils, the windows, and the doorway contain additional examples of studied classical detailing. The entrance to this estate is marked by a gatekeepers' lodge which is an informal version of the same design with a simplified molding atop its second story and a corbeled, hooded, shell-filled roof over the front door. On the second story of the wings that project to the east and the west are open porches with delightful trellis work.

Continue north on Sheridan Road 1½ blocks. On the NW corner of Sheridan Road and Humboldt Avenue is

5. **CHRIST CHURCH AND GARLAND CEMETERY**
784 Sheridan Road—grounds from 1870s
This cemetery was begun in 1876 after a church had been established here in 1869. The grounds surrounding the church and containing the cemetery are exquisite. This church was one of the first churches in the area to use crypts. Stone markers along the ivy covered wall identify the remains buried there. The present church building dates from the twentieth century.

Continue north 1 block. On the NW corner of Sheridan Road and Lloyd Place is

6. **830 SHERIDAN ROAD**
The Wayside—Henry Demarest Lloyd House
—1850s, with additions
This National Historic Landmark once served as an inn and stopping place for those interested in lively conversation. The original section was built in the 1850s, across the road, and moved here a generation later. It was added to from time to time. The portions visible now are from the 1870s. The site is historically significant as the home of Henry Demarest Lloyd, a very prominent citizen of the country, at one time economics editor of the *Chicago Tribune*. He had married into the Medill family which controlled the *Tribune*. His books and pamphlets from the 1890s and early twentieth century assisted in promoting both liberal and libertarian causes and in bringing reform to politics, government, and economics. The house was given by the Lloyd family to the Landmarks Preservation Council of Illinois which established a means to assure its preservation and, with the Lloyd Fund, assists in preserving other historically and architecturally significant structures. Facing Sheridan Road, on the southeast corner of the property, is a monument that commemorates Henry Demarest Lloyd's ideals; its base is inscribed with quotations from his works.

Walk west on Lloyd Place past Bryant Avenue on your left to a triangular island with street signs demarcating the intersection of Bryant Avenue and Lloyd Place. Veer left, still on Lloyd Place. The first house on your right is

7. **822 BRYANT AVENUE—1901**
This is a fine example of the Shingle style as it grew through the Arts and Crafts movement in the direction of the basic horizontality and openness of the Prairie style. It represents an important variant of the exploration of

7. 822 Bryant Avenue

domestic architecture of progressive architects at the turn of the century, here by Augustus B. Higginson. It opens its L-shaped plan to the corner with a broad entry porch that also serves as a sunporch and has broad, sloping, pitched roofs and groupings of windows that form unified strips marked off by clear plain surrounds that fit nicely into the shingle planes of the wall. The upper sashes have leaded glass. As the walls approach the ground, they flare slightly, and various courses of the shingles are layed more tightly in order to allow the house to settle onto the ground. A pair of gables, one extending beyond the other, looks to the south; the eastern pitch in each is raised, with that in the eastern wing forming dormer windows.

Directly across the street, on the south side of Lloyd Place, is

8. 800 LLOYD PLACE—1901

This is another illustration of the search for a domestic architectural style parallel to the Prairie School but taking a slightly different direction. The traditional cubic block of the 1901 structure is covered by a hipped roof broken in the front of a hipped dormer which, like the main roof, has slight flares near the eaves. Extending to the east is a polygonal bay and to the west a one-story sunporch. The front of the house has a polygonal bay on one side and a hipped roof entry on the other. The ground floor, up to the sill level of the second story windows, is stucco; the one above that is shingled.

Continue on Lloyd Place to the corner. Turn right (north) on Prospect Avenue. The fifth house on your left is

9. 824 PROSPECT AVENUE—c. 1900

This turn-of-the-century house rises through two stories of a masonry mass to a prominent cornice with a garland frieze below the modillions that support the hipped, tiled roof in the middle of which is a Palladian window with rich foliate relief. The ground floor has a porch extending across the entire front supported by swelling columns with undersized Ionic capitals. This is a typical touch of the period, especially in the way it sweeps around the south side to the bay that projects to the south. This bay has a half-round plan and, on the second story, an area which was originally an open sunporch defined by the extension of the building's cornice, sustained here by Ionic columns.

Cross the street and continue north. The third house on your right is

10.   853 PROSPECT AVENUE—1890

This fine house, designed by Augustus B. Higginson in 1890, has a shingled gambrel second story (lacking a full attic) that stands above the brick ground floor and has a T-shaped plan. Projecting toward the street is a wing whose face has strips of windows on the ground floor covered by a slightly sloped shingle roof and another row of casement windows in the gambrel gable. Overlooking the lawn on the south is the entrance, under an arch, set into a chimney which follows the reentrant angle where the two wings meet. Projecting before it is a glass conservatory above which is a slight bay window molded out of the lower slope of the gambrel. Extending to the east is another wing with windows set into the lower gambrel slope opening up the inside rooms. The smooth planes of shingles topped by eaves and gables lacking projections but lined with shingles is typical of the best quality of Shingle style work.

Backtrack south on Prospect Avenue. On the NW corner of Prospect Avenue and Eldorado Street is

11.   844 PROSPECT AVENUE—1885 and later

The central kernel of this house, the section topped by the steeply pitched roof, apparently dates from 1885. Since then it has acquired numerous additions. Today it conveys a sense of the combination of the Queen Anne style and the Classical Revival styles that became popular after the Columbian Exposition of 1893. The tall building has a pitched roof with a prominent flare at its base and, on the south facade, a chimney rises to the level of the roof peak. The entrance is under a shouldered segmental arch held by two Roman Doric columns, the same order that holds the sunporch on the eastern end. The sunporch slides into the two-story porch in the center of the east facade which is sustained by columns of the Ionic order. The metal siding on the structure detracts from its original character.

Continue south on Prospect Avenue. Just before Humboldt Avenue, on the NE corner of Humboldt and Prospect avenues, is

12.   759 PROSPECT AVENUE—1899

This 1899 building is an excellent example of the Tudor style adapted to American tastes and needs in anticipation of the Prairie style. The ground floor is covered with tightly spaced clapboards; above is stucco, with girts placed below the sills and near the middle of the upper sash level, except in the gables and on the section that projects on the eastern side where full half-timbering appears. Especially notable here is the timber frame construction from the top of the second floor and into the eaves of the gables where notched and interlocked beams carry the loads. The dormer on the western end and the gable on the west facade have diamond pane leaded glass which is repeated at a larger scale in the upper sash of all of the other windows.

Continue south on Prospect Avenue. The fourth house on your right is

13. 696 PROSPECT AVENUE—1884

Set well back from the street is a shingled 1884 house rising to a steeply pitched roof above the second story which, in the center section, slides down through the second story to provide a roof for the entrance. The section on the south rises through the first and second floors through a polygonal bay, repeated in the second floor level in the center. On the north end the bay in the center has a round-headed window whereas the others have square windows. Above the center and southern wall dormer is a roof dormer covered by a hipped roof.

Continue south on Prospect Avenue following its curve around to its junction with Lincoln. Continue south on Lincoln 1 long block to Elm Street. Turn left (east) on Elm Street and continue 2 blocks to the Village Green.

This concludes the Winnetka Walking Tour.

Drive west on Elm Street 3 blocks, across the bridge, to Green Bay Road. Turn right (north) .8 miles to Tower Road. Turn left (west) .8 miles. The first house on your right, past Vernon Avenue, is

14. 1407 TOWER ROAD
Schmidt Cabin—1820

This cabin is thought to be the oldest remaining building in Cook County and may also be the oldest building in the six-county area. The original portion is the front section; probably built in 1820, it is a fine example of a pioneer log cabin. The section behind is a later addition. Notable are two aspects of the building: one is the general proportions and the composition,

14.   Schmidt Cabin
1407 Tower Road

with windows placed one above the other in the pitch side of the gabled roof, which follows a general Greek Revival type common in the early part of the nineteenth century. The other is the squared timbers used in the construction which still bear the adz marks, showing the tool used for making timbers when saws were unavailable or before power saws made their use economical.

Backtrack east to Vernon Avenue. Turn left (north) 1 mile to South Avenue.

GLENCOE

GLENCOE

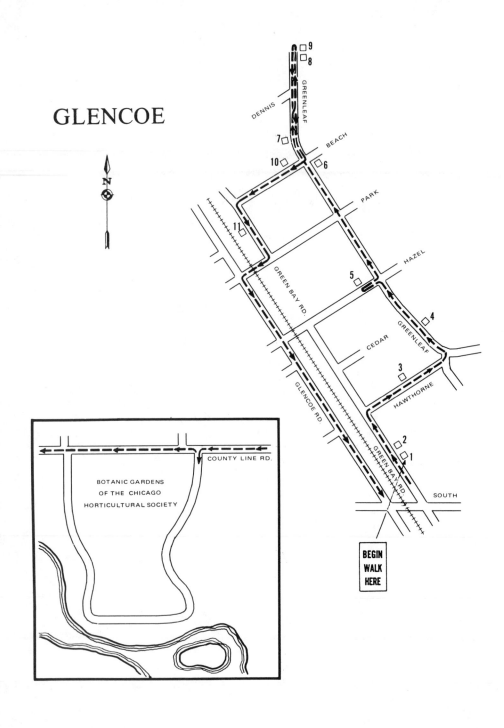

BEGIN
WALK
HERE

Turn right (east) on South Avenue to Glencoe Road. Stop.

GLENCOE WALKING TOUR

Walk east, across the tracks, and turn immediately left (north) on Green Bay Road. The fifth house on your right is

1.   535 GREEN BAY ROAD—1865

Built in 1865, this Gothic style building, although unfortunately covered by modern asbestos shingles, portrays very clearly the characteristics of the English Cottage style popularized by Andrew Jackson Downing. Note the extremely steeply pitched roofs with a gable facing the front, near the center of the massing, flanked on either side by wall dormers. These, like the rest of the roofs, are steeply pitched and have flared eaves. The proportions of the windows are the tall, skinny proportions associated with the Gothic, but here they lack the pointed arch features. On the south side is a porch with square posts, high brackets, open fillets in the lintels, and (on the south end) a polygonal bay with similar brackets.

Continue north. The next house on your right is

2.   557 GREEN BAY ROAD—1860s

This structure from the 1860s is a variation on the previous structure (Glencoe #1) but has been covered by stucco and its front window on the ground floor has been replaced with a modern picture window. The variation is noticeable here; it is the jerkin-head roof on the south. The porch is also a modern reconstruction.

Continue north to the corner. Turn right (east) on Hawthorne Avenue. The fifth house on your left (north side of the street) is

3.   245 HAWTHORNE AVENUE—c.1872

This "guest cottage" was built about 1872. Its clapboard siding rises the full two stories to the steeply pitched roof which contains another complete floor. The front gable there is especially interesting with its very early Palladian window framed with a very simple molding with both shoulders and feet, characteristic of the Italianate. It is in a field filled with thin vertical siding with a saw-tooth bottom which rises through a hip in the central section. The second story windows are again quite simple with shoulders and, in the centers of their pitched lintels, a broad pinnacle. The ground floor porch turns down the side to the east to look across the broad lawn. The additions to the north are later as are, most likely, the dormers.

Continue east on Hawthorne Avenue, veering left, then turn left (north) on Greenleaf Avenue. The second house on your right is

4.   599 GREENLEAF AVENUE—late 1860s

This large, two-story, frame, clapboard-covered mansion was built shortly before 1870. It rises through a full two stories to a high hipped roof. The roof is intersected on both the north and south sides by a pair of dormers with scallop shingled pediments. A larger dormer serves in place of a pediment on the west slope of the roof. The mass of the structure is encased at each corner by full-height Ionic pilasters with squat capitals. Across the south half of the front and turning around the south facade is a porch sustained by somewhat delicate, fluted, Doric columns. The graciousness of the design is completed by detailing around the windows, which have pitched lintels and feet and shoulders, and by the cornice with its garland enrichment.

Continue north to Hazel Avenue. Turn left (west). The second house on your right (north side of the street) is

5.   243 HAZEL AVENUE—1889

This 1889 house achieves its Queen Anne character more through the manipulation of surface texture than through the variations in projections, recessions, and silhouette. It does have a broad bow on the ground floor in the center and a polygonal bay on the west side, but the main interest is provided by the variation of the alternating strips of shingle and clapboard, concluding in shingles in the gable, and the variety of shingle treatment. The peak of the gable on the front is especially interesting with its sunrise motif split asunder by a strip of four windows.

Backtrack east on Hazel Avenue to Greenleaf Avenue. Turn left (north) 2 blocks. On the SE corner of Greenleaf Avenue and Beach Road is

6.   739 GREENLEAF AVENUE—pre-1857

This very fine, frame, clapboard-clad house was built prior to 1857 and

6. 739 Greenleaf Avenue

shows a very fine integration of several often disparate elements. The central core is a cube topped by a Second Empire Mansard roof complete with flare and, on the west and north faces, a dormer topped by a fully rounded eared hood. Projecting to the west and to the north are pitched roofed wings which merge into the Second Empire roof shape without a transition. They are, however, integrated into the other mass by the continuous cornice with sharp moldings that act as a collar for the entire mass. Projecting to the south is a polygonal bay with a polygonal roof. The windows on that bay and above the entrance facing west have segmental eared heads. The windows on the west projection on the second floor are bifore windows set under a small hood. It has a Second Empire shape supported by large brackets with generous pendant knobs and trimmed with a scroll-cut frieze. The frieze has a scalloped bottom and a double eared motif alternating with a knobbed stem which is characteristic of the period. Below it, on the ground floor, is a polygonal bay broad enough to allow its outer face to repeat the bifore motif slightly more generously as is appropriate for the ground floor. The only change visible is in the north and west faces; the entrance has been moved forward from its original location, but when the front door was moved, the original porch was retained and enclosed as the entrance. The

6.   739 Greenleaf Avenue

original configuration of the porch including its posts and balusters is there-fore still visible on the north side. The original double doors were replaced by a single door with sidelights, but the generous rope molding in the jamb and the fully rounded head were retained. The lower service wing projecting to the east has recently received a side porch extending out from the original service porch. Other minor modifications at the east hardly detract from the outstanding quality of this early structure.

Continue north on Greenleaf Avenue. The second house on your left (west side of the street) is

7.   766 GREENLEAF AVENUE—c. 1890

This elaborate Queen Anne structure from about 1890 achieves its excellent effect through deceptively simple means. The basic block is a cube topped by a pitched roof. Projecting toward the east is a large gable with a bib flaring below the eave line of the roof. It projects as it rises into a boss field flanked by two windows. Next are halves of sunrise motifs, and above them is a shingle field producing a variation on the boss pattern. The octagonal-cut shingles in the flared bib vary the pattern as does the shingle cornice of the second story. The clapboard field on the second story acts as a pause before the ground floor where some of the variety of the upper floor reappears. The north side is recessed only to break out into a polygonal bay on the north facade. The entrance is marked by a grid pattern pediment slightly off center from the entrance door. Additional original elements are the multi-pane casement windows, the multi-pane upper sash in the attic, the fringed-pane upper sash elsewhere on the front facade, and the sidelights at the door.

Continue north past Dennis Lane. Then, the third house on your right is

8. 815 Greenleaf Avenue—c.1858

This clapboard Italianate house is a slightly diluted version of the structure seen earlier at 739 Greenleaf Avenue (Glencoe #6). It was built by the owner of that property, who erected this structure immediately after the earlier one, probably in 1858. This house lacks some of the decorative detail but retains the same general character: a cube with a Mansard roof and pitched roof gables. Paired brackets with large modillions in between trim the gables and the cornice around the entire structure. Mansard hoods protect the windows. The large porch, which covers most of the front, is held by large square posts supporting a lintel with brackets. The double entrance is within a molding with shoulders and feet and a segmental top set against a projecting section that terminates at the upper level of the cornice. This suggests a truncated tower of the Italian Villa type popular at the middle of the century, a suggestion continued by the larger size of the dormer compared to that of the smaller dormer immediately to its left.

Continue north. The next house on your right is

9. 823 Greenleaf Avenue—1870s

This brick structure on large grounds represents the kind of structure often built during the period of prosperity that followed the Civil War, in this case in the mid-1870s. The brick renders in very simple form the segmental shouldered moldings characteristic of the Mansarded Italianate style while the cornice, perhaps originally more elaborate, is the base of a Mansard roof with twin dormers on the west facade. The double doored entrance stands in an entry porch. On the south side is a two-story polygonal bay like the one in the front, and lower service wings extend to the back. Especially interesting here is the chimney rising on the north face with its highly sculpted brick work.

Backtrack south on Greenleaf Avenue to Beach Road. Turn right (west). The first house on your right is

10.   247 BEACH ROAD—c.1880

This is a fine example of the Stick style as it was rendered in the Midwest. It is a simple frame structure, L-shaped in plan, with a projecting reentrant angle containing an additional projection on the ground floor to house the entrance. The surfaces are covered with fields of boards, framed at their edges and containing clapboards, with a pair of windows in the center. The ground floor is separated from the second story by tooth-cut shingles. The gable of the south wing has scallop-cut shingles and a flared upper section over a pair of windows like those below. The cornice there, as at the main roof area, has simple modillions. Set along them are bulging corbels with incising in the bulge. On the east wing on the second story is a porch with cut-out fillets. The house probably dates from about 1880 but its ample front porch is from the turn of the century.

Continue west to the corner. Turn left (south) on Green Bay Road. On your right is

11.   GLENCOE TRAIN STATION—1890s

Built in the early 1890s, this structure is a fine example of a suburban train station probably by Frost and Granger. The long structure is covered with a low hipped roof rising from walls that are supported by battered wall buttresses in limestone. The limestone is also used for the segmental arches on the south facade. Projecting in the southern section is a more steeply pitched roof to indicate the waiting room inside. It retains its original vertical grooved wainscoting. The roof, supported by brick walls, projects over the track to provide a shelter for the passengers. The station master's office projects through the roof as a circular turret with a conical roof.

Continue south to the corner. Turn right (west) on Park Avenue, across the tracks. Turn left (south) on Glencoe Road to South Avenue.

This concludes the Glencoe Walking Tour.

Drive north on Glencoe Road, veering to the left as it becomes Green Bay Road, 2 miles to Lake Cook Road (County Line Road). Turn left (west).

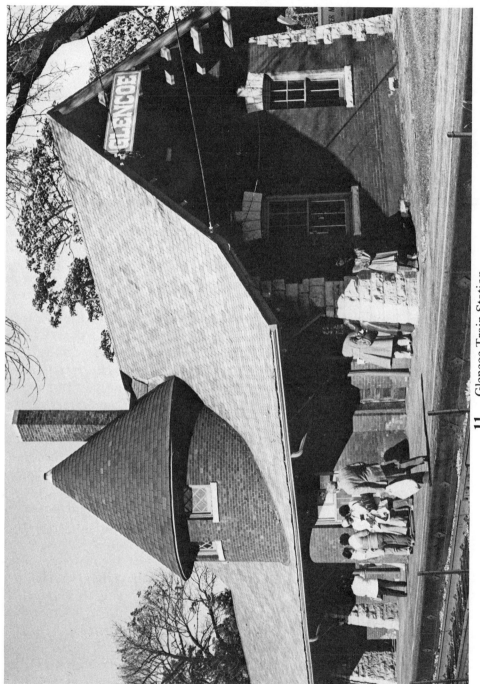

11. Glencoe Train Station

The first road on your left is the entrance to

12.   BOTANIC GARDEN OF THE CHICAGO
HORTICULTURAL SOCIETY—1976

Three hundred acres of landscape and lakes comprise the garden. The administrative and exhibition center is set onto the rolling landscape. A structure suitable for the site, it is dominated by a centrally placed, high, pyramidal roof rising into a tall, square lantern. The north section is the administrative center with an auditorium, meeting rooms, and so on. The south part has a U-shaped configuration leading through a sequence of ten greenhouse lobes, each with a pyramidal roof much smaller in size than the one in the center over the central exhibition hall. The greenhouses reveal a respect for traditional greenhouse construction which requires a structural frame and independent glass membranes for walls and roofs. Here the structure is simplified into a welded, steel tubular frame and the glass is standard-curtain walls of glass construction similar to that found on tall commercial office buildings. To the east and west of the central exhibition hall are two large courtyards, one with a thundering fountain, the other with a peaceful coppice made from a variety of trees both deciduous and nondeciduous.

The building was opened in 1976 and was designed by Edward Larabee Barnes, a prominent East Coast architect with Chicago origins. It shows an expansion across the landscape with wings spreading out from a central dominant structure and a disciplined merging of interior and exterior spaces. These are important legacies of Prairie School architects which show a link to the tradition of this region. The idiom of the construction, however, is anything but Prairie School. It has walls of Chicago common brick used as broad planes, broken for openings, left undressed by moldings or other elaboration and, serving as doors and windows, a device taught by the International Style architects. A final contribution to the design came from Scandinavian architects. They showed how to achieve quality in design by being particularly careful in the simple detailing given the materials. They also explored the use of wood as it is handled here in the ceilings with battens of hemlock strips spaced evenly along cyprus dowels tying them together. These three aspects of design, that is, the Prairie School, the International Style, and the lessons of Scandinavian designers, have been the most important in the recent twentieth century.

Highlights include: the Main Island, an educational center with demonstration gardens located in the modern building at the center of the island;

an annual flower garden and a dramatic fountain; prairie restoration established on several acres; an herb garden, a vegetable garden, a children's garden, and a learning garden for the disabled are operated as demonstration gardens; three Japanese islands are under development, one to feature a home, one a viewing arbor, and one a mystical island of happiness where "man does not walk"; and Illinois' one hundred varieties of trees are planted in another area. Woodland animals and wildlife abound. There are also tram-train tours that leave from the west portico of the Education Center. The tram operates April 15-October 31. Adults: $1.00; Children: 50¢. The Botanic Garden is open daily except Christmas Day from 8:00 A.M. to about sundown. $1.00 parking fee per car.

Turn left (west) on Lake Cook Road (County Line Road) and drive 6.8 miles to Milwaukee Road (Routes 21 and 45).

NORTHBROOK

NORTHBROOK

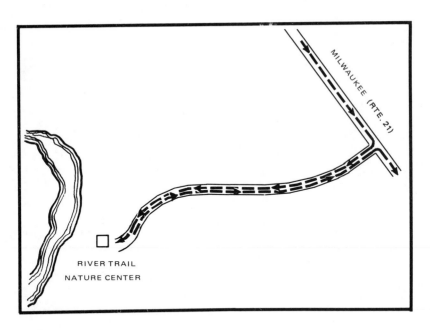

Turn left (south) on Milwaukee Avenue (Routes 21 and 45) 3.7 miles to the fork in the road. Take the left fork (Route 21) .8 miles. On your right is the River Trail Nature Center in the forest preserve. Turn right (west) to the parking lot.

RIVER TRAIL NATURE CENTER
Forest Preserve District of Cook County

The nature center has exhibits that change seasonally. There are also several animals including a coyote and a ferret, outdoor exhibits, wild deer, and self-guided trails that tell stories about the area. There are over thirty varieties of trees on the grounds some of which are maple sugar trees. The trees are tapped annually. At the end of March, usually on the second or the third weekend, there is a maple syrup festival. Pancakes with the syrup and coffee are available. In the fall, usually during the second weekend in October, there is a honey festival. Both festivals take place from 9:30 A.M.-6:00 P.M. The museum is open 8:30 A.M.-4:30 P.M. Monday-Thursday except holidays. Grounds are open 8:30 A.M.-5:00 P.M. Closed Thanksgiving, Christmas, and New Year.

Return to Milwaukee Avenue. Turn right (south).

GLENVIEW

GLENVIEW

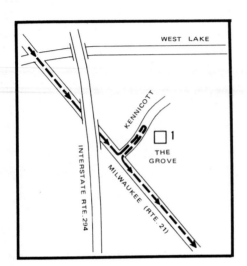

WEST LAKE

KENNICOTT

INTERSTATE RTE. 294

MILWAUKEE (RTE. 21)

□ 1
THE
GROVE

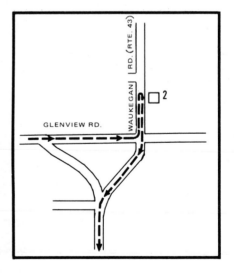

WAUKEGAN RD. (RTE. 43)

GLENVIEW RD.

□ 2

Continue south 1.3 miles on Milwaukee Avenue. On your left, just after the underpass, (east side of the road) is

1. THE GROVE
1421 Milwaukee Avenue
Kennicott's Grove—1856

The 1856 house is in the process of being made into a museum to be run by the Glenview Park District. There will also be a nursery operated here. The house was built by the Kennicott family who were pioneers in many ways. The large, rambling structure occupying the top of a rise in the ground is representative of an earlier generation than its date of 1856 would suggest. The steeply pitched roof of the central section, the board and batten walls, the wall dormers, and the simple hood moldings over the tall double-hung windows recall the Gothic Revival, but the near austerity of the forms belongs to rustic frontier buildings rather than to the settled period following mid-century. Also archaic is the seemingly haphazard massing with a tall central block which includes a second story projection above the front porch and which is flanked by lower, unequal wings. Another wing with additional service spaces projects at the back. The house and grove are a National Historic Landmark; extensive rebuilding has restored the house to the condition it had when it was built by an important early physician and naturalist. The Kennicott's descendants were involved in exploring Alaska, developing modern floriculture, and founding the Chicago Academy of Sciences. The Grove Heritage Society is also very active. Plans are underway to restore the land to its mid-nineteenth century condition and operate a nineteenth century working farm.

Leaving The Grove, turn left (south) on Milwaukee Avenue .8 miles. Turn left (east) on Glenview Road, over the bridge, 3 miles to Waukegan Road (Route 43). Turn left (north) on Waukegan Road ¾ block. The first house on your right is

2. GLENVIEW HISTORIC SOCIETY
1121 Waukegan Road—1865

The back core of this frame clapboard house is old, apparently dating from 1865. The front sections are newer and were added in a sequence up to the turn of the century. The interior is displayed as a turn-of-the-century house. Displays include costumes, spinning wheels, antique typewriters, Indian and Civil War artifacts, antique cameras, and a wonderful toy and doll collection. Sundays: 2:00 P.M.-5:00 P.M. Free.

Drive south on Waukegan Road (Route 43) 1.3 miles to Golf Road. Turn right (west) 4.7 miles. Turn left (south) on River Road (Des Plaines Avenue).

DES PLAINES

DES PLAINES

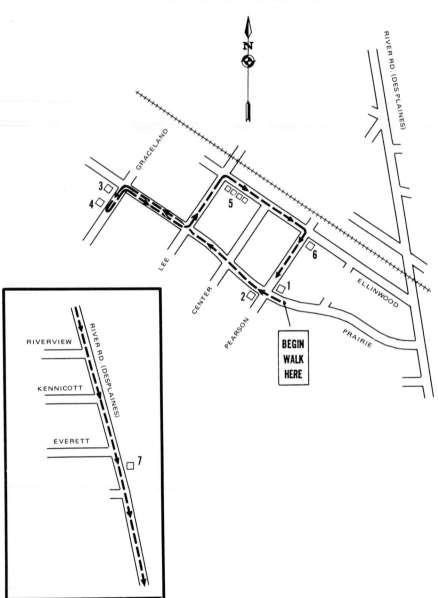

Drive south on Des Plaines Avenue (River Road) 1.2 miles to Prairie Avenue. Turn right (west) one very long, winding block to Pearson Street. Stop.

DES PLAINES WALKING TOUR

On the NE corner of Pearson Street and Prairie Avenue is

1. DES PLAINES HISTORICAL SOCIETY
789 Pearson Street—1906

This red brick house is being restored and is to be displayed as a home at the turn of the century. Built in 1906, it shows the late remaining vestiges of the Queen Anne style rendered in brick with a neo-classical severity. The cubic block is broken forward on the south and west faces with projections covered by gables which, with their continuous cornices below, provide steep pediments. The south projection has splayed corners. The west projection contains the front entrance; the front is being restored. Projecting from the corner is a large round bay rising into the roof zone and topped by a conical roof whose simple sheet-metal pinnacle towers above the rest of the building. The building, which was moved to its present site in 1979, has beautiful original woodwork and leaded glass windows.

Exhibits dealing with a variety of historical subjects are changed regularily. For researchers, a local history library is available. There is also an extensive costume collection. Wednesdays, Saturdays, and Sundays: 2:00 P.M.-4:00 P.M. Free.

On the SW corner of Pearson Street and Prairie Avenue, is

2. 794 PEARSON STREET—c. 1870 and 1906

The foundations of this red brick building with Greek Revival influence probably date from about 1870, but the present structure was built in 1906 as the cornerstone clearly indicates. The simple two-story structure, covered by a pitched roof, served as the rectory for St. Mary's Church and faces to the east with a projecting bay running through two stories to a pitched roof slightly lower than that of the gable. Its corners, like the rest of the building, have massive brick quoins. Midway along the south face of the building is an arched religious window and, on the second floor of the west end, a polygonal apsidal device which helps to convey the religious character of this structure.

Walk west on Prairie Avenue 3 blocks. On the SW corner of Prairie and Graceland avenues is

3.   MASONIC TEMPLE
1345 Prairie Avenue—1870s

This church, made of locally produced red brick in the 1870s, was the First Congregational Church. The original section is the simple pitched roofed sanctuary. Its windows, along the side and on the east face, are sheltered under protruding bricks which describe the pointed arches with pinnacles at their peaks. The circular window, in the projecting section in the center of the east facade, is also part of the original construction. The corners are brought out to suggest buttresses, and the top of the wall has a corbel table rising with the roof. At some later date, perhaps shortly after the turn of the century, the stubby tower on the north side with its diagonally placed entrance and ancillary rooms on the northwest corner and the slight gabled projection on the east face were added to the original structure. At a later date the windows were bricked up to convert it to its present use.

Walk south on Graceland Avenue. The second house on your right is

4.   704 GRACELAND AVENUE—1873

This small, one-and-one-half-story, frame structure has a pitched roof facing the street intersected on both the north and south facades by projections with full gables. The two on the north facade and the less extensively projecting one on the south facade date from 1873. The western one on the south facade is probably from about twenty years later, as is the square projecting bay with the pent roof rising above it. Both of these have decorative shingle fields while the large projection has an especially fine split sunrise motif below its vertical board gable with applied diagonal struts. The wall under the double gable on the north side, as well as the projection on the east side, displays the original window heads which are simple pediments attached above the windows. The entry projection is of yet more recent origin.

Backtrack north to Prairie Avenue. Turn right (east) 1 block to Lee Street. Turn left (north) 1 block. Turn right (east) on Ellinwood Street. On your right (south side of the street) is

5. **1507–1517 ELLINWOOD STREET**—1880s and later
These storefronts date from a thirty-year period beginning in the 1880s. The one farthest west (1507 Ellinwood Street) uses rough red brick, juxtaposed against white glazed brick, with standard catalogue item terra-cotta decorations inserted in the central sections of the parapets. It is a good example of the terra-cotta storefronts for which the Chicago area was famous during the period just following World War I. The next structure east (1511 Ellinwood Street) is a neo-classical storefront from the turn of the century with smooth-faced red brick juxtaposed against light colored limestone to produce a distinct neo-classicism. The next structures east (1513–1517 Ellinwood Street) were originally one building with cast iron storefronts. The section surviving at 1517 Ellinwood is an excellent example of the storefront design from the 1880s with extensive, brick, shouldered, segmental arches for the window heads.

Continue east on Ellinwood Street to Pearson Street. On the SE corner of Pearson and Ellinwood streets is

6. **1545 ELLINWOOD STREET**
Kinder Hardware Store—1881
Established in 1873, the hardware business moved to this site in 1881. A portion of the building from that time is visible along Pearson Street, the west facade with its simple brick wall and limestone lintels. Sometime about 1910, the present front (the north facade facing Ellinwood Street) was added. It has the neat, rough brick facade touched up with light colored limestone to provide a neo-classical image. The ample store windows have copper fittings and a copper bulkhead with windows to light the basement spaces. Inside is a charming interior with its original tin roof.

Walk south on Pearson Street 1 block to the historical society on your left.

This concludes the Des Plaines Walking Tour.

Drive east on Prairie Avenue one very long, winding block until it ends at River Road (Des Plaines Avenue). Turn right (south) 1.3 miles. On your right, just past Everett Avenue, is

7. Izaak Walton League
1841 S. River Road

7. 1841 S. RIVER ROAD
Izaak Walton League—1859

This is the headquarters for the Izaak Walton League, which is concerned with preserving and studying the waterfowl in the area. The surrounding grounds are a wildlife preserve.

This substantial red brick structure, in a secluded grove next to the river, is a handsome monument built in 1859. The main section of the house has a T-shaped plan with the stem facing west. It originally contained the entrance which is still visible there although the original porch is gone. The openings display the characteristic segmental arches built of a variety of brick projections to reproduce a normal stone pattern. Note how the upper sash and the double-hung windows fit snugly into the semicircular arch. On the north side, under a recently added porch, is the side entrance to the structure; beyond it and farther to the east is the original service entrance leading to the service wing beyond. In the gables are full circular windows which originally contained a quatrefoil pattern in front of the window glass, a fragment of which remains in the west face.

Drive south on Des Plaines Avenue (River Road) .8 miles. Just past Touhy Avenue, veer right on Route 294 (Tri-State Tollway South) towards Indiana. Continue south 1.2 miles to Route 90 East (Kennedy Expressway) towards Chicago. Exit right, then bear immediately left, to Chicago.

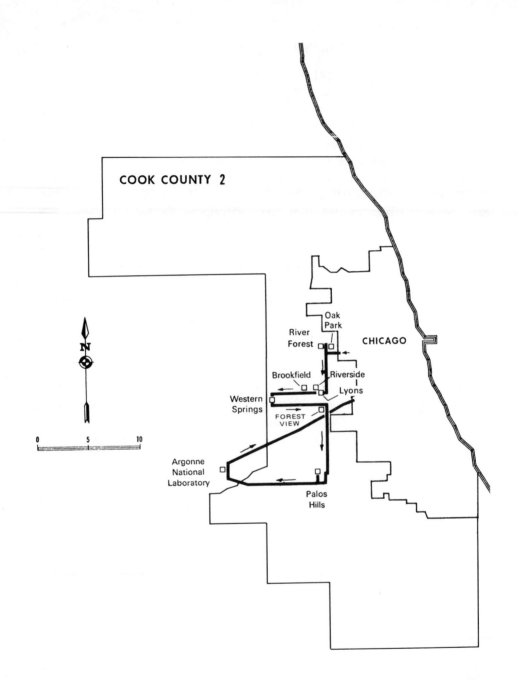

COOK COUNTY 2

N

0   5   10

Oak
Park

River
Forest

CHICAGO

Brookfield

Riverside

Lyons

Western
Springs

FOREST
VIEW

Argonne
National
Laboratory

Palos
Hills

Cook County 2

RIVER FOREST

RIVER FOREST

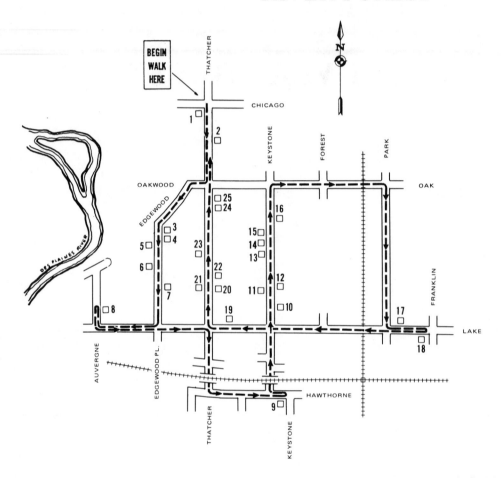

From Chicago, drive west on the Eisenhower Expressway (Route 290) to Harlem Avenue (Route 43). Exit left, then turn right (north) on Harlem Avenue 1½ miles. Turn left (west) 1 mile on Chicago Avenue to Thatcher Avenue. Turn left (south). Stop.

RIVER FOREST WALKING TOUR

On the SW corner of Thatcher and Chicago avenues is

1. TRAILSIDE MUSEUM OF NATURAL HISTORY, COOK COUNTY FOREST PRESERVE
738 Thatcher Avenue—1874

Built in 1874, this is an excellent example of an asymmetrical Italian villa. Only the original porch is lacking, although there may have originally been brackets under the eaves, and the brick structure was not painted. The two-story block has floor-to-ceiling windows on the ground floor and slightly smaller ones on the upper floor. A three-story tower sits in the reentrant angle of the L-shaped plan which is extended on the south side by a flat-fronted bay. The window heads, which are brick segmental shouldered arches springing from brick corbels, are larger on the ground floor than on the second floor. Notice that on the back of the house these projecting segmental arches are lacking because the back was unimportant in conveying the dignity that the Italianate style rendered so well. Notice also, in the south face of the hipped roof on the south wing, the small gable with the pair of simple windows with the suggestion of a segmental arch above them rendered in boards.

Housed here is a collection of over a hundred animals; the larger ones are in outside cages. Go inside to see an assortment of wild and tame, domestic and unusual residents. A pet cat often nurses litters of squirrels. There is also a large display of stuffed birds of prey. 10:00 A.M.-noon and 1:00 P.M.-5:00 P.M. except Thursday.

Walk south on Thatcher Avenue. The fifth house on your left is

2. 719 THATCHER AVENUE—1890s

This quite dignified Queen Anne structure shows an L-shaped frame block covered with a full pitched roof to provide an attic story and scalloped shingles in the gable with a simulated Palladian motif in the gable which is terminated by a pent roof. Tucked under the pent roof on the south side of the front facade is a round corner bay. On the ground floor a porch stretches beyond it as far as the projecting wing at the back of the house. The porch parapet and its corner posts are covered in thin clapboard as is the rest of the ground floor, while the second floor shows a standard sheathing. The building shows the late 1890s taming of the Queen Anne style.

Continue south to the corner. Turn right (west) on Oakwood Avenue, continuing on Edgewood Place. The sixth house on your left is

3.   603 EDGEWOOD PLACE—1908

Designed by Frank Lloyd Wright in 1908, but remodeled in the 1950s, the building presents a marvelously harmonious presentation of the mature Prairie style forms. The plan is a basic cross shape with the east-west section two stories high and the north-south section one story. The prominent hipped roofs are extended with broad plastered soffits. The intersection of the cross shape is marked by a broad flat chimney, while the two-story front, facing the street on the west side, is glazed with a two-story tier of windows exhibiting the delicate horizontal diamond pattern used so effectively by the Prairie style architects. Especially notable here is the fine integration of materials with stucco used in the eave soffits and at the rear of the building, tawny brick walls (topped by an extremely dense, finely surfaced cement coping) used for the areas below the sills on the wings, and timbers used for the fenestration.

Continue south on Edgewood Place. The first house on your left is

4.   559 EDGEWOOD PLACE—1911

This 1911 Prairie School house was designed by William Drummond. The building's massing is basically a hipped roof block with broad stuccoed soffits, but it shows a marked contrast with the earlier design (River Forest #3) by Frank Lloyd Wright by having less fenestration and a more decorative use of the wall. The stucco walls are articulated by boards which cross the heads and sills of the strips of casement windows and turn down from the second story to frame the front wall. On the north and south faces generous flat-fronted bays project on the second floor under the soffits to be answered on the ground floor on the west facade by a deep projection covered by a flat roof. These are tied into the block behind by garden wall extensions which in turn connect with the boards descending from the second story window sills. Notice that the chimney projecting to the north of the center of the block is articulated with stucco and boards. The structure is listed on the National Register of Historic Places.

On the west side of the street is

5. 560 EDGEWOOD PLACE—1910

This 1910 building, also by William Drummond, is a slightly simpler version of the other house (River Forest #4). Here the two-story block is again covered by a hipped roof. It has projections, to the south of one story and to the north of two stories. Facing the street on the east facade, instead of an extension of the interior space there is a planter box with piers rising on either end and penetrating into the window grouping. That window grouping, here as in the rest of the building, alternates a large fixed sash with sidelights of three panes, one above the other, in narrow strips. That motif is repeated on the second floor on the front and as long strips on the other faces. Again, a chimney penetrates through the house to anchor its horizontal extensions to the earth in the typical Prairie School manner.

Continue south. The fifth house on your right is

6. 530 EDGEWOOD PLACE—1895

Designed by Frank Lloyd Wright in 1895, this building shows the independent manner that Wright had developed in using the styles of the 1890s before he had evolved his Prairie style approach. It combines some of the simplified massing of the Shingle style with some of the motifs popularized by Louis Sullivan which is most evident in the arched entrance with its ornamented frieze. The general massing shows a masonry base, a stucco section in the upper half of the ground floor, and a very high steeply pitched roof terminating in polygonal planes covering the polygonal projections on the north end and on the short extension toward the street at the opposite end. In that tall roof are two dormers with similar steeply pitched roofs, slightly projecting polygonal windows, and above them a deep extension of the dormer cornice providing a shading window hood. The front parapet of the porch and the lowest sections of the masonry, including a build-up toward the entrance, has large random rubblestone, above which begins the smooth brick wall of the long horizontal Roman brick. This combination of a heavy rustic basement and smooth, sophisticated masonry forms a striking contrast. Notice that within the general Shingle style massing is included a discrete reference to the Tudor Revival in the quatrefoil window next to the entrance.

Continue south. The fourth house on your left is

7. 511 Edgewood Place—1858

Built in 1858 and moved a little over twenty years later from its original location a few blocks away, this building contains the basic features of the early Italianate style. The L-shaped plan is topped by a pitched roof with its eaves supporting pairs of simple elongated brackets. Enlarged versions of those brackets are used to support the balcony before the second story windows on the west face of the front wing. The balcony has a fine, scroll-cut balustrade and a decorative lintel between the brackets. The pair of windows opening on the balcony is topped by an entablature. The windows on the ground floor beneath the balcony are fronted by a matching parapet and, like the windows opening into the porch, are full height, running from floor to ceiling. The front entrance has an unusual configuration for the Italianate with sidelights and transom with additional sidelights flanking the transom. Notice the decorative corbel flanking the transom and the pilasters flanking the entrance. The porch was probably built when the house was moved to this site. Its square, chamfered, porch posts holding a relatively elaborate lintel suggest the slightly later period in the Italianate style as does the pitch of the roof that reaches to the sills of the second story windows. The brick structure is neatly dressed by the fine limestone lintels and sills used for the windows.

Continue south to the corner. Turn right (west) on Lake Street 1 block. Turn right (north) on Auvergne Place. The second house on your right is

8. 515 Auvergne Place
William H. Winslow House—1893

Designed in 1893 by Frank Lloyd Wright soon after he had set up his independent practice, this building is one of the first mature manifestations of his style. It was extremely important in bringing fame and renown to the young architect. The client was an important industrialist who operated the

8. 515 Auvergne Place

(detail)

foundry that produced the metal pieces for buildings designed by Louis Sullivan (for example the shopfronts on State and Madison streets of the Carson Pirie Scott and Company building in Chicago).

In this design Wright was able to establish an harmonious and fine relationship with a sympathetic client who sought a design that would combine the spaces of the house into a setting that could draw the members of the family together around their common interest in music. Thus inside, in front of the fireplace marked on the outside by the chimney, is a small stage where musicales could be held. The outside presents a quite formal composition with a long block topped by a hipped roof with broad soffited eaves. The sill level of the second story windows is marked by a continuous cornice, and the zone between it and the roof is sheathed in a richly patterned terra-cotta surface. The three, large, double-hung windows in that zone each have geometric leaded glass in the upper sash. Each of those windows is answered on the ground floor by an opening, the outer ones framed by a molding that acts as a frame around the window rather than as a structural device with a sill with one form and a lintel with another. These frames are set into the orange tawny brick wall built of broad, low, Roman brick. The wall plane breaks forward in two steps in the center to contain the entrance. The entrance motif repeats the composition of the house as a whole with a central door flanked on either side by windows, and that section is framed by a decorative pattern supplementing the pattern of the terra-cotta second story running around its outer frame but moving up over the central door. The windows meanwhile remain unframed, but the reveals of the jambs, sills, and heads repeat the decorative pattern. The stone of that element is then extended around the house as a mudsill decorated only by a broad cyma molding. Projecting to the south on the ground floor only is a polygonal bay answered on the north by a porte-cochere. This repeats the broad hipped roof and has in its brick structure a large, stone frame which opens in a broad, low arch. Its soffits are decorated with the rich foliate motif common to the Queen Anne style of the period, the only reference in this structure to that then-current style.

The design of the house is extended across the landscape with the broad front area marked by urns on the porch podia and by podia close to the curb. The central section of that broad paved area is treated as a planter. Already visible in this design are the basic elements of the horizontality and the extension of the design across the landscape which will permeate the Prairie style. The house is listed on the National Register of Historic Places.

Backtrack south on Auvergne Place. Turn left (east) on Lake Street 2 blocks. Turn right (south) on Thatcher Avenue, under the railroad tracks. Turn left (east) on Hawthorne Avenue 1½ blocks. On the SW corner of Hawthorne and Keystone avenues is

9. 344 KEYSTONE AVENUE—c.1870

This fine example of the Italianate style probably was built in 1870. It is much closer to the symmetrical formality of the Italianate than to the asymmetrical Italian villa-type, although it contains aspects of both types of Italianate composition. The building is almost a cubic block with a central tower rising in the center, but the north section of the block is brought forward almost to the face of the tower, a movement that is accentuated by the flat-fronted bay on the ground floor and by the porch on the opposite side between the front of the tower and the main mass of the brick house. That porch moves around to the south side and is supported by square piers with small impost blocks between the pier capitals and the simple lintel. Continuing the line of each post is a pair of diminutive brackets echoing the pair of brackets in the cornice.

The roof is a Mansard roof with a dormer in each face flanking the tower. These dormers have pointed arches carried by small freestanding columns and jerkin-head roofs with incising on the arched faces. They are taken from the High Victorian Gothic style. The tower in its third floor, the level equivalent to the story in the Mansard roof, has a trifoil arch above its pair of windows and is topped by a corbeled cornice. Standing atop it, beyond the wrought iron railing, is a cupola or lantern with pairs of windows, each with a trifoil arch. This is then topped by a square bell roof extending into a broad overhang with single brackets.

Throughout the building the openings are brick with corbeled shoulders and prominent limestone keystones. The north face of the building contains the side entrance and an asymmetry which complements the asymmetry of the main, or east, face. Slightly to the west of center, the building projects forward and has a small entrance porch with a pair of windows under a trifoil arch. On the second story, protected by a truncated gable intersecting the cornice above it and centered in the roof on either side of the projection, is another of the Victorian Gothic jerkin-head dormers.

Backtrack west on Hawthorne Avenue, turning right (north) on Keystone

9. 344 Keystone Avenue

Avenue under the railroad tracks. The third house on your right past Lake Street is

10. 517 KEYSTONE AVENUE—1915

This 1915 house, designed by William Drummond, is a simple version of the basic cube covered with a pitched roof elaborated in the Prairie style. The ground floor is extended up to the sill level of the second story windows as a board sheathing with alternating narrow and thick boards. The zone above that is stucco which extends into the eave soffits, including the soffits of the pent roof of the gable, and it is crossed by a board set at the sill level of the second story windows. In the gables facing the sides of the lot lines are windows set at a 45° angle to accentuate the angle of the pitched roof. The entrance is on the south side and is marked by a flat-fronted bay on the second story. Projecting toward the street on the west side is a one-story extension of the interior space covered by a low hipped roof. Notice the care with which the casement windows are designed, divided as they are into tall thin panes with a constantly diminishing set of squares in the lower outer or upper outer corner.

Cross to the west side of the street and continue north. The third house on your left is

11. 530 KEYSTONE AVENUE—1909

This L-shaped house covered in a low hipped roof with a stuccoed soffit was designed by Robert Spencer, Jr., in 1909. It is a fine brick example of the Prairie School used within a relatively traditional framework. The Prairie style is especially manifest in the restraint of the detailing. The windows are grouped into strips, the second story ones resting on a stone stringcourse that continues around the entire structure. The windows have especially fine abstracted floral patterns. Attention is called to the entrance by a number of devices which begin with the square urns atop the podia at the porch set behind the front face of the front wing and is continued by the slight projection of a balcony. It is then extended by the recession containing the entrance and the deeper recession for the second story balcony. The final emphasis on the entrance comes in the simple dormer. The asymmetry of the L-shaped plan is redressed somewhat by the extension on the south side of a one-story porch and by the chimney between it and the main block of the house, answered on the other side by a pair of chimneys.

Directly across the street is

12.   535 KEYSTONE AVENUE—1860s (possibly 1870)
A very early River Forest house from after 1860, this building has had a number of alterations, most recently the addition of siding, but its original character, a somewhat enlarged, L-shaped Gothic cottage with the low shapes of the Italianate, may still be perceived. The front wing projects with a broad bay window with simple surrounds and low pedimented lintels, the same device used above the pair of windows in the second story.

Cross back to the west side of the street and continue north. The fourth house on your left is

13.   558 KEYSTONE AVENUE—c. 1860
Built about 1860, this is an excellent example of a large Gothic cottage. The two-story frame structure is entirely sheathed in thin clapboards complete with corner boards. The gables fronting the three faces of the T-shaped plan have cut-out bargeboards and at their peaks probably the longest pendant that could be attached to such a structure. On each side of the front wing are porches, one for the main entrance and the other slightly smaller for the side entrance, their posts elaborated by cut-out fillets. The ends of the wings have projecting ground floors with hood moldings above their square-topped windows while the second story windows are paired, have segmental arches on the upper sash, and are enclosed under a single segmental pediment.

Continue north. The next house on your left is

14.   562 KEYSTONE AVENUE—1909
This 1909 house, designed by Frank Lloyd Wright, is an excellent example of the mature Prairie style as it had evolved from the basic hipped roofed cube. The hipped roof is prominent with its simple fascia and stuccoed soffits on both the south and north sides. On the second story a balcony projects between the zone defined by the second story sills and the ground floor heads. The second story sills are continued across the entire stucco surface and, in the front, continue out for the strip of five windows. At that sill level is the peak of the hipped roof for the ground floor projection on the front facade which serves as an open porch. The coping of the porch is extended out on either side to continue the horizontal emphasis of the design as a

whole. The windows contain the excellent Prairie glass of the period, and the entire building shows the restraint and discipline of the Prairie School.

Continue north. The next house on your left is

15. 606 KEYSTONE AVENUE—1905

This large Tudor style house, designed by E. E. Roberts, an important Oak Park-based architect of the period, in 1905, has brick on the ground and second stories and an ample attic story in a very simple half-timbering. The windows on the ground floor are set in strips and those on the attic story are grouped as strips within the half-timbered pattern. The building is basically a block with a projection on the south side with a low pitched roof repeated on the north side with the entrance there marked by the very tall chimney rising next to it. The restraint of the design, the lack of archaeological references to the Tudor style, and the pattern of the leaded glass in the casement windows all betray the discipline and the stylistic characteristics of the Prairie style.

Cross back to the east side of the street and continue north. The first house on your right is

16. 611 KEYSTONE AVENUE—c.1877

This one-and-one-half-story cottage, built about 1877, has been altered somewhat, primarily by the probable loss of a porch, but it indicates the use of the Italianate forms within a basic Gothic cottage framework. Note the heavy pediments over the segmental-headed windows and the small corbels holding the ears of the segmental hood over the transomed entrance.

Continue north to the corner. Turn right (east) on Oak Avenue under the railroad tracks. Turn right (south) on Park Avenue 1 long block. Turn left (east) on Lake Street. The first building on your left is

17. 7776 LAKE STREET
The Old Harlem School—1860

Built in 1860, this is the oldest public building still standing in River Forest. A fine representative of the monumental style used in the nineteenth century for public buildings, this brick structure has the basic configuration of the Colonial New England church-type with a two-story block in brick and a

17. 7776 Lake Street

steeple in the front, but it has been modified to bring it into accord with the Italianate style popular at the period. Notice that the side walls on the front section of the building are stepped forward slightly on both the east and the west sides and that the corners there and at the north end are marked by projecting sections of brick which seem to define large pilasters. These rise to a brick corbel course that begins the entablature which, in the front facing south, rises to a pediment with the stunted steeple on top. The corners of that steeple are splayed, and in the front is a triplet of half-circular blind windows, the center one larger than the other two. That same motif is repeated on the ground floor. The double doors of the entrance are sheltered under a fully-rounded arch and flanked on each side by segmental shouldered arches like the four on each side of the ground floor. Above is an equal number of openings all the same size, all with half-circular arches which like the openings below are of stone, now painted.

Cross to the south side of Lake Street and walk east. The second building on your right is

18. 7751–7773 LAKE STREET and 426 FRANKLIN AVENUE

River Forest Bank Building—1912

This long commercial structure, designed in 1912 by William Drummond, represents one of the few applications of the Prairie style to this building type. Along the ground floor are shops (many with their original shop windows still in place) and above, entered through a series of ground floor indentations, are two stories of apartments. The broad horizontality, characteristic of the Prairie School, is rendered by the extension of limestone stringcourses above the shopfront windows at the level of the second story window sills and, at the third story, along the window heads. It is further emphasized by the simple soffited eaves of the roof. Another characteristic of the Prairie style, that of grouping windows into strips, is clear in the upper level above each of the indented entrances. Finally, the lack of historical ornament and the careful squaring off of the limestone with let-in squares from place to place convey the characteristics of the style. Notice also the name of the building in the terra-cotta frieze facing Lake Street. The building bears comparison with George Grant Elmslie's later commercial structures in Aurora, for example, Aurora #7 and #13.

Backtrack west on Lake Street 3 blocks. Past Keystone Avenue, on your right, is

19.   7970 LAKE STREET
River Forest Methodist Church—1912

Designed by William Drummond in 1912, this building is an excellent example of the merging of the Prairie style with the Tudor. The general configuration, an L-shaped plan with a tower containing the entrance marking the reentrant angle, derives from the pattern for designing English churches based upon medieval English practice. This source probably also accounts for the pointed arches over the windows and at the doorway, for the suggestion of buttresses in the corners and along the walls between the windows, and for the brick construction with disciplined stone copings. Attributable to the Prairie style however is the general horizontality of the massing, the quite idiosyncratic interpretation of the Tudor vocabulary, and the Prairie style glass especially noticeable at the entrances in the sanctuary dormers and in the small windows in that same level in the tower.

Continue west on Lake Street to the corner. Turn right (north). The fourth house on your right is

20.   527 THATCHER AVENUE—c.1890
Built in about 1890, the building originally had a porch across a large section of the south side of its front facade but the removal of the porch was done with great care and the integrity of the wall cladding restored. Later alterations over time added sections to the back.

Across the street is

21.   532 THATCHER AVENUE—c.1887
This fine Queen Anne house, probably from 1887, has a broad porch from the polygonal bay on the north side which extends across the front and breaks at an angle to turn down to the wing projecting toward the back on the south side. That angular break of the porch is reflected above in the splayed corner window which is marked by a pendant at the outer corner. The hipped roof above carries a gable at its peak and swells out in pitches over the polygonal bay at the corner. Notice that two of the windows on the second story, as well as the ones on the ground floor, retain their original transoms.

Cross back to the east side of the street and continue north. The next house on your right is

22.   535 THATCHER AVENUE—1887

Built in 1887, this clapboard frame structure is representative of the Queen Anne during its earlier, more subdued period. It has a simple shingle pattern in the lower part of the gables, the peaks of which contain either cut-out boards or a Stick style pattern adding interest to that section. Notice how the smaller gable and the gable on the south wing extend beyond the face and are carried by very flat modillions. The ample veranda across the entire front and part of the south side has fine turned posts and a beautifully maintained spindle lintel.

Cross to the west side of the street and continue north. The second house on your left is

23.   544 THATCHER AVENUE—c.1890

This structure from about 1890 is a simple box elaborated by an oversized polygonal bay through two stories on one corner and a two-story veranda overlapping it and taking up the rest of the front face. The clapboard sections on the first and second stories are separated by a scalloped shingle band that flares above the ground story window heads. Notice, in the area between the first and second floor along the porch and below the flared polygonal roof above the bay, the heavy boss and square paten elements which are derived from the rich bulbous forms of the "U.S. Grant" style but here are considerably simplified.

Cross back to the east side of the street and continue north. The seventh house on your right is

24.   615 THATCHER AVENUE—1869

Built in 1869, this one-and-one-half-story, L-shaped, clapboard-clad, Gothic cottage has sparsely applied but delicately done elaboration. Note that in the pair of windows in the second story, the pointed heads of the outer frames extend up to make a combined pointed head that then extends down on each side to suggest a hooded molding. The ground story has a porch across the entire front returning down the south side to terminate at the back wing (the sections beyond that are later additions). That porch is supported by turned posts with scalloped cut-out fillets and a sparse spindled lintel. The entrance on the north side is marked by a pediment with cut-out and attached board decoration.

Continue north. The next house on your right is

25.   623 THATCHER AVENUE—1867

Although the porch on this structure is probably from the 1890s, the original building has two features of great interest. One is in the attic where a Stick style surface is used for sheathing. The other is the use of window shades above the second story windows. Notice that they are very simply construct-ed but quite effectively do the job of shielding the interior from the harsh rays of the summer sun. These are extremely rare now although many of the house pattern books of the nineteenth century show them as standard fea-tures on the buildings they helped to popularize.

Continue north 1 block to the Trailside Museum on your left.

This concludes the River Forest Walking Tour.

Turn right (east) on Chicago Avenue.

OAK PARK

OAK PARK

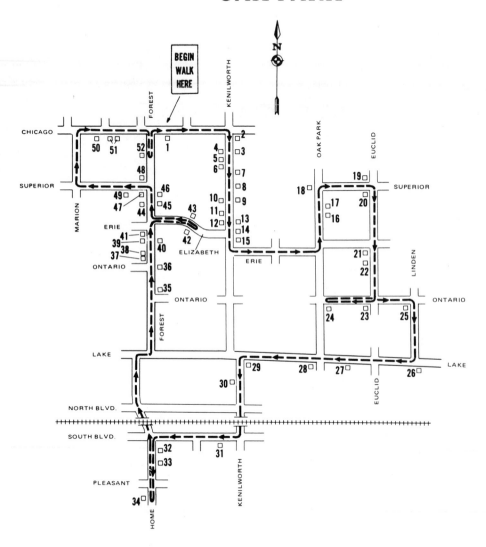

Drive east on Chicago Avenue 1.4 miles to Forest Avenue. Stop.

OAK PARK WALKING TOUR

Most of the area covered in this walk is within the Frank Lloyd Wright-Prairie School of Architecture Historic District, which is roughly bounded by Harlem Avenue, Division Street, Clyde Street, and Lake Street. The district is listed on the National Register of Historic Places.

On the SE corner of Chicago and Forest avenues is

1. FRANK LLOYD WRIGHT HOME AND STUDIO
947 Chicago Avenue—1889 and 1898

The original section of this house, which Wright used as an experiment in building, faces to the west onto Forest Avenue. Built in 1889, it is a Shingle style composition of utter simplicity and formality. A tall pitched roof faces the street and encloses the second story which extends into an unused attic. Across the front of the second story extends a balcony supported at each end by brick and stone piers and, in between, square wooden piers. Beyond the balcony is a strip of casement windows with diamond paned glass. The entrance porch is underneath the balcony tucked within the overhanging gabled front. The sheltered central door is flanked by broad bow windows. Beyond this section is a cross pitched roof which encloses the remainder of the house. At this point in Wright's career it would be possible to anticipate neither his future designs nor his future greatness because this is simply a competent Shingle style design, but it was done by a man only slightly more than twenty years old.

Wright lived here for more than twenty years, maintaining his studios and establishing himself as an architect of world fame. Here he employed a number of young architects who learned his principles, contributed to his own ideas, and remained in the area after he left. This group constituted the core of the Prairie School of Architecture. In this building Wright continued to experiment by adding, subtracting, rebuilding, and modifying elements in this design.

Walk around the building on the north side facing Chicago Avenue and you will see examples of his later style. The entrance here is indicated by a flat overhanging roof left open above the sidewalk with grills and other open

1. Frank Lloyd Wright Home and Studio

areas to define this as the entrance. The overhang is flanked on either side by steps defined by flat-topped urns; these clearly and decisively mark the entrance. Beyond it, on the north side, is an octagonal space with brick and a shingle top which contained a pleasant room looking out over the garden to the west. On the opposite side is a tall cubic structure with an octagonal top in shingles; this was the drafting room. Especially nice is the large central window facing to the north, flanked on either side by terra-cotta sculpture with figures supporting a foliated abacus which sustains the flat-fasciad roof line. Notice on this side of the building the variety of materials including shingles, terra-cotta, limestone, brick, wood, and cast concrete each (according to Wright's philosophy) used in the inherent nature of that material itself, but disciplined by the geometric rigor that underlay the Prairie School principles.

The building, which is a National Historic Landmark, is in the process of being renovated. The interior includes furniture and artifacts by and of Wright. There is an hour-long tour and a very well stocked bookstore concentrating on architecture. Call 848–1978 for tour information. Adults: $3.00; seniors and children: $1.50.

Walk east on Chicago Avenue 1 long block. Turn right (south) on Kenilworth Avenue. The second house on your left is

2. 432 KENILWORTH AVENUE—1909

Built in 1909 and designed by Tallmadge and Watson, this simple cubic block is developed in the Prairie style with a broad, low, truncated, hipped roof and stucco soffits for the eaves. The entrance is a two-story motif with its own low gable and battered walls attached in the center of the building. The small sidelights immediately next to the door and containing Prairie glass are complemented by larger ones beyond them which extend into the second story, just as the door is suggested in the upper story by a broad window. Flanking that motif on each story is a single Chicago window with narrow sidelights and a broad central window. The simple boards set against the rough-faced stucco provide an appropriate simplicity for this Prairie-derived design.

Walk south on Kenilworth Avenue. The second house on your left is

3. 420 KENILWORTH AVENUE—c.1880

This building from about 1880 is also a simple cube but very different in design, topped by a very steeply pointed hipped roof. It has a gabled dormer set in the front with half-timbering at the top and a wavy pattern of shingles in its gable. Below the eaves over small brackets is a high frieze with a patterned shingle course and, between it and the porch roof, two pairs of double-hung windows. The porch stretches across the entire front with a pedimented entrance slightly to the north of center with delightful applied spindle work marking the entrance. In the south section within the porch is a broad, slightly polygonal bay window protruding from the cubic block on the front. Another is found on the south side toward the rear rising two stories to a gabled roof answered on the north side by a flat-fronted projection.

Across the street is

4.   423 KENILWORTH AVENUE—c. 1903

This cubic block is again very different in design. From about 1903, it shows the workings of the Classical Revival style very individually interpreted within a broad compositional framework that suggests the remnants of the Queen Anne. The block is extended into a long rectangular plan and topped by a flared, pitched roof facing the street. In its center is a steep gabled element with a broad Palladian window extended with a pair of flat-topped windows on each side, and faced across the bottom with a parapet. Beyond it, on the second story within the eave overhang, is a polygonal bay projecting from the clapboard covering. The composition is tied together by the columnar porch stretching across the entire front.

Continue south. The next house on your right is

5.   417 KENILWORTH AVENUE—1894

This building from 1894 was designed by E. E. Roberts. It is a delightful combination of motifs. Quite striking are the very steeply pitched roofs in a cross-gabled pattern. The roof planes are broken only above the entrance and on the south side of the front projection by steeply pitched gabled dormers. The front facing gable has a group of three windows within a single hooded lintel. The gable rafters terminate in foliated ends meeting the cornice supported by paired consoles. The corners of the wings are marked by pilasters rising to small Ionic capitals. Across the entire front and extending down the wing on the north side to the entrance is a broad porch with a low

5. 417 Kenilworth Avenue

foliated pediment marking the entrance. The pairs of Ionic columns supporting it stand on high pedestals and are connected by shouldered balustrades with tightly ranked, thin spindles. The steep pitches and some of the
details in this building will be found in modified forms in some of the buildings from this period designed by Prairie School architects.

Continue south. The next house on your right is

6.   407 KENILWORTH AVENUE—1894

This design is also by E. E. Roberts and is from the same year as Oak Park
#5. It shows a variation on the motifs of the other building with the steeply
pitched roofs and combination of windows in the front facing gable, but
here are five windows under a pediment topped by a keystone and a broader
flare for the gable cornice. Consoles here are grouped rather than paired and
the entire design has a greater asymmetry below the roof line. A broad bow
window swells out in the north section in a projecting field while on the
south corner is a polygonal projecting bay. The entire front is crossed by a
porch which sweeps through a broad circular arc at the south end before
rejoining the building. The porch has been modified but its original configuration is still clear.

*Cross to the east side of the street and continue south. The first house on
your left is*

7.   400 KENILWORTH AVENUE—c. 1872 and early 1900s

This is an older structure from about 1872 with modifications from the early
1900s by E. E. Roberts, but its original Italianate character survives. Originally it was a T-shaped structure, the entrance tucked into one side and three
windows on each floor of the front stem. These windows have segmental
heads, broad but simple window surrounds with feet and shoulders, and an
incised keystone motif attached in the center of the cornice. The ground
floor windows lack this device; they were perhaps removed when Roberts
built the porch. Its pairs of columns with a simple combined capital and
pairs of low gouged modillions complement the original design. So, too,
does the new entrance vestibule which is tucked in the reentrant angle on the
north. It has a fully rounded head over the door to repeat, with the second
story window, the design found in the attic of the original building.

Continue south. The next house on your left is

8. 344 KENILWORTH AVENUE—c.1880

This structure from the 1880s shows the broken forms that will become characteristic of the full-blooded Queen Anne. Here the steeply pitched roofs, including those on the gables and on the polygonal projection on the south side of the front facade, provide marked verticalities suggestive of the retention of the Gothic Revival. Across the entire front is a porch extended to the south and projecting forward for a large veranda and, on the north, marked by a decorated pediment. The pairs of thin columns also display the combined capital which is a relatively rare motif and, strangely, is found here on two buildings side by side. This one perhaps suggested its use on its neighbor to the north.

Continue south. The second house on your left is

9. 334 KENILWORTH AVENUE—1897

This 1897 building designed by Frank Lloyd Wright again shows the highly stylized Tudor growing from the Queen Anne. It has a steeply pitched gable on the front wing backed against the steeply pitched roof of the main block. The gable has thin half-timbering and a pointed-headed attic window with diamond paned glass. The second story has incised strapwork on its corner pilasters which support the broad gable beam. Below it is a group of three diamond paned casement windows. Across the entire front and stretching down the north side to the entrance is a timbered porch which on the north side is cantilevered in a half-circular extension to act as a porte-cochere. That half-circular extension is answered on the south by a half-circular termination to the porch extended beyond the south face. It is glazed to serve as a sunporch.

Across the street is

10. 317 KENILWORTH AVENUE—1893 (possibly 1885)

This Queen Anne building probably from 1893 and almost certainly by E. E. Roberts shows some of the taming of that style attributable to the Colonial Revival. The central block rises to a flared hipped roof covered in slates and extends back to a cross hipped roof for the western block of the building. In the front hip is a large dormer with a shingled field and rounded corners extending into the mass to provide a balcony. It is fronted by a pair of columns. The second story has a projecting bay on the south face, its balcony cut from the porch roof. The porch roof extends across the entire face and to the north to provide a porte-cochere and to the south to extend the veranda. Its clusters of stout columns stand on podia formed from the irregular rough-faced ashlar that provides the foundation and turns forward for the porch podia. Tightly spaced simple spindles on the second story balcony and on the porch provide a simple rhythmic pattern to augment the stark grandeur of the design.

Continue south. The second house on your right is

11.   309 KENILWORTH AVENUE—c.1887

This Queen Anne building from about 1887 is set beneath a broad and very high pitched roof. Its pitch faces the street and is intersected on the north side by a large gable which on its south side has a half gable attached to it above the flat-fronted projection in the center of the front facade. That projection is acknowledged by an extension of the roof, of the full width porch, and by a flat-fronted projection on the ground floor containing the entrance. The entrance is marked by a pediment with foliate and bossed decoration and supported by long punctured consoles rising from the porch posts. From the south can be seen the elaborateness of the face that originally looked over the side street. A pair of broad projecting bays, lacking a window on the extreme south face, projects within the confines of the overhanging gable roof. Below its upper half is another projecting bay. Broad consoles, like those on the front but simpler, support these projections. Between the lintels of the ground floor and the sills of the second floor is a flared shingle field with a circular pattern different from the wave pattern found in the gable. It in turn sets off, with its texture and pattern, the quite different texture and pattern of the tightly ranked clapboards.

Continue south. The second house on your right is

12.   245 KENILWORTH AVENUE—c.1890

This blocky Queen Anne house from about 1890 by Patten and Fisher is interesting for the departures it makes from the block. The hipped roof is extended to the south as a gable and has a small projecting bay at its corner kept under its flared eaves. On the north side, turning the corner at what originally was a street intersection, is a broad two-story polygonal bay extending beyond the face of the building and topped by a polygonal bell roof with shouldered half-circular dormers in each face. The front of the hipped roof of the main block is covered by a steep, fishscale shingled gable marking the entrance, which is indicated on the porch by a foliated pediment.

Across the street is

13. 312 KENILWORTH AVENUE—1868 and 1905

This simple, geometrically precise, Colonial Revival structure started in 1868 as a farmhouse. Its present appearance came after its move in 1905 and when it was remodeled by E. E. Roberts. It provides a marked contrast to the other buildings on the street. Its corners are defined by Ionic capitals. The five openings on each of the two floors are simple, the ones on the ground floor with slightly more elaborate lintels. The central opening is the doorway. It is sheltered by a pedimented porch carried by columns, the front ones of which have lost their Ionic capitals. Contrasting with the five openings on the facade are the three dormers in the front pitched roof, each flanked by pilasters and with a shell motif in the circular head above the window and rising into the broken pediment field. Notice the entablature here, a distinct type with the architrave level obscured now by having been painted the same color as the clapboard siding below. It has a swelling frieze level and a simplified cornice level.

Continue south. The next house on your left is

14. 308 KENILWORTH AVENUE—c. 1868

This building from about 1868 was originally a farmhouse and was moved to this location. It is a good example of a style rare in the six-county area, the Stick style. The simple, T-shaped plan has a low pitched roof facing the street with the elaborate board decoration characteristic of that style. The top section projects and is carried on consoles. Notice the bosses in its barge-boards and its sculpted gable rafters. The zone immediately below has diagonal siding intersected by boards, the ones in the center describing a tree branch motif. Below it, acting as a broad frieze at the eave line, is a series of fields with alternating types of shingle patterns; below those with the truncated saw-tooth pattern are windows; below those with the keystone pattern are clapboards. These zones are separated again by boards intersecting the siding. Across the entire front and extending down the south side is a deep porch carried by clusters of Tuscan columns standing on a rough-faced random ashlar foundation.

Continue south. The next house on your left, on the NE corner of Kenilworth Avenue and Erie Street, is

15. 300 KENILWORTH AVENUE—c.1890

This Queen Anne building from about 1890 is very interesting for the variety of materials used. The clapboards on the first and second floors contrast with the shingles in the low pitched roof gable facing the front. The gable is complemented by the small polygonal projection with its steeply pitched roof on the north side. Across the entire front and extending well toward the street on the south side is a broad porch with Cyclopean masonry as its base and extending well upward to act as bases for the porch roof supports. These are brick piers extending outward beyond the somewhat low columns supporting the lintels. A broad, low pediment with foliate decoration centered in a scallop shell marks the entrance.

Walk east on Erie Street 2 blocks. Turn left (north) on Oak Park Avenue. Past the apartment building, the first house on your right is

16. 308 OAK PARK AVENUE—c.1870

This is a fine Italianate design from the 1870s, symmetrical in configuration, with a great simplicity and clarity in its form. The front has three windows on the upper floor and two on the lower. Its entrance has larger forms on the second story than on the ground story although of the same type. The shallow surrounds have feet and the large lintels above are carried by corbels. The building is topped by a high paneled cornice with pairs of angle-cut brackets. Notice, on the south side, the extension of the building; its long projection has a distinct central emphasis by having larger windows between the pairs of windows on each floor. On the ground floor the larger windows break forward slightly in a flat-fronted bay while above is a pair of windows under a single entablature which rises into a pediment and is the largest window covering on the building. The porch is a turn-of-the-century addition but it is quite sympathetic to the original design.

Continue north. The second house on your right is

17. 316 OAK PARK AVENUE—c.1900 (possibly c.1870)

This simple cubic block has its corners defined by flat-faced pilasters rising through both stories to a simple cornice. It is topped by a flared hipped roof with the simplicity yet heaviness characteristic of one of the region's turn-of-the-century interpretations of the Colonial Revival. Designed about 1900, it perhaps has an older building acting as an armature for what one now sees. The building has a gabled dormer in the front with the suggestion of a Palladian motif obtained by covering the central two windows of the group of four with a segmental pediment with a high pediment with a high keystone set within the broken pediment of the gable. Below it, a pair of bays lined by broad pilasters opens onto a circular balcony in the porch, originally probably with a balustrade. Crossing the entire front is a simple porch with Ionic capitals that are very low.

Cross to the west side of the street and continue north. The second house on your left is

18.   339 OAK PARK AVENUE—1887
This Queen Anne house was the birthplace of Ernest Hemingway.

Walk east on Superior Street 1 block. On the NW corner of Superior Street and Euclid Avenue is

19.   405 N. EUCLID AVENUE
Unity Church of the Daily Word—1912
Originally a residence and designed in 1912 by George Washington Maher, one of the most original and independent spirits within the Prairie School, this masonry block is an excellent example of his style. The broad horizontality is reinforced by the simple limestone mudsill and by the broad hipped roof with its unbroken cornice below its soffits. The central block is recessed slightly on each end where groups of windows including those on the first and second floors are set back slightly within the brick block. On each side of the main block on each floor is a pair of Chicago windows with delicate Prairie School leaded glass in the smaller sidelights. That motif is repeated in the group of six windows in the second story, in the center, separated by very simple wooden piers. The central entrance has a broad segmental arch extended on each side and then set back. Within the arch is a doorway with the same configuration and surrounded by sidelights and top lights. The simple, uncovered porch is marked on each corner by broad urns with a simple geometric pattern in their upper lip. Projecting on the north end and set well back beyond the face of the building is a recent addition, sympathet-

ically subdued relative to the strength of the simple original block. The building is now in adaptive reuse as a church.

On the SW corner of Superior Street and Euclid Avenue is

20. 333 N. EUCLID AVENUE—1898

This simple design from 1898 by Pond and Pond forms an interesting comparison with a similar building by the same architects (Evanston #23). It has a brick ground floor rising to the level of the second floor sills where the upper section is shingled. The corners and various bay divisions there are marked by broad, gouged boards. The pitched roofs do not overhang but are terminated by very simple molded fascia. In the front roof is a pair of dormers with half-circular roofs and shingled tympana, a motif echoed and expanded for the projecting entrance porch where a half-circular hood is set between a thin flat roof on each side and carried by a pair of simple square piers. Next to it is a polygonal projecting bay with half-timbering of board and brick extending into the second story. On the facade facing the side street is a polygonal bay descending from the second story in shingles and reaching only halfway down the ground floor wall. It has round-headed windows on each face on the ground floor but small double-hung windows on the second story. The second story roof is a balcony for the attic space which is marked by the gable of a small projecting wing beyond which is another dormer like the one in the front.

Walk south on Euclid Avenue. On the SW corner of Euclid Avenue and Erie Street is

21. 231 EUCLID AVENUE—1907

Designed in 1907 by Robert Spencer, Jr., this brick building shows a subdued masonry design brought alive by fine proportion and detailing. The design begins at the sidewalk with the low brick wall rising to large podia caps at the walkway. The broad walkway has a planter box in its center. Next comes a broad porch with two very low steps and its extremities marked by low, square planting urns. The entrance is marked by a slight forward projection topped by a broad limestone sill, the squares at either end embedded in the wall marked by a geometric pattern. A more elaborate version of that pattern is in the limestone frame and lintel of the door. Notice the Prairie glass in the entrance door, where similar geometric motifs are worked out, and related ones in the other windows. The entrance is set eccentrically in a hipped roof projection on the front face. It has four casement windows directly above and three tall, thin casement windows lighting the stairhall on the north side of that projection. At the level of the larger casement windows, paired on the extremes of the second story, is a simple limestone stringcourse which is answered at the top of the wall by the simple cornice extending out to the eave soffits of the broad hipped roof. Extending along the side street on the north beyond the main block is a low one-story service wing set at the sidewalk.

Continue south. The next house on your right is

22.   223 N. Euclid Avenue—1897

Designed in 1897 by Frank Lloyd Wright, this curious design makes very interesting use of brick and contains a quite idiosyncratic interpretation of Tudor forms. The main block of the building is covered by a low hipped roof. It has projections erupting at its front, at each corner; these are covered by low flared conical roofs. The geometric plan of the projections is fitted within the extension of those flares on the north and south faces of those projections. The windows extend from the low sill all the way to the flares, but on the inner diagonals of those projections the windows are confined to the second story. These windows and the ones on the second story in the center of the house are framed by timbers set at an angle with bulbous capitals. The porch, extending to the front with its broad low hipped roof, provides a marked contrast to the exuberance of the forms behind. The building contains an octagonal living room which cannot be deduced from the configuration of the exterior.

Continue south. On the SW corner of Euclid Avenue and Ontario Street is

23.   175 N. Euclid Avenue—1886

This large building was built in 1886. It faces the street with a porch across the entire front and has a high, stone, rough-faced basement rising to the porch parapet and slightly higher for the pairs of square tapered piers holding the lintel. The ground floor has a swelling bay at one corner and a projecting entrance. The second story has variations in its shingle pattern and is topped by a vertical board cornice. A tower has probably been lost from the southeast, square, projecting corner. The middle of the hipped roof has a large dormer. East of the polygonal projection on the side facade's ground floor, which is flared on its flat-fronted base and rises to a split gable, is a series of three tall windows rising to mark the location of the stairhall within. Notice above it the quadrant motif with low relief wooden patterns within it. Along the side street sidewalk is a fine cast iron fence with forms predating the design of the building, carrying as it does the various "U.S. Grant" style motifs.

Walk west on Ontario Street. On the SE corner of Ontario Street and Oak Park Avenue is

24. OAK PARK CLUB
721 Ontario Street—1923

This 1923 building designed by Holmes and Flynn presents a quite personal and individualistic interpretation of the formal grandeur associated with private clubs and the variety of motifs often used in the suburbs for classical architecture when applied to domestic designs. The high, long, two-story block, topped with a hipped roof in Spanish tile, is utterly simple. Flanking the entrance on each side are large windows paired within their arched or linteled openings. In the center of the second story a group of three windows with additional arches set above them call attention to the projecting porch below. The porch has a truncated hipped roof carried by a free interpretation of classical architecture. The freedom of interpretation visible there is found also in the brick work and in the limestone trim. Along Oak Park Avenue the building presents a long facade with pavilions connected by a loggia with abstracted Palladian windows on the second story and an extended Chicago window motif on the ground floor.

Backtrack east on Ontario Street 2 blocks. On the SW corner of Ontario Street and Linden Avenue is

25. 175–181 LINDEN AVENUE and
643–645 ONTARIO STREET
Linden Apartments—1914–1916

This is a rare and quite fine example of a large three-story apartment building in the Prairie style, rare because those who built apartment buildings believed that conservative designs such as those in the Tudor or the classical styles would more easily attract and hold tenants. There was apparently a suspicion that the Prairie style represented progressive trends that might not be popular and acceptable to a broad market.

The design is by John S. Van Bergen, and it contains many of the elements in the standard three-story apartment building types done in conservative styles, for example, the solaria or projecting sunporches that opened up the interior space to the outside and the collection of the apartment entrances into a series of vestibules rather than into a single entrance for the entire building. The Prairie School design can be seen in the simplicity of the forms, the lack of historical references in the decoration, in the decorative effect that comes from the disciplined handling of the materials, and from the overall horizontality of the design. Note that the roof of the main block and of the solaria project beyond the face to provide extensive lids for the brick below. The simple limestone lintels and sills are extended across the wall to reinforce the horizontality, a quality also stressed by the projecting and recessing courses of brick in the top floor. Contrasting with those horizontalities are the verticalities at the corner entrance set into the reentrant angle. The walls paralleling the side street project into this area to provide a semblance of a pylon. Next to it are the broad flanks of chimneys and, at the 45° splay of the inner corner where the entrance is located, is a group of three tall vertical windows on each floor set between projecting piers. The glass here represents the geometric design of the Prairie style and was probably originally found in windows elsewhere in the building. The present windows are metal replacements of the originals. They deprive the design of the rhythm given by the original casements and whatever subdivisions of the panes which they held.

Walk south on Linden Avenue 1 block. On the south side of Lake Street, at Linden Avenue, is

26. FRANCISCO TERRACE APARTMENTS—1895 and 1978
This building represents a last resort in the preservation of landmarks. The original building on which this design is based was built in 1895, in Chicago, by Frank Lloyd Wright. It was an attempt by the prominent Chicagoan James B. Waller to provide dwelling units in which the poor could find a start in life. He expected only a minimal return on his investment rather than the massive profits often available in apartment construction at that time. The building was extremely successful in providing small clean apartments for working class couples. While living in it they could, and did, save money

26. Francisco Terrace Apartments

in the first few years of their marriages and then move on to a better home. The building was threatened with destruction despite the fact that it was an internationally known architectural monument to Frank Lloyd Wright's early design ability and to Waller's notions about how to help the working class. When the building was destroyed, several pieces were salvaged, and finally an opportunity was found to use them. They appear here in a reproduction, by Harry Weese and Associates in 1978, of the original design with the apartment units modified to meet the higher standards of today's society.

The building presents a broad face to the street with entrances to apartments at each side and a broad arch in the center opening to an interior court. Above each side apartment's entrance, on the second story, is a window from Wright's building. It has a column between two skinny windows set on a high base of terra-cotta elaborately worked with low foliate and geometric design. A richer treatment of that same design motif is found in the spandrels of the central arch, also from Wright's building. It is delicately worked with nicely scaled moldings of foliate and geometric design and has the name of the apartment building set into the terra-cotta voussoirs. The arch leads to the interior court which has a number of apartments opening onto it. At the base of the court are corner projections marking the stair towers, covered by hipped roofs supported by a superelevation flanked by terra-cotta pilasters, also original pieces. They rise from a motif that shows a richly worked geometric pattern vaguely based on Tudor forms, also original.

Walk west on Lake Street. The highrise on your left, past Euclid Avenue, is

27. 715 LAKE STREET
Medical Arts Building—1929

Designed in 1929 by Roy Hotchkiss, this building represents the incursion into the suburbs of the skyscraper building types commonly associated with the dense downtown cores of metropolitan areas. Although only eight stories high with an additional two stories in a central tower, it would be a relatively low building in Chicago's loop but here it is a tower. Its street facade presents a dramatic example of the Set-Back-Style with Art Deco ornament in the spandrels and with various zig-zag and abstracted spiral and wave motifs suggesting energy, industry, and velocity. The verticality in the composition is formed by the towers and by the continuous vertical rise of the thin sections between the windows and the thicker ones at the corners. The two-story entrance recess is set forward slightly and flanked on each side by angled, streamlined light fixtures. The materials along the ground floor are shiny and hard as if made by machines to reinforce the overall character of the seemingly machine made, modern design.

Continue west. On the SW corner of Lake Street and Oak Park Avenue is

28. 317 N. OAK PARK AVENUE
Scoville Square—1908

This is a fine example of the merging of the Prairie style with the Classical Revival style in a building type that seldom received Prairie style designs, a commercial structure in a downtown area. Designed by E.E. Roberts in 1908, it faces east on Oak Park Avenue then extends for an entire half block with a unified composition that provides a striking contrast to the older buildings in the next half block to the south. The central section is set back and raised into a four-story block, covered by a hipped roof. To the sides of that entrance stretch three-story blocks also covered by hipped roofs. The upper stories originally had both professional offices and apartments while the ground floor contained commercial spaces. The blocks are articulated by clusters of pilasters at the corners stretching from the strong string-courses above the ground floor up to the copper eave soffits. The ends of the long bays are marked by a single pilaster set against a pier to form a triplet of windows with seven windows between each end pavilion. The third story windows are fully rounded. They spring from limestone blocks which cap the slightly projecting pier between the windows. The second story windows are double-hung windows with six lights in the upper sash and a single one in the lower. These form essential parts of the proportional rhythm with the semicircles contrasted with the flat-topped windows and with the rhythmic sequence of piers pierced by the greater projection and greater upward extension of the pilasters, themselves rhythmically disposed. The central block accentuates that rhythm by moving the round-headed windows to the fourth floor and replacing those on the third floor with flat-topped windows. Additional rhythmic interest comes from grouping the windows into pairs with each pair covered by an arch set out from the wall and springing from piers with a projection similar to that of the pilasters. The building, long a familiar landmark in Oak Park, is currently being restored to its original condition. Its local architect was associated with the Prairie School. His design bears comparison to Drummond's bank building in River Forest and to Elmslie's commercial structures in Aurora (River Forest #18 and Aurora #17 and #13).

Continue west 1 block. On the SE corner of Lake Street and Kenilworth Avenue is

29. UNITY TEMPLE
Unitarian Universalist Church
875 Lake Street—1906

This 1906 building by Frank Lloyd Wright is the first example of his style done for a major building other than a residence. He received the commission through his family's connections with the congregation that built it, and he was allowed to design what, at the time, was a very bizarre building only because of the generally liberal outlook of that religious group. It contains no references anywhere to any traditional forms or symbols associated with religion. Instead it is a purely abstract design that grows out of the requirements of the congregation and the materials from which it was built as they were subjected to the geometric planer discipline characteristic of his outlook on architecture at that time.

The material is poured concrete, one of the first uses of that material in an important building constructed in this country. The surface has recently been restored to its original appearance; its texture emphasizes the planer qualities of the design. The congregation required a sanctuary and a parish or assembly hall. The sanctuary is set next to Lake Street and takes the form of a cube with each face projected outward and a tall cubic block set in each reentrant angle. The projections between those blocks rise higher and are extended outward by flat roofs supported by square piers with an abstracted geometric design descending from their abstract geometric capitals. The fascia of that projection with its let-in panel provides a firm horizontality. This visual quality is reinforced by the coping of the inner central cube, by the coping above the cubic blocks, and by the two-step mudsill. To the south of the main block is the lower parish house. It too is cubic, but it is longer in its east-west direction and has smaller, lower projections at each end. It is connected to the main block by a low flat-roofed connecting area which also serves as the entrance to the complex. That entrance is clearly identified by the abstracted cubic shapes piled up to form a termination to the podium of the wall separating the entrance area from the sidewalk. The interior of the

29. Unity Temple
875 Lake Street

structure continues the character of the exterior. It has been carefully restored to reproduce the original Frank Lloyd Wright design. The main sanctuary is lit with light flooding down from a skylight. It is ornamented with abstract geometric squares and rectangles made from carefully contrived moldings, some of which incorporate electrical light fixtures in an early example of the integration of electric lighting with decorative schemes. The building is a National Historic Landmark. Tours: Saturdays and Sundays: 2:00 P.M.

Walk south on Kenilworth Avenue. The first structure past the post office, on your right, is

30.   115–121 N. KENILWORTH AVENUE—c.1885–1890

This group of four row houses was built between 1885 and 1890. It illustrates the variety of Queen Anne designs that gave class and character to this type of residential construction. Each has a porch (the southernmost one is mostly gone) each of which is different, just as the materials and the designs of each is different. From the north, there is one with a polygonal bay and step gable; next is one with a swelled bay and a projecting pedimental gable; next is a flat-fronted one opening to a broad semicircular arch, a segmental arch above, and a semicircular pointed gable above; and the final one has a polygonal bay projecting to a pyramidal roof.

Continue south, under the railroad tracks. Turn right (west) on South Boulevard. The third house on your left is

31.   915 SOUTH BOULEVARD—c.1870

This clapboard-clad cube, topped by a low hipped roof, is a simple Italianate building from the 1870s with delicately thin forms in its detailing. The only break in the cubic shape is in the low service wing extending to the back and the flat-fronted projection on the west side. The front windows, three on the second story, two on the lower one, as well as those on the front of the side projection have thin cornices held by tiny brackets that echo the diminutive brackets in the eaves. The transomed doorway is the typical Italianate double-valve door, and the porch protecting it crosses the entire front. Its square, thin, paneled posts support the largest brackets in the design as well as broadly shouldered struts with pendant keystones in the form of arrowheads, a delightful abstraction of a structural motif converted into a wooden decorative form.

Continue west on South Boulevard to Home Avenue. Turn left (south). On your left is

32.   100–110 S. Home Avenue—1880s

Built in the middle of the 1880s, this group of row houses represents the Romanesque interpretation (as Oak Park #30 represented the Queen Anne interpretation) of this building type. Here the only original porches are on the southern four units. Again, there is a contrast of materials with brick, stone of two colors, and stone and brick combined, and a variety of roofs breaking the silhouette. The brick structures originally had cornices, as on the southernmost unit, which would have provided the proper completion for the design.

Continue south. The next building on your left is

33.   112 and 114 S. Home Avenue—1880s

This Romanesque Revival building, originally a six-flat, is representative of a Chicago rather than of a suburban building type. Built in the 1880s, it has a stone foundation (slightly battered) and three broad arches across the front, the outer ones supported by very short columns, the middle one supported by longer columns to mark the entrance. The arches are built by many layers of thin brick acting as voussoirs. Each corner is polygonal allowing the central section to be set back behind a balcony across the first floor. The polygonal corners rise to flared pyramidal roofs, and a broad flared pitched roof connects them. The building is representative of the first style of apartment buildings built in Chicago beginning in 1881 and 1882, during what was called the "flat-craze." Chicagoans had refused to live in apartments before that, but under the increased pressure of higher land costs, greater distance to unbuilt land, and rapidly increasing population, flat buildings suddenly became popular. Thousands were built in a few years' time, virtually transforming the appearance of Chicago. This flat building is a far-distant pioneer into the suburbs and was not followed by later settlers.

Continue south. On the SW corner of Home Avenue and Pleasant Street is

34.   217 Home Avenue
Farson-Mills House—1897

Built in 1897 to the design of George Washington Maher, this large home

34. Farson-Mills House
217 Home Avenue

occupies very expansive grounds and stands at the end of a street which provides an axial direction that leads ultimately to the entrance of the building. The grounds are surrounded by an especially noteworthy fence, designed by Maher, with large corner posts containing the name Pleasant Home in raised plaques set within half-circular hoods. The fence is an excellent example of Maher's design. Tall panels topped and bottomed with triangles are attached to the stiles by spheres which rise to spherical tops. At both top and bottom is a pair of rails. On the axis of Pleasant Street the fence is set back to contain the steps leading to the entrance. That setback is marked by broad, flanged urns with a repetition at the base and around the lip of motifs found in the fence.

The house itself is a broad block crossed by a low porch across the entire front sustained by only four piers. Here the hood motif found in the porch posts is repeated but the medallion within it is a highly abstract geometric foliate design characteristic of those who were impressed by the designs of Louis Sullivan. The second story has only three windows, each very large and each framed with broad limestone frames set into the tawny-colored brick. Immediately above those frames is the broad horizontal cornice which is extended outward in a thin lip before continuing upward to form the parapet for the broad hipped roof. The block is framed at each end by great slab-like chimneys. The middle of the hipped roof carries a dormer, also with a hipped roof, with three elaborate stained glass windows set well into its reveal. At the front of the reveal is a pair of thin columns with flat-topped capitals. The reveal is framed by a geometric device which itself is framed by lions' heads atop the pilasters. The entrance, set within the porch, has three arched openings; two of them have stained glass windows with limestone sills; the middle one has a broad arched doorway. The openings are separated from one another by columns. The porch extends on the south side to a half-circular extension arched and glazed to serve as a sunporch which looks across the extensive landscaped grounds with their beautiful mature trees. On the opposite side, projecting from the middle of the mass, is a porte-cochere with a thick flat roof carried by stout piers. Above it is a group of three windows, and above that group is a circular window with a panel between it and the broad flat limestone frame that surrounds the triplet of windows. The mudsill around the entire block rises through a cove to form the porch parapet which established the mudsill's level around the building. That limestone base is answered at the top by the limestone head on the chimney.

Inside may be seen the extensive scheme of superior quality stained glass. Also visible are the furniture and fixtures Maher designed. Note the interesting tiles on the floor of the east porch and of the entrance hall. The house is on the National Register of Historic Places.

The building also houses the Historical Society of Oak Park and River Forest. Hemingway and Wright displays are featured along with antique toys and furniture. Fridays and Sundays: 2:00 P.M.-4:00 P.M. Free.

Backtrack north on Home Avenue, under the train tracks, continuing north on Forest Avenue, through the mall. Then, turn left on Forest Avenue and continue north. The first building on your right, past Ontario Street, is

35. 200–206 N. FOREST AVENUE—1880s

This group of four row houses from the late 1880s is designed as a single unit but individual identity is given each by the porches. These have been re-worked, but the original pediments on three of them, with their foliate deco-ration, survive. Note that the overall design emphasizes rounded corners rising above the hipped roof of the main mass and is emphasized in the center by a gabled element with two round-cornered bays projecting below it. In the roof, a pair of dormers stands on either side with the same foliate motif as the one found in the porch pediments but set within a steeper roof pitch. These bear an interesting comparison to the previous sets of row houses encountered (Oak Park #32 and #33).

Continue north. The next house on your right is

36. 210 FOREST AVENUE—1901

This 1901 house is one of the earliest designs by Frank Lloyd Wright to contain some of the motifs found in his fully developed Prairie style houses from just a few years later. It begins as a simple, two-story block with a hipped roof. A sequence of Chicago windows has been tucked under the roof soffits and contained within a zone defined by horizontal boards set into the stucco surface. That basic pattern is then expanded with the tre-mendous horizontality associated with the Prairie style. The projection to the west (toward the park) has complex corners which feature freestanding piers. The sills of its casement windows are combined into a stringcourse which becomes the coping for the porch extending to the north across the entire front of the house and beyond the main block to an open porch at the north end. Its eave line is extended across the main block to connect with the eave line of the western projection, thereby reinforcing the horizontality of the main block. Again the decorative posts support the fragment of the roof extending across the main block. The ornament worked into the design is extremely simple with bead moldings running into larger ornaments made from larger spheres. The entrance to the house reinforces the horizontality of the main block by being extended out to the sidewalk with stucco parapets topped by boards. These lead back to a low arch that opens under the terrace. It is the only form breaking that long horizontal stucco plane. Especially notable is the design of the glass in the casement windows which extends the motif of the posts into brilliant displays of geometry and color. An extention to the rear, not visible from the street, was designed by Tallmadge and Watson. The house is listed on the National Register of Historic Places.

Across the street, on the NW corner of Forest Avenue and Ontario Street is

37.   203 N. FOREST AVENUE—c.1880

This frame structure from about 1880 makes fine use of its corner site by extending a gable to both streets. The larger gable faces east and marks the entrance. It has an extended upper section, carried by long volutes crossing the shingle field, covered with a variety of shingles. The second story is an interesting version of the Stick style with a coved cornice springing from a lower level where blocks with incised bosses mark the intersection of the boards that frame the openings and line the corners. The splayed corners have long, gouged struts ending in pendants to carry the load above. Across the fronts and facing both streets is a veranda with turned posts and with bosses on the upper, unturned sections. The corner is splayed at 45° and has a small pediment with a textured shingle field. Notice the fence that survives along the Forest Avenue sidewalk. It has cast iron gate posts with "U.S. Grant" forms and intersecting loops put through the rails to provide an economical but attractive fence.

Continue north. The next house on your left is

38.   209 FOREST AVENUE—c.1895

This fine Queen Anne building has a limestone base and a brick ground floor with limestone lintels. The upper part is shingled. The north corner of the front is a three-story round bay rising into a conical roof. Next to it is a broad gable, flared at the base and containing a balcony and a bowed window. From the round corner across the entire front and turning down the side is a porch carried by highly tapered posts carrying a broad, flat lintel decorated at the top with a frieze made of small roundels.

Continue north. The second house on your left is

39. 219 FOREST AVENUE—1865

The oldest house on the block, this simple Italianate building from 1865 has a broad front projection which, on the ground floor, extends into a polygonal bay. The cornice has single brackets set into the paneling. The windows are topped by simple lintels. The porch across the ground floor is later. It is characteristic of porches from just after the turn of the century with its fine Roman Doric columns probably ordered from a catalogue.

Across the street, on the east side, is

40. 238 FOREST AVENUE—1906

Designed by Frank Lloyd Wright in 1906, this is one of the finer, very formal Prairie School designs. The main block has a gable roof intersecting in the center of each face while each corner is covered by a flat section. The motif of the west facade is repeated, in slightly simplified form, twice along the north side. That motif has brick rising to the level of the second story sills where five casement windows are set within large timbering to span the entire distance of the gable. On either side of it and extending down to the level of the heads of the ground floor windows are stucco panels framed with boards. The center of the brick motif carries a long lintel with a Chicago-type window beneath it. To either side extend planters also capped by concrete copings, an example of the integration of concrete into the formal vocabulary of the Prairie School. Well back on the south side of the building is a one-story open porch carried by brick piers extended outward as planters to allow the building to grasp the landscape.

Cross to the west side of the street and continue north. On the SW corner of Forest Avenue and Erie Street is

41. 231 FOREST AVENUE—c.1870

This simple, L-shaped, Gothic cottage from about 1870 has a projecting bay window on the ground floor and a pair of windows under a simple lintel on the second story. The scroll-cut bargeboard is quite simple, being quite small in scale. The porch on the reentrant angle is probably a later addition from the turn of the century, but it works well with the overall design.

Walk east on Elizabeth Court. The third house on your right is

42. 6 ELIZABETH COURT—1909

Designed in 1909 by Frank Lloyd Wright, this frame and stucco building becomes an almost completely abstract composition of horizontal planes and cubic spaces. The basic cubic block, covered by a flat roof with simple fascia, is extended out on the first and second stories by broad, flat, balcony fronts beyond which are strips of casement windows. Extending on either side from the block are pylons topped by broad square urns. Beyond them similar projections extend out from the mass and are tied back into it by the obligatory chimney, which here is extended as an anchoring abstract plane. It has its stucco surface enlivened by setting thin strips of wood into it, strips only sparsely used elsewhere on the building. The house is listed on the National Register of Historic Places.

Across the street is

43. 5 ELIZABETH COURT—before 1875 (perhaps 1861)

This early brick building, perhaps the oldest brick building in Oak Park, was here in 1875 and perhaps as early as 1861. Its simple T-shaped design was modified in 1907 by the addition of the porch but the original design is still clear. It has a pair of tall, thin windows topped by segmental arches with their three brick courses projecting beyond one another, then topped in the attic by a bull's-eye window with a similar layering of brick, this time fully rounded. The eave and gable cornice has a cut-out pattern applied to produce a descending drapery pattern.

Backtrack west on Elizabeth Court to the corner. Turn right (north) on Forest Avenue. The third house on your left is

44. 313 FOREST AVENUE—c.1896 and 1906

Designed by Frank Lloyd Wright about 1896 and modified by him in 1906, this building suffered a disastrous fire in the mid-1970s during the course of restoration. Neighbors in the area helped to raise funds for its restoration following Frank Lloyd Wright's drawings.

The building is a basic cube topped by a hipped roof and extended on the south section of the east face by a projection which is reflected in the roof and further accentuated by the dormer. The broad angled fascia of the dormer roof is repeated by the main roof. The roof form as a whole is repeated for the entrance which projects at the south end of the east facade to form a porch, then extends down the north face to an entrance. This motif of an entrance projecting toward the street with the doorway set well back into the house is often encountered in Wright's designs. The central section of the front projection in the upper story has a group of projecting windows in timber framing while below, on the ground floor, the windows are set back beyond an enframement formed by stucco piers. Similar contrasts of timber, boards, and stucco are found throughout the design.

Across the street is

45.   308 FOREST AVENUE—1905
This broad building designed by W. Fifield has undersized detailing worked into its broad stucco walls to make the large block seem even larger than it actually is. Derived from the Tudor is the collecting of casement windows into groups standing above a broad stringcourse supported by small corbels. These are framed by board strips which are repeated where there are no windows. Also Tudor is the timber construction of the porch, but that style is so modified by abstraction that the building becomes a suitable companion for the Prairie style neighbors.

Continue north. The next house on your right is

46.   318 FOREST AVENUE—1902
When Frank Lloyd Wright designed this house in 1902 he introduced entirely new concepts in design. The basic block covered by a low hipped roof is familiar but the extension of it into the landscape is a first clear indication of what would become characteristic of Prairie School designs. The brick walls are slightly battered as they rise with strips of projecting brick to the sill level of the second story windows. These are casement windows set in continuous strips and with fine Prairie glass. They span between the clear brick pylons that mark the corners of the basic block. Similar pylons and windows mark

the slightly off-center projection from the front facade. North of that projection is a low arched entrance, fronted by an open porch that extends toward the street with a prow-like front wall. The simplicity, the lack of historical reference, the suggestion of abstract shapes and forms rather than of historical styles, and the coherence of the design brought great and early fame to this building.

Across the street, on the SW corner of Superior Street and Forest Avenue, is

47.   333 FOREST AVENUE—1895 and 1923

This house by Frank Lloyd Wright was first designed in 1895 and following a fire at Christmas in 1922 was redesigned. Those two moments caught Wright when he was in his most decorative phases, but the sources of his decoration had two different origins; the earlier was the Tudor popular at the time, the later the Aztec or Mayan with which he had become infatuated upon his return from Japan when he had a number of important commissions in Los Angeles. The result is that this house contains elaborate representations of both decorative styles which are so intertwined with one another that it is extremely difficult to separate them. The general character and configuration, with a long pitched roof covering the second and attic stories intersected on the south facade by two wings each with similar pitched roofs that extend only in the attic story, is clearly indebted to the Tudor style, but the very steep pitch comes from the 1923 rebuilding. The gable on the east is half-timbered and projected over a terra-cotta ground floor with clear, almost archeologically correct Gothic references with their pointed, cusped arches. The facade facing the large gardens on the west has a porch across the ground floor and a terrace on the second with large globular shapes used as balusters. The forms lining the windows, which stretch well into the gables, clearly represent the Aztec sources of the later period. The curious dormers set in the roof beyond the projecting gables contain a mixture of Queen Anne devices and the expected Queen Anne variety of materials, but again they are Aztec. The two great chimneys are treated as slabs with limestone cappings and elaborate terra-cotta ornament worked into each end.

In marked contrast to the exuberance of the garden facade is the relatively subdued character of the entrance facade facing north. Here a broad central gable, spanning the entire length of the roof, extends beyond the brick base to protect the entrance. It is also marked by light fixtures hanging from the edges of the projecting central section of the gable. The combination of brick and masonry forms defining the entrance lack historical precedents, but immediately to its east is a terra-cotta bay window like the Gothic one on the east facade. At the west end are servants' quarters beyond the garage where the stucco wall contains rather straightforward half-timbering.

In the roof at the second story level, placed close to each side of the great central gable, is a dormer of extremely original invention. Its flat front is crossed at its top and outer sides by a curb molding in terra cotta with excellent floriate ornamentation. Beyond it is an extension in plain brick. The middle of it however projects forward into elaborate carpentry to provide a thin, two-faced, polygonal bay intersected by a slat (itself intersected at right angles) of a highly ornamental but strictly geometric cut-out pattern. This is the formal version of a similar, informal elaboration found on the south facade facing the garden.

On the NW corner of Superior Street and Forest Avenue is

48. 403 FOREST AVENUE—1890s

This large Queen Anne house from the early 1890s shows the usual exuberance with its broken silhouette and projecting section, but it has a quite unusual veranda which stretches across the two street facades forming an angle at the corner to complement the angle of the polygonal bay beyond it. This veranda is supported by octagonal columns with two necking-rings with sharp profiles set below the dentiled capital. The entrance porch is given emphasis by having pairs of these columns connected by arches with very thin intrados, moldings, and small keystones. Above that section is a large porch on the second story with three octagonal columns and, between them, octagonal planter boxes. The parapet above the flat roof of this porch has podia in line with the columns below in the balustrade which, like the others, is made of thin spindles.

Walk west on Superior Street. The second house on your left is

49. 1019 SUPERIOR STREET—1911

Designed in 1911 by E.E. Roberts, this is a fine example of his Prairie School mode. The simple cubic block is topped by a low pitched roof faced to the street and angled out at the bottom in a lower pitch. The central section of the stucco-covered block projects with a thin, flat roof immediately atop the polygonal bay set within the second floor. The same form is repeated in a variation by the thin slab cantilevered over the entrance to protect the side-lighted central doorway. Note the excellent Prairie glass in the central windows. The porch roof has its response in the parapet that defines the porch which, like the house, has its central section set slightly forward. The brick used for this porch parapet is also used for the foundation of the building and for the parapet of the lower porch landing which is marked by a large urn to indicate that the entrance is to one side. Smaller versions of the podium supporting that urn are repeated at the corners, and another one is next to the walkway, each of these topped by a large sphere. The design of the house is completed by having a group of three windows in simple surrounds set on each side of center on each floor and by the integration of the copper downspouts set in from the outer corners.

Continue west to the corner. Turn right (north) on Marion Street 1 block. Turn right (east) on Chicago Avenue. The fourth structure on your right is

50.   1031 Chicago Avenue—1893

This 1893 house designed by Frank Lloyd Wright shows his early experience with the Queen Anne style which was current when he was beginning his practice. This is as personal an interpretation of the style as any Queen Anne house is, but this one already indicates the direction in which Wright's designs will go. A basic geometric rigor pervades the design with the block topped by a pitched roof covering both the second story and the full attic. It swoops down as a hipped roof on the west face to shelter the porch, which lacks any other roof and provides a strong horizontal frame for its run along the west and north faces. The extension of the balusters below the level of the porch to form a tight pattern texture shows Wright's inventiveness. The geometric rigor is reinforced by the oversized bay that swells across fully half of the front facade, rising through two stories to a flared conical roof. The ground floor windows have oversized lintels that are extremely plain. The second story windows are arranged as a continuous strip reinforcing the roundness of that element. Further emphasizing the roundness of the bay is the thinness of the two-story dormer occupying the other half of the roof. Its thinness is accentuated by the broad swell of the polygonal bay on the ground floor which does not extend beyond the lip of the roof flare. The house is listed on the National Register of Historic Places.

Continue east. The next house on your right (and the second building on your right east of that) are

51. 1027 CHICAGO AVENUE and
1019 CHICAGO AVENUE—1892

These two buildings are identical to one another and were built as rental houses in 1892 to the design of Frank Lloyd Wright. 1019 Chicago Avenue retains its original porch. The basic block is topped here by a very steeply pitched hipped roof that descends through the second story to erupt across a low hipped roof forming the porch. The second story above the porch is lit by a dormer tucked into that roof. Its polygonal shape is expanded in the huge projection at the northeast corner, topped by its own steeply pitched pyramidal roof with a slight flare at the base. The ground story has large windows with rectangular frames around the central pane, and the second story has pairs of windows, similarly subdivided, set in each face. The clear geometric shapes of the building are accentuated by the contrast of the very thin clapboards and of the very high, flat, unornamented lintel above the ground floor windows which is carried across the porch as the lintel. That lintel is supported by simple tapered piers. The balusters extend from the bannister all the way to the ground level and have steps in the middle, the railings of which are horizontal and are set only slightly higher than the porch level. This produces a counterbalance to the dormer above, and it introduces an unexpected touch of originality and flourish in an otherwise quite simple design.

Continue east to the corner. Turn right (south) on Forest Avenue. The fourth house on your right is

52. 415 FOREST AVENUE—1904

This excellent design from 1904 by E.E. Roberts is a simple cubic block played with in a Prairie style manner that still retains traces of the Tudor style. On the north section a wing breaks forward as is acknowledged in the roof by its hipped roof projecting from that of the main block. The dormer, in line with the flat-fronted projection on the second floor, also has a hipped roof. The diamond-pane glass in the dormer, and on the second story casement windows, is lined with an outer rectangular frame, a typical Prairie School adaptation of Tudor forms. Projecting toward the south from the wing on the north is a two-faced polygonal bay kept within the confines of the ample soffited eaves. The projecting bay on the ground floor has a po-lygonal projecting bay, the outer face of which provides the fascia for the porch extending across the entire front. It is enclosed only in the greater part of the central section in order that a polygonal bay may extend beyond the face of the building to the south. The brick of the ground floor extends upward to the sill level of the second story where an extremely simplified half-timbering scheme takes over.

Backtrack north to Chicago Avenue to the Frank Lloyd Wright Home and Studio on your right.

This concludes the Oak Park Walking Tour.

Drive west on Chicago Avenue 3 blocks to Harlem Avenue (Route 43). Turn left (south).

LYONS

LYONS

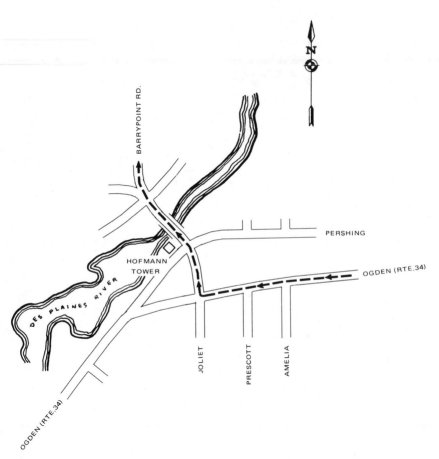

Drive south on Harlem Avenue (Route 43) 5.2 miles to Ogden Avenue (Route 34). Turn right (west) 1 mile. Turn right (north) on Joliet Avenue 1 block. Stop.

At the river, on your left, is

HOFMANN TOWER
Lyons Tower
3910 Barry Point Road—1908

This tall, gaunt, reinforced concrete tower was built in 1908 by George Hofmann to capitalize on the development of the western suburbs in the early 1900s. In 1905 the Cicero plant of the Western Electric Company had been built, and in 1906 the Chicago and Joliet Railway Company had opened a recreation area in Lockport, many miles from Chicago but accessible along its inter-urban railroad. Even at that great distance it drew 80% of its visitors from Chicago. Hofmann built the tower as a landmark for the enjoyment of those who would come to the recreation and beer garden* that spread around his tower. One of the attractions was a pond, created by a dam Hofmann built across the river, where he operated excursion boats and rented canoes. Within a decade the Des Plaines River, the source of the major attraction in his recreation settlement, began to show high degrees of pollution and Hofmann soon had to close his facility because it was no longer attractive. In 1946 the tower became the property of the Cook County Forest Preserve District. It is listed on the National Register of Historic Places and on the Illinois Register.

Continue north, across the bridge.

---

* Across the road from the tower can be seen a small, castellated triangular-shaped tavern. The ground floor has been drastically alterated, but still visible above the entrances are logos of the beer sold here. In the undisturbed one is an "H" in the escutcheon topped by an eagle. It beckoned the prospective elbow benders to enter and enjoy.

RIVERSIDE

RIVERSIDE

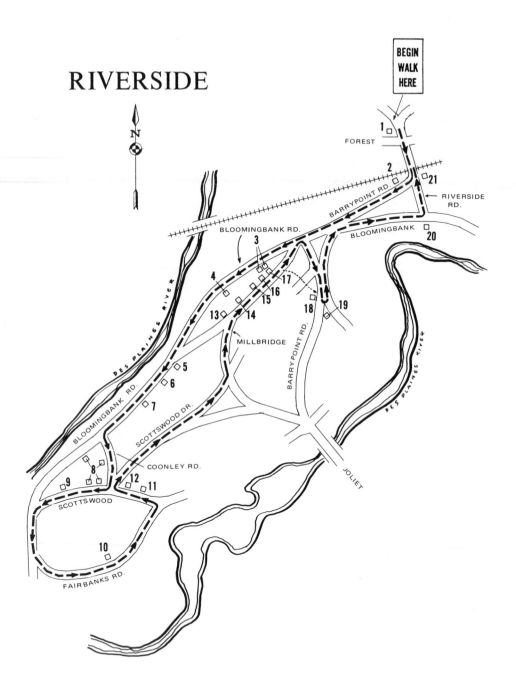

As you cross the bridge you will be on Barry Point Road. After you cross the bridge, stay on the center one of the three roads (Barry Point Road), curving around to the right a total of ½ mile to Riverside Road. Turn left (north) one block, crossing the tracks, and stop.

RIVERSIDE WALKING TOUR

The town of Riverside was designed by Olmsted, Vaux, and Company in 1869. Frederick Olmsted was the landscape designer of the firm, while Calvert Vaux did the architecture. This speculative development was the first landscaped suburb connected to an industrial metropolis by a railroad line and meant to be only a domestic enclave rather than a complete urban settlement with industry, commerce, and the other characteristics of a major city. It became a model for many such communities, but not until the twentieth century. The architects were chosen on the basis of their reputation based upon their design for Central Park in New York City. Most of Riverside is listed on the National Register of Historic Places as an historic district.

On your left, just north of the railroad tracks, is

1. OLD WATER TOWER
Riverside Museum—1870

This 1870 building was designed by William LeBaron Jenney. It was and still is the most prominent landmark in this important suburb. The design of the large middle tower (the top of which burned in a fire in 1913 and was rebuilt) and of the two low round structures flanking it provide a semblance of a medieval German settlement.

    The larger tower has a strongly battered freestone limestone basement and rises through brick, now painted, to a pier arcade featuring pointed arches and incised keystones. A blind arcade, whose arches are half the size of the arcade below, is near the top with a catwalk carried on large stone corbels projecting from the upper area and surrounding the water tank. The catwalk that burned, began much lower at the crown of the lower larger pointed arches. The present arcade has punctured spandrels and rises through a flared candle-snuffer roof to a great knobular finial. Attached on the south side of the main water tower is a later civic structure designed to work well with this central ensemble of Riverside. The lower towers are random ashlar or freestone with similar roofs immediately below which runs a cornice with delicately detailed scroll-cut applique.

The museum is in the low, freestanding structure on the northeast part of the site. The interior has been cleverly designed to contain as much as possible while disguising it from sight. There is an exquisite geometric Tiffany lamp from the Babson estate. The exhibits change regularly. Saturdays: 10:00 A.M.-2:00 P.M. Free.

Walk south across the railroad tracks. On your right is

2.   RIVERSIDE RAILROAD DEPOT—1901

Built in 1901 and designed by the Chicago, Burlington, and Quincy Office of the Engineer of Buildings, this building illustrates the high quality which a corporation's anonymous designers could achieve when they were surrounded by a generally high level of architectural practice. It displays a delightful combination of the conservatism of railroad architects, the substantiality of their construction techniques, and the broad horizontalities and care in handling materials which were permeating from the Prairie School experiments of that moment. It replaces an earlier structure. This one has the main structure on the south side of the tracks and a subsidiary sheltered platform on the north side. The broad, tiled, hipped roofs with flared eaves terminate with soffits spreading out from brick walls that in a sense have no particular style but display a mastery of design. Note the slight difference in brick color for the section below the stringcourse at the window sill level from the brick above. The brick on the upper section is laid so that every sixth course is inset to provide horizontal shadow lines. Notice also the lintels with their rosette bosses spanning the openings. The design is carried into the interior with quarter-sawn golden oak wainscoting and other fine carpentry work which has been beautifully restored. The original ticket window is also preserved. Part of the interior is in adaptive reuse as the Lyons Savings and Loan.

Walk west on Barry Point Road, continuing west on Bloomingbank Road. The third and fourth houses on your left are

3.   107 BLOOMINGBANK ROAD and
111 BLOOMINGBANK ROAD—c.1890

This pair of buildings in the Queen Anne style from around 1890 illustrates variations on the same basic design. The ground floor of the basic structure has a porch across the entire front with different kinds of projections through it to hold the second story and the attic. Each has a porch, but one has a tower on the east side and the other has an unbroken gable. Both have the same kinds of clapboard and shingle sheathing.

Continue on Bloomingbank Road. The third house on your left is

4.   143 BLOOMINGBANK ROAD—1869

Built in 1869, the year the suburb was established, this early house sits on the protuberance of the roadway giving it a very distinctive site. It is very well designed in the Italianate style. Its complex massing and steep roof pitches reveal the continuing vigor of the Gothic Revival style. Distinctive to the Italianate, however, are the pairs of large brackets and the tall windows with distinctive feet and shoulders for their jambs and segmental points. The pair of windows on each side of the front facade is matched on the ground floor by a larger, transomed, sidelighted window. Beneath each pair of windows on the second story on the outer sides, are equally large ground floor windows. Projecting on each end are bays, either flat-fronted and one-story or polygonal and two stories. The entire front is covered by a veranda with its original carpentry still intact.

Continue on Bloomingbank Road to the corner. Cut left diagonally, intersecting the triangle of park. Directly in front of you is

5.   201 BLOOMINGBANK ROAD—c.1870

This is a prime example, from about 1870, of the T-shaped Gothic Revival plan worked up with quite simple carpentry to give it great dignity. The stem of the "T" faces the street and is surrounded on all three sides by a veranda. The windows extend from floor to ceiling and are topped by Italianate lintels. The porch posts also indicate the Italianate style but the angularity of the brackets atop the posts' capitals indicate the Carpenter's Gothic style as a source. On the second story the stem has a pair of windows under a hood molding. The attic is lit by a small pointed-lintel window set close to the top of the gable created by the steeply pitched roofs. Note that the roof here is lower than that of the top of the "T" farther back. On each end of that section is a square-fronted bay topped by a flared roof.

Continue on Bloomingbank Road. The second house on your left is

6. 213 BLOOMINGBANK ROAD—c.1905

This simple frame structure from about 1905 is a two-story cube, clad in clapboards on the ground floor and shingles on the second story, topped by a low hipped roof. In the front is a dormer with a hipped roof, below it a pair of windows with round heads, and across the entire front (protecting broad polygonal bays on the ground floor) is an august porch with four great piers. Especially notable here are the pier capitals which contain a variety of almost whimsical, but quite geometrically disciplined, moldings to provide a distinctive (if not unique) capital form. These touches are characteristic of the search for originality of the first few years of the twentieth century.

Continue on Bloomingbank Road. The third house on your left is

7. 253 BLOOMINGBANK ROAD—c.1890

This large Queen Anne structure from about 1890 has a basic cubic block covered with a gambrel roof and fronted by a wing with its own gambrel roof. The porch on the right side is protected by a flared roof descending from that front, its left half marked by a steeply pitched gable. An open porch is on the second story on the left side. The variety of original surfaces with clapboards and shingles has been disturbed by the replacement of the ground floor with stucco, but this building is a rare example of the use of the gambrel roof form within the Queen Anne style.

Continue on Bloomingbank Road to the corner. Across Coonley Road, on your left, is

8. AVERY COONLEY ESTATE—1909

281 BLOOMINGBANK ROAD is the first section of the extensive Avery Coonley estate, designed by Frank Lloyd Wright in 1909, to be encountered on this walk. The estate is a National Historic Landmark. This section, facing to the north and set well back from the street, gives only a small indication of the extent of the estate. The design begins at the street, where a broad low urn sits on a podium that terminates a planter strip running back to the broad low structure beyond. Here can be seen quite well the broad stucco walls, trimmed in simple boards on the ground floor, and the colorful tile used on one wing as a facing material, all set below the broad, tiled, hipped roofs. This section of the estate was severely damaged in a fire in 1978 and, although the exterior was restored to its original appearance, several changes were made inside.

Walk south on Coonley Road. The second structure on your right is

336 COONLEY ROAD is another major section of the Coonley estate. Here the garden is set off from the street by stuccoed walls topped by board copings. Notice as you approach the structure the pergola made from stucco piers and board lattice work. Also notice how carefully the landscaping is integrated with the architecture consisting of broad planes and flat walls. This is a modification to the original design to adapt the original carriage structures and entrance area to a separate dwelling unit.

Continue to the corner and turn right on Scottswood Road. The first structure on your right is

290 SCOTTSWOOD ROAD is a freestanding structure, added a little later. It is another example of the Prairie style, this time used for a simple domestic structure with an L-shaped plan covered by broad hipped roofs.

Continue on Scottswood Road. The next structure on your right is

300 SCOTTSWOOD ROAD is the main block of the Avery Coonley estate. It reveals the integration of the stucco boards, tile and Prairie glass and broad horizontals below low hipped roofs characteristic of the greatest achievements of the Prairie School.

Continue on Scottswood Road. The third house on your right is

9.   322 SCOTTSWOOD ROAD—1897
This small stone house, built in 1897, represents the English Cottage style with a large attic story immediately above the ground floor stone walls. Strips of diamond-pane casement windows, a half-timbered gable next to its gambrel roof, and its timber porch recreate the character which wood craftsmen were thought to have given the medieval cottages which inspired this design.

Continue to the corner. Turn left on Fairbank Road. The ninth house on your left is

10.   AVERY COONLEY PLAYHOUSE
350 Fairbank Road—1909
Originally built as a progressive school and designed by Frank Lloyd Wright

in 1909, the building has subsequently been altered by enclosing the wings on either side with sliding glass doors. They provide only a minimal disturbance to the plan which is still clearly basically a "T" with its stem projecting toward the street. The stem is higher than the wings. It is opened to the outside by three windows shaded by an extensive brow from the flat roof which, with its flat fascia, continues the lines of the fascias for the lower roofs and produces a distinct horizontality in this simple stucco structure. The clerestory windows lighting that interior space above the lower wing roofs can be seen from the east, as can be the large chimney terminating that wing.

Continue on Fairbank Road to Coonley Road. Turn left. Across the street, on your right (although the address is on Fairbank Road, this house is actually located on Coonley Road) is

11.   308 FAIRBANK ROAD—c.1910
Designed about 1910 by Guenzel and Drummond, important figures in the Prairie School and associated with Frank Lloyd Wright, this small structure is representative of their style. A one-story hipped roofed block, it extends slightly on the left with a glazed porch with the extremely broad stuccoed soffits of the eaves providing a shelter for the entrance. The windows are strips of casement windows, the three opening to the living room with triangular Prairie patterns. The section below the window sills has a board siding pattern; the area above is stuccoed.

Continue around to your right on Coonley Road. The next house on your right is

12.   283 SCOTTSWOOD ROAD
Thorncroft—c.1910
This building provides a more elaborately developed scheme based on the same pattern as the previous structure (Riverside #11). Also by Guenzel and Drummond and from the same time, it was built for the teachers of the Coonley School conducted at the Coonley Playhouse. Here the block is two stories high, again topped with a hipped roof with a recessed section on two sides of the second story, balanced by a projecting section on the left side of the front facade. Below it, a low extension projects forward with very broad extensions of the eaves matched at the ground level by the concrete founda-

tion containing planting beds. Originally an open porch, it has subsequently been glazed.

To the left is a one-story extension. Instead of the characteristic Prairie leaded glass, the panes are divided into small geometric patterns by muntins and rails.

Continue to your right, around the corner, and continue on Scottswood Road. Take the left fork to Millbridge Road. Turn left on Millbridge Road, then veer right. The first house on your left is

13. 166 Scottswood Road—c.1870

This is another of the earlier buildings built in this suburban development. Notice that its site is the best in the immediate area, sitting as it does on a slight rise in the land and overlooking the public park created within the street pattern. A tall frame structure in the Italianate style probably from about 1870, it nonetheless has the steeply pitched roofs identified with the Gothic Revival. The ground floor has the idiosyncratic interpretation of the Tuscan order, so much liked by the Italianate designers, supporting the veranda. It covers the entire front and extends across one side to a porte-cochere where two of the original posts have been replaced by later wrought iron posts. The second story has Italianate windows with thin frames complete with feet and shoulders; the one on the foremost front wing originally had a pair of windows under the pedimented lintel. Above it is a fully rounded arch covering the attic vent sheltered by the robustly bracketed gable.

Notice the large coachhouse at the back of the property which betrays evidences of at least two building periods. The general massing and the cupola are characteristic of the Italianate period of the house while the stucco surface and the lumpy, blocky forms on its ground floor and gable windows indicate the free interpretations of the classical styles fashionable just after the turn of the century.

Continue on Scottswood Road. The second house on your left is

14. 144 Scottswood Road—c.1870

This also is an early building in the suburb from about 1870, often thought to be by William LeBaron Jenney. A fine example of the merging of the Gothic Revival style almost to the point of becoming a Stick Style building,

14. 144 Scottswood Road

it displays an overall excellence in the handling of wooden forms. The roofs have a relatively low pitch and are decorated with dormers and gables with half-circular fillets connected by turned cross spars and kingposts. The extensive overhang in the entire eave zone is supported by milled brackets which foot on vertical boards intersecting the tightly ranked clapboard siding. On the side of the house near the entrance the brackets are closely spaced and the boards divide an ascending series of windows lighting the stairhall in a zone set out slightly from the face of the wall. Just beyond that stairhall is a projecting polygonal porch. Before it, and turning to cross the entire front of the building, is a broad veranda with turned posts supporting a lintel, itself supporting a series of small pointed arches and supported by broad milled struts. The porch railing has extremely simple but tightly spaced and robust balusters. The skirt below the porch has a cut-out pattern which emulates the form of the balusters above. The entrance is set at 45° to project from the corner to make it quite prominent. The veranda extends beyond the house into a porte-cochere, beyond which is a quite simple carriage house.

Stop for a moment to notice how the streets in Riverside follow the contour of the land, how the buildings are sited to take advantage of the view across the parks, and how much the plantings contribute to the overall effect.

Continue on Scottswood Road. The second house on your left is

15. 124 SCOTTSWOOD ROAD—1871

Designed in 1871 by William LeBaron Jenney, this is an excellent example of a board and batten Gothic Revival cottage with strong indications of the later Gothic Revival, also known as the High Victorian Gothic, but rendered in wood. The massing of the house is extremely picturesque with several wings projecting to different distances on different faces and with extensive eaves carried by projecting modillions. The second story windows are either tabernacle windows but rendered in Carpenter Gothic form or, on the front face, are wall dormers with jerkin-head roofs projecting deeply from the wall and carried by broad sides constructed from boards with decorative incising including cut-out quartrefoils. A veranda stretches across the front and the left side and is carried by chamfered square posts with milled brackets. The entrance is marked by the pair of wall dormers flanking it, by the square window set diagonally in the gable, by the pair of pointed-headed windows

15. 124 Scottswood Road

in the second story, and by the pedimented porch carried by scroll-cut and spindle work and projecting slightly from the face of the veranda. Notice the wooden window awning on the ground floor, something that survives very rarely, as does the board and batten siding which is so well maintained and displayed in this building.

Continue on Scottswood Road. The next house on your left is

16. 118 Scottswood Road—1880s

This Queen Anne house from the late 1880s has a basic symmetry which is disrupted in the center. It rises two stories with a pitched roof set at the level of the second story window heads. It includes a full attic lit by dormers and a window in the front gable. That dormer is on the right; on the left is an eyebrow dormer. The front gable is below a gambrel roof; on the left side it erupts into a half-circular bay covered by a conical turret. The truncated hipped roof of the porch acknowledges the bay. The entire central section is set slightly to the left of center of the overall mass.

Continue on Scottswood Road. The next house on your left is

17. 112 Scottswood Road—1870s

Probably from the late 1870s, this is an extremely sophisticated design within a very simple format. A basic cube is topped by a steeply pitched hipped roof, flattened at the top. The second story has a splayed corner with cut-out fillets and a pendant knob forming a small balcony. The incursion into the cube is compensated for on the ground floor by the projection outward of a flat-fronted entrance vestibule. The entrance is framed by sidelights and simple pilasters carrying a simple lintel. Those forms reflect the forms of the veranda which stretches across the entire front, is splayed at 45° across the corner in front of the entrance, and then continues one bay along the side of the house. Its columns are irregularly spaced to add an interesting pattern and to reveal the variation in the fenestration on the ground floor where one large and one normal window sit below the three normal size windows of the second story. The entrance is further emphasized by the pediment set on the splayed angle. Here at the splayed corner the porch lintel is carried by posts with a pentagonal cross section to reveal two aspects of the design, one being the route of the lintel, the other being the axial approach to the front door. Beyond the veranda is a polygonal bay on the ground floor. The result of the design is one of restraint and sophistication.

Continue to the corner. Turn right (or cut across the park to your right before the corner). The church in front of you is

18. RIVERSIDE PRESBYTERIAN CHURCH
116 Barrypoint Road—1872

This building, designed by F. C. Withers and finished in 1872, is a fine amalgamation of Gothic Revival and Italianate forms. The stone mass of the sanctuary has steeply pitched gables rising high into the pitched roof to mark the transepts and chancel and to mark the entrance which projects slightly and contains the pointed arched entrance. At the corner stands the stone base for the tower with carefully dressed stone describing the corner buttress and rising to a steep timber belfry topped by a thin roofed steeple. The bell is clearly visible behind the pointed arched openings on each face which are topped by prominent moldings, terminating in the corner pilasters. The extensions to the left are twentieth-century construction but are done in harmony with the original design.

Across the street from the front of the church, on the corner of Barrypoint and Fairbank roads, is

19. 100 FAIRBANK ROAD—1869

This 1869, clapboard, Carpenter Gothic house was designed by Calvert Vaux of Olmsted, Vaux and Company, the original planners of the town. This is one of few extant examples in the United States (and the only one in the Midwest) of the work of this very important architect. It is the only building by them in Riverside and was one of the earliest residences built here. It is a fine example of East Coast architecture, the kind that was illustrated in house pattern books published on the East Coast, sent to the Midwest, and used rather more freely by local builders than was the case on the East Coast, making this not a Midwest but rather an East Coast building. It has a strict formality with a higher ground floor and lower second story. A low, broad, pitched roof is intersected in the front by a gabled roof supported by a projecting porch on the second story which is carried by struts continuing into the Gothic Revival carpentry work forming the balcony. A similar balcony appears at each end of the structure above a flat-fronted projecting bay on one end and a polygonal projecting bay on the other. These extend the entire width of those building faces. The clapboard sheathing is edged by vertical boards at the corners. The faces project slightly at the second floor level, and the sheathing is intersected by a vertical

19. 100 Fairbank Road

board carrying the outer brackets defining the porch on the front facade. A final definition for the porch occurs with the low, cut-out porch parapet. A final finish for the design is provided by the window frames with small corbels beneath the jambs and a thin lintel atop the tall, narrow openings.

Notice here the care given to the detail in the design of the suburb. The streets lack curbs, and often the sidewalk does not parallel the street but takes its own path across the landscape. Large lots often allowed the houses to be set far back from the street, and ample open space takes advantage of the Des Plaines River flowing through the site provided in idyllic setting, already heavily forested at the time it was planned. Many of the trees survive.

Backtrack on Barrypoint Road toward the railroad tracks, curving to the right. Turn right on Bloomingbank Road. The second building on your right is

20. RIVERSIDE TOWN HALL
27 Riverside Road—1895

The town hall, designed in 1895 by George Ashby, shows the Richardsonian Romanesque style as it was tamed by Queen Anne delicacy in its midwestern application. The large structure rises to a steeply pitched, hipped roof with tawny-colored brick on the second story and random rough-faced ashlar on the ground floor. In the midsection, wall dormers of different sizes rise into the third story level while on the east end a polygonal turret extends from the corner. Toward the west end a three-story block stands forward of the building face. It carries dormers in its hipped roof, the front one with a clock. The copper cornices end in volutes rather than cross the wall dormers; below the uppermost cornices are terra-cotta cornices with rich foliate decoration, a motif repeated in plaques in various parts below the windows on the third floor of the dormers. Colonettes, stringcourses, and dressed stone around the ground floor openings complete this design which is both picturesque and august at the same time.

Walk north on Riverside Road toward the tracks. The second building on your right is

21. ARCADE BUILDING
1 Riverside Road—1871

The first commercial structure built in the new suburb, this 1871 structure designed by F.C. Withers provided the suburb's shopping center which was conveniently located next to the railroad stop. It was the first structure of a series which later grew in the area, all having a general medieval homogeneity (except for the commercial block from the turn of the century immediately east of the water tower). A similar medieval town square was imposed in one design, of 1913, by Howard Van Doren Shaw in Lake Forest (Lake Forest #32). This building, which remains remarkably intact, displays the merging of the later Gothic Revival and the Italianate. The polychromatic treatment with light brick, red brick, and Joliet limestone mixed to construct the pointed arches and the walls with their projecting cornices and stringcourses indicates the architect's penchant for the so-called streaky bacon style of the High Victorian Gothic. The general composition, however, is that of the Italianate with hipped roof pavilions in the center and at each corner. Also worked in is a reference to the Second Empire with the dormered Mansard windows between the pavilions. The ground floor is much simpler. Note the excellent stained glass in the upper sections of the shopfront windows.

Continue across the tracks. On your left is the Riverside Museum.

This concludes the Riverside Walking Tour.

Drive west on Forest Avenue .6 miles to Golf Road Avenue (at the high school on your right).

BROOKFIELD

BROOKFIELD

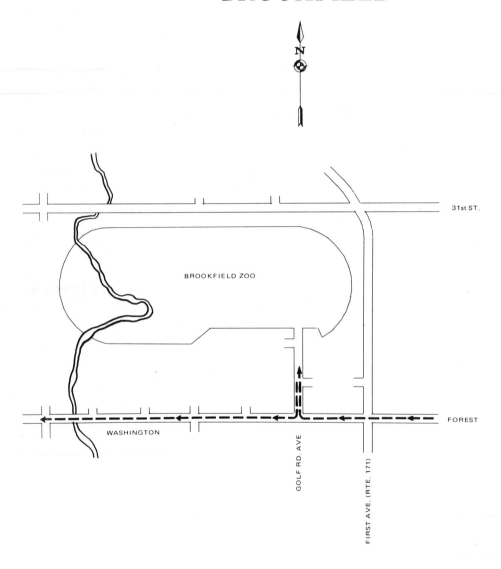

Turn right (north) on Golf Road Avenue into the zoo entrance.

BROOKFIELD ZOO

This outstanding zoo has over twenty-four major exhibits housed on 200 acres of land. New exhibits include: The Australia House; Predator Ecology, a nocturnal addition to the lion house; the Ellen Thorne Smith Trail around Indian Lake; and walks through five natural habitats (guided tours only).

Special attractions include: a narrow gauge railroad which runs through many parts of the zoo normally inaccessible to visitors; a narrated motor safari tour through the zoo; tape casettes and recorders are available for rent from the attendant at the information booth just inside the entrance gate; by advance appointment, the zoo will provide a free trained guide; a children's zoo with plenty of animals to touch; a bookstore with 4,000 titles is the most extensive assortment of natural history books for sale at any zoo; and the Seven Seas Panorama where dolphins can be viewed at any time through porthole windows in the tank of the main building but a separate admission is charged for the dolphin show, the first of its kind away from the sea coast, which provides an aquatic arena in which the dolphins perform. Shows are at 11:30 A.M. and 2:30 P.M. weekdays and Saturdays; 11:30 A.M., 1:00 P.M., and 3:00 P.M. Sundays and holidays. The zoo is open 10:00 A.M.-5:00 P.M. Adults: $1.50, children: 50¢. Free Tuesday.

Turn right (west) onto Washington Avenue, continuing 1 mile. Drive through the traffic circle, exiting on Maple Avenue (southbound). Continue south on Maple Avenue .7 miles to Ogden Avenue.

WESTERN SPRINGS

WESTERN SPRINGS

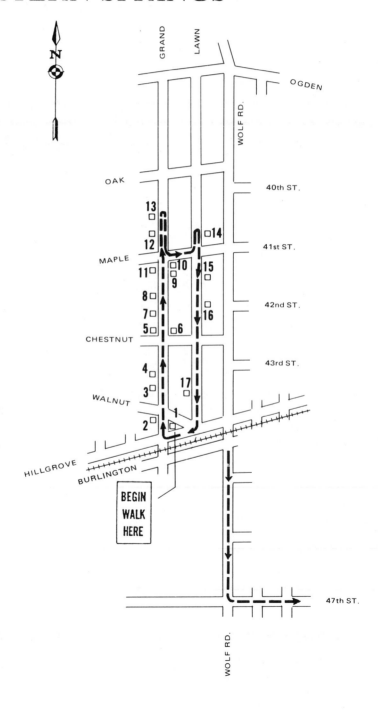

Turn right (west) on Ogden Avenue 2.6 miles to Wolf Road. Turn left (south) .7 miles to Hillgrove Avenue. Turn right (west) 1½ blocks. Stop.

WESTERN SPRINGS
WALKING TOUR

On the north side of Hillgrove Avenue, in the park, is

1. WESTERN SPRINGS HISTORICAL SOCIETY
Old Water Tower—1892

The water tower once housed the village hall, courthouse, and police station. The building combined into one prominent landmark in this early suburb all of the requirements of an early town with special emphasis given to the importance of a source of water for the prosperity of a new settlement on the prairie. Built in 1892 it rises with battered, irregular, rough-faced limestone walls to a corbel course where brick enclosing the water tank begins. The brick cylinder has a tall blind arcade adding interest to its surface. At the top is a deeply projecting eave supported by quadrant brackets between which are let-in panels as if to suggest battlements. Atop the tower is a polygonal pyramidal roof.

The historical society has an excellent collection of artifacts from the town. Among the permanent collections are: an 1892 grocery store with phone, cash register, and merchandise; a Burlington railroad display with the original ticket office and the stationmaster's desk; home furnishings; and dollhouse-like miniatures. There are also rotating displays. Tuesdays and Saturdays: 10:00 A.M.-2:00 P.M. Free.

Leave the Water Tower, heading northwest. On the SW corner of Grand Avenue and Walnut Street is

2. 4364 GRAND AVENUE—1873 and later

This frame structure, built in 1873, began as a typical Italianate cubic block topped by a low truncated hipped roof. Note the Italianate paired brackets and the shallow window frames with shoulders around the windows which on the ground floor rise from the floor to the ceiling. The entrance to the building was probably in a porch set deep within the south side which, on the second story, had a corresponding porch. At some later date, perhaps about

1. Old Water Tower

1885, the veranda across the front was added to the structure, probably replacing a foursquare Italianate porch. The veranda was extended to the north to form a porte-cochere. It has turned posts and a delicate spindle bracket with square foliate cut-outs at its ends supported by delicate fillets. At that time the large polygonal bay on the south side toward the back was added, probably replacing an original Italianate bay. The bay on the north side, however, which is shallow and kept within the projection of the cornice, appears to be from the original Italianate period. The railing across the roof of the veranda is recent construction.

Walk north on Grand Avenue. The second house on your left is

3. 4344 Grand Avenue—c. 1873

The original structure, built about 1873, rises through two full stories to a broad pitched roof in the wing projecting forward and has additional space in other construction farther back. On the ground floor is a broad bow window within the porch. The porch, probably added about the turn of the century, extends to the south and returns toward the back to connect with the wing. Its stout Ionic columns are connected by tightly spaced square-rung balusters. The recently added metal siding detracts only slightly from the simplicity of this design.

Continue north. The third house on your left is

4. 4326 Grand Avenue—c. 1874

This clapboard-covered house was built about 1874. It is a fine example of the massing and detailing of the T-planned Gothic Revival structure with its high pitched roof and elaborately framed windows. Uncharacteristic of the Gothic Revival are the brackets under the eaves. The boss, in the middle of the hump between the pair of thin windows on the second story, is a "U.S. Grant" style detail. Unfortunately the original porch has been lost and the doorway rebuilt, but the tall windows on the ground floor and the doorway retain their original window heads.

Continue north. On the NW corner of Grand Avenue and Chestnut Street is

5. 4224 Grand Avenue—1892

Built in 1892, this frame structure shows the taming of the Queen Anne style by the neo-classical revival attitudes becoming current toward the end of the

2. 4364 Grand Avenue

nineteenth century. The large central projection on the second floor is flanked by smaller dormers set into the steeply pitched roof that slopes down and flattens slightly to extend over the ground floor porch. It is supported across the front by a row of stout piers quite capable of doing the job. Within the porch, in the center, is a polygonal projection containing the entrance. The symmetry of the design introduces a disciplining formality that is enlivened by the complexity of the forms, for example in the flares of the dormer roofs with their flared shingled gables and the intersecting diamond heads which form a molding in the cornice of the polygonal bell-shaped roof. The windows on the ground floor, within the porch, have been altered.

On the NE corner of Grand Avenue and Chestnut Street is

6. GRAND AVENUE SCHOOL
1020 Chestnut Street—1887 and 1906

This irregular ashlar, rough-faced limestone structure, rising two stories high, shows the lingering indebtedness to the Italianate style for public buildings of this sort, but its broad eaves and the Palladian windows, seen in the gables projecting in the center of each face, betray an awareness of the Queen Anne style. The entrance facing Grand Avenue sets a segmental arch between two wall piers connected by a coping rising to form a gable. The heads of other openings vary with rough-faced, single stone lintels on the west face left plain while some of those on the south face on the ground floor have hooded drip moldings. Unusual in this design is the irregularity in the fenestration with the windows forming various groupings rather than displaying a strictly formal symmetry. The hipped roof is topped by a belfry cupola. The small wing on the north was added in 1906 and was carefully designed to match the original structure. The extension to the west is much more recent, but still sympathetic. The windows in the entire building have been replaced.

Continue north on Grand Avenue. The second house on your left is

7. 4216 GRAND AVENUE—1890

This small house, built in 1890, has clapboards on the lower level and scalloped shingles in the gable marking the entrance. The hipped roof dormer works well with the cubic hipped roofed block, extended toward the back by projecting wings and in the front of an ample veranda. Scallop shingles also decorate the top zone of the second story.

6. Grand Avenue School
1020 Chestnut Street

Continue north. The fourth house on your left is

8.   4146 GRAND AVENUE—1890

This clapboard, Colonial house was built in 1890.

Cross to the east side of the street and continue north. The fifth house on your right is

9.   4123 GRAND AVENUE—c.1905

This simple cubic structure from about 1905 is topped by a pitched roof facing the street and flared slightly at its soffited eaves. An ample dormer with the same forms occupies the attic. The ground floor is crossed by a full porch supported by simple Ionic columns.

Continue north. On the SE corner of Grand Avenue and Maple Street is

10.   4115 GRAND AVENUE—1902

Like its neighbor (Western Springs #9), this is a simple cubic block, now topped by a hipped roof with dormers in each face. The full porch, with a Doric column apparently replacing the original Ionic column on the corner, erupts into a fully rounded bay at the corner. Additional protuberances occur as polygonal bays elsewhere on the clapboard-clad structure.

Across the street, near the SW corner of Grand Avenue and Maple Street is

11.   4118 GRAND AVENUE—1890

Built in 1890 and now covered with metal siding, this simple formal structure has a large polygonal bay with a high pyramidal roof occupying the center of the front. The porch on its north face is covered by a roof sloping down from the pitched roof behind it.

Continue north. The second house on your left is

12.   4058 GRAND AVENUE—c.1895

Built about 1895, this building is a simple cube with a high hipped roof extended by a broad polygonal bay on the second story. It has its own gabled roof with a Palladian window set in a patterned shingle field. On the ground floor, extending to the south beyond the building, is a broad porch sustained by simple porch piers.

Continue north. The second house on your left is

13.   4040 Grand Avenue—1874

Although much disfigured by later work, particularly by the reconstruction of the porch and the inappropriate siding which managed to find its way into the second story window pediments, this 1874 building is nonetheless noteworthy as a rare example of a one-story Mansard structure with large tabernacle windows in the Mansard roof. Their frames have been stripped of their original ornament.

Backtrack south on Grand Avenue to Maple Street. Turn left (east) 1 block. Turn left (north) on Lawn Avenue. The first house on your right is

14.   4069 Lawn Avenue—c.1888

This house was built about 1888 and has a steeply pitched roof above the second story, where a small window lights the attic and three larger windows light the second story. Crossing the entire ground floor, and protecting the polygonal bay within it, is a full width porch. The entrance is marked by a pediment with thin vertical grooved boards.

Backtrack south past Maple Street. The sixth house on your left is

15.   4137 Lawn Avenue—c.1875

Built about 1875, this narrow, one-and-one-half-story, hipped roof structure contains traces of the Greek Revival but is expanded by adding elements from the later, picturesque styles. On the south is a polygonal bay with a full pedimented roof projecting over its corners. In the front, on the ground floor, a flat-fronted bay projects in the center. Next to it is a porch with a sunrise motif in the pediment which is supported by thin Tuscan columns. The oversized scale of that front window and porch introduce a charming disproportion in the scale of the building.

Continue south. The sixth house on your left is

16.   4209 Lawn Avenue—c.1875

Built about 1875, and probably originally with its entrance in the front, this frame structure has a pitched roof with a gable over the northern half protecting the flared pedimented element above the pair of windows. A single window on the ground floor probably marks the original entrance. Next to it is a broad polygonal bay with tightly spaced, small, quadrant brackets in its cornice. The cornice of the main roof is especially interesting with its central frieze level set at a slight angle and carrying attached cut-out forms to introduce an interesting pattern.

Continue south past Chestnut Street. The eighth house on your right is

17.   4334 LAWN AVENUE—c.1889

Built about 1889, this building is a late example of the simple Italianate cube with a hipped roof. The expected brackets have given way to simple consoles above the paneled cornice. The Italianate window frames also failed to survive to this late date. The porch has been rebuilt with an inappropriate Williamsburg-inspired lintel, but the original double door configuration survives. On the north face are two small square windows set diagonally, the upper one of which has its corners marked by square blocks.

Continue south to the corner. On your right is The Western Springs Historical Society.

This concludes the Western Springs Walking Tour.

Drive south across the railroad tracks, turning left (east) immediately on Burlington Avenue to Wolf Road. Turn right (south).3 miles to 47th Street.

FOREST VIEW

FOREST VIEW

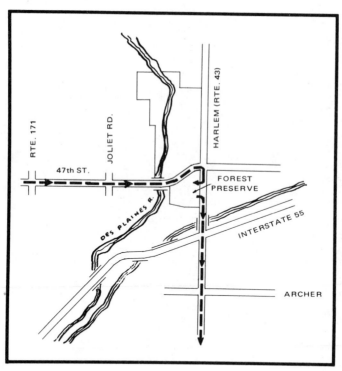

Turn left (east) on 47th Street 5.3 miles to Harlem Avenue (Route 43). Turn right (south) .2 miles. Turn right (west) into

CHICAGO PORTAGE NATIONAL HISTORIC SITE
West side of Harlem Avenue at 48th Street

Located in the Cook County Forest Preserve is the site where, in 1673, Marquette and Joliet, the first explorers of Illinois, landed. In days gone by, this place on the Des Plaines River was a portage for Indians and later for traders. A large stone boulder, behind the parking lot, marks the site. Tourists may also enjoy hiking or picnicking in the forest preserves. The site is listed on the National Register of Historic Places.

Turn right (south) on Harlem Avenue (Route 43) 5.3 miles to 95th Street (Routes 12 and 20). Turn right (west) 3 miles to LaGrange Road (Route 45).

PALOS HILLS

PALOS HILLS

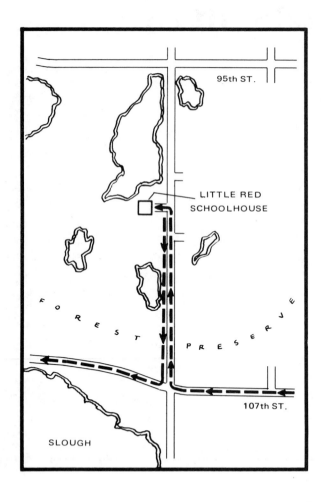

95th ST.

LITTLE RED
SCHOOLHOUSE

F O R E S T   P R E S E R V E

107th ST.

SLOUGH

Turn left (south) on LaGrange Road (Route 45) 1.6 miles to 107th Street. Turn right (west) 1 mile. Turn right (north) on Willow Springs Road (104th Avenue) .9 miles. Turn left (west) into the parking lot of

LITTLE RED SCHOOLHOUSE NATURE CENTER—1886

This building was built in 1886 and moved to its present site in 1952. It illustrates a typical one room schoolhouse of the nineteenth century. Illinois was one of the first states in the Union to pass an act requiring that local school districts be formed and provide education which was compulsory. This called for standards to be set for the design of schoolhouses, and the important Chicago architect W.W. Boyington was asked to provide the standard designs for these school buildings which then proliferated across the state after the 1870s. This typical structure has ample windows along the sides set high to allow light to flood into the rooms and with ample ventilation provided by having windows in all four walls. The small belfry originally provided space for a bell to call scholars to their lessons. Lacking, in this setting, are the outhouses which would have been at some distance beyond the back of the building; otherwise the building is a good representative of the schoolhouse type.

The building now houses an excellent nature center along with a large assortment of indigenous mammals and reptiles, and an unusual exhibit: an inside beehive. There are several exhibits about the ecology of the area. An excellent assortment of books on nature and ecology is for sale. Also at the forest preserve is Saganashkee Slough, a stopping place for migrating waterfowl. Fifteen- thirty- and sixty-minute nature trails offer a look at wildlife and wild flowers. Also visit the farm garden and orchard. Mondays through Thursdays: 9:00 A.M.-4:30 P.M.; Saturdays, Sundays, and holidays: 9:00 A.M.-5:00 P.M.*

Leaving the Little Red Schoolhouse Nature Center, turn right (south) on Willow Springs Road .9 miles. Turn left (east) on 107th Street 1 mile to LaGrange Road (Route 45). Turn left (north) 5 miles to Route 55 North, to Chicago.

* You are now as close as the route takes you to Argonne National Laboratory which is in DuPage County. If you wish to go there now,

Turn right (south) on Willow Springs Road .9 miles. Turn right (west) on 107th Street 3.3 miles until it ends. Turn right (north) on Route 83, .9 miles. Turn left (west) on Bluff Road until it ends. Turn right (north) on Cass Avenue 1/3 mile to the Visitors Reception Center on your right.

ARGONNE NATIONAL LABORATORY

Argonne National Laboratory is the direct offshoot of the World War II Metallurgic Laboratory at the University of Chicago which was instrumental in enabling scientists to demonstrate the sustained nuclear chain reaction and to control it. With a change in parent agent from the Atomic Energy Commission (AEC) to the Department of Energy (DOE), Argonne changed from a "nuclear energy laboratory" to an "energy research laboratory" and now a large part of their work is in developing alternate energy sources. Tours are available by advance reservation (972–2771) on Saturdays at 9:00 A.M. and 1:30 P.M. Tours take 3–3½ hours. Free.

Drive north on Cass Avenue 1.3 miles. Turn right onto Route 55 North, toward Chicago.

This concludes the six-county tours. It is the hope of the author that you have found the tours enjoyable and that a new insight and appreciation of the architectural and historical heritage of the area is yours.

Argonne
National
Laboratory

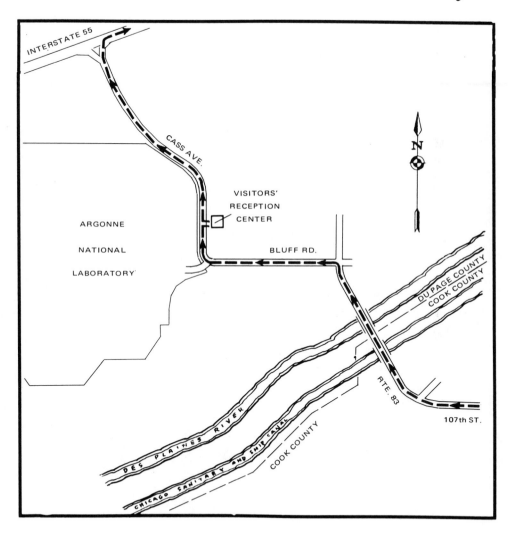

APPENDIX OF HISTORICAL SOCIETIES AND MUSEUMS

Aurora Historical Museum, 323
Barrington Historical Museum, 67
Batavia Depot Museum, 306
Brookfield Zoo, 683
Cantigny Museum and Gardens, 389
Chicago Horticultural Society, Botanic Garden of the, 584
Des Plaines Historical Society, 597
Dundee Township Historical Museum, 245
DuPage County Historical Museum, 367
Elmhurst Historical Museum, 348
Evanston Arts Center, 530
Evanston Historical Society Museum, 475
First Division Museum, 390
Fort Sheridan Museum, 143
Frankfort Historical Society Museum, 475
Fullersburg Woods Nature Preserve, 419
Geneva Historical Society, 285
Glenview Historical Society, 593
Graue Mill, 419
Grove, The, 593
Haines House Museum, 110
Henry Mansion, 455
Highland Park Historical Society Museum, 149
Illinois and Michigan Canal Museum, 438
Illinois Railroad Museum, 165
Joliet Park District Conservatory, 466
Kenilworth Historical Society, 551
Little Red Schoolhouse Nature Center, 703

Lizzardo Museum of Lapidary Art, 347
Lombard Historical Museum, 355
Martin-Mitchell Museum, Caroline, 397
McCormick Museum, 389
McHenry County Historical Society, 166
Morton Arboretum, 415
Oak Park and River Forest Historical Society, 649
(Palos Hills) Little Red School House Nature Center, 703
Peotone Historical Museum, 483
Pilcher Park Nature Center and Museum, 466
(River Forest) Oak Park and River Forest Historical Society, 649
Riverside Museum, 665
River Trail Nature Center, 589
St. Charles Historical Museum, 279
Seven Acres Antique Village and Museum, 149
Trailside Museum of Natural History, 597
Victorian Manor, 455
Waukegan Historical Society, 110
Western Springs Historical Society, 687
Will County Historical Society, 438
Willowbrook Wild Life Haven, 415
Wilmette Historical Society, 535
Woodstock Opera House (historical exhibits on 1st floor), 192

707

APPENDIX OF NATIONAL HISTORIC LANDMARKS AND NATIONAL REGISTER OF HISTORIC PLACES

Boldface type indicates picture pages.

National Historic Landmarks

Evanston #1, 499-501, **500**
Glenview #1, 593
Oak Park #1, 625-27, **626**
Oak Park #29, 643-45, **644**
Riverside #8, 688-70
Winnetka #6, 569

National Register of Historic Places

Aurora #1, 323
Aurora #7, 326-27, **327**
Aurora #12, 329-30
Aurora #13, 330, **331**
Aurora #18, 333-35, **334**
Aurora #20, 335-37, **336**
Barrington #5, 68, **69**
Batavia #1, 305
Batavia #3, 306
Batavia #19, 313-15, **314**
Carpentersville #1, 233
Crystal Lake #2, 206, **207**
Crystal Lake #3, 207-9, **208**
Elgin #3, 249-50
Elgin #16, 256-58
Elgin #23, 261
Elmhurst #2, 345-46

Evanston Lake Shore Historic District, 499
Evanston #61, 530, **531**
Fort Sheridan Historic District, 143
Fort Sheridan #5, 144, **146**
(Forest View) Chicago Portage National Historic Site, 699
Frankfort Historic District, 472
Frank Lloyd Wright—Prairie School of Architecture Historic District, 625
Geneva #1, 285, **286**
Geneva #38, 301-2
Glen Ellyn #1, 363
Highland Park #17, 157
Joliet Historic District, 455
Joliet #1, 455-**456**
Joliet #3, 457-58
Joliet #4, 458-60, **459**
Kenilworth #1, 551, **552**
Kenilworth #3, 553
Lake Forest Historic District, 125
Lockport Historic District, 448
Lockport #1, 438
Lockport #9, 441-43, **442**
Lombard #9, 359
Lyons (Hofmann) Tower, 661
Marengo #2, 171, **172**
Marengo #9, 176, **177**

Naperville Historic District, 399
Naperville #1, 397, **398**
Oak Brook (Graue Mill), 419-20
Oak Park Historic District, 625
Oak Park #34, 646-49, **647**
Oak Park #36, 649-50
Oak Park #42, 652
Oak Park #50, 656
Plainfield #7, 432
River Forest #4, 608-9
River Forest #8, 610-12, **611**
Riverside Historic District, 665

St. Charles #18, 278
St. Charles #23, 280-81
Waukegan (Bowen Park), 109-10
Wayne (Dunham Castle), 267-68
Wayne (Oaklawn Farm), 267-68
Wayne (Village of), 377
Wheaton #3, 368, **369**
Wheaton #12, 372-73
Wheaton #17, 375, **376**
Wilmette #1, 535
Wilmette #3, 536
Wilmette #21, 545

INDEX

Adler, David, 134
Alloway, Wilmore, 511
Arcada Theater, 278
Arcade Building, 678
Argonne National Laboratory, 704
Ashby, George, 678
Aurora Historical Museum, 323
(Aurora) First Baptist Church, 323-24
Baha'i House of Worship, 535
Baker, Hotel, 278-79
Barfield and Hubbell, 502
Barnes, Edward Larabee, 584-85
Barnes, Julian, 460
Barnum, P. T., 508
Barrington Historical Museum, 67
Batavia Congregational Church, 309
Batavia Depot Museum, 306
Batavia Institute, 313-15, **314**
Batavia Library, 308
Batavia Methodist Church, 306-8, **307**
Baumann and Cady, 512
Beers, Clay, and Dutton, 514, 515
Beith House, 280
Bell, Mifflin E., 375, 409
Bellevue Mental Hospital, 313-15, **314**

Beman, Solon S., 306-8
Benevolent and Protective Order of Elks, 329-30
Benny, Jack, Center, 110
Betts, William (Betts and Holcomb), 73
Birth of a Nation, 528
Blanchard Hall (Wheaton College), 372-73
Botanic Garden of the Chicago Horticultural Society, 584-85
Bourgeois, Louis, 535
Boyington, William W., 465
Bowen Park, 109
Brookfield Zoo, 683
Burnham, Daniel, 462, 525
Burnham, Franklin (firm of), 505
Burnham, Franklin (Edbrooke and Burnham), 287, 551, **552**, 553-54, 556, **557**
Burnham (Lord and Burnham), 466
Cady (Baumann and Cady), 512
Calvary Episcopal Church, 316, **317**
Campana Factory, 305
Canal Works (Lockport), 438-39
Cantigny Museum and Gardens, 389-90
Catlow Theater, 73
Cauley, Frank W., 517

Chase, Frank (Childs and Smith), 305
Chatten, Melville C. (Chatten and Hammond), 513, 525
Chicago and Alton Railroad Station (Lockport), 445
Chicago & Northwestern Railroad Depot (Wilmette), 536
Chicago, Burlington, & Quincy Roundhouse and Locomotive Shop, 335-37, **336**
Chicago Horticultural Society, Botanic Garden of the, 584-85
Chicago Portage National Historic Site, 699
Childs and Smith, 305
Church of the Holy Spirit Episcopal Church, 137
Clas, A. C., 508
Clausen, H. Ring, 515
Clay (Beers, Clay, and Dutton), 514, 515
Cobb, Henry Ives, 128, 132
cobblestone houses, 211-12, **212**, 214, 256-58
Compton, Henry Dann, 368
Coolidge, Charles A., 389
Coolidge, Charles A. (Coolidge and Hodgkins), 522
Coolidge, Charles A. (Shepley, Rutan, and Coolidge), 133
Coonley, Avery, estate, 668-70
Cupola House, 176, **177**
Dawes, Charles Gates, Mansion, 499-501, **500**
Deknatel, William, 526
Des Plaines Historical Society, 597
Disciples of Christ Meeting House, 299
Dole Mansion, 214
Downing, Andrew Jackson, 19, 25, 215
Drummond, William, 608, 609, 615, 619, 620
Drummond, William (Guenzel and Drummond), 670, 671
Dundee Township Historical Society Museum, 245
Dunham Castle, 267-68
DuPage County Courthouse, 56, 375
DuPage County Historical Museum, 367
Durand Art Institute (Lake Forest College), 132

Durant House, 280-81
Dutton (Beers, Clay, and Dutton), 514, 515
Edbrooke, Willoughby J. (Edbrooke and Burnham), 287, 551, 553, 556
Elgin Academy, Old Main, 249-50
Elgin National Watch Company, 261
Elgin Mental Health Center, 263-64
Elks Lodge, 329-30
Elmhurst College Campus, 345-46
Elmhurst Historical Museum, 348-49
Elmhurst Public Library, 345
Elmslie, George Grant, 57, 325, 326, 330, 335
Elmslie, George Grant (Purcell and Elmslie), 109
Evanston Arts Center, 530
Evanston Historical Society, 499-501, **500**
Evanston Lake Shore Historic District, 499
Fabyan Forest Preserve, 301-2
Farnsworth House, 57-61, **58**
Farson-Mills House, 646-49, **647**
Fermilab, 319
Fermi National Accelorator Laboratory, 319
Ficken, Henry Edwards, 499-501
First Church of Lombard, 359
First Division Museum, 390
First Universalist Church (Elgin), 261
Fisher (Patten and Fisher), 632-33
Flynn (Holmes and Flynn), 638
(Forest View) Chicago Portage National Historic Site, 699
Fort Sheridan, 141-46, **145**
Fort Sheridan Museum, 143
Fowler, Orson Squire, 54, 68
Francisco Terrace Apartments, 639-41, **640**
Frankfort Historic District, 472-75
Frankfort Historical Society Museum, 475
Frank Lloyd Wright Home and Studio, 625-27, **626**
Frank Lloyd Wright—Prairie School of Architecture Historic District, 625
Frost, Charles, 130-31, 136, 137, 367
Frost, Charles (Frost and Granger), 126, 127, 128, 132, 138, 582
Fullersburg Woods Nature Preserve, 419

Galena Hotel, 332

Ganster, William A. (Ganster and Pereira), 110-11

G. A. R. Hall, 324

Garfield Farm and Tavern, 285, **286**

Geneva Historical Society, 285

Gifford House, 256-58

Glencoe Train Station, 582, **583**

Glenview Historic Society, 593-94

Glessner House, 41

Glos Mansion, 348-49

Grace United Methodist Church, 121

Graham Building, 325-26

Granger, Alfred, 137

Granger, Alfred (Frost and Granger), 126, 127, 128, 132, 138, 582

Graue Mill, 419-20

Griffin, Walter Burley, 349, 350

Grosse Pointe Lighthouse and Nature Center, 530-**531**

Grove, The, 593

Guenzel, Louis (Guenzel and Drummond), 670, 671

Haeger Pottery, 231

Haines House Museum, 110

Halfway House (Plainfield), 432

Hammond, Charles H. (Chatten and Hammond), 513, 525

Harper (Wolf, Sexton, Harper, and Trueax), 278, 279

Harvey, George L., 528

Hauptgebäude, 345-46

Henry, Jacob A., Mansion, 455-56, **456**

Hibbard, Charles H., House, 176

Highland Park Historical Society Museum, 149

Hoag, Smith, 192-93, 267-68

Hodgkins, Charles (Coolidge and Hodgkins), 552

Hofmann Tower, 661

Holcomb, Richard (Betts and Holcomb), 73

Holmes and Flynn, 638

Hotchkiss, Jed (Lake Forest Landscape Architecture), 125

Hotchkiss, Roy, 641-42

Hubbell (Barfield and Hubbel), 502

Hunt, Jarvis, 457-58

Hunt, Myron, 508-9, 516

Illinois and Michigan Canal, Lock No. 1 (Lockport), 437, 444

Illinois and Michigan Canal Museum, 438

Illinois Railroad Museum, 165

Immanuel Lutheran Church (East Dundee), 233

Indian marker tree, 563

Izaak Walton League, **600**-1

Jenney, William LeBaron (Jenney and Mundie), 205, 665, 671, 673

Jennings, J. T. W., 515

Jennings, Stephen A., 509

Johnson, W. K., 514

Joliet Historic District, 455-56

(Joliet) Methodist Episcopal Church, 461-62

Joliet Park District Conservatory, 466

Joliet Public Library, 462

(Joliet) Union Station, 457-58

(Joliet) Universalist Church, 460

Kane County Courthouse, 56, 286

Kenilworth Club, 553

Kenilworth Historical Society, 551-53

Kenilworth Railroad Depot, 551, **552**

Kenilworth Union Church, 555

Kennicott's Grove, 593

Keystone Building, 326-27, **327**

Kingsley, George S. (and/or Harvey L. Page), 528

Lake Forest City Hall, 138

Lake Forest Campus, 127-32

Lake Forest Historic District, 125

Lambs Farm, 91

Lane, J. C., 512

Lapidary Art, Lizzardo Museum of, 347

Latz, Leonard J., Sr., 103, 107, 109

Lilacia Park, 360

Linthicum House, 502-3

Little Red Schoolhouse Nature Center, 703

Lizzardo Museum of Lapidary Art, 347

Lloyd, Henry Demarest, House, 569

(Lockport) Congregational Church, 440, **441**

Lockport Historic District, 448-51
(Lockport) Methodist Church, 446
(Lockport) North Public Landing, 438
Locks, Illinois and Michigan Canal, 437
log cabins, 157, 166, 438, 573
Lombard Historical Museum, 355
Long Grove Church, 83
Long, John Turner, 503, 520
Lord and Burnham, 466
Lyons Tower, 661
Maher, George Washington, 542, 553, 635, 646-49
Market Square (Lake Forest), 138, **139**
Mariott's Great America, 95
Martin-Mitchell, Caroline, Museum, 397, **398**
Mayo, Ernest, 502, 506-8, 515, 517-19, 521, 523, 526
McCormick Museum, 389-90
McHenry County Historical Society, 166
McNally, Frank (McNally and Quinn), 518
Mies van der Rohe, Ludwig, 57-61, 110
mills, 301-2, 419-20, 487-89, **488**
Morton Arboretum, 243, 415
Mundie, William Bryce (Jenney and Mundie), 205
Naper Settlement, 397-99, **398**
Naperville Historic District, 399
Newton, Erastus, House, 441-43, **442**
Nichols Library (Naperville), 409
North Central College, Old Main, 399-401, **400**
North Public Landing (Lockport), 438
Northwestern University Campus, 529
Norton Store, 449-51
Norton Warehouse and Store, 449, **450**
Oaklawn Farm, 667-68
Oak Park and River Forest Historical Society, 649
Oak Park Club, 638
Oak Park Historic District (Frank Lloyd Wright-Prairie School of Architecture Historic District), 625
Octagon House, 68, **69**

Old Central Grade School (Lockport), 439-40
Old Harlem School (River Forest), 617-19, **618**
Old McHenry County Courthouse and Jail, 185, **186**
Old Second National Bank (Aurora), 330, **331**
Old Water Tower (Riverside), 665-66
Old Water Tower (Western Springs), 687, **688**
Olmsted, Frederick Law (Olmsted, Vaux, and Company) (Riverside Landscape Architecture), 665
Page, Harvey L. (and/or George S. Kingsley), 528
Page, Harvey L., and Company, 515
(Palos Hills) Little Red Schoolhouse Nature Center, 703
Paramount Arts Centre, 333-35, **334**
Patten and Fisher, 632
(Peotone) First United Presbyterian Church, 492
Peotone Historical Museum, 483
Peotone Public Library, 483
Periera, William L. (Ganster and Periera), 110-11
Perkins, Dwight Heald, 121
Perkins, Frederick, 133
Pilcher Park Nature Center and Museum, 466-67
Pine Craig, 397, **398**
(Plainfield) Congregational Church, 430, **431**
(Plainfield) Sharon United Methodist Church, 428
(Plainfield) United Methodist Church, 430
(Plainfield) Universalist Church, 427
Pond and Pond, 509, 636
Presbyterian Church (Lake Forest), 130-**131**
Purcell, William Gray (Purcell and Elmslie), 109
Quinn, James Edwin (McNally and Quinn), 518

Rapp, C. W., 521

Rapp, C. W. (Rapp and Rapp), 333, 458

Rapp, George (Rapp and Rapp), 333, 458

Rathje Mill, 487-89, **488**

Ravinia Park, 158

Rialto Square Theatre Building, Rubens, 458-60, **459**

Riverside Historic District, 665

Riverside Museum, 665-66

Riverside Presbyterian Church, 676

Riverside Railroad Depot, 666

Riverside Town Hall, 678

River Trail Nature Center, 589

Roberts, E. E., 617, 628, 630, 633 (remodeled by), 642, 655, 657

Robie House, 60

Robinson, Harry, 405, 406

Rogers, Orson, House, 171, **172**

Rookery Building, 56

Rubens Rialto Square Theatre Building, 458-60, **459**

Rutan (Shepley, Rutan, and Coolidge), 133

St. Charles City Building, 271, 272

St. Charles Historical Museum, 279

St. Charles Municipal Center, 279

St. Dennis Church (Lockport), 445

St. Francis Convent (Joliet), 465-66

St. John's Episcopal Church (Lockport), 446

Saint Mary of the Lake Seminary, 87

St. Mary's Catholic Church (Joliet), 462

Sanctuary, The, 427

Schlacks, H. J., 505

Scoville Square, 642-43

Seven Acres Antique Village and Museum, 165

Sexton (Wolf, Sexton, Harper, and Trueax), 278, 279

Shaw, Howard Van Doren, 138, 678

Shaw, Howard Van Doren (or Ernest Woodyat), 518

Shepley, Rutan, and Coolidge, 133

Silsbee, Joseph Lyman, 501, 526

Smith (Childs and Smith), 305

Spencer, Robert, Jr., 520, 523, 615, 636

Stickney House, 206, **207**

Stacy's Tavern, 363

Stupey Cabin, 157

Sullivan, Louis, 48, 57, 205, 272

Tallmadge, Thomas, 50, 499, 543

Tallmadge, Thomas (Tallmadge and Watson), 108, 121, 156, 502, 519, 521-22, 627, 650

Tanner, William A., House, 323

Terwilligar House, 206-9, **208**

Thompson, C. H., 516

Tomlinson, Webster, 120

Trailside Museum of Natural History, 607

Trinity Episcopal Church (Wheaton), 368-69, **369**

Trueax (Wolf, Sexton, Harper, and Trueax), 278, 279

Turnoch, Enoch, 513

Underground Railroad station, 176, 243

Unitarian Church (Geneva), 288

Unitarian Universalist Church (Unity Temple), 643-45, **644**

United Church of Christ (Wayne), 383

Unity Temple (Unitarian Universalist Church), 643-45, **644**

Van Bergen, John S., 516, 639

Van Osdel, John Mills, 185

Vaux, Calvert, 676

Vaux, Calvert (Olmsted, Vaux, and Company) (Riverside Landscape Architecture), 665

Victorian Manor, 455-56, **456**

Walton, Izaak, League, **600**-1

Ward's, Lee, Creative Craft Center, 249

Warren, Julius, House, 393

Watson, Vernon (Tallmadge and Watson), 108, 121, 156, 502, 519, 521, 522, 627, 650

Waukegan Historical Society, 110

Wayne Congregational Church, 383

Wayne United Church of Christ, 383

Wayne Historic District, 377-85

Wayside, The, 569

Weese, Harry, and Associates, 641

West Dundee Village Hall, 237

Western Springs Historical Society, 687, **688**

Wheaton College campus, 372-74

Wilmette Historical Society, 535

Will County Historical Society, 438

Willowbrook Forest Preserve, Wild Life Haven, 415

windmills, 301-2, 487-89, **488**

Winslow, William H., House, 610-12, **611**

Withers, F. C., 676, 678

Wolf, Sexton, Harper, and Trueax, 278, 279

Woodstock Opera House, 192, **193**

Woodyat, Ernest (or Howard Van Doren Shaw), 518

Wright, Frank Lloyd, 36, 60, 157, 300, 302, 305, 350, 545, 608, 609, 610, 612, 616, 622, 625-27, 631, 637, 639-41, 643-45, 649, 651, 652, 653, 654, 656, 657, 668-70

Wright, Frank Lloyd, Home and Studio, 625-27, **626**

Zimmerman, William Carbys, 329

Zook, R. Harold, 279

GLOSSARY

ABACUS: flat, square slab forming the top part of a classical capital

ACANTHUS LEAVES: richly moulded foliage form used to enrich classical capitals and other elements

ADAMESQUE: based on the rich, elegant classical forms of the brothers Adam active in the second half of the eighteenth century in England; see Introduction

AEDICULA (PL.: AEDICULAE): large indentation in a wall with a half circular plan and, usually, a half domed top; also, a box-like form attached to a gothic-style structure, usually fronted by a pair of columns holding a gable

ALLÉE: long road-like landscape feature, either grassed or paved as a path, flanked by trees planted in straight lines

AMERICAN-GOTHIC STYLE: see Introduction

ANCILLARY: subsidiary subordinate elements

ANTHEMION: ornament based on honeysuckle flower and leaves, sometimes used repetitively to form a moulding decoration, sometimes as a single element to decorate a console or a projection above a cornice

APSIDAL: apse-like, i.e., a projection of a wall usually with a half-circular end

ARCHITRAVE: lowest of the three levels of an entablature, usually with a flat face

ART DECO: style of the late 1920s with smooth surfaces, non-historical forms, and often with zig-zag and whip-like curved patterns

ART MODERNE: style of the late 1920s with smooth surfaces, non-historical forms, and emphasis on basic geometric shapes such as circles and squares

ASHLAR: stone construction using regular blocks with opposite sides parallel to one another; if all blocks are the same size, it is regular ashlar; if blocks come in a few different sizes, it is irregular ashlar; if blocks come in a great variety of sizes, it is random ashlar

717

ASTRAGAL: thin moulding wrapped around a column and with a half-round cross section; like a torus but quite small

BALLOON FRAME: see Introduction

BALUSTER: a support used for a railing, usually round, often in a shape resembling a bottle or vase

BALUSTRADE: a railing support made from a series of identical balusters or other repetition of elements which leaves open spaces

BARGEBOARD: also verge boards; decorative gable rafter

BARONIAL: resembling the character of rambling country seats of English nobility

BEAD MOLDING: made up of a series of tightly spaced beads as if they are strung along a string

BEDFORD LIMESTONE: see Introduction

BELL ROOF: bell-shaped covering for an element, usually circular in plan, sometimes polygonal, with flared base and a tendency to flatten at the top

BELT COURSE: also stringcourse; a continuous horizontal line drawn across a facade, as, for example, by a string of stones in a brick wall or a projecting brick course in a brick wall

BEVELED: at an angle other than 90°

BIB: element with greater degree of finish used to dress up the center of a facade

BOARD AND BATTEN: siding made of vertical boards with their joints covered by thin strips of wood

BOSS: projecting flattened knob, usually circular, sometimes decorated, often marking the intersection of other elements, sometimes used as ornaments on the face of elements such as gable rafters

BRACED FRAMED CONSTRUCTION: see Introduction

BUNGALOW STYLE: see Introduction

BUTTRESS: thickened section of wall used to give added strength

CANONIC: standards for composition of designs based on earlier, long-standing practice and tradition

CANTED: a plane placed at an angle

CANTILIVER: structural element projecting beyond a wall with no additional support beyond the wall

CAPITAL: top, decorative element of a column or pier

CARPENTER GOTHIC STYLE: see Introduction

CARTOUCHE: ornamental panel with decorative edges

CASTELLATED: composition with castle-like forms, for example with towers and crenelations

CAVETTO: a moulding with a simple concave cross-section

CHAMFERED: having the corners of a rectangular post cut back at 45°

CHANCEL: the area in a church containing the altar, choir, and director of services (preacher, priest)

CHATEAUESQUE STYLE: see Introduction

CHICAGO WINDOW: window placed in an opening forming a horizontal rectangle and composed of a large central fixed pane and moveable sash on each side

CHORD: a straight line connecting any two points on an arc

CLAPBOARD: siding composed of the boards attached horizontally and overlapping one another to form a seal

CLASSICAL REVIVAL: see Introduction

CLERESTORY WINDOW: a window placed along a side of a building above a lower pitched roof and below an upper pitched roof

COLONETTE: a thin column usually bunched into groups, usually attached to a wall

CONSOLE: projecting support usually with a curved shape and with its height greater than its projection; compare "modillion"

"CONTRACTORS-PRAIRIE": see Introduction

COPING STONE: stone placed atop a wall to provide a seal for the wall and to throw the rain away from the wall

CORBEL: a block-like form projecting to hold something above

CORINTHIAN COLUMN: see "orders"

CORNICE: the top, projecting horizontal element ornamenting a wall or an entablature, usually the most decorative of the various horizontal courses

CRENELATION: the gaps in a battlement at the top of a wall

CRESTING: a lacy, decorative iron work topping of a wall or roof

CUPOLA: a small structure, usually square, placed at the top of a roof and usually with windows

CUSP: the point where semicircular indentations in the intrados of an arch or window jamb come together

CYCLOPEAN MASONRY: stone construction made up of blocks lacking parallel sides

CYMA MOLDING: a molding whose cross-section is made up of contrary curves

DENTIL: tooth-like block used in an evenly spaced sequence just beneath the top overhanging part of a horizontal member such as a cornice or lintel

DORIC COLUMN: see "orders"

DORMER: a window set into a roof pitch

DRESSED STONE: finished, smooth-faced ashlar or other stone pieces

DUTCH COLONIAL STYLE: see Introduction

EASTLAKE STYLE: see Introduction

EASTERN STICK STYLE: see Introduction

EAVES: projection beyond the wall of a flat roof as of a roof pitch

ECHINUS: the convex curved element just below the abacus in the Doric or Tuscan order

ENGLISH COUNTRY GOTHIC STYLE: see Introduction

ENGLISH TUDOR: see Introduction

ENGLISH VICTORIAN GOTHIC: see Introduction

ENTABLATURE: horizontal structural member in classical architecture usually composed of an architrave, frieze, and cornice

Entasis: slight bulge in the silhouette of a column shaft or pier

Eschutcheon: shield-like shape used to hold a coat of arms and often used alone as a decorative panel

Extrados: outer line of an arch

Facade: outer face of a building

Fanlight: semicircular window above an entrance

Fascia: face, usually flat or sparsely ornamented, placed across the eaves

Federal style: see Introduction

Feet (on window frames): outward projection along the wall surface at the bottom of a window frame; see also "shoulders"

Fenestration: the composition or character of the windows on a facade

Festoon: decorative element made to resemble a band of fruit, flowers, or foliage tied at each end usually by ribbons and hanging in a gentle curve between those ties

Filagree work: intricate pierced decorative pattern

Fillet: small element, often decorative, placed in the angle where a support and a beam intersect

Finial: upward-projecting decorative element atop a roof's peak

Fleche: tall spire atop the intersection of a church's nave and transept

Flute: indentation with semicircular cross section running on a column's face

Foliated: decorated with foliage forms, often based on the acanthus leaf

Foursquare: cubic; blocky

French window: window with sash hinged at the outer edges and extending to the floor, the bottom usually fronted by a balcony rail unless opening to a porch

Frieze: middle section of an entablature, usually ornamented, and lacking a projecting element; also used independently as a horizontal decorative band

Frontispiece: an element with the form of a temple front attached to and usually projecting from the center of a facade

Gable: triangular shape for a facade created by pitched roofs

Gable rafter: wooden member set out from the wall face following the pitched roof which projects beyond the wall to hold it

Gambrel roof: pitched roof with each plane broken to form two pitches, the lower steeper than the upper

Georgian Revival: see Introduction

Gingerbread: informal term referring to rich ornamental forms usually in wood

Girts: small girder-like or truss-like structural forms used in conjunction with gable rafters

Gothic cottage: see Introduction

Gothic Revival: see Introduction

Grate: rectangular grid

Greek Revival: see Introduction

Hipped roof: roof with pitched planes rising from each wall

Historical styles: see Introduction

In antis: columns standing in the plane of a wall which is broken into to form an opening for a porch or aedicula

Incising: carving into a surface to form a decorative pattern

Italian Renaissance Revival: see Introduction

Italian Villa style: see Introduction

Italianate style: see Introduction

International style: style of the late 1920s and later which used no historical forms and stresses the juxtaposition of planes, large areas of glass, and a regular structural pattern of thin elements

Intrados: inner line or surface of an arch

Ionic column: see "orders"

Jeffersonian: see Introduction

Jerkin-head: pitched roof plane placed at right angles to and at the gable peak of a pitched roof

Keystone: stone, usually larger than the others, placed at the top of an arch

King-pin: see "kingpost"

Kingpost: vertical post in a truss placed in the center directly under the peak

Knee fillet: same as fillet, which see

Lancet: tall, thin window topped by a pointed arch

Lannon stone: stone in varying tones of yellow used with rough face and irregular ashlar forming only a facing veneer

Lapped-board: wide clapboards (which see) with flat surfaces and square edges

Lattice: criss-cross rectangular pattern usually made from thin boards

Let-in: carving out an indentation from the surface usually to form a panel

Lintel: horizontal structural member over a door or window opening unless it is made of voussoirs in which case it is a flat arch

Loggia: open covered porch with a row of columns or piers across the front

Luxifer prism: piece of glass usually about four inches square used with others in a panel above a shopfront window, moulded with forms that project daylight into the store; invented in Chicago in the 1890s

Mansard (or Mansart) roof: a hipped roof with a steep lower pitch containing an extra floor and a top roof so close to being flat it is not visible from the street

Masonry: construction using brick, stone, or both

Massing: the composition of the building's major three-dimensional elements

Meeting house style: the appearance of a building type characterized by a rectangular volume entered from the short end and covered with a low pitched roof

Milled: the result of using power driven woodworking tools to give various angled and curved edges and shapes to larger pieces of lumber

MILLRACE: the channel from a source of water that directs the water to a waterwheel

MISSION STYLE: a revival style popular during the World War I period and later on the adobe and stucco structures of the southwest

MODERNE: see "Art Moderne"

MODILLION: projecting support usually in a cornice with its projection greater than its height; compare "console"

MONITOR ROOF: a low superstructure with windows placed atop and following the ridge of a pitched roof

MOORISH STYLE: style popular during the 1880s and 1890s usually used within the Queen Anne style which features colorful, rich surface patterns and windows with arches forming a horseshoe shape

MOTIF: a collection of smaller elements into a composition which makes a major contribution to a composition

MUDSILL: the lowest level of a masonry wall, usually in stone, which projects slightly providing a visual base for the wall and protecting the upper sections from the mud splashed by rainwater

MUNTIN: the thin vertical member within a sash holding a glass pane; the similar horizontal member is called a rail

NAVE: the major, central volume within a church

NECKING RING: an incised ring running around the shaft just below the capital, usually used in twos or threes in the Doric order

NEO-CLASSIC: a quality in a design which indicates that the classical architecture of an earlier period, usually that of ancient Greece or Rome, served as an important source for the designer

NEO-GEORGIAN STYLE: see Introduction

NORMAN STYLE: see Introduction

OBELISK: a vertical element with a square section tapering slightly and ending in a pyramidal top

OGIVE ARCH: pointed arch

ONION DOME: a dome that bulges outward and usually moves upward to a pointed top

ORDERS: the canonic assemblage of posts and beams into a finished architectural form established by the Greeks and used, with modifications, by the Romans, and subsequently identified with classical and neo-classical architecture. The three Greek orders were the Doric, using a simple capital with an echinus and abacus and no base beneath the shaft; the Ionic, using volutes at the corners of the capital; and the Corinthian, the slimmest of the three, using small volutes which are overwhelmed by lush acanthus leaves around the capital. The entablatures follow a similar change from rugged to delicate. The Romans added two more orders: the Tuscan, like the Doric but with a base and an astragal in place of the Greek's necking rings and with smooth shafts rather than fluted ones, and the Composite which combines the volutes of the Ionic and the rich acanthus of the Corinthian

ORIEL: a circular projection from a corner rising from above the top of the ground floor and extending into the roof area

PALLADIAN WINDOW: a window form invented in the sixteenth century in Italy using a larger central section topped by an arch and side sections with linteled heads placed at the spring point of the central arch

PALMETTE: a decorative form often used in a series and resembling a palmette leaf

PARAPET: the low, horizontal top of a silhouette placed above a cornice

PARGING: covering a masonry wall with stucco

PAVILION: a section of a facade at the end or center which projects forward and upward; a small free standing structure open on all sides

PEDIMENT: a low triangular element enclosed with cornices standing above an entablature or lintel; when carried by columns or pilasters it forms part of a frontispiece and resembles a temple front

PENT ROOF: a thin pitched roof crossing a wall

PERGOLA: a covered walkway open on the sides extending across a garden or along the side of a building and attractive to vines; also, a free standing garden pavilion also called a gazebo

PIAZZA: a large open porch, usually covered

PIER: a square pillar resembling a column and too stout to be called a post

PIER ARCADE: a motif made from a series of piers carrying arches

PILASTER: a column flattened out and attached to a wall

PITCHED ROOF: a roof made from two planes rising from walls opposite one another and meeting at the center in a ridge

PODIUM: a wall-like element at one end of stairs leading to a porch and usually rising no higher than the porch floor

PORTAL: a large entrance, often arched

PORTE-COCHERE: a covering protecting a driveway

PORTICO: an element protecting an entrance with a roof held by columns, piers, or posts

PRAIRIE SCHOOL: see Introduction

PRAIRIE STYLE: see Introduction

PYLON: stout corner elements with sloping sides

QUADRANT: a quarter of a circle

QUARRY-FACED STONE: stone with a rough face appearing as if it had come undressed from the quarry

QUARTREFOIL: a form made of four segments of circles meeting in cusps

QUEEN ANNE: see Introduction

QUOINS: larger dressed ashlar blocks often projecting slightly and set in the corner of a masonry wall

Rafter: structural members running from the wall to the ridge to hold a roof pitch and extending beyond the wall to form the eaves

Random ashlar: see "ashlar"

Redstone: a soft stone with a deep red, almost brown color and granular surface

Reentrant angle: the inner corner where two wings meet

Richardsonian Romanesque: see Introduction

Riverstone: see Introduction

Romanesque: see Introduction

Rope molding: a molding with a curled form resembling a rope

Rosette: an ornamental form, often incised, sometimes projecting, based on that of a fully blooming rose but with only four to six curled petals

Roundel: a round ornamental form

Rubblestone: stone seemingly brought directly from the quarry or field and lacking planer, straight faces

Sash: the part of a window with the pieces holding the glass; if hinged at the sides, it is a casement sash; if it slides up and down, it is a hung sash; if immovable, it is a fixed sash

Saw-tooth motif: a horizontal zig-zag resembling the teeth of a saw

Scroll-cut: cut with a scroll saw (or jig saw) which allowed the easy cutting of curved forms in boards

Second Empire: see Introduction

Segmental arch: an arch turning through less than a half circle

Serlian door: a door framing based on the designs of Sebastiano Serlio, a sixteenth century Italian architect, featuring columns or piers supporting large-scale entablatures and pediments or arches

Shake sheathing: a wall or roof covering composed from hand hewn slabs of wood forming a much rougher surface than the one formed by using machine-cut shingles

Shed roofed: a pitched roof attached to a wall and sloping outward

Shingle style: see Introduction

Shoulders (on window frames): outward projection along the wall surface at the top of a window frame; see also "feet"

Sidelights: windows as tall as the door flanking it on each side

Soffit: the underneath plane of an overhang or other span

Solarium (pl. solaria): a projecting bay window with large windows to catch the sunlight and large enough to be considered an extension of the room within

Spandrel: the area defined by the extrados of an arch, a horizontal extended from its keystone, and a vertical projected upward from its spring block

Spar: a small connecting member, for example forming part of a girt in the decoration of a gable

Spindle-work: small, skinny pieces of wood, turned on a lathe, assembled to form a larger decorative element

SPIRE: a tall pointed termination atop a tower

SPRING BLOCK: a block, usually stone, upon which an arch rests or from which it rises or springs

STEPBACK: a recession in a wall or along a gable that suggests a step, often used in a series to suggest steps

STICK STYLE: see Introduction

STICK-WORK: flat boards, often milled, assembled to form a larger decorative element

STRAP-WORK DECORATION: an ornamental enrichment in stone or stucco made up of broad bands with curled edges

"STREAKY-BACON STYLE": an informal term for the Victorian Gothic style when its walls are made from alternating layers of brick and stone

STRINGCOURSE: see "belt course"

STRUT: a small member running between larger members, for example in a girt decorating a gable or between a post and a lintel in a porch

SWAG: simplified festoon

SWAN'S-NECK PEDIMENT: a segmental pediment broken in the center and with each side rising slightly vertically to suggest the shape of a swan's neck

SWINGBRIDGE: a bridge that can swing aside either from a pivot on the bank or one on a pier on the center to allow a boat to pass

TABERNACLE WINDOW: a window framed on all four sides with the appropriate elements, that is, a sill, piers on each side with pilasters or half columns, and a lintel at the top in the form of a cornice or entablature, often topped by a pediment

TERRA COTTA: literally, baked earth; clay like that used for making bricks moulded into special forms and sometimes with glazing to produce a shiny surface and rich colors

TERRAZZO: a special kind of concrete using small colored stones which after it has set is ground down to a smooth surface to produce a colorful floor

TIE ROD: a rod of metal, usually wrought iron, strung between opposite walls and attached at the outside with anchor plates to prevent the walls from collapsing outward

TIERS: layers one atop another

TORUS: doughnut-like moulding; fat moulding wrapped around a column with a half-round cross section; like an astragal but fat

TOURELLE: an oriel but much taller in proportion to its breadth and affixed to walls as well as to corners

TRACERY: the stone pattern holding the glass within a larger window opening

TRANSEPT: a space within a church similar to the nave in size and intersecting it at right angles just in front of the chancel or choir

TRANSOM: the horizontal rectangle forming a window above a door

TRIFOIL: a form made of three segments of circles meeting in cusps

TRELLIS: open work made up of thin wooden members in a rectangular pattern

TRUNCATED: a cut-off form, as for example in a hipped roof which rises to a flat top rather than to a point

TRUSS: a structural device made up of a number of straight pieces of timber or metal using various engineering principles to span a great distance with a minimum of material

TUDOR STYLE: see Introduction

TURRET: a projecting element usually circular or polygonal in plan and rising from the ground or from an upper section of the wall and extending into the roof zone

TUSCAN COLUMN: see "orders"

TYMPANUM (PL.: TYMPANA): the area beneath the arch and above the lintel of the door within the arch

URN: a large, squat vase

U.S. GRANT: see Introduction

VARIEGATED: having a variety, for example, of colors, shapes, forms, or elements

VAULTED: covered by a vault, that is, a ceiling spanning the space with a half-circular cross section or a series of such shapes intersecting one another at right angles

VESTIBULE: a small recess in front of or just beyond an entrance

VICTORIAN GOTHIC STYLE: see Introduction

VOLUTE: a curling form unwinding in ever larger continuous circles

VOUSSOIR: one of the wedge-shaped pieces used in building an arch

WAINSCOT: the lower section of a wall, usually in a different material from the upper section, often darker in color and in wood to facilitate maintenance